ANNOTATED

HANDBOOK OF

BIBLICAL QUOTATIONS,

VERSES, AND

PARABLES

Robert P. Vichas

For he looked for a city which hath foundations, whose builder and maker is God.

HEBREWS 11:10

Prentice-Hall, Englewood Cliffs, NJ 07632

Prentice-Hall International, Inc., *London*
Prentice-Hall of Australia, Pty. Ltd., *Sydney*
Prentice-Hall Canada, Inc., *Toronto*
Prentice-Hall of India Private Ltd., *New Delhi*
Prentice-Hall of Japan, Inc., *Tokyo*
Prentice-Hall of Southeast Asia Pte. Ltd., *Singapore*
Whitehall Books, Ltd., Wellington, *New Zealand*
Editora Prentice-Hall do Brasil Ltda., *Rio de Janeiro*
Prentice-Hall Hispanoamericana, S.A., *Mexico*

© 1986 *by*

PRENTICE-HALL, INC.

Englewood Cliffs, N.J.

Library of Congress Cataloging-in-Publication Data
Vichas, Robert P.
Annotated handbook of biblical quotations, verses,
and parables.
Bibliography: p.
Includes index.
1. Bible—Indexes.   2. Christian life—Biblical
teaching.   3. Christian life—Biblical teaching—Indexes.
I. Title.
BS432.V48   1985   220.3'21   85-19346

ISBN 0-13-037870-4

Printed in the United States of America

Honour your father and your mother: that your days may be long upon the land which the Lord your God gives you."

Exodus 20:12

To the Memory of

PETER and IDALENE

The world passes away, and the lust thereof: but he who practices the will of God abides forever.

1 John 2:17

ACKNOWLEDGMENTS

The author thanks the following persons for taking time to review critically portions of the manuscript, whose comments and suggestions challenged him to rethink portions of the book: Dr. Edmund Opitz, author of *Religion and Capitalism: Allies, Not Enemies;* and Dr. Gary North, author of *An Introduction to Christian Economics.* Both works influenced the author to undertake the challenge of writing this book.

The author also owes an intellectual debt to many persons and many published works, some of which have been referenced in footnotes throughout the book. He especially wishes to mention several persons on whose works he drew heavily for inspiration and ideas: Dr. Rousas John Rushdoony (president, Chalcedon); Dr. D. James Kennedy (senior pastor, Coral Ridge Presbyterian Church); Dr. Gary North (president, Institute of Christian Economics); and Dr. Edmund Opitz (officer, Foundation for Economic Education).

The author also personally thanks the purchaser of this book and hopes that the reader experiences many years of benefit from referring to it.

HOW TO USE THIS BOOK PROFITABLY

The unusual volume you now hold in your hands is a powerful reference tool. Its trenchant design enables you to tap, in a rather unique manner, the most influential Book ever written. Whether you are a businessperson, speaker, minister, writer, manager of others or a home, concerned citizen, just beginning your career, or a serious student of the free society under the rule of God, this book has been patterned expressly for your everyday use.

What can you expect to discover in the following pages? First, considering the antiquity of the Bible, the question arises whether it speaks to the concerns of a modern society: For instance, inflation, welfarism, military draft, foreign aid, economics, business profits, honesty, bribery, economic growth, private property, egalitarianism, law and order, and strategic planning. It definitely does! It also addresses feminism, poverty, Hippies, productivity, work and wages, taxes, inheritance, and even the free market and socialism. Did you know that?

Second, you will discover what kind of economic system, government system, welfare system, court system, military system, and business system is consistent with what God intended. Further, you will unravel advantages of godly order and disadvantages of having it man's way when something more monumental than hamburgers is involved.

Third, you will discover that challenges confronted two thousand, three thousand, four thousand, or five thousand years ago were no different than those we face every day in the present. The language has changed, the actors have changed, but God's remedies have not changed. You will learn that the Bible applies even more on Monday through Friday than on Saturday or Sunday. It is the most practical book of solutions we have. If you have experienced difficulty extracting those solutions from the Bible in a rapid, time-saving manner, you now have answers at hand.

This book has been organized to save you time and to provide you quickly and easily with practical information that relates to yesterday, today, and tomorrow. It has been organized like an encyclopedic dictionary, with entries listed alphabetically. Each entry begins with a brief discussion of the subject. Cross-references encourage you to pursue any topic of interest in further detail. Then several biblical quotations, verses, or parables support the entry. You will notice that contemporary language heads these entries, with terms such as abortion, bureaucracy, rape, United Nations, and so on. Although the Bible does not employ this terminology, it addresses these issues. Nearly 300 main entries and cross-references have been selected, and many cross-references assure locating the right term for the right occasion.

It has been organized to save you considerable time and to allow you to penetrate the heart of a matter. It is not a concordance of the type used in scholarly investigations. It is not a theological work. The writer-editor, businessman, and lecturer is interested in the moral power of the Bible and its practical, supercharged counsel for daily living and confrontation of daily challenges.

Its frequent usage can add vigor and style to your speeches, management meetings, conference presentations, personal discussions, letters, and other written communications, because now, not only can you quote with the strength of authority, but what you say or write will be a new and dynamic view or fresh approach for your listener or reader.

Let's consider a few cameos on profitably using this reference tool. For instance, suppose you have been called upon to give a talk. You need to include something incisive about inflation to make your point. In the first place, few people truly understand inflation, its cause, and its solution. This has been one of the most badly abused words of our generation. Looking up *inflation* in this book, not only will you learn exactly what it is, but studying the introduction may generate additional thoughts for your presentation. Then, for a final touch of tonicity and eloquence, you may want to select a choice biblical verse to nail down your point. See how easy it is?

Another example: You are a salesmanager planning to conduct a forceful sales meeting. First you decide to discuss sales commissions and production. Read entries on "Work" and "Tinstaafl" for openers. Then, when you move on to customer relations in your meeting, stressing honesty, admonishing your sales team not to take shortcuts for the quick buck, encouraging them to render full value to customers for money received and to fulfill promises, the power of your words and the range of your ideas will have been enriched from reading "Honesty," "Golden Rule," "Value," and "Contract." Finally, you choose to end your talk by encouraging your salespeople to work harder and better. Topics such as "Abundance," "Prosperity," and "Return on Investment" support those exciting and intense ideas you want to convey to your sales team.

Many young people interested in business often question the morality of business activities. They want to know they are doing the right thing. (A person need not be young to have these preoccupations.) These are the kind of people we want in business! Whether in a discussion group, talking with friends or business associates, or needing hard proof that God does not frown on people in business, you can uncover answers here. Many who want to destroy the free society and replace it with a totalitarian one use the tactics of inducing guilt. Replace guilt with facts, and for starters, explore what the Bible says about "Profit," "Materialism," "Free Enterprise," "Demand and Supply," "Price Mechanism," "Business," "Savings," and "Private Property."

Presume you are a corporate executive preparing a memo or an address to a group of workers to mitigate potential labor problems. You may want to prepare yourself with prayer and by examination of eye-opening entries on "Work," "Wages," "Labor Market," "Stewardship," "Freedom," "Productivity," "Market Economy," "Division of Labor," and "Savings."

You may be an elected official of a legislative body or a staff member, government agency departmental manager, or judge. Before making an important decision in haste, while those affected by your decision must repent at leisure, take time to persue appropriate entries. There is really no rush to promulgate laws or to devise regulations or to please the press. Others before you met those same crises. Find out about it. Why hurry to go nowhere?

Ministers of the Gospel! With hardly any effort at all—assuming you have backgrounds or experience in fields other than your doctrinal specialization—you have enough material here for six months of sermons, which further study and amplification can translate into years of ideas to put ebullience into your sermons and vitality into your Bible study groups.

It is hard to imagine anyone speaking or writing to the public who would not want to add verve and vivacity to his or her pronouncements. This volume is not duplicated elsewhere either in this format or extensiveness of coverage. Further, it is hard to imagine how anyone concerned with issues such as abortion, feminism, the family, education, marriage, social security, and so forth will not make at least modest effort at self-education on this pivot of society—freedom.

This book facilitates discovery of what the Bible says about a multitude of concerns that involve you and me, our friends, associates and loved ones, as well as those who may be in opposition. Using it often will soon make you appear an expert, because you will become an expert on the Bible's message for living in a free society today.

Robert P. Vichas

THEMATIC LOCATER

This user-friendly annotated handbook presents several approaches to locate quickly a word, topic, or theme: (1) Topics appear alphabetically; look it up as you would in any similarly organized reference book. (2) Each entry lists several additional references; pursue an interesting topic in further detail. (3) The *Thematic Locater* that follows organizes all entries into thirty-three broad themes; save time with this versatile planner.

ACCOUNTABILITY AND RESPONSIBILITY

Accountability	Honesty	Restitution
Compensation	Individualism	Risk Aversion
Contract	Liability	Self-Discipline
Discipline	Libertarianism	Stewardship
Freedom	Maturity	Tinstaafl
Golden Rule	Responsibility	

BUSINESS AND LABOR

Business	Free Market	Return on Investment
Contract	Labor Market	Service
Cooperation	Persuasion	Specialization
Demand and Supply	Price	Supply
Division of Labor	Production	Technology
Employee	Profit	Value
Exchange	Rent	Work

CHILDREN AND INHERITANCE

Abortion	*Education*	*Marriage*
Children	*Family*	*Private Property*
Creation	*Hippies*	*Youth Cultism*
Discipline	*Inheritance*	

CIVIL GOVERNMENT SYSTEMS AND -ISMS

Bureaucracy	*Humanism*	*Rule of Law*
Communism	*Inflation*	*Social Security*
Cradle-to-Grave	*Keynesianism*	*Socialism*
Demagoguery	*Liberalism*	*Statism*
Directed Economy	*Libertarianism*	*Terrorism*
Draft (Military)	*Military Defense*	*U.S.A.*
Elitism	*One Worldism*	*United Nations*
Environmentalism	*Peace Treaty*	*War*
Evolutionism	*Planned Economy*	*Welfarism*
Free Society	*Power of State*	*World Government*
Government	✓ *Rule by Decree*	*Xenophobia*

CRIME AND PUNISHMENT

Abortion	*Golden Rule*	*Rape*
Capital Punishment	*Idolatry*	*Responsibility*
Compensation	*Judgment*	*Restitution*
Corruption	*Kidnapping*	*Rule of Law*
Discipline	*Law*	*Theft*
Dishonesty	*Perjury*	

DEBTS AND LOANS

Bankruptcy	*Investments*	*Poverty*
Collateral	*Liability*	*Profit*
Debts	*Losses*	*Return on Investment*
Foreign Aid	*Pledge*	*Risk Aversion*
Interest	*Poor Nations*	*Surety*

ECONOMICS AND ECONOMIC SYSTEMS

Barter	*Demand and Supply*	*Economic Growth*
Capital Formation	*Directed Economy*	*Economics*
Cycles	*Division of Labor*	*Equality*
Demand	*Economic Forecasts*	*Exchange*

FREEDOM AND LIBERTY

Abundance
Capital Punishment
Cooperation
Foundation
Freedom
Free Enterprise
Free Market
Free Society
Honesty
Individualism
Inequality
Inheritance

Investments
Justice
Law
Libertarianism
Liberty
Market Economy
Maturity
Military Defense
Persuasion
Private Property
Prosperity
Responsibility

Rule of Law
Say's Law
Self-Discipline
Source
Stewardship
Strategic Planning
Supply
Tinstaafl
U.S.A.
Voluntarism
Zain

GOD, GOLD, GUNS, AND GROCERIES

Barter
Capital Punishment
Debts
Food Storage
Foundation
Gold

Gotham City
Inflation
Investments
Military Defense
Money
Private Property

Remnant
Responsibility
Savings
Source
Stewardship
Strategic Planning

HUMAN GOVERNMENTS AND THEIR LIEUTENANTS

Bribery
Bureaucrat
Census
Communist
Conspiracy
Corruption
Cradle-to-Grave
Cycles
Daylight Saving Time
Demagogue
Double Standard
Elitism
Expropriation
Foreign Aid

Gotham City
Government
Heroes
Idolatry
Inflationist
Liberal
Military
Nonalignment
Nothing Is Forever
Planned Economy
Politician
Pollution
Poverty
Power

Randomness
Redistribution
  of Income/Wealth
Rule by Decree
Slavery
Socialist
Statist
Subsidies
Tax Collector
Terrorism
Theft
War
Welfarist
World Government
Xenophobia

INTERNATIONAL TRADE AND AID

Bribery
Business
Demand
Demand and Supply

Foreign Aid
Free Enterprise
Imports
International Trade

Poor Nations
Price Mechanism
Say's Law
Specialization

JUSTICE AND EQUITY

Capital Punishment
Compensation
Ethics
Foundation
Free Society

Inequality
Inheritance
Justice
Law
Private Property

Productivity
Restitution
Rule of Law
Self-Discipline
TINSTAAFL

LAW AND LEGAL SYSTEM

Bankruptcy
Capital Punishment
Collateral
Contract
Court System
Discipline
Ethics

Inequality
Law
Law and Order
Liability
Organization
Peace Treaty
Perjury

Pledge
Private Property
Restitution
Rule of Law
Surety
Testimony
Theft

MANAGEMENT AND ORGANIZATION

Business
Character
Communication
Cooperation
Debts
Division of Labor

Forecasting
Golden Rule
Harmony
Management
Productivity
Quality

Responsibility
Return on Investment
Specialization
Stewardship
Strategic Planning
Value

OPPRESSORS AND SLAVERS

Alcoholism
Communist
Corruption
Crowd Psychology
Demagogue
Directed Economy

Elitism
Envy
Evolutionism
Expropriation
Fury of a
    Bureaucrat Scorned

Idolatry
Inflationist
Nonalignment
Perjury
Power of State
Property Taxes

SAVING AND INVESTING

Capital Formation
Economic Growth
Equality
Exchange
Food Storage
Inequality

Inheritance
Interest
Investments
Law of Increase
Money
Productivity

Profit
Return on Investment
Risk Aversion
Savings
Self-Discipline
Social Security

SOCIAL SECURITY AND WELFARISM

Census
Cradle-to-Grave
Crowd Psychology
Demagoguery
Envy

Humanism
Inflationism
Keynesianism
Law of Opposites
Liberalism

Socialism
Social Security
Tinstaafl
Welfarism
Welfarist

SOCIETY: ETHICS AND MORALITY

Abortion
Bribery
Capital Punishment
Character
Corruption
Crowd Psychology
Double Standard
Environmentalism

Ethics
Family
Free Society
Golden Rule
Hippies
Homosexuality
Honesty
Moral Principles

Persuasion
Prostitute
Responsibility
Restitution
Rule of Law
Stewardship
Testimony
Voluntarism

TAXATION AND PRIVATE PROPERTY

Directed Economy
Envy
Expropriation
Inequality
Inflation
Kidnapping
Liberalism
Pollution
Poor Nations

Poverty
Power of State
Private Property
Property Taxes
Redistribution
   of Income/Wealth
Rule by Decree
Slavery
Social Security

Statism
Subsidies
Taxation
Tax Collector
Terrorism
Theft
Welfarism

WAGES AND WORK

WAR AND PEACE

WEALTH AND ABUNDANCE

WOMEN AND SOCIETY

ABORTION

Proabortionists hold that each woman has the right to do whatever she wishes with her own body. How does that square with the issue of moral accountability? What does the Bible say? Almost a nonissue, abortion is not a subject open to question or debate in the Bible. Destruction of a human embryo or fetus, by biblical standards, is murder. Therefore, the fetus is protected by the sixth commandment: "Thou shalt not kill." However, you may want further evidence.

Let's start with DEUTERONOMY 22:6–7. It clearly tells us that tampering with a mother bird and her eggs or young is a serious matter. We know, too, from MATTHEW 10:31, that each human is worth more than many birds.

Yet, in the United States, we have stringent laws protecting the eggs of eagles, for example. Destroy an egg, and you will be arrested, subject to fine and jail, plus condemnation by the environmentalists. Still, the same government pays for aborting human babies, which is similar to saying that one eagle's life is worth many human lives, the inverse of MATTHEW 10:31.

Now read EXODUS 21:22–23, quoted below. Reverend Rousas Rushdoony points this out as an example of case law. Therefore, if the penalty is so severe for *accidental abortion*, we must conclude that *deliberate abortion* is forbidden. If the penalty for accidental abortion is death to the one who caused it, can we reasonably presume that the penalty for deliberate abortion is anything less? Reverend Rushdoony writes, "The essence of the demand for abortion is to return to pagan statism, to place life again under the state rather than under God."[1]

Further, Dr. Francis Schaeffer (authority on modern culture from the perspective of biblical Christianity and author of twenty-two books) and Dr. Everett Koop (Surgeon General of the United States) believe that current events and trends will lead to the disintegration of human dignity. Abortion-on-demand leads to infanticide, which leads to euthanasia—all of which are taking place right now. "Cultures

[1]Rousas John Rushdoony, *The Institutes of Biblical Law* (Nutley, N.J.: The Craig Press, 1973), Vol. 1, p. 267.

can be judged in many ways, but eventually every nation in every age must be judged by this test: How did it treat people?"[2]

(See Also: Capital Punishment, Creation, Family, Feminism, Homosexuality, Marriage, Rape, Women)

> You shall not kill.
>
> EXODUS 20:13.

> If men strive and hurt a pregnant woman, so that her fruit depart from her, and yet no harm follows: he shall surely be punished, according as the woman's husband will decide; and he shall pay as the judges determine. And if any harm follows, then you shall give life for life.
>
> EXODUS 21:22–23.

> If a bird's nest happens to be before you in the way in any tree, or on the ground, whether they be young ones, or eggs, and the dam sitting upon the young, or upon the eggs, you shall not take the dam with the young.
>
> DEUTERONOMY 22:6.

> Fear not therefore, you are of more value than many sparrows.
>
> MATTHEW 10:31.

ABUNDANCE

Does the Bible promise us riches and abundance of health, wealth, and happiness? Yes, indeed! There is ample evidence of this promise. A few representative verses follow. Too many Christians interpret Jesus' message as a plea for poverty. Nowhere in the Bible will you find a statement in which God said that we must be poor, miserable creatures. Absolutely, nowhere!

Frank Goines has pointed out in his monthly, *The Frank Goines Report* (5314 S. Yale, Suite 500, Tulsa, Oklahoma 74135) that God's prophets were often rich. He has estimated the net worth of a couple of those outstanding prophets by today's money standards and discovered that they were multimillionaires. Reverend Norman Vincent Peale (*Guideposts*, Carmel, New York 10512) has written books and scores of articles that not only reaffirm our right to our Father's inheritance but provide us

[2]Francis A. Schaeffer and C. E. Koop, *Study Guide for Whatever Happened to the Human Race?* (Old Tappan, N.J.: Fleming H. Revell, 1979), p. 19.

with directions for better living. Dr. Jack Addington's Foundation for Abundant Living (Box 100, San Diego, California 92138) has file drawers of testimonies proving that God provides for His people. Dr. Pat Robertson of the CBN 700 Club (Virginia Beach, Virginia 23464) gives us continuous public examples of the miracles that can occur when we walk in the ways of the Lord.

These writers refer to individual abundance. However, Deuteronomy 28:1–14 deals with blessings of obedience, the national, aggregate wealth our country will experience as long as we diligently obey the voice of the Lord: "The Lord will grant you plenty of goods...." "The Lord will open to you His good treasure...." Or, as a nation, we can exercise our free will and choose the curses of disobedience described in Deuteronomy28:15–68.

If you are not experiencing abundance, perhaps you ought to reexamine your goals and your personal relationship with God, instead of blaming Him. Although we have the formula for abundance, the fundamental issue—perhaps even the precondition—is the use to which we intend to put our good fortune as individuals and as a nation.

(*See Also:* Capital Formation, Economic Growth, Inheritance, Prosperity, Savings, Source, Wealth)

> *Be fruitful, and multiply; bring forth abundantly in the earth, and multiply therein.*
>
> Genesis 9:7.

> *If you walk in my statutes, and keep my commandments, and practice them; then I will give you rain in due season, and the land shall yield her increase, and the trees of the field shall yield their fruit. And your threshings shall reach until the vintage, and the vintage shall reach until the sowing time; and you shall eat your bread to the full, and dwell in your land safely. And I will give you peace in the land, and you shall lie down, and none shall make you afraid; and I will rid evil beasts out of the land, neither shall the sword go through your land. And you shall chase your enemies, and they shall fall before you by the sword. And five of you shall chase a hundred, and a hundred of you shall put ten thousand to flight. For I will respect you, and make you fruitful, and multiply you, and establish my covenant with you. And you shall eat old store, and bring forth the old because of the new. And I will set my tabernacle among you: and my soul shall not abhor you. And I will walk among you, and will be your God, and you shall be my people. I am the Lord your God, who brought you forth out of the land of Egypt, that you should not be their slaves; and I have broken the bands of your yoke, and made you go free.*
>
> Leviticus 26:3–13.

Behold, I set before you this day a blessing and a curse; a blessing, if you obey the commandments of the Lord your God; and a curse, if you will not obey the commandments of the Lord your God.

DEUTERONOMY 11:26–28.

If you diligently obey the voice of the Lord your God, to observe carefully all His commandments which I commanded you today, that the Lord your God will set you high above all nations of the earth.

The Lord will command the blessings on you in your storehouses and in all to which you set your hand, and He will bless you in the land.

The Lord will grant you plenty of goods, in the fruit of your body, in the increase of your livestock, and in the produce of your ground.

The Lord will open to you His good treasure, the heavens to give rain to your land in its season, and to bless all the work of your hand. You shall lend to many nations, but you shall not borrow.

DEUTERONOMY 28:1, 8, 11, 12.

They shall call the people to the mountain; there they shall offer sacrifices of righteousness, for they shall suck of the abundance of the seas, and the treasures hid in the sand.

DEUTERONOMY 33:19.

How excellent is your loving-kindness, O God! Therefore the children of men put their trust under the shadow of your wings. They shall be abundantly satisfied with the fatness of your house.

PSALM 36:7–8.

A good man leaves an inheritance to his children's children, but the wealth of the sinner is stored up for the righteous.

PROVERBS 13:22.

Tribulation and anguish, upon every soul of man that does evil, but glory, honor, and peace, to every man who works good.

ROMANS 2:9–10.

For our rejoicing is this, the testimony of our conscience, that in simplicity and godly sincerity, not with fleshly wisdom, but by the grace of God, we have behaved ourselves in the world, and more abundantly toward you.

2 CORINTHIANS 1:12.

By an equality, that now at this time your abundance may be a supply for their want, that their abundance also may be a supply for your want: that there may be equality.

2 CORINTHIANS 8:14.

No man should blame us in this abundance which is administered by us.

2 CORINTHIANS 8:20.

ACADEMICIAN

Then certain philosophers of the Epicureans, and of the Stoics, encountered him. And some said, What will this babbler say? Others, He seems to set forth strange gods, because he preached to them of Jesus and the resurrection. And they took him, and brought him to Aeropagus, saying, May we know what this new doctrine of which you speak, is? For you bring certain strange things to our ears, we would know therefore what these things mean.

ACTS 17:18–20.

(*See:* Educator, Professor)

ACCOUNTABILITY

Each of us is accountable for our thoughts and actions despite the words to the *Psychiatric Folksong:*

> *At three I had a feeling of*
> *Ambivalence toward my brothers,*
> *And so it followed naturally*
> *I poisoned all my lovers.*

But now I'm happy; I have learned
The lesson this has taught;
That everything I do that's wrong
Is someone else's fault.[1]

Freud saw neurosis as illness, not as sin. His error does not release us from moral accountability.[2] "Innocent by reason of insanity," "I'm only carrying out orders," or "I don't make the laws (policies), I just execute them" are excuses that hardly release us from judgment of our deeds, or misdeeds. When Marxists take over a government, they rather thoroughly purge the bureaucracies; they are not in the least ambivalent over accountability. After the Marxist revolution in Nicaragua, for instance, some who began working for the new government told me that they did so, not because they believed in Marxism but to earn a living. Does earning a living excuse them from God's judgment?

The tax collector, police officer, judge, soldier, and town clerk are just as accountable for their decisions, acts, and judgments as those who passed the laws, decrees, and regulations. On the other hand, you who accept subsidies, favors, and special privileges from an apostate government are equally accountable. "Every one of us shall give an account of himself to God" (ROMANS 14:12). As Gabriel Meurier put it: "He sins as much who holds the sack as he who fills it."

(*See Also:* Character, Compensation, Judgment, Nonalignment, Responsibility, Restitution, Rule of Law)

Cease from man, whose breath is in his nostrils: for wherein is he to be accounted of?

ISAIAH 2:22.

Woe to you who spoil, and you were not spoiled, and deal treacherously, and they dealt not treacherously with you! When you shall cease to rob, you shall be robbed; and when you shall make an end to deal treacherously, they shall deal treacherously with you.

ISAIAH 33:1.

I, the Lord, search the heart, I try the reins, even to give every man according to his ways, and according to the fruit of his doings. As the partridge sits on eggs, and hatches them not; so he who gets riches, and not be right, shall leave them in the midst of his days, and at his end shall be a fool.

JEREMIAH 17:10–11.

---

[1]Quoted in O. Hobart Mowrer, *The Crisis in Psychiatry and Religion* (New York: D. Van Nostrand, 1961), p. 49.
[2]*Ibid.*

Either make the tree good, and its fruit good; or else make the tree corrupt, and its fruit corrupt: for the tree is known by its fruit.

MATTHEW 12:33.

Now also the axe is laid to the root of the tree: every tree therefore which brings not forth good fruit is hewn down, and cast into the fire.

LUKE 3:9.

Every one of us shall give account of himself to God. Let us therefore not judge one another any more, but rather judge this, that no man put a stumbling-block or an occasion to fall in his brother's way.

ROMANS 14:12–13.

Be not deceived; God is not mocked, for whatsoever a man sows, that shall he also reap.

GALATIANS 6:7.

ADMINISTRATION

For we are laborers together with God.

1 CORINTHIANS 3:9.

(*See:* Management, Organization, Strategic Planning)

ADVERTISING

Therefore, let us keep the feast, not with old leaven, neither with the leaven of malice and wickedness, but with the unleavened bread of sincerity and truth.

1 CORINTHIANS 5:8.

(*See:* Market Economy, Persuasion)

ALCOHOLISM

The Bible makes no direct comment on the two- (three- or four-) martini lunch, because distilled alcoholic beverages and libationary concoctions are distinctly modern in invention. But alcoholism is not a modern malady, and the Bible has a few things to say about that issue.

Although wines were an acceptable part of the diet, temperance in consumption of such genies in a bottle was the rule. In biblical times, wines were available for festive occasions, where the custom was to serve the vintage wine first and *vin ordinaire* after taste glands had become less alert to nectarous distinctions. When Jesus, at His mother's wish during a wedding reception, turned water into a gustatory pleasure when no more wine was available, the governor of the feast said, "Aha, you've been saving the good stuff until now." (See JOHN 2:1–10.)

Wines were an appropriate adjunct to meals. Recall that St. Paul even suggested that Timothy drink some wine for health (1 TIMOTHY 5:23). Wines could even appropriately be included with the offering to God (See NUMBERS 15:5–10 and DEUTERONOMY 14:26). But woe to those who had a heavy hand with the bottle! Temperance was the byword then, as now.

Why is drunkenness evil? Alcoholism was, and still is, an issue of ethics. Such excesses distort perception and cloud personal responsibility. We are all familiar with the statistics on vehicular accidents. In the majority of fatal automobile and boat accidents, alcohol has been the prime cause. In a godly society, survivors of such accidents would not escape punishment and payment of restitution. Recall DEUTERONOMY 21:18–21, the verses dealing with the rebellious son. "This son of ours is stubborn and rebellious; he will not obey our voice; he is a glutton and a *drunkard*." Therefore alcoholism is a sign of rebellious behavior. The son in Deuteronomy was stoned to death.

Due to the heavy responsibility carried by our national and state leaders, they too should not drink (see PROVERBS 31:4–5). Also, alcoholism is destructive to family life, the very foundation of a free society under God's law. Therefore, it is not a question of touch not, taste not. EPHESIANS 5:18 applies to all self-imposed distortions, whether induced by drugs, alcohol, or fantasies, that result in irresponsible action. Self-discipline and prayer acknowledging God as the Creator and Source provide the answer.

(*See Also:* Accountability, Family, Foundation, Responsibility, Self-Discipline)

> *His father and his mother shall say to the elders of his city, This son of ours is stubborn and rebellious; he will not obey our voice; he is a glutton and a drunkard. Then all the men of his city shall stone him to death with stones; so you shall put away the evil person from among you.*
>
> *DEUTERONOMY 21:20–21.*

Woe to them who rise up early in the morning in order to follow strong drink, who continue until night, until the wine inflames them!

ISAIAH 5:11.

They also have erred through wine, and through strong drink are out of the way; they err in vision, they stumble in judgment.

ISAIAH 28:7.

For all tables are full of vomit and filthiness, so that there is no place clean.

ISAIAH 28:8

It is not for kings, O Lemuel, it is not for kings to drink wine, nor for princes intoxicating drink; lest they drink and forget the law, and pervert justice of all the afflicted.

PROVERBS 31:4–5.

Do not be drunk with wine, wherein is excess; but be filled with the Spirit.

EPHESIANS 5:18.

Deacons must be reverent, not double tongued, not given to much wine, not greedy for money.

1 TIMOTHY 3:8.

The older women likewise, that they be reverent in behavior, not slanderers, not given to much wine, teachers of good things,...

TITUS 2:3.

For we have spent enough of our pasttime in doing the will of the Gentiles, when we walked in licentiousness, lusts, drunkenness, revelries, drinking parties, and abominable idolatries.

1 PETER 4:3.

ATHEISM

Saying to a tree, You are my father, and to a stone, You gave birth to me....

JEREMIAH 2:27.

The fool has said in his heart, There is no God....

PSALM 14:1.

(*See:* Evolutionism, Idolatry)

AUTOMATION

(*See:* Technology)

BALANCED BUDGET

For we stretch not ourselves beyond our means.

2 CORINTHIANS 10:14.

(*See:* Capital Formation, Inflation, Stewardship)

BANKRUPTCY

To many persons, bankruptcy connotes personal failure, lack of responsibility, and a violation of contract and trust of the lender or creditor. Still, the Bible speaks of a release from obligations every seventh year. This implies that the lender shares risk and responsibility with the borrower. The seventh-year release, equivalent to bankruptcy, prevents people from selling themselves into slavery due to onerous financial burdens (see GENESIS 47:18–19). Otherwise, persons acting irresponsibly or impulsively may sell their birthright for food stamps or a bowl of stew (see GENESIS 25:29–34).

Neither consumer debt nor financial leverage are encouraged in the Bible. (Read DEUTERONOMY 15:1–6.) When debt is contracted, an escape clause lets the borrower off the debt hook in the seventh year. Statutes of limitation and various bankruptcy and receivership acts in our federal law today reflect intent of this ancient law of sabbatical release.

The point is more easily understood with business credit. For example, a supplier of materials who sells goods on credit knowingly accepts some risks. The likelihood of a business error leading to insolvency is ever-present. After business discontinuance, should insufficient assets remain to cover all liabilities, partial or complete loss to creditors ensues. A supplier who extends credit to a business already in financial trouble merits no sympathy or special considerations. On the other hand, a debtor who secures credit by fraud deserves the harshest of penalties.

(*See Also:* Collateral, Contract, Cycles, Debts, Exchange, Pledge, Private Property, Responsibility)

> ...*when money failed in the land of Egypt, and in the land of Canaan, all the Eygptians came to Joseph, and said, Give us bread: for why should we die in your presence? for the money fails. And Joseph said, Give your livestock and I will give you bread for your livestock, if the money is gone.*
>
> GENESIS 47:15–16.

> *When that year was ended, they came to him the second year, and said to him, We will not hide it from my lord, how that our money is spent; my lord also has our herds of cattle; there is nothing left in the sight of my lord, but our bodies, and our lands: Wherefore shall we die before your eyes, both we and our land? buy us and our land for bread, and we and our land will be servants to Pharoah.*
>
> GENESIS 47:18–19.

> *At the end of every seven years you shall make a release. And this is the manner of the release: Every creditor who lends anything to his neighbor shall release it; he shall not exact it of his neighbor, or of his brother.*
>
> DEUTERONOMY 15:1–2.

> *There were also those who said, We have borrowed money for the king's tax, and that upon our lands and vineyards. Yet now our flesh is as the flesh of our brethren, and our children as their children: and, lo, we bring into slavery our sons and our daughters to be servants, and some of our daughters are brought into bondage already; neither is it in our power to redeem them; for other men have our lands and vineyards.*
>
> NEHEMIAH 5:4–5.

> *Tekel; thou art weighed in the balances, and art found wanting.*
>
> DANIEL 5:27.

> *Owe no man anything....*
>
> ROMANS 13:8.

BARTER

Barter—an exchange of goods or services for other goods or services—represents the only peaceful means of trade when no universally acceptable monetary system exists. If a monetary system breaks down due to inflation, barter becomes the increasingly preferred alternative because goods are safer to hold than a currency deteriorating in value.

There are several disadvantages to bartering:

1. It is more difficult to find a partner who wants to exchange what you want to acquire and vice versa. This is less difficult in a predominately agrarian economy; but should you desire to sleep at the Hyatt Regency in downtown San Francisco, the hotel management may not appreciate your bringing live pigs into the lobby in exchange for a room.
2. It becomes less practical in a modern, diversified economy. A producer of specialized bearings that have application only in a limited type of equipment will soon run out of exchange partners in direct trade.
3. Transaction costs are higher. Several trades may occur before each of several parties actually ends up with what each wants. International brokers who had to barter with communist countries found they had to engage in a series of trades before they ended up with either money or goods that could be readily converted into a desired currency.
4. Many trades are indivisible. If you need dental work but have only one cow to trade, to exchange value for value either the dentist must keep books and provide your family with dental services over some period or offer something else in kind.

Money, whether gold, clam shells, cattle, or pieces of paper with pictures of politicians, circumvents these problems as long as the money is acceptable to all parties in exchange. Gold boasts the longest history of universal acceptance as a currency, followed by silver. In other words, one good—gold—has most often become the standard by which the value of all other goods are measured because it is the most marketable commodity.

(*See Also:* Division of Labor, Exchange, Gold, Food Storage, Inflation, Money, Price Mechanism, Say's Law, Supply, Value)

And Jacob served seven years for Rachel.

Genesis 29:20.

And Joseph said, Give your cattle; and I will give you for your cattle, if money fail. And they brought their cattle; and Joseph gave them bread in exchange for horses, and for the flocks, and for the cattle of the herds, and for the asses; and he fed them with bread for all their cattle that year.

GENESIS 47:16–17.

So Hiram gave Solomon cedar trees and fir trees according to all his desire. And Solomon gave Hiram twenty thousand measures of wheat for food to his household, and twenty measures of pure oil: thus gave Solomon to Hiram year by year.

1 KINGS 5:10–11.

Now therefore the wheat, and the barley, the oil, and the wine, which my lord has spoken of, let him send to his servants; and we will cut wood out of Lebanon, as much as you shall need; and we will bring it to you in rafts by sea to Joppa; and you shall carry it up to Jerusalem.

2 CHRONICLES 2:15–16.

So I brought her to me for fifteen pieces of silver, and for a homer of barley, and a half homer of barley.

HOSEA 3:2.

BELIEF

All things, whatsoever you will ask in prayer, believing, you shall receive.

MATTHEW 21:22.

(*See:* Foundation, Judgment, Source)

BOTTOM LINE

Tekel; you are weighed in the balance, and are found wanting.

DANIEL 5:27.

(*See:* Profits, Return on Investment)

BRIBERY

Bribery is a transaction cost or tollgate tax necessarily paid to overcome artificial barriers usually raised by the bureaucracy. In a free market, bribes are rare: One just offers a higher bid than his competitor. Bribery became such a significant issue in the United States, especially with respect to American companies doing business overseas, that Congress passed the Foreign Corrupt Practices Act in December 1977. In an article on this act, the author writes:

> The new ethics hardly expresses any real concern for a return to morality, either in business or governmental transactions, but reflect a scalene attack on business bribery together with an international kinship among politicians and bureaucrats unmatched by the divine rights of international medieval royalty.
>
> The philosophy implicitly underlying the Foreign Corrupt Practices Act appears to stem from the view that all persons associated with governments—elected, appointed, or employed—are of high morals except where they have been tempted by bribes of colubrine businessmen who corrupt honest officials and rob people of their officials' loyalty. Although punishment in Eden turned out differently, American businessmen and firms, under the new ideology, may be fined and punished because of the moral weaknesses of the foreign officials who accept tendered payments (bribes).
>
> It is a perverse code of ethics that relieves persons in position of public trust from accountability for their actions. Some of those very same politicians who voted for this piece of legislation also voted for massive transfer payments to select groups (housing, e.g.), just prior to election time, in order to secure their own reelection. Using public funds for private gain, to assure continuance in office, these politicians exempt themselves from charges of corruption and bribery.[1]

An ungodly government creates the opportunity for and necessity of bribery in ordinary transactions. An economy made inefficient by government restrictions, red tape, licensing, and inspection requirements invites bribery. Eliminate artificial economic barriers, and several positive things will result:

1. The price of goods will fall.
2. The supply of goods will tend to be more abundant in the marketplace.
3. The need or opportunity for bribery disappears as competitive bidding replaces bribery.

Still quoting from the same article, the author concludes:

> The Foreign Corrupt Practices Act, a misdirected attack on American business, reflecting the inconsonance of situational ethics, is itself a corrupt act that may change

[1]Robert P. Vichas, "The 'Corrupt' Foreign Corrupt Practices Act," *Tradelook* (January–February 1979).

the form of bribery in dealing with corrupt governments but will not alter its indispensability, and, may, in its new forms, actually increase both the need for it and the amount of bribes paid. The Foreign Corrupt Practices Act is not the solution.[2]

The Bible clearly indicates that it is illegal to take a bribe (see Proverbs 17:23; 21:14). Nothing less than submitting ourselves to God's requirements for living in a free society will suffice.

(*See Also:* Bureaucracy, Corruption, Envy, Power of State, Price Mechanism, Risk Aversion, Taxation)

If it must be so now, do this; take of the best fruits in the land in your vessels, and carry down to the man a present, a little balm, and a little honey, spices, and myrrh, nuts, and almonds, and take double money in your hand.

GENESIS *43:11–12.*

Keep far from a false matter; and the innocent and the righteous slay not; for I will not justify the wicked. And you shall take no gift: for the gift blinds the wise, and perverts the words of the righteous.

EXODUS *23:7–8.*

Neither take a gift: for a gift does blind the eyes of the wise, and pervert the words of the righteous.

DEUTERONOMY *16:19.*

It came to pass afterward, that he loved a woman in the valley of Sorek, whose name was Delilah. And the lords of the Philistines came to her, and said to her, Entice him, and see wherein his great strength lies, and by what means we may prevail against him, that we may bind him to afflict him: and we will give you, every one of us, eleven hundred pieces of silver.

JUDGES *16:4–5.*

And his sons walked not in his ways, but turned aside after lucre, and took bribes, and perverted judgment.

1 SAMUEL *8:3.*

Of whose hand have I received any bribe to blind my eyes therewith?

1 SAMUEL *12:3.*

[2]Ibid.

And Menahem exacted the money of Israel, even of all the mighty men of wealth, of each man fifty shekels of silver, to give to the king of Assyria. So the king of Assyria turned back, and stayed not there in the land.

2 KINGS 15:20.

And he said to the judges, Take heed what you do, for you judge not for man, but for the Lord, who is with you in judgment. Wherefore now let the fear of the Lord be upon you; take heed and do it: for there is no iniquity with the Lord our God, nor respect of persons, nor taking of gifts.

2 CHRONICLES 19:6–7.

Gather not my soul with sinners, nor my life with bloody men: in whose hands is mischief, and their right hand is full of bribes.

PSALM 26:9–10.

A wicked man takes a gift out of the bosom to pervert the ways of judgment.

PROVERBS 17:23.

A gift in secret pacifies anger: and a bribe behind the back, strong wrath.

PROVERBS 21:14.

Your princes are rebellious, and companions of thieves; everyone loves gifts, and follows after rewards: they judge not the fatherless, neither does the cause of the widows come before them.

ISAIAH 1:23.

He who despises the gains of oppressions, that shakes his hands from holding of bribes, he shall dwell on high.

ISAIAH 33:15–16.

That they may do evil with both hands earnestly, the prince asks and the judge asks for a reward; and the great man, he utters his mischievous desire; so they wrap it up.

MICAH 7:3.

Then they secretly bribed men, who said, We have heard him speak blasphemous words against Moses, and against God.

ACTS 6:11.

BUREAUCRACY

At a marketing club meeting on a recent trip to India, I remarked to a retired Indian army colonel about the absence of any British imprint on the Indian society, despite their long period of occupation and domination. "We kept one thing British—" he said, smiling, "their bureaucracy."

Bureaucratic management is the method applied to conduct administrative affairs, the result of which has no cash value on the market. Whereas profit management is limited by its own resources and profits and losses, bureaucratic management has no such limitation. It is bound by changing rules and regulations, formulated by some supreme body, which is seldom directly accountable to those who pay the bills—the taxpayers. Profit management must rely on persuading its customers to buy products and services; bureaucratic management uses coercion and compulsion.

In a simplified example, assume ten producers of strawberries, of which three producers appointed to a newly created Federal Strawberry Market Control Board cease growing berries. Because these three no longer produce, they must depend on others for their financial support. With strawberries now supplied by seven, not ten, we might expect these seven to expand production. Since they now carry the added burden of filling forms and complying with extensive, complex regulations of the Strawberry Market Control Board, they have neither time nor resources available to increase strawberry production, assuming, of course, that the Federal Strawberry Board would even grant permission for expansion. The supply of strawberries decreases, prices rise, and consumers eat fewer but higher-priced strawberries than before the board's formation. So, like a well-kept woman, the bureaucracy must be regaled, while the taxpaying public feigns vicarious pleasure with "leaked" accounts in the press or other public ululations about the *fille de joie*. Like a demanding mistress, it imposes a greater burden on the economy with its rules, regulations, and forms, and raises the cost of production.

To carry our illustration a step further, bureaucrats may notice that strawberries are not only in shorter supply but are extremely high priced. Someone decides that this unfairly burdens The Poor People. From that point, schemes for product redistribution proliferate. (See the story on butter under "Welfarist.")

Huge bureaucracies are a relatively recent phenomenon in American history. (Newly independent countries avoid this blessing that an earlier, limited-government America enjoyed; they remain poor, drained of productive resources by their burdensome bureaucracies.) Bureaucracies proliferate because every special interest group wants representation in the government along with the special privileges, subsidies, and handouts. A new board is created in response to demands of a minority segment, and it grows and grows. (The United States Tea Advisory Board may be an exception.)

When we place our faith in bureaucracies instead of the Lord, this is clearly idolatry. Perhaps the Department of Energy does not erect a golden oil pump above its building for all to bow down and worship, but when we place faith in bureaucracies to provide needs instead of doing it God's way—by producing and working, we can expect shortages, famines, and heavy taxation.

(*See Also:* Bureaucrat, Demagoguery, Fury of a Bureaucrat Scorned, Power of State, Redistribution of Income/Wealth, Rule by Decree)

Howbeit every nation made gods of their own, and put them in the houses of high places...
                                                                    2 KINGS 17:29.

Of a truth, Lord, the kings of Assyria have destroyed the nations and their lands, and have cast their gods into the fire, for they were no gods, but the work of men's hands.
                                                                    2 KINGS 19:17–18.

For all the gods of the people are idols; but the Lord made the heavens.
                                                                    1 CHRONICLES 16:26.

There were also those who said, We have borrowed money for the king's tribute, and upon our lands and vineyards. Yet now our flesh is as the flesh of our brethren, our children as their children; and lo, we bring into slavery our sons and daughters to be servants, and some of our daughters are brought into bondage already; neither is it in our power to redeem them, for other men have our lands and vineyards.
                                                                    NEHEMIAH 5:4–5.

I have seen the wicked in power, and spreading like a green bay tree.
                                                                    PSALM 37:32, 35.

Because sentence against an evil work is not executed speedily, therefore the heart of the sons of men is fully set in them who do evil. Though a sinner do evil a hundred times, and his days be prolonged, yet surely I know that it shall be well with them who fear God.
                                                                    ECCLESIASTES 8:11–12.

Your princes are rebellious, and companions of thieves: every one loves gifts, and follows after rewards.
                                                                    ISAIAH 1:23.

We roar all like bears, and mourn sore like doves. We look for judgment, but there is none.

ISAIAH 59:11.

Such as do wickedly against the covenant shall he corrupt by flatteries; but the people who do know their God shall be strong, and do exploits.

DANIEL 11:32.

O generation of vipers, how can ye, being evil, speak of good things? for out of the abundance of the heart the mouth speaks.

MATTHEW 12:34.

For we wrestle not against flesh and blood, but against principalities, against powers, against the rulers of darkness of this world, against spiritual wickedness in high places.

EPHESIANS 6:12.

BUREAUCRAT

While driving back to my hotel in New Delhi, an Indian government minister and I were discussing economic development. He complained bitterly against bureaucrats as the biggest obstacles to economic growth. Whether at home or abroad, the bitterest complaints and criticisms against bureaucrats often come from other bureaucrats: perhaps because they deal with one another daily.

Bureaucrats seem to be of two types: (1) those who thrive in that kind of environment, and (2) those who use the system but immunize themselves from it when away from the office. In some of the United Nations bureaucracies, the socialists and communists, or those of like mind, often function best. They learn to control and manipulate the bureaucracies to personal advantage.

Professor Glenn L. Pearson writes: "It is a law of bureaucracy that the most evil men are the best at appearing good. Another bureaucratic law is that power corrupts most people. So, even if we replace bad bureaucrats with good ones, many of the good [*sic*] ones will get bad by and by."[1]

What are some basic criticisms of bureaucrats and the systems they perpetuate? Essentially, they engage in activities that have no market value, but that divert valuable resources away from God's work for their maintenance. Similarly, when they entangle believers in expensive court cases, they steal from God. Some become dictocrats, erecting idols enveloped in red tape and complex procedures and

[1] Glenn L. Pearson, "Mixed Economies a No-Man's Land," *The Freeman* (August 1982).

regulations, replacing God's laws promising health, happiness, and eternal prosperity. Some use their power to obtain lavish prerequisites that are paid for, of course, by forced redistribution of income. Hence, some of the following verses may be most appropriate.

(*See Also:* Bribery, Bureaucracy, Demagogue, Envy, Fury of a Bureaucrat Scorned, Heroes, Power, Statist, Tax Collector)

They meet with darkness in the daytime and grope in the noonday as in the night.

JOB 5:14.

They are enclosed in their own fat; with their mouth they speak proudly. They have now compassed us in our steps; they have set their eyes bowing down to earth; like a lion that is greedy of his prey, and as it were a young lion lurking in secret places.

PSALM 17:10–12.

Their inward thought is, that their houses shall continue for ever, and their dwelling places to all generations; they call their lands after their own names. Nevertheless, man being in honor abides not: he is like the beasts that perish. This their way is their folly; yet their prosterity approve their sayings.

PSALM 49:11–13.

But to the wicked God says, What have you to do to declare my statutes, or you should take My covenant in mouth? Seeing you hate instruction, and cast my words behind you. When you saw a thief, then you consented with him, and have been partaker with adulterers. You give your mouth to evil, and your tongue frames deceit. You sit and speak against my brother; you slander your own mother's son.

PSALM 50:16–20.

A fool's voice is known by his multitude of words.

ECCLESIASTES 5:3.

Surely the princes of Zoan are fools, the counsel of the wise counsellors of Pharoah is become brutish... They have also seduced Egypt.

ISAIAH 19:11, 13.

You eat the fat, and you clothe yourself with wool, you kill them who are fed; but you feed not the flock. The diseased you have not strengthened, neither have you healed that which was sick; neither

*have you bound up that which was broken, neither have you brought
again that which was driven away, neither have you sought that which
was lost; but with force and cruelty have you ruled them.*

                                                                    EZEKIEL 34:3–4.

*And he spoke a parable to them, Can the blind lead the blind? shall
they not both fall into the ditch?*

                                                                        LUKE 6:39.

*But what went you out for to see? A man clothed in soft raiment?
Behold, they who are gorgeously apparelled, and live delicately, are in
kings' courts.*

                                                                        LUKE 7:25.

*Woe unto you, Pharisees! for you love the uppermost seats in the
synagogues, and greetings in the markets. Woe unto you, scribes and
Pharisees, hypocrites! for you are as graves which appear not, and the
men who walk over them are not aware of them.*

                                                                   LUKE 11:43–44.

*And there was also a strife among them, which of them should be
accounted the greatest.*

                                                                       LUKE 22:24.

Professing themselves to be wise, they became fools.

                                                                      ROMANS 1:22.

*For though there be those who are called gods, whether in heaven or in
earth,…but to us there is but one God, the Father, of whom are all
things.*

                                                              1 CORINTHIANS 8:5–6.

BUSINESS

A Soviet Counsul said that he would hate to be an American businessman. If he does
wrong, he's arrested. If he does right, he's taxed.

Ever since the rise of a class of mercantilists and entrepreneurs, business has
managed to receive much of the blame for the woes of the world while people in the
government and bureaucracies receive most of the credit for the quantities of goods
and services generated by the business sector. So well embedded is social revolutionary fiction learned fifteen to twenty years ago, that the nihilistic generation of the

1960s still deprecate business (although seldom openly) though they themselves may hold excellent salaried positions. To many of this ilk, business simply provides a vehicle for skinning others out of their income.

Business is an organizing vehicle. Although goods and services have always been produced, they were not manufactured in any appreciable quantity until labor was combined with natural resources, machinery, and equipment in such a way to take advantage of time; that is, the chief function of a business organization is to produce things in the most efficient (read, cheapest) way for the most people, considering the value of time.

Hence, the expression *mass production* means production for the masses! Notice that government programs are usually elitist—that is, designed for a privileged minority. Manufactured goods, on the other hand, are mass produced and sold without distinction of race, religion, or hereditary rights. It is nonelitist. In a free market system, a person can rise through the ranks of wealth. In a system of special privileges, a person rises by heredity, by who he can do in or who he knows—not by *what* he knows. Is it any wonder that God's system provides for equality of opportunity unequaled by that ostensibly offered by humanistic governments?

(*See Also:* Exchange, Free Enterprise, Investments, Management, Market Economy, Organization, Private Property, Profit, Strategic Planning, Supply, Work)

It came to pass about this time, that Joseph went into the house to do his business.

GENESIS 39:11.

And he had much business in the cities of Judah.

2 CHRONICLES 17:13.

Those who go down to the sea in ships, who do business on great waters, they see the works of the Lord, and his wonders in the deep.

PSALM 107:23–24.

Do you see a man diligent in his business? he will stand before kings; he will not stand before unknown men.

PROVERBS 22:29.

For a dream comes through the multitude of business; and a fool's voice is known by multitude of words.

ECCLESIASTES 5:3.

When I applied my heart to know wisdom, and to see the business that is done upon the earth, (even though one sees no sleep day or night) then I saw all the work of God, that a man cannot find out the work that is done under the sun.

ECCLESIASTES 8:16–17.

And Jesus answered him, saying, It is written, That man shall not live by bread alone, but by every word of God.

Luke 4:4.

Be not slothful in business.

Romans 12:11.

BUSINESS PHILOSOPHY

(*See:* Ethics, Free Society, Moral Principles)

BUSINESS POLICY

(*See:* Strategic Planning)

CAPITAL FORMATION

Formation of capital, the accumulation of means of production—that is, tools, machinery, equipment, buildings employed to produce a final product—requires a present sacrifice in order to have a greater future production. Capital equals land and labor over time. It allows more production for each unit of resource employed; more output can be obtained with less labor.

Imagine that you are alone in the mountains. The weather is icy cold. You need firewood for your immediate survival. Your axe handle has just broken. Both your axe head and axe handle represent capital. Unless you have beaver teeth, your choices are either to spend the day scrounging for scattered dry twigs and branches (a consumption good), or fashioning a new axe handle (a capital good). If you do not gather firewood, you will freeze. If you do not make a new axe handle, you will be pegged to a hand-to-mouth existence. One bad day can spell disaster. You need a reserve (savings) of firewood in order to take the day off from firewood hunting to create capital (the new axe handle).

Capital formation, therefore, represents a current sacrifice; it requires abstinence today from consuming. More capital eases our tomorrows. Our high standard of living derives from capital formed and technology and sacrifices of our past. Taxing away savings for nonproductive uses, or consuming everything today, reduces available capital. Disinvestment results in lower material welfare and higher unemployment.

A free society, under God's laws, allows for private accumulation of capital and the higher material standards of living that accompany these acts of saving. It allows us to pass along this accumulation to future generations without restrictions or taxation of inheritances.

If we reject God's system for providing, we can expect our standard of living to drop. The question boils down to whether we prefer branch and twig gathering or swinging the axe (capital) and doing in an hour what would take days to achieve by more primitive methods.

(See Also: Division of Labor, Economic Growth, Free Market, Private Property, Productivity, Savings)

Thou shall not muzzle the ox when he treads out the corn.
                                                                DEUTERONOMY 25:4.

And the rest of the acts of Hezekiah, and all his might, and how he made a pool, and a conduit, and brought water into the city, are they not written in the book of the chronicles of the kings of Judah?
                                                                2 KINGS 20:20.

Also he built towers in the desert, and [dug] many wells: for he had much cattle, both in the low country, and in the plains, husbandmen also, and vine dressers in the mountains, and in Carmel, for he loved husbandry.
                                                                2 CHRONICLES 26:10.

A good man leaves an inheritance to his children's children...
                                                                PROVERBS 13:22.

I made [myself] great works; I built houses; I planted vineyards; I made gardens and orchards, and I planted trees in them of all kinds of fruits. I made pools of water, to water therewith the wood that brings forth trees; I got myself servants and maidens, and had servants born in my house; and also I had great possessions of great and small cattle above all that were in Jerusalem before me.
                                                                ECCLESIASTES 2:4–7.

And he shall judge among the nations, and shall rebuke many people. and they shall beat their swords into plowshares, and their spears into pruninghooks: Nation shall not lift up sword against nation, neither shall they learn war any more.
                                                                ISAIAH 2:4.

The he who had received the five talents went and traded with the same, and made them another five talents.
                                                                MATTHEW 25:16.

According to the grace of God which is given to me, as a wise masterbuilder, I have laid the foundation, and another build thereon. But let every man take heed how he build thereupon.
                                                                1 CORINTHIANS 3:10.

CAPITAL PUNISHMENT

Executing someone certainly must be a distasteful task. Who would want to torch the brush, or pull the switch, or squeeze the trigger, or inject the venom? Yet, . . .

"Thou shalt not kill" commands the Lord, to provide protection from evil-doers. Quite clearly, without exception, the death penalty is prescribed in the Bible for murder, adultery, incest, sodomy, rape, perjury in a capital offense, kidnapping, offering human sacrifice, striking parents, incorrigible juvenile delinquents, blasphemy, sacrificing to false gods, witchcraft, bestiality, and the committing of fornication by a priest's daughter.

The message given us is: To deny the death penalty is to insist on life for evil. If the criminal goes unpunished, we adhere to a system that denies life to those whose persons were violated. This grants life to those who commit evil acts.

(*See Also:* Accountability, Discipline, Justice, Law and Order, Perjury, Rape, Restitution, Rule of Law)

Whoever sheds man's blood, by man shall his blood be shed.
GENESIS 9:6.

He who smites a man, so that he die, shall be surely put to death.
EXODUS 21:12.

And he who smites his father, or his mother, shall be surely put to death. And he who steals a man, and sells him, or if he be found in his hand, he shall surely be put to death. And he who curses his father or his mother, shall surely be put to death.
EXODUS 21:15–17.

And if he smite him with an instrument of iron, so that he die, he is a murderer: the murderer shall surely be put to death. And if he smite him by throwing a stone, wherewith he may die, and he die, he is a murderer: the murderer shall surely be put to death. Or if he smite him with [a] hand weapon of wood, wherewith he may die, and he die, he is a murderer: the murderer shall surely be put to death. The revenger of blood himself shall slay the murderer: when he [meet] him, he shall slay him. But if he thrust him of hatred, or hurl at him by laying of wait, that he die; or in enmity smite him with his hand, that he die; he [who] smote him shall surely be put to death; for he is a murderer: the revenger of blood shall slay the murderer, when he [meet] him.
NUMBERS 35:16–21.

Ye shall take no satisfaction for the life of a murderer, which is guilty of death: but he shall surely be put to death.

NUMBERS 35:31.

If a man find a betrothed damsel in the field, and the man force her, and lie with her: then the man only that lay with her shall die.

DEUTERONOMY 22:25.

If a man be found stealing any of his brethren of the children of Israel, and maketh merchandise of him, or sell him; then that thief shall die; and you shall put evil away from among you.

DEUTERONOMY 24:7.

The fathers shall not be put to death for the children, neither shall the children be put to death for the fathers: every man shall be put to death for his own sin.

DEUTERONOMY 24:16.

CAPITALISM

(*See:* Free Enterprise, Market Economy)

CENSUS

In a free society, census-taking is difficult to justify, because civil governmental activities are limited primarily to two essential areas: military defense and a civil court system. According to the letter and intent of the U.S. Constitution, census meant only a head-counting task. To enumerate a population by sex and district—perhaps for determining the number of judges and for military draft—may provide, at best, justification for an occasional census. To require, under threat of fine and imprisonment information on the number of baths, television sets, rooms one has, and personal financial data on occupants and property suggests nothing is sacrosanct or secure from state prying. The fact is that the census is used to make state planning "rational." Without it, planners could not plan. Therefore, census-taking is an arm of state power.

Information-seeking organizations (whether profit or nonprofit) should pay for their own raw data and secure it voluntarily; social researchers can gather their own statistics (with their own money, not with public grants), and even if we missed being inundated with the latest few thousand "scientific findings," we would hardly be the poorer for it; and civil governments under the rule of God simply cannot justify accumulating extensive information on inhabitants under some guise or another.

An in-depth census and genealogical survey was undertaken on the tribes of Israel for the singular purpose of establishing rights of inheritance on lands that God gave them. In the Old Testament, census meant counting the number of males for military defense purposes or for payment of a head tax (the only civil government tax). A most interesting verse is found in 1 CHRONICLES 21:1: "Satan stood up against Israel, and provoked David to number Israel." God did not like that. King David had sinned. We would have to conclude that God's people are counted by God, not by man.

(*See Also:* Bureaucracy, Directed Economy, Draft (Military), Freedom, Inheritance, Justice, Libertarianism, Taxation)

Take the sum of all the congregation of the children of Israel, after their families, by the house of their fathers, with the number of their names, every male by their polls.

And they assembled all the congregation together on the first day of the second month, and they declared their pedigrees after their families, by the house of their fathers, according to the number of names, from twenty years old upward, by their polls.

NUMBERS 1:2, 18.

Number the children of Levi after the house of their fathers, by their families: every male from a month old and upward you shall number them.

NUMBERS 3:15.

And Satan stood up against Israel, and provoked David to number Israel.

And God was displeased with this thing; therefore he smote Israel. And David said to God, I have sinned greatly, because I have done this thing; but now, I beseech you, do away with the iniquity of your servant, for I have done very foolishly.

1 CHRONICLES 21:1, 7–8.

CENTRAL PLANNING

(*See:* Census, Directed Economy, Rule by Decree)

CHARACTER

Character-building begins at home, in the family, based on Christian morals. God's people are characterized by their blamelessness, faithfulness, godliness, and holiness (see PHILEMON 2:15; REVELATION 17:14; 2 PETER 2:9; COLOSSIANS 3:12). According to Scripture, they are loving, humble, sincere, courteous, hospitable, generous, peaceable, patient, and steadfast. The character of the wicked is evident by their attitude toward God: They are disobedient, hostile, and deny His existence. (See TITUS 1:16; ROMANS 8:7; PSALM 14:1.) According to Scripture, they are full of evil, boastful, sensual, slaves to sin, and they despise the Gospel.

When the Kentucky Military Institute existed, the school motto was: Character Makes the Man. Development of good character and good habits was a matter of daily reminder and reinforcement. Today the question arises whether good character formation is the responsibility of the family or the dictate of the state. It is not a new issue. Herbert Spencer wrote about it in the 1890s.

> Of the many reasons for restricting the range of governmental actions, the strongest remains to be named. The end of which the statesman should keep in view as higher than all other ends, is the formation of character. And if there is entertained a right conception of the character which should be formed, and of the means by which it may be formed, the exclusion of multipled state agencies is necessarily applied....
>
> Whether the chosen ideal of a citizen, and the chosen process for producing him, be good or bad, the choice inevitably has three implications, any one of which condemns it.
>
> The system must work towards uniformity.
>
> Another concomitant must be the production of a passive receptivity of whatever form the state decides to impress.
>
> One further necessary implication is that either there exists no natural process by which citizens are being molded, or else that this natural process should be superseded by an artificial one.
>
> Anyone who says this must say that the varieties of mankind have arisen without cause; or else have been caused by government action.[1]

[1]Herbert Spencer, *The Principles of Ethics,* Vol. II (Indianapolis, Ind.: Liberty Classics, 1978), pp. 271-73.

Most important, believers must set themselves apart by their character. Although most television programs, for instance, establish the character of the wicked as a norm, God's people stand out in sharp contrast—a rich opportunity to demonstrate by example as well as a deep responsibility to maintain character.

(*See Also:* Ethics, Family, Honesty, Maturity, Moral Principles, Self-Discipline, Stewardship)

But the Lord said to Samuel, Look not on his countenance, or on the height of his stature, because I have refused him: for the Lord sees not as man sees; for man looks on the outward appearance, but the Lord looks on the heart.

1 SAMUEL 16:7.

He who refuses instruction despises his own soul: but he who hears reproof gets understanding. The fear of the Lord is the instruction of wisdom; and before honor is humility.

PROVERBS 15:32–33.

Even a child is known by his doings, whether his work be pure, and whether it be right.

PROVERBS 20:11.

A good name is better than precious ointment.

ECCLESIASTES 7:1.

For where your treasure is, there will your heart be also … if your eye be evil, your whole body shall be full of darkness. If therefore the light that is in you be darkness, how great is that darkness! No man can serve two masters: for either he will hate one, and love the other; or else he will hold to the one, and despise the other. You cannot serve God and mammon.

MATTHEW 6:21, 23–24.

Behold, I send you forth as sheep in the midst of wolves: be therefore wise as serpents, and harmless as doves.

MATTHEW 10:16–17.

A good man out of the good treasure of the heart brings forth good things; and an evil man out of the evil treasure brings forth evil things.

MATTHEW 12:35.

…it is required in stewards, that a man be found faithful.

1 CORINTHIANS 4:2.

CHARITY

In the Soviet Union, any charitable activity is strictly forbidden to religious groups.[1] Collecting money and goods and distributing them to needy members of the community create a power independent of the state. Charity, therefore, has been preempted by the state in its march toward totalitarianism. In Marxist Nicaragua, the Sandinista government intervenes in church collections and takes 40 percent in its march toward totalitarianism.[2] Many charitable functions now attempted by the American government were generously provided by private organizations and churches just a few decades ago.

Charity, it appears, is a direct obligation of each person, not only as a moral duty but also as a necessity for preserving the Christian way of life. Let's conclude with a glimpse at Jewish charity.

> The survival of the Jews through the centuries has been due to the centrality of the family and also to its perpetuation of a taxation outside the state. While such taxation has become humanistic, its strength has been phenomenal in not only preserving but advancing Jewish faith and culture. Many people, bitter about Jewish power, fail to recognize that it rests on this form of taxation. To cite two examples, Jewish immigrants in New York City, numbering 1.5 million by 1915, had created 3,637 institutions and agencies to administer charity, social welfare, educational enterprises, and the like. Again, during the Six Day War, at one luncheon alone, $1 million a minute was pledged for 15 minutes; the total American Jewish giving to that war effort was $230 million. The Puritans, and Americans of some years back, have alone rivalled the Jews in this respect.[3]

(*See Also:* Character, Compensation, Faith, Free Society, Inequality, Materialism, Poverty, Zain)

> *And when you reap the harvest of your land, you not wholly reap the corners of your field, neither shall you gather the gleanings of your harvest. And you shall not glean your vineyard, neither shall you gather every grape of your vineyard; you shall leave them for the poor and stranger.*
> *Leviticus 19:9–10.*

[1]*An Illustrated Digest of the Church and State Under Communism* (Staten Island, N.Y.: St. Mary's School of Religion for Adults).

[2]"Nicaragua Today," *The Envoy* (November–December 1981).

[3]Rousas John Rushdoony, *Law and Society* (Vallecito, Calif.: Ross Books, 1982), p. 386.

For the poor shall never cease out of the land: therefore I command you, saying, you shall open your hand wide unto your brother, to your poor, and to your needy, in your land.

Deuteronomy 15:11.

Blessed is he who considers the poor: the Lord deliver him in time of trouble.

Psalm 41:1.

Whoever mocks the poor reproaches his Maker: and he who is glad at calamities shall not be unpunished.

Proverbs 17:5.

He who has pity upon the poor lends to the Lord; and that which he has given will He pay him again.

Proverbs 19:17.

Learn to do well; seek judgment, relieve the oppressed, judge the fatherless, plead for the widow.

Isaiah 1:17.

Knowledge puffs up, but charity edifies.

1 Corinthians 8:1.

Though I speak with the tongues of men and of angels, and have not charity, I am become as sounding brass, or a tinkling cymbal. And though I have the gift of prophecy, and understand all the mysteries, and all knowledge, and though I have all faith, so that I could remove mountains, and have not charity, I am nothing. And though I bestow all my goods to feed the poor, and though I give my body to be burned, and have not charity, it profits me nothing. Charity suffers long, and is kind; charity envies not; charity vaunts not itself, is not puffed up, does not behave itself unseemly, seeks not her own, is not easily provoked, thinks no evil; rejoices not in iniquity, but rejoices in the truth; bears all things, believes all things, hopes all things, endures all things. Charity never fails.

And now abides faith, hope, charity, these three; but the greatest of these is charity.

1 Corinthians 13:1–8, 13.

Every man according as he purposes in his heart, so let him give, not grudgingly, or of necessity: for God loves a cheerful giver.

2 Corinthians 9:7.

If a brother or sister be naked, and destitute of daily food, and one of you say to them, Depart in peace, be warmed and filled; notwithstanding you give them not those things which are needful to the body; what does it profit?

JAMES 2:15–16.

CHILDREN

Children and property are two major areas of family social function. Humanistic governments primarily attack these two areas in order to make the state superior to the family, the reverse of God's order.

Counselors tell us that problem children often come from those very homes where parents have relinquished their responsibilities for religious and educational training and where discipline is absent or inconsistently administered. Without moral training, children are set adrift. In later years, they become vulnerable to every type of strange philosophy in their quest for a firm foundation of right and wrong and the meaning of life.

Creation of a Children's Bill of Rights directly attacks family and church and the Christian faith. Parents who abdicate their child-rearing responsibilities contribute to this warfare against society. Thus, by their irresponsible behavior, they give tacit support to a statist form of government. In communist countries, as wards of state, children are encouraged to inform on parents.

Parental obligations toward children are nourishment (1 SAMUEL 1:22), training (PROVERBS 22:6; EPHESIANS 6:4), instruction (GALATIANS 4:1–2), responsibility (1 SAMUEL 17:15), and inheritance (LUKE 12:13–14). Duties of children include obedience (EPHESIANS 6:1–3), honor to parents (EXODUS 20:12, HEBREWS 12:9), respect for age (PROVERBS 23:22; 1 PETER 5:5), care for parents (1 TIMOTHY 5:4), obedience to God (DEUTERONOMY 30:2), remembering God (ECCLESIASTES 12:1).

(*See Also:* Abortion, Discipline, Education, Family, Hippies, Inheritance, Maturity, Youth Cultism)

Honor your father and your mother: that your days may be long upon the land which the Lord your God gives you.

EXODUS 20:12.

He who smites his father, or his mother, shall be surely put to death. And he who curses his father, or his mother, shall surely be put to death.

EXODUS 21:15, 17.

Behold, children are a heritage of the Lord, and the fruit of the womb is His reward. As arrows are in the hand of a warrior, so are the children of one's youth. Happy is the man who has his quiver full of them.

PSALM 127:3–5.

Train up a child in the way he should go: and when he is old, he will not depart from it.

PROVERBS 22:6.

Hearken unto your father who begot you, and despise not your mother when she is old.

PROVERBS 23:22.

The rod and reproof give wisdom: but a child left to himself brings his mother to shame.
Correct your son, and he shall give you rest; yea, he shall give delight unto your soul.

PROVERBS 29:15, 17.

Now I say, that the heir, as long as he is a child, differs nothing from a servant, though he be lord of all, but is under tutors and governors until the time appointed by the father.

GALATIANS 4:1–2.

Children, obey your parents in the Lord: for this is right. Honor your father and mother, which is the first commandment with promise, that it may be well with you and you may live long on the earth. And you, fathers, do not provoke your children to wrath; but bring them up in the nurture and admonition of the Lord.

EPHESIANS 6:1–4.

If any widow have children or nephews, let them learn first to show piety at home, and to requite their parents: for that is good and acceptable before God.

1 TIMOTHY 5:4.

If you are without chastisement, whereof all are partakers, then you are bastards, and not sons. Furthermore, we have had fathers of our own flesh which corrected us, and we gave them reverence. Shall we not much rather be in submission to the Father of Spirits, and live?

HEBREWS 12:8–9.

Likewise, you younger, submit yourselves to the elder. Yea, all of you, be subject one to another, and be clothed with humility: for God resists the proud, and gives grace to the humble.

                                                              1 PETER 5:5.

CITIZENSHIP

The stranger who dwells with you shall be to you as one born among you, and you shall love him as yourself.

                                                              LEVITICUS 19:34.

(*See:* Equality, Justic, Law)

CLASS WARFARE

Mark those who cause divisions and offenses [contrary to the doctrine which you have learned]; and avoid them, for they who are such serve their own belly; and by words and fair speeches deceive the hearts of the simple.

                                                              ROMANS 16:17–18.

(*See:* Communism, Demagoguery, Liberalism)

COERCION

The king answered and said to the Chaldeans, The thing is gone from me. If you will not make known to me the dream, with its interpretation, you shall be cut in pieces, and your houses shall be made a dunghill.

                                                              DANIEL 2:5.

(*See:* Power of State, Statism)

COLLATERAL

Collateralized loans are secured by any marketable asset. The pledged property, or title to it, ordinarily is transferred to the lender.

The borrower expects to repay the loan with proceeds anticipated from future income or from sale of other assets. However, always at risk, income may be generated later or less than anticipated, or not at all. Also at risk, the borrower may be a poor steward of assets. Hence, the lender likes to be reassured that there are two sources of loan repayment: (1) repayment from future income, or (2) sale of collateral. Since collateral lowers risk to the lender, interest rates tend to be slightly lower for secured loans.

Collateral trust bonds are secured entirely by a pledge of other securities such as leaseholds, rents, franchises, and patents, which enable the trustee to reimburse bondholders when debt becomes due.

In ancient times, personal items such as clothing were often pledged as loan security, as we shall read in the following verses.

(*See Also:* Contract, Debts, Pledge, Private Property, Risk Aversion, Surety)

If you at all take your neighbor's raiment to pledge, you shall deliver it to him before the sun goes down; for that is his covering only, it is his raiment for his skin.

EXODUS 22:26–27.

No man shall take the nether or the upper millstone to pledge, for he takes a man's life to pledge.

DEUTERONOMY 24:6.

Take his garment that is surety for a stranger: and take a pledge of him for a strange woman.

PROVERBS 20:16; 27:13.

COMMITTEES

In all labor there is profit; but the talk of the lips tends only to penury.

PROVERBS 14:23.

(*See:* Crowd Psychology, Expert, Organization)

COMMON SENSE

If the clouds be full of rain, they empty themselves on the earth; and if the tree fall toward the south, or toward the north, in the place where the tree falls, there it shall be. He who observes the wind shall not sow; and he who regards the clouds shall not reap.

                                                                      ECCLESIASTES 11:3–4.

(*See:* Forecasting, Harmony, Moral Principles)

COMMUNICATION

"I know you believe you understand what you think I said. But I am not sure you realize that what you heard is not what I meant."

The president of a large multinational corporation complained to me not long ago about some recent college graduates, staff assistants to the president. "They have trouble communicating," he said. In the political arena, miscommunication rises to a level of science. When someone in politics deliberately twists meanings, he, more than being just a menace to those who hear and believe him, is a threat and danger to a free society.

Consider the word *capitalism.* To some the word means free enterprise, where honorable men and women engage in willing exchange of labor and goods and voluntarily cooperate and compete in response to consumer demand. To others, the word connotes monopoly, cutthroat competition, law of the jungle, exploitation of workers, greed—in other words, quite the opposite. A nineteenth-century liberal believed in the free enterprise system. Today, a liberal mostly opposes the free enterprise system.

Libor Brom writes:

> Marxism-Leninism is particularly effective on the semantic level where it exhibits a devastating duality. It lulls its adversaries to sleep, while at the same time it mobilizes its followers to revolutionary action. The Communist International's Seventh Congress concluded that open use of revolutionary terminology does not promote the Marxist-Leninist drive for world domination. Therefore, "revolution" has been changed to "liberation," "world conquest by the proletariat" has been changed to "peace and socialism," "armed seizure of power and liquidation of the bourgeoisie" has been

rephrased to read, "peaceful and gradual transition to socialism." Even the word "Communism" has been changed into "progressive," "antifascist," or "liberal."[1]

Effective communication requires that we say what we mean. Integrity requires that we mean what we say. Without effective communication, a society is headed for turmoil and chaos. Without integrity, there can be no free society under the rule of God.

(*See Also:* Character, Demagoguery, Honesty, Perjury, Persuasion, Testimony, Truth)

Woe to them who call evil good, and good evil; who put darkness for light, and light for darkness; who put bitter for sweet, and sweet for bitter.

ISAIAH 5:20.

There are, it may be, so many kinds of voices in the world, and none of them is without signification. Therefore if I know not the meaning of the voice, I shall be to him that speaks a barbarian, and he who speaks shall be a barbarian to me.

1 CORINTHIANS 14:10–11.

Yet in the church I had rather speak five words with understanding, that by my voice I might teach others also, than ten thousand words in an unknown tongue.

1 CORINTHIANS 14:19.

If any man speak in an unknown tongue, let it be by two, or at most by three, and that by course; and let one interpret.

1 CORINTHIANS 14:27.

Be not deceived: evil communications corrupt good manners.

1 CORINTHIANS 15:33.

COMMUNISM

Communism, a variation of socialism, is neither biblical nor realizable. Even the devils know that, and have said so, but too many professed Christians do not.

[1]Libor Brom, "Where Is Your America?" *Imprimis* (August 1982) (published by Hillsdale College, Hillsdale, Mich.).

Voluntary communalism hardly compares to the coercive nature of the communist state. Certainly Jesus and His band of itinerant preachers pooled resources and operated from a common fund—similar to investment pooling done in a modern corporation today. Those are voluntary acts, a matter of convenience for a group constantly on the road. It no more establishes a biblical precept than to command that we all become traveling ministers of the Gospel.

However, the whole argument for Christian communism (a true pairing of opposites) arises from ACTS 5:1–11. Because Ananias and Sapphira secretly held back part of their private property from the apostles, they were struck dead. Therefore, the communists argue, private ownership of property is unbiblical. But nothing is further from the truth! Ananias and Sapphira had made a covenant with the Lord. They failed to fulfill their end of the contract. Theirs was a fair-weather commitment to God, holding back something—just in case.

Peter did *not* say, "Private ownership is evil; you must surrender everything to the state." Peter did say, "Why hath Satan filled thine heart to lie to the Holy Ghost, and to keep back part of the price of the land? While it remained, was it not thine own? and after it was sold, was it not in thine own power? why hast thou conceived this thing in thine heart? thou hast not lied unto men, but unto God." (ACTS 5:3–4). Notice the emphasis on *lying to God, not lying to men or to the state.*

Communism bulldozes the lazy, uninformed, guilt-ridden Christian. Read what David Chilton writes about inducing *guilt.*

> Guilt produces *passivity,* and makes man *programmed for defeat.* The importance of this for totalitarianism cannot be overemphasized. If a whole society can be made to feel guilty, it will be unable to withstand an enslaving state: it is ripe for conquest. This has long been recognized as the most successful method of rendering men passive and pliable, incapable of resistance to statist domination and control. As guilt produces impotence, it also leads people to call for more and more controls from the state. The passive population is not only malleable, yielding, submissive; it positively *welcomes* state intervention. The guilty, unable to solve life's problems, will be *saved by the state.*
>
> The churches also have become enslaved. Regardless of all the hoopla over Moral Majority, most pastors are toeing the government line. When was the last time your minister spoke out against unbacked paper money and the expansion of credit? Does he even want to know what those words mean?[1]

We hope he does, especially when this reference book has made it so easy to discover what such modern expressions mean within a biblical context. We'll end with a few sentences from a funeral eulogy for Eugene Davis, Socialist Party, spoken by Gus Hall, Communist Party of America:

> I dream of the hour when the last preacher is strangled to death on the guts of the last congressman. And since Christians like to sing about blood, let's give them a little of

---

[1]David Chilton, *Productive Christians in an Age of Guilt-Manipulators: A Biblical Response to Ronald J. Sider,* rev. ed (Tyler, Tex.: Institute of Christian Economics, 1982), pp. 218–220.

it. Slit the throats of their children and drag them across the mourner's bench and see whether or not they still enjoy singing their hymns.

(*See Also:* Communist, Conspiracy, Envy, Evolutionism, Expropriation, One Worldism, Power of State, Slavery, Socialism, Statism)

I have seen servants upon horses, and princes walking as servants upon the earth.

ECCLESIASTES 10:7.

For the land is full of adulterers; for because of swearing the land mourns; the pleasant places of the wilderness are dried up, and their course is evil, and their force is not right. For both prophet and priest are profane;... Wherefore their way shall be to them as slippery ways in the darkness: they shall be driven on, and fall therein, for I will bring evil upon them, even in the year of their visitation, saith the Lord.

I have seen also in the prophets of Jerusalem [a] horrible thing: they commit adultery, and walk in lies: they strengthen also the hands of evildoers, that none does return from his wickedness: they are all of them to me as Sodom, and the inhabitants thereof as Gomorrah.

JEREMIAH 23:10–12, 14.

To crush under his feet all the prisoners of the earth, to turn aside the right of a man before the face of the most High, to subvert a man in his cause, the Lord approves not.

LAMENTATIONS 3:34–36.

As for us, our eyes as yet failed for our vain help: in our watching we have watched for a nation that could not save us. They hunt our steps, that we cannot go in our streets; our end is near, our days are fulfilled; for our end is come. Our persecutors are swifter than the eagles of the heaven: they pursued us upon the mountains, they laid wait for us in the wilderness. The breath of our nostrils, the anointed of the Lord, was taken in their pits, of whom we said, Under his shadow we shall live among the heathen.

LAMENTATIONS 4:17–20.

Our inheritance is turned to strangers, our houses to aliens.... We have drunken our water for money; our wood is sold to us. Our necks are under persecution; we labor, and have no rest.

Servants have ruled over us; there is none who delivers us out of their hand.

Princes are hanged up by their hand: the faces of elders were not honored.

They took the young men to grind, and the children fell under the wood. The elders have ceased from the gate, the young men from their music. The joy of our heart is ceased; our dance is turned into mourning.

LAMENTATIONS 5:2, 4–5, 8, 12–15.

Woe to them who devise iniquity, and work evil upon their beds! when the morning is light, they practice it, because it is the power of their hand. And they covet fields, and take them by violence, and houses, and take them away: so they oppress a man and his house, even a man and his heritage. Therefore thus saith the Lord; Behold, against this family do I devise evil, from which you shall not remove your necks; neither shall you go haughtily: for this time is evil.

MICAH 2:1–3.

And fear not them who kill the body, but are not able to kill the soul: but rather fear him who is able to destroy both soul and body in hell.

MATTHEW 10:28.

And you shall be betrayed both by parents, and brethren, and kinsfolks, and friends; and some of you shall they cause to be put to death. And you shall be hated of all men for my name's sake.

LUKE 21:16–17.

Because that, when they knew God, they glorified him not as God, neither were thankful; but became vain in their imaginations, and their foolish heart was darkened. Professing themselves to be wise, they became fools. And changed the glory of the uncorruptible God into an image made like to corruptible man, and to birds, and fourfooted beasts, and creeping things. Wherefore God also gave them up to uncleanness through the lusts of their own hearts, to dishonor their own bodies between themselves: who changed the truth of God into a lie, and worshipped and served the creature more than the Creator, who is blessed for ever.

ROMANS 1:21–25.

And there went out another horse that was red: and power was given to him that sat thereon to take peace from the earth, and that they should kill one another; and there was given unto him a great sword.

REVELATION 6:4.

COMMUNIST

You Can Trust the Communists (To Be Communists), a book by Dr. Fred Schwarz, whose thesis is that communists are communists, true to their beliefs.[1] Once we comprehend their strategic plan, and communist morality, and not interpret what they say and do within a framework of Christian morality, what they do, how they do it, and why they do it are "perfectly understandable and almost mathematically predictable."[2] Schwarz also tells us, "The Communists invariably tell the "truth," but it is the Marxist-Leninist "truth." Those who believe that the communists will lie in the interests of Communism are mistaken. In fact, it is not possible for a Communist to lie in the interests of Communism. By definition, if a statement is in the interests of Communism, it is the truth."[3]

Communists believe that a state of war exists; the Communist party was created to win this war against the state. Which state? Any state that acknowledges any power higher than the Communist party. They war with God; they conspire to destroy the free market system. The communist state must bring about social justice according to principles of truth discovered by and entrusted exclusively to communists in charge. Anyone who questions these truths is an enemy of the state.

Treating communism as a competing religion, its religious fervor is comprehensible. Former communist leader Douglas Hyde has written about recruitment techniques of communists in his book, *Dedication and Leadership.*[4] The source of Communist recruitment and retention techniques? The Bible!

Dr. Pat Robertson, in "A Christian Action Plan for the 1980s" writes:

> The Communists, who espouse a false religion, after only 60 years dominate the world. The reason is simple—they were dedicated to their cause and they worked at it. Except for our Lord's return we cannot expect our nation or our world to be freed from tyranny in one year or even 10 years. But if we are faithful and diligent, with His blessing, it will be done.[5]

Communism is the modern satanic banner under which statists by whatever name have gathered since Adam and Eve. "Ye shall not surely die," the serpent said to Eve (Genesis 3:4). God is the mythical father of chaos; the state is the only reality

[1]Fred Schwarz, *You Can Trust the Communists (To Be Communists),* Christian Anti-Communism Crusade (Long Beach, Calif.), 1969.

[2]Ibid., p. 1.

[3]Ibid., p. 8.

[4]Douglas Hyde, *Dedication and Leadership,* University of Notre Dame Press, 1966.

[5]Dr. Pat Robertson, *A Christian Action Plan for the 1980s* (Virginia Beach, VA: CBN, n.d.), p. 5.

and giver of law, say the communists. Verses that follow describe 6,000 years of tactical variations of the same scheme to replace God's laws with human laws.

(*See Also:* Communism, Humanism, Idolatry, Poor Nations, Redistribution of Income/Wealth, Slavery, World Government)

The wicked plot against the just, and gnash upon him with his teeth.

The wicked have drawn out the sword, and have bent their bow, to cast down the poor and needy, and to slay such as be of upright conversation.

PSALM 37:12, 14.

Your tongue devises mischiefs; like a sharp razor, working deceitfully. You love evil more than good; and lying rather than to speak righteousness. You love all devouring words, O deceitful tongue. God shall likewise destroy you for ever, he shall take you away, and pluck you out of my dwelling place, and root you out of the land of the living.

PSALM 52:2–5.

The fool has said in his heart, There is no God. Corrupt are they, and have done abominable iniquity: there is none who does good. God looked down from heaven upon the children of men, to see if there were any who did understand, who did seek God. Every one of them is gone back: they are altogether become filthy; there is none who does good, no, not one. Have the workers of iniquity no knowledge? who eat up my people as they eat bread: they have not called upon God.

PSALM 53:1–4.

They only consult to cast him down from his excellency: they delight in lies; they bless with their mouth, but they curse inwardly.

PSALM 62:4.

Woe to them who call evil good, and good evil; who put darkness for light, and light for darkness; who put bitter for sweet, and sweet for bitter!

ISAIAH 5:20.

Their works are works of iniquity, and the act of violence is in their hands. Their feet run to evil, and they make haste to shed innocent blood: their thoughts are thoughts of iniquity; wasting and destruction are in their paths.

ISAIAH 59:6–7.

For among my people are found wicked men; they lay wait, as he who sets snares; they set a trap, they catch men. As a cage is full of birds, so are their houses full of deceit.

JEREMIAH 5:26–27.

By swearing, and lying, and killing, and stealing, and committing adultery, they break out, and blood touches blood. Therefore shall the land mourn, and every one who dwells therein shall languish, with the beasts of the field, and with the fowls of heaven; yea, the fish of the sea also shall be taken away.

HOSEA 4:2–3.

Shall horses run upon the rock? will one plow there with oxen? for you have turned judgment into gall, and the fruit of righteousness into hemlock: you who rejoice in a thing of nought, who say, Have we not taken to us horns by our own strength?

AMOS 6:12–13.

Be not unequally yoked together with unbelievers: for what fellowship has righteousness with unrighteousness? and what communion has light with darkness?

2 CORINTHIANS 6:14.

COMPENSATION

Man rewards man because God rewards man (see 1 CORINTHIANS 3); and man punishes man because God punishes man (see LUKE 12:47–48). The principle of compensation is illustrated repeatedly in the Bible: the Golden Rule, MATTHEW 7:12: "Therefore, whatever you want men to do to you, do also to them, for this is the Law and the Prophets"; justice, EXODUS 21:24: calling for an eye for eye, tooth for tooth, measure for measure; or in 2 THESSALONIANS 2:6: "...since it is a righteous thing with God to repay with tribulation those who trouble you..." Of course, we know, too, that "He who leads into captivity shall go into captivity; he who kills with the sword must be killed with the sword" (EXODUS 13:10).

When things become imbalanced, compensatory forces work to restore balance. This compensatory action is more apparent in a free society because nothing really inhibits the adjusting process. In any other kind of society, equilibrating forces are offset, thwarted, and rechanneled long enough to create the delusion that man, not God, is in control. In fact, many people really doubt the existence and operation of this basic universal law. They lack faith and ability to reason out long-term consequences of any action. Hence, the public may not recognize relationships between inflation and disinvestment, compulsory unionism and unemployment, obedience to God's laws and economic prosperity. Although rain falls on the wicked and just alike, repeated historical examples link prosperity and obedience to God. "For the Lord knows the way of the righteous, but the way of the ungodly shall perish" (PSALM 1:6).

To illustrate, if more of a product is demanded than has been produced, what is the sequence of events in a free market? First, price rises. Higher prices mean more profits to producers so production is expanded. Supply of product increases. Price begins to fall. Finally, equilibrium is restored once again, bringing matters back into balance.

If we believe it in economics and in physics, then might it not be true everywhere else? Can we really escape judgment? To those who still believe in free lunches (i. e., food stamps)—perhaps! But, no, a price must be paid. Elsewhere I pointed out the tremendous price Puerto Rican Islanders pay for living on the dole.[1]

If we truly believe in compensation for thoughts and deeds, then we need to heed ECCLESIASTES 5:4–5:

> *When you make a vow to God,*
> *do not delay to pay it;*
> *For He has no pleasure in fools.*
> *Pay what you have vowed.*
> *It is better not to vow*
> *than to vow and not pay.*

(*See Also:* Accountability, Contract, Discipline, Justice, Price Mechanism, Restitution, Tinstaafl)

> *A blessing, if you obey the commandments of the Lord your God,*
> *which I command you this day: And a curse, if you will not obey the*
> *commandments...*
> >   DEUTERONOMY 11:27–28.

> *Even as I have seen, they who plow iniquity, and sow wickedness, reap*
> *the same.*
> >   JOB 4:8.

> *Woe to you who spoils and was not spoiled; and deals treacherously,*
> *and they dealt not treacherously with you! when you shall cease to*

---

[1]Robert P. Vichas, "Puerto Rico: Land of Food Stamps," *Human Events,* 38 (June 1978).

spoil, you shall be spoiled, and when you shall make an end to deal treacherously, they shall deal treacherously with you.

ISAIAH 33:1.

And first I will recompense their iniquity and their sin double…

JEREMIAH 16:18.

In those days they shall say no more, The fathers have eaten a sour grape, and the children's teeth shall be set on edge. But every one shall die for his own iniquity; every man who eats the sour grape, his teeth shall be set on edge.

JEREMIAH 31:29–30.

Render to them a recompence, O Lord, according to the work of their hands.

LAMENTATIONS 3:64.

And my eye shall not spare you, neither will I have pity; but I will recompense your ways upon you: and you shall know that I am the Lord.

EZEKIEL 7:4.

As you have done, it shall be done to you; your reward shall return upon your own head.

OBADIAH 1:15.

He who receives a prophet in the name of a prophet shall receive a prophet's reward; and he who receives a righteous man in the name of a righteous man shall receive a righteous man's reward.

MATTHEW 10:41.

Judge not, and you shall not be judged; condemn not, and you shall not be condemned; forgive, and you shall be forgiven. Give, and it shall be given to you; good measure, pressed down, and shaken together, and running over, shall men give to your bosom. For with the same measure that you mete, it shall be measured to you again.

LUKE 6:37–38.

And that servant, who knew his lord's will, and prepared not himself neither did according to his will, shall be beaten with many stripes. But he who did not know, and did commit things worthy of stripes, shall be beaten with few stripes. For to whomsoever much is given, of him much will be required: and to whom men have committed much, of him they will ask the more.

LUKE 12:47–48.

But Abraham said, Son, remember that in your lifetime you received your good things, and likewise Lazarus evil things: but now he is comforted, and you are tormented.

LUKE 16:25.

We receive the due reward of our deeds.

LUKE 23:41.

Be not deceived; God is not mocked: for whatsoever a man sows, that shall he also reap. For he who sows to his flesh shall of the flesh reap corruption; but he who sows to the Spirit shall of the Spirit reap life everlasting.

GALATIANS 6:7–8.

But he who does wrong shall receive for the wrong which he has done…

COLOSSIANS 3:25.

For we know Him who has said, Vengeance belongs to me, I will recompense, saith the Lord. And again, The Lord shall judge his people. It is a fearful thing to fall into the hands of the living God.

HEBREWS 10:30–31.

And, behold, I come quickly, and my reward is with me, to give every man according as his work shall be.
Blessed are they who do his commandments, that they may have right to the tree of life, and may enter in through the gates to the city. For without are dogs, and sorcerers, and whoremongers, and murderers, and idolaters, and whosoever loves and makes a lie.

REVELATION 22:12, 14–15.

COMPETITION

Do you not know that they who run in a race run all, but one receives the prize? So run, that you may obtain.

1 CORINTHIANS 9:24.

(*See:* Exchange, Free Enterprise, Market Economy)

CONSCRIPTION

(See: Draft, Military; Military Defense)

CONSPIRACY

There are major conspiracies; there are minor conspiracies. There are conspiracies within conspiracies, circles within circles. We all know of the communist conspiracy. The conspiracies of international bankers have captured imaginations of socialists and libertarians alike. Today we read of the conspiracy of trilateralism. Two hundred years ago it was Weishaupt's Illuminati. Or 2,000 years ago the enemies of Jesus conspired to murder Him.

Why do the nations rage (PSALM 2:1)? "The nations rage against their bondage to God, and they take counsel or conspire against God and His Christ, planning to create their own world order and law in contempt of Him."[1] In PSALM 2:10–12, "The nations are exhorted to abandon the conspiracy against God and His Christ or else face destruction."[2] As we move backward through historical time, we finally come to the conspiracy of Eve and Adam against God, in their quest for power. Then, in GENESIS 3, we discover the origin of these conspiracies: Satan conspires against God, promising his co-conspirators *total control* if they will engage in total war against God.

"The Bible as a whole presents a view of *history as conspiracy,* with Satan and man determined to assert their 'right' to be gods, knowing, or determining, good and evil for themselves."[3] The issue is theological. When the state will not submit to and enforce God's law, conspiracies flourish. Man must live by the whole counsel of God if he is to live free. Conspirators, on the other hand, in their drive for power, seek control of the minds of men through controlled news media, public schools, and cooperative churches or private schools and other cooperating private institutions. They seek economic control primarily through the monetary system. Hence, "the building of a Christian resistance movement cannot legitimately be based on a

---

[1] Rousas J. Rushdoony, *The Nature of the American System* (Fairfax, Va.: Thoburn Press, 1978), p. 140.
[2] Ibid.
[3] Ibid.

program of initiation into a secret hierarchy of power,"[4] but on adherence to the principles of righteous action revealed in our handbook, the Bible.

(*See Also:* Communism, One Worldism, Rule by Decree, Statism, Terrorism, United Nations, Xenophobia)

And when they saw him afar off, even before he came near to them, they conspired against him to slay him.

GENESIS *37:18.*

And one told David, saying, Ahithophel is among the conspirators with Absalom. And David said, O Lord, I pray to you, turn the counsel of Ahithophel into foolishness.

2 SAMUEL *15:31.*

And they conspired against him, and stoned him with stones at the commandment of the king in the court of the house of the Lord.

2 CHRONICLES *24:21.*

Why do the nations rage, and the people plot a vain thing? The kings of the earth set themselves, and the rulers take counsel together, against the Lord, and against His anointed, saying, Let us break their bands asunder, and cast away their cords from us.

PSALM *2:1–3.*

They also who seek after my life lay snares for me; and they who seek my hurt speak mischievous things, and imagine deceits all the day long.

PSALM *38:12.*

For they have consulted together with one consent: they are confederate against you.

PSALM *83:5.*

And the Lord said to me, A conspiracy is found among the men of Judah, and among the inhabitants of Jerusalem. They are turned back to iniquities of their forefathers, which refused to hear my words; and they went after other gods to serve them: the house of Israel and the house of Judah have broken my covenant which I made with their fathers. Therefore thus saith the Lord, Behold, I will bring evil upon

---

[4]Gary North, "Editor's Introduction," in *Tactics of Christian Resistance,* Vol. 3 (Tyler, Tex.: Geneva Divinity School Press, 1983), p. x.

them, which they shall not be able to escape; and though they shall cry unto me, I will not listen to them.

JEREMIAH 11:9–11.

There is a conspiracy of her prophets in the midst thereof, like a roaring lion ravening the prey; they have devoured souls; they have taken the treasure and precious things; they have made her many widows in the midst thereof.

EZEKIEL 22:25.

Jesus answered him, I spoke openly to the world; I ever taught in the synagogue, and in the temple, where the Jews always resort; and in secret have I said nothing.

JOHN 18:20.

CONSULTANT

In multitude of counsellors there is safety.

PROVERBS 24:6.

(*See:* Expert)

CONTINGENCY PLANNING

(*See:* Risk Aversion, Strategic Planning)

CONTRACT

The basis of human contract is God's covenant. The Ten Commandments establish the foundation of the contract between man and God. In DEUTERONOMY 28:1–14, we are promised the many blessings for diligently obeying God's commandments. By the same token, for not observing carefully all His commandments, the remainder of that chapter describes the many curses that will befall us. Legally, a contract (an agreement between one or more persons in which each promises to do or not to do something) may be oral or written. Four conditions must be fulfilled for a contract to be valid:

1. There must be an express offer and an unequivocal acceptance. If an acceptance differs from the original offer, this constitutes a counteroffer, which requires acceptance by the original offeror before there is a valid contract.
2. All parties to the contract must be competent, that is, have legal capacity to contract. Corporations may enter into contracts as persons but ability to contract is limited by the charter, various statutes, and bylaws of the corporation.
3. Something of value must flow among persons contracting.
4. There must be an absence of fraud, duress, and extraordinary mental and physical pressure.

A contract may be express or implied. An *express contract* specifically details terms of agreement. An *implied contract* is one implied by law. For instance, when you order lunch at your favorite restaurant, it is implied that you will pay for the meal after eating it. God expects us to honor our promises and contractual commitments, for whatever commitments are made on earth are heavenly obligations as well (MATTHEW 18:18).

(*See Also:* Collateral, Exchange, Justice, Law, Responsibility, Rule of Law, Stewardship)

You shall not commit adultery.

EXODUS 20:14.

If Balak would give me his house full of silver and gold, I cannot go beyond the word of the Lord my God, to do less or more.

NUMBERS 22:18.

Every vow, and every binding oath to afflict the soul, her husband may establish it, or her husband may make it void. But if her husband altogether holds his peace at her from day to day, then he establishes all her vows, or all her bonds, which are upon her; he confirms them, because he held his peace at her in the day that he heard them. But if he shall any ways make them void after he has heard them, then he shall bear her iniquity.

NUMBERS 30:13–15

If a man vow a vow to the Lord, or swear an oath to bind his soul with a bond; he shall not break his word, he shall do according to all that proceeds out of his mouth.

NUMBERS 30:2

When you shall vow a vow to the Lord your God, you shall not slack to pay it: for the Lord your God will surely require it of you; and it would be sin in you.

DEUTERONOMY 23:21.

That which is gone out of your lips you shall keep and perform, even a freewill offering.

DEUTERONOMY 23:23.

My covenant will I not break, nor alter the thing that is gone out of my lips.

PSALM 89:34.

When you vow a vow to God, defer not to pay it; for he has no pleasure in fools: pay that which you have vowed. Better is it that you should not vow, than that you should vow and not pay.

ECCLESIASTES 5:4–5.

I bought the field and weighed him the money, even seventeen shekels of silver. And I subscribed the evidence, and sealed it, and took witnesses, and weighed him the money in the balances. So I took the evidence of purchase, both of which was sealed according to the law and custom, and that which was open; and I gave the evidence of the purchase to Baruch the son of Neriah, in the sight of my uncle's son, and in the presence of witnesses who subscribed to the book of the purchase, before all Jews who sat in the court of the prison.

Thus saith the Lord of hosts, the God of Israel; Take these evidences, this evidence of the purchase, both which is sealed, and this evidence which is open; and put them in an earthen vessel, that they may continue for many days.

JEREMIAH 32:9–12, 14–15.

They who observe lying vanities forsake their own mercy. But I will sacrifice unto you with the voice of thanksgiving; I will pay that which I have vowed. Salvation is of the Lord.

JONAH 2:8–9.

Whatsoever you shall bind on earth shall be bound in heaven: and whatsoever you shall loose on earth shall be loosed in heaven.

MATTHEW 18:18.

About the eleventh hour he went out, and found others standing idle, and said to them, Why do you stand here all day idle? They said to him, Because no man has hired us. He said to them, Go also into the vineyard; and whatsoever is right, that you shall receive. So when evening came, the lord of the vineyard said to his steward, Call the laborers, and give them their hire, from the last to the first. And when they came who were hired about the eleventh hour, they received every one a penny. But when the first came, they supposed that they should receive more, and they likewise received every man a penny. And when they had received it, they murmured against the goodman of the house. Saying, These last have wrought but one hour, and you have made them equal to us, who have borne the burden and heat of the day. But he answered one of them and said, Friend, I do you no wrong: did not you agree with me for a penny?

MATTHEW 20:6–13.

COOPERATION

Jerry Buchanan tells an interesting story about cooperation. A fireman (no pun!) was given the grand tour of Hell and Heaven. He visited hell first. In hell's huge dining hall were rows of tables loaded with every imaginable kind of nutritious food. Seated around them sat emaciated, sad souls. No one had any elbows. So, being unable to bend their arms to put food into their mouths, they were starving.

Then the fireman visited heaven, where the situation was identical: a huge dining hall with rows of tables covered with deliciously prepared food. Here, everyone, happy and healthy, really enjoyed themselves, despite the fact that they, too had no elbows. The difference between hell and heaven pivoted on one word: *cooperation.* In heaven, everyone fed someone else.

Cooperation and organization, within the framework of a free society under God's commandments, result in peace, harmony, and better living. Don't confuse what passes for cooperation in a statist society with cooperation in a free society. There is plenty of apparent cooperation in a bee society or an ant society. Females run the bee society; ants live in a military dictatorship. They "cooperate" all right but so do people in communist countries.

In a free society, cooperation provides the means to individual ends. No one knows how to satisfy someone else's goals. That is an individual decision. No conflict arises between self-interests and goals of individuals and those of the free society. Society is only another name for the combination of individuals cooperating to satisfy distinct ends of each member of that society. Abundance, not poverty, results.

(*See Also:* Demand and Supply, Division of Labor, Free Market, Harmony, Honesty, Organization, Service)

And the Lord said, Behold, the people are one, and they have all one language; and this they begin to do: and now nothing will be restrained from them, which they have imagined to do.

GENESIS 11:6.

For if they fall, the one will lift up his fellow: but woe to him who is alone when he falls; for he has not another to help him up.

ECCLESIASTES 4:10.

Can two walk together, except they be agreed?

AMOS 3:3.

Jesus knew their thoughts, and said to them, Every kingdom divided against itself is brought to desolation; and every city or house divided against itself shall not stand.

MATTHEW 12:25.

If I then, your Lord and Master, have washed your feet, you also ought to wash one another's feet.

JOHN 13:14.

Every branch in Me that bears not fruit He takes away; and every branch that bears fruit, He prunes it, that it may bring forth more fruit.

Abide in Me, and I in you. As the branch cannot bear fruit of itself, except it abide in the vine; no more can you, except you abide in Me. I am the vine, you are the branches. He who abides in Me, and I in him, the same brings forth much fruit for without Me you can do nothing. If a man abide not in Me, he is cast forth as a branch, and is withered; and men gather them, and cast them into the fire, and they are burned.

Herein is my Father glorified, that you bear much fruit; so shall you be my disciples.

JOHN 15:2, 4–6, 8.

For none of us lives to himself, and no man dies to himself.

ROMANS 14:7.

For the body is not one member but many. If the foot shall say, Because I am not the hand, I am not of the body, is it therefore not of the body? And if the ear shall say, Because I am not the eye, I am not of the body, is it therefore not of the body? If the whole body were an eye, where were the hearing? If the whole were hearing, where were the smelling? But now has God set the members every one of them in the body as it has pleased Him. And if they were all one member which were the body? And the eye cannot say to the hand, I have no need of you; nor again the head to the feet, I have no need of you. Nay, much more those members of the body, which seem to be more feeble, are necessary.

1 CORINTHIANS 12:14–22.

For brethren, you have been called to liberty; only use not liberty for an occasion to the flesh, but by love serve one another.

GALATIANS 5:13.

Submitting yourselves one to another in the fear of God.

EPHESIANS 5:21.

CORRUPTION

Corruption, like many evils, springs from taking shortcuts, which, in turn, arise from failure to practice the laws of God daily. A little corruption down at Metro Center may seem like a minor affair. And it often is—to start with. But by the fruits of their labor we shall know them (*see* MATTHEW 7:16; 12:33).

Why must we take drastic action to rid our homes or society of corruption? In Luke and Matthew we read that evil is the product of corruption. We should not delude ourselves: Good works never come out of corrupt action (MATTHEW 7:17–20; Luke 6:43). How do we deal with corruption? Get rid of it. "Every tree that brings not forth good fruit is hewn down, and cast into the fire" (MATTHEW 7:19).

A sinful nation may run corruption up the flagpole and salute it, but it will hardly destroy it. In fact, from evidence available, apostates will more likely deal harshly with those who keep the commandments and judgments of God. "Thy princes are rebellious, and companions of thieves" (ISAIAH 1:23). Now, be careful that *you* can distinguish between corruption and good. Just because Congress, or a judge, or a bureaucratic agency, or the news media declare something bad, or good, or corrupt, does not necessarily make it so.

Immorality leads to corruption. Corruption leads to slavery. Slavery leads to death. A free society requires unending work, discipline, and adherence to that great model of societal organization blueprinted in the Bible. Although mingling with the troubled waters of the regenerate may seem like the fast road to riches and merriment, those waters cast up the mire and dirt of corruption. Creation itself will be delivered *from* the bondage of corruption into the glorious *liberty* of the children of God (see ROMANS 8:20–21.)

(*See Also:* Demagoguery, Dishonesty, Elitism, Foundation, Rule by Decree, Statism, Theft)

> We have dealt very corruptly against You, and have not kept the commandments, nor the statutes, nor the judgments, which You commanded your servant, Moses.
>
> NEHEMIAH 1:7.

> That which is crooked cannot be made straight.
>
> ECCLESIASTES 1:15.

> Ah, sinful nation, a people laden with iniquity, a brood of evildoers, children who are corrupters, they have foresaken the Lord; they have gone backward.
>
> ISAIAH 1:4.

> Your princes are rebellious, and companions of thieves. Every one loves gifts, and follows after rewards. They judge not the fatherless, neither does the cause of the widow come to them.
>
> ISAIAH 1:23.

> The wicked are like the troubled sea, when it cannot rest, whose waters cast up mire and dirt. There is no peace to the wicked.
>
> ISAIAH 57:20–21.

> A corrupt tree brings forth evil fruit. A good tree cannot bring forth evil fruit, neither can a corrupt tree bring forth good fruit. Every tree that brings not forth good fruit is hewn down, and cast into the fire. Wherefore by their fruits you shall know them.
>
> MATTHEW 7:17–20.

> Because the creature itself also shall be delivered from the bondage of corruption into the glorious liberty of the children of God.
>
> ROMANS 8:21.

> Be not deceived: evil communications corrupt good manners.
>
> 1 CORINTHIANS 15:33.

> Now this I say, brothers, that flesh and blood cannot inherit the kindom of God; neither does corruption inherit incorruption.
>
> 1 CORINTHIANS 15:50.

COST

For which of you, intending to build a tower, does not sit down first and count the cost, whether he has sufficient to finish it?

LUKE 14:28.

(*See:* Exchange, Price, Strategic Planning, Supply)

COURT SYSTEM

Considering Jesus' comments on law suits (MATTHEW 5:25, 40) and lawyers (LUKE 11:45–52), it is better to settle quickly and privately with an adversary than involve the judicial system. Good advice then and now! The Bible refers to three kinds of court systems: circuit (1 SAMUEL 7:15–17), superior and inferior (EXODUS 18:21–26), and ecclesiastical (MATTHEW 18:15–18). Each system had its layers of lesser courts.

In a free society under the rule of God, the family is the basic institution, the building block of society. Beyond the family, a network of voluntary associations for worship and justice has limited powers and provides for basic government. Therefore, the court system really begins in the family and between families, with appeal to a *Christian court* for mediation.

St. Paul tells us (1 CORINTHIANS 6:1–8) that Christians should only appear before Christians. A judge or court premised on anything but God's laws is untrustworthy in the administration of justice. Certainly Paul would not approve of our administrative law system created and controlled by various bureaucracies; he would treat them as pagan courts administering humanistic laws. God's law must be sought in God-appointed courts. Too often Christians go to an ungodly court (itself an ungodly act), hoping that an ungodly judge may favor them.

Regarding witnesses, the Bible applies some strict rules. To convict a person of a serious crime, two or three solid witnesses must testify. The testimony of one witness is insufficient (DEUTERONOMY 17:6; 19:15–21). For perjury, witnesses suffer the same penalty as the accused (EXODUS 23:1–3; DEUTERONOMY 19:18–19). (See also the Ninth Commandment: EXODUS 20:16.) The sentence was final in perjury cases, even requiring the death penalty for failure to accede to the sentence (DEUTERONOMY 17:8–13). Although mercy was granted for a proven accidental murder, murderers could not escape punishment by pleading insanity.

(*See Also:* Accountability, Capital Punishment, Justice, Law, Restitution, Rule of Law)

Moreover you shall provide out of all the people able men, such as fear God, men of truth, hating covetousness; and place such over them, to be rulers of thousands, and rulers of hundreds, rulers of fifties, and rulers of tens: and let them judge the peoples at all seasons: and it shall be, that every great matter they shall bring unto you, but every small matter they shall judge: so it shall be easier for yourself, and they shall bear the burden with you. If you shall do this thing, and God command you so, then you shall be able to endure, and all these people shall also go to their place in peace. So Moses chose able men out of all Israel. And they judged the people at all seasons; the hard causes they brought to Moses, but every small matter they judged themselves.

Exodus 18:21–26.

You shall not raise a false report: put not your hand with the wicked to be an unrighteous witness. You shall not follow a multitude to thwart judgment. Neither shall you favor a poor man in his lawsuit.

Exodus 23:1–3.

At the mouth of two witnesses, or three witnesses, shall he who is worthy of death be put to death; but at the mouth of one witness he shall not be put to death. The hands of the witnesses shall be first upon him to put him to death, and afterward the hands of all the people. So you shall put the evil away from among you. If there arise a matter too hard for you in judgment, between blood and blood, between plea and plea, and between stroke and stroke, being matters of controversy within your gates: then shall you arise, and get to the place which the Lord your God shall choose; and you shall come to the priests and Levites, and to the judge who shall be in those days, and inquire; and they shall show you the sentence of judgment; and you shall do according to the sentence, which they of that place which the Lord shall choose shall show you; and you shall observe to do according to all that they inform you, according to the sentence of the law which they shall teach you, and according to the judgment which they shall teach you, and according to the judgment which they shall tell you, you shall do. You shall not decline from the sentence which they shall show you, to the right hand, not to the left. And the man who will do presumptuously, and will not hearken to the priest who stands to minister there before the Lord your God, or to the judge, even that man shall die: and you shall put away the evil from Israel. And all the people shall hear, and fear, and do no more willfully.

Deuteronomy 17:8–13.

One witness shall not rise up against a man for any iniquity, or for any sin, in any sin that he sins: at the mouth of two witnesses, or at the mouth of three witnesses, shall the matter be established. If a false witness rise up against any man to testify against him that which is wrong, then both the men, between whom the controversy is, shall stand before the Lord, before the priests and the judges, which shall be in those days; and the judges shall make diligent inquisition, and behold if the witness be a false witness, and has testified falsely against his brother; then shall you do to him, as he had thought to have done to his brother: so shall you put the evil away from among you.

DEUTERONOMY 19:15–20.

Samuel judged Israel all the days of his life. And he went from year to year in circuit to Bethel, and Gilgal, and Mizpeh, and judged Israel in all those places.

1 SAMUEL 7:15–17.

Agree with your adversary quickly, while you are in the way with him, lest at any time the adversary deliver you to the judge, and the judge deliver you to the officer, and you be cast into prison.

And if any man sue you at the law, and take away your coat, let him have your cloak also.

MATTHEW 5:25, 40.

Moreover if your brother shall tresspass against you, go and tell him his fault between you and him alone; if he shall hear you, you have gained a brother. But if he will not hear you, then take with you one or two more, that in the mouth of two or three witnesses every word may be established. And if he shall neglect to hear them, tell it to the church; but if he neglect to hear the church, let him be to you as a heathen and a publican. Verily I say to you, Whatsoever you shall bind on earth shall be bound in heaven; and whatsoever you shall loose on earth shall be loosed in heaven.

MATTHEW 18:15–18.

If Demetrius, and the craftsmen who are with him, have a matter against any man, the law is open, and there are deputies; let them implead one another. But if you inquire any thing concerning other matters, it shall be determined in a lawful assembly.

ACTS 19:38–39.

Dare any of you, having a matter against another, go to law before the unjust, and not before the saints? Do you know that the saints shall judge the world? And if the world shall be judged by you, are you unworthy to judge the smallest matter? Know you not that we shall judge angels? How much more things that pertain to this life? If then you have judgments of things pertaining to this life, set them to judge who are least esteemed in the church. I speak to your shame. Is it so, that there is not a wise man among you? No, not one that shall be able to judge between his brethren? But brother goes to law with brother, and that before the unbelievers. Now there is utterly a fault among you, because you go to law one with another. Why do you not rather take wrong? Why do you not rather suffer yourselves to be defrauded? Nay, you do wrong, and defraud, and even your own brethren.

1 CORINTHIANS *6:1–8.*

CRADLE-TO-GRAVE

Call it cradle-to-grave, womb-to-tomb, or security from want and need; but seductive promises of lifetime insulation from the stimulation of living in an uncertain world rob us of the chance for achieving greatness and lead us to mediocrity: mediocrity in thinking, in desiring to succeed, in working, in studying, in even questioning the cradle-to-grave philosophy. It is a cheap and unenduring imitation of God's power to sustain life. It establishes a rival god, the quest for a providential god on earth. It creates an imitation society—one in imitation of the real freedom, abundance, and security promised by our Creator.

What naively begins as "security" ends as slavery. There are no free gifts in this uncertain world; God organized it this way. He expects us to mature and accept responsibility. The cradle-to-grave idea of security exacts a high price for allowing state planners to think and plan and take risks for us. "In proportion as you give the State power to do things *for* you, you give it power to do things *to* you; and the State invariably makes as little as it can of the one power, and as much as it can of the other."[1]

"The ultimate result of shielding men from the effects of folly is to fill the world with fools."[2]

"...We are not beggars; that [pain] is the hard coin which must be paid for everything valuable in this life, for our power, our wisdom, our love; that in pain is symbolised the infinite possibility of perfection. The eternal unfolding of joy; and the man who loses all pleasure in accepting pain sinks down to the lowest depth of penury and degradation."[3]

---

[1]Albert Jay Nock, *Memoirs of a Superfluous Man* (Chicago: Henry Regnery Co., 1964), p. 181.

[2]Herbert Spencer, "State Tamperings with Money." *Essays* (1891), in John Bartlett, *Famous Quotations* 15th ed. (Boston: Little, Brown, 1980), p. 579.

[3]Rabindranath Tagore, "The Problem of Evil" *Sadhana* (Tucson, Ariz: Omen Press, 1972), pp. 64-65.

(*See Also:* Equality, Humanism, Power of State, Redistribution of Income/ Wealth, Welfarism)

> *They said to Moses, Because there were no graves in Egypt, have you taken us away to die in the wilderness? wherefore have you dealt thus with us, to carry us forth out of Egypt? Is not this the word that we did tell you in Egypt, saying, Let us alone, that we may serve the Egyptians? For it had been better for us to serve the Egyptians, than that we should die in the wilderness.*
>
> EXODUS 14:11–12.

> *If you buy a Hebrew servant, six years he shall serve: and in the seventh he shall go out free for nothing.*
> *And if the servant shall plainly say, I love my master, my wife, my children; I will not go free; then his master shall bring him unto the judges; and he shall also bring him to the door, or to the door post; and his master shall bore his ear through with an awl; and he shall serve him forever.*
>
> EXODUS 21:2, 5–6.

> *He becomes poor who deals with a slack hand; but the hand of the diligent makes rich.*
>
> PROVERBS 10:4.

CREATION

Why has creation come under such heavy attacks? Nonbeliever, scientist, and believer alike recognize the untenable position of evolutionists. In the first place, the evidence is overwhelmingly against the probability of a chance combination of molecules—organic or inorganic. In the second place, to define a new species means that we must have a fairly concrete idea of what a species is to begin with. But the fundamental issue is *sovereignty*. (See COLOSSIANS 1:15, 17.) Who created us? Who sustains us? The state? Or God? Is our creation a random act of nature? Are we now sustained by the beneficence of the state?

Professor Charles Eugene Guye estimated the probability of four atoms—not all the elements in the periodic chart or life, but only four elements: carbon, hydrogen, oxygen, and nitrogen—combining to form a simple protein molecule. For this random event to occur, the sphere of atomic material needed would be so large that light traveling across would take 1×10^{82} years. Compare that with the outermost limits of the known universe, which is only about 1×10^{10} light years across. Further, the likelihood that this imaginary molecule would form on a body the size of earth would be 1×10^{243} years, compared with the assumed age of the universe of 1×10^{10}.[1] Darwin's hypothesis is based on randomness occurring in the universe. In other words, he is committed to indeterminacy. The Mayan Indians of Mexico and Central America, with their pagan rituals, human sacrifices, and autocratic government, had formulated a theory of evolution 2,000 years before Darwin. The data reject the acceptance of this hypothesis.

Furthermore, we discover there is no definition of the term *species*. Darwin denied any limits on genetic variation within any arbitrarily defined species grouping as well as any reliable definition of species. Darwin writes, "I look at the term *species* as one arbitrarily given, for the sake of convenience, to a set of individuals closely resembling each other, and it does not essentially differ from the term *variety*."[2] In other words, if it looks like a monkey, then it must have been a monkey.

So Darwin blew apart his own hypothesis in Chapter 2 of his *Origin*. Why is evolutionism such an important issue today? After all, even the atoms had to be created to come into existence, didn't they? Are our friendly supreme courts not telling us something?

Evolutionism is predicated on randomness. The universe is chaotic. Therefore, man imposes his imprimatur and creates order: the earth today, the universe tomorrow. Hence, there is no law higher than the law of man, because reasoning man puts purpose into the meaning of life. There is no cosmological purpose prior to the evolutionary advent of man.

Creation denies randomness. It uses terms such as God's purpose, God's plan, God's order, God's immutable laws. Evolutionism allows, at least intellectually, for an escape from God-ordained purpose. Creation restricts criminal activities of man, which run counter to a free society. It enlarges the greater freedom and productivity of believer and nonbeliever alike in a society that functions within the laws and ordained purpose of God.

Evolutionism—a license to kill, destroy, and enslave—denies purpose and higher laws. Statists must outwardly commit themselves to evolutionism, because this provides them with the rationale to war, eliminate believers (i.e., the opposition), confiscate property, regulate production, tax, and commit all kinds of unjustifiable acts that lead to poverty and slavery. Man now becomes god. In order to become a god, first man must deny any higher authority or purpose.

The larger question is not simply one of dealing with the theories of evolution and creation. The issue is, Who rules—God or man? In order to accept evolutionism, we must surrender the benefits of living in a free society under God's rule.

(*See Also:* Conspiracy, Evolutionism, Power of State, Randomness, Source, Statism, Strategic Planning)

---

[1] Cited in Lecomte du Noüy, *Human Destiny* (New York: Longmans, Green, 1947), p. 34.

[2] Charles Darwin, *The Origin of Species and the Descent of Man* (New York: Modern Library ed.), chap. 2, p. 46.

...God created the heaven and the earth.

God created great whales, and every living creature that moves...after their kind, and every winged fowl after its kind.

And God said, Let us make man in our image, after our likeness.

GENESIS 1:1, 21, 26.

Hezekiah prayed before the Lord, and said, O Lord God of Israel, who dwells between the cherubims, you are the God, even you alone, of all the kingdoms of the earth; you have made heaven and earth.

2 KINGS 19:15.

For all the gods of the people are idols; but the Lord made the heavens.

1 CHRONICLES 16:26.

By the word of the Lord were the heavens made; and all the host of them by the breath of His mouth.

PSALM 33:6.

Know that the Lord he is God: it is He who has made us, and not we ourselves; we are his people, and the sheep of his pasture.

PSALM 100:3.

You hide your face, they are troubled; you take away their breath, they die, and return to their dust. You send forth your spirit, they are created: and you renew the face of the earth.

PSALM 104:29–30.

Behold, all souls are mine; as the soul of the father, so also the soul of the son is mine; the soul that sins, it shall die.

EZEKIEL 18:4.

In the beginning was the Word, and the Word was with God, and the Word was God. The same was in the beginning with God. All things were made by Him; and without Him was not any thing made. In Him was life; and the life was the light of men.

Which was born, not of blood, nor of the will of the flesh, nor of the will of man, but of God.

JOHN 1:1–4, 13.

Saith the Lord:...has not My hand made all these things?

ACTS 7:49–50.

God made the world and all things therein, seeing that He is Lord of heaven and earth, dwells not in the temples made with hands.

ACTS 17:24.

For we are his workmanship, created in Christ Jesus to good works, which God has before ordained that we should walk in them.

EPHESIANS 2:10.

Who is the image of the invisible God, the firstborn of every creature. He is before all things, and by Him all things consist.

COLOSSIANS 1:15, 17.

...he who built the house has more honor than the house. For every house is built by some man; but he who built all things is God.

HEBREWS 3:3–4.

CREDITOR

At the end of every seventh year, you shall make a release. Every creditor who lends anything to his neighbor shall release it; he shall not exact it of his neighbor, or of his brother.

DEUTERONOMY 15:1–2.

(*See:* Bankruptcy, Debts, Interest)

CRIMINAL

It is not good to accept the person of the wicked, to overthrow the righteous in judgment.

PROVERBS 18:5.

(*See:* Capital Punishment, Justice, Restitution)

CROWD PSYCHOLOGY

"I do not believe in the collective wisdom of individual ignorance," wrote Thomas Carlyle.[1] Majoritarianism is based on majority opinion, majority rule. While the ignorance of a minority remains ignorance, transformed into a majority the same opinions become irreproachable and resulting legislation irrepressible. As Horace Mann said, "We go by majority vote, and if the majority are insane, the sane must go to the hospital."[2]

In crowds and mass societies, the individual loses his uniqueness, his importance. He feels helpless until he becomes part of the crowd or joins a pressure group. The crowd, then, becomes his god. He feels secure in numbers but pays the price of loss of judgment. More fundamentally, running with the pack is a quest for power through numbers—a human power that denies the absolute principles of God and the discipline of living in a free society according to His law.

In a democratic society of simple majority rule, as few as 51 percent can impose their will on the other 49 percent. Now 49 percent is no small number. Moving to a system of representative democracy, where legislators are elected from each district, the trick is to elect a majority of the legislators. It is now mathematically possible for minority rule under pretense of majority rule. Figure it out, and you will discover 26 percent of the voters can control 51 percent of the votes and 100 percent of the legislation. We shift, therefore, from a potential dictatorship by the majority to one by a minority—completely severing responsibility from voting power.

They say the secret to successful investing is buy low and sell high to the next fellow who wants to buy low. As prices rise, new investors are drawn into the game by "bargains" and the opportunity to become rich. So, each, believing they buy low and sell high, fails to recognize that in order to sell, there must be buyers eager and waiting. Rising prices, driven upward as long as buyers exceed sellers, require ever-increasing new money in the game. If the number of buyers and sellers equates, prices stabilize. At the end of a rapid price rise of stock or commodity futures, quite suddenly sellers vastly outnumber buyers, which accounts for the sudden ensuing price collapse. Who made the money? Those in and out early in the game! They were not the majority—for the majority was right but at the wrong time. Mark Twain said, "Whenever you find that you are on the side of the majority, it is time to reform (or pause and reflect)."[3]

Bernard Iddings Bell spoke on crowd culture. He said, in April 1952, at Ohio Wesleyan University, "Our crowd-mindedness renders us suggestible, manipulatable, easy meat for almost any propagandist who is willing to flatter, to encourage

---

[1] Thomas Carlyle, as cited in Herbert V. Prochnow & Herbert V. Prochnow, Jr. *A Treasure Chest of Quotations for All Occasions* (N.Y.: Harper & Row, 1983), p. 79.

[2] Horace Mann, U.S. House of Representatives, and first president of Antioch College (1796–1859).

[3] Mark Twain, pseudonym of Samuel Langhorne Clemens, a master of American literature.

animality, to promise ease and opulence with a minimum of labor expended to get them, and freedom from responsibility."

Bell makes a point in his book that when the Soviet Union leagued itself with Nazi Germany, the American public thought of the Soviets as fiends. Bell, at a dinner, seated next to a corporate officer of a news service, said, "I suppose now that the Muscovites are on our side, the American people will have to be indoctrinated so as to stop thinking of them as devils and begin to regard them as noble fellows." The news service executive replied, "Of course. We know what our job is in respect to that. We of the press will bring about a complete and almost unanimous *volte-face* in the belief of the Common Man about the Russians. We shall do it within three weeks."[4] And they did!

Thomas B. Reed, Speaker of the House of Representatives, 1839-1902, summed it up well: "One, with God, is always a majority, but many a martyr has been burned at the stake while the votes were being counted."[5]

(*See Also*: Cycles, Demagoguery, Expert, Foundation, Idolatry, Individualism, Remnant, Self-Discipline)

> You shall not follow a multitude to do evil; neither shall you testify in a dispute so as to turn aside after many to pervert justice.
>
> *EXODUS 23:2.*

> Let not the anger of my Lord wax hot: you know the people, that they are set on mischief.
>
> *EXODUS 32:22.*

> According to all the works which they have done since the day that I brought them out of Egypt, even to this day, wherewith they have forsaken Me, and served other gods, so they do also to you.
>
> *1 SAMUEL 8:8.*

> To you it is commanded, O people, nations, and languages, that you fall down and worship the golden image that Nebuchadnezzar the king has set up, and whoever falls not down and worships the same hour be cast into the midst of a burning fiery furnace. Therefore at that time, when all the people heard the sound of the cornet, harp, sackbut, psaltery, and all kinds of music, all the people, the nations, and the languages, fell down and worshipped the golden image that Nebuchadnezzar the king had set up.
>
> *DANIEL 3:4—7.*

[4]Bernard Iddings Bell, *Crowd Culture: An Examination of the American Way of Life* (Freeport, N.Y.: Books for Libraries Press, 1970), pp. 25–26.

[5]Thomas B. Reed, in W.A. Robinson, *Life of Thomas B. Reed,* cited in George Seldes, *The Great Quotations* (Secaucus, N.J.: Citadel Press, 1983), p. 580.

There are wells without water, clouds that are carried with a tempest, to whom the mist of darkness is reserved for ever.

2 PETER 2:17.

Raging waves of the sea, foaming out their own shame; wandering stars, to whom is reserved the blackness for ever.

JUDE 13.

CYCLES

Some major religions hold that creation is cyclical, in endless repetition. Christianity is rectilinear, an unfolding of God's plan from beginning to end. However, within that unfolding, periods of evolution and devolution and cycles of all types arise. Gary North writes:

> The fulfillment [of the dominion covenant] would of necessity be linear, but the new law of nature was cyclical. To overcome this cyclical restraint, covenantally faithful men must apply the principles of biblical law. Linearity of economic growth, of the growth of both human and animal populations, is now a product of ethically faithful societies (EXODUS 23:26). *Linear development is the product of a philosophy of life, a religious outlook, and few cultures in history have maintained anything like it.*[1]

If we do not learn about and remember history, then certainly we get another chance to learn. As a commodity trader and fund manager, I observed the same people making the same mistakes week after week, which led me to derive another of my not-so-famous laws: *One thing about life, if at first you do not succeed, you get another chance to fail.*

Cyclical periodicity is reflected in Oswald Spengler's thesis that historical cycles run: bondage—spiritual faith—courage—liberty—abundance—selfishness—complacency—apathy—dependency—bondage.[2]

Trade cycles, the boom-bust syndrome, have been studied for decades and decades. Reputable, intellectually honest economists have traced the cause of these cycles directly to governmental monetary policies and have laid the dead rat right at the doorstep of politicians who do not act responsibly to prevent inflation.

Must we be victims of endless cycles? Must good times become rebellious times? Must blessings necessarily turn into curses? (See DEUTERONOMY 8.) The Bible says there is creation, time, and judgment. In other words, creation is linear. The theology of cycles is no beginning, no final judgment. Cycles mean that growth must

---

[1]Gary North, *The Dominion Covenant: Genesis* (Tyler, Tex.: Institute for Christian Economics, 1982), p. 114.

[2]Oswald Spengler, *The Decline of the West* (N.Y.: Alfred A. Knopf, 1953), Vols. 1 & 2.

end. But in a free society under God's law, growth implies linear development, responsibility, and blessings for obedience.

(*See Also:* Demand and Supply, Market Economy, Say's Law, Strategic Planning)

Behold, there comes seven years of great plenty throughout all the land of Eygpt. And there shall arise after them seven years of famine; and all the plenty shall be forgotten in the land of Egypt; and the famine shall consume the land.

GENESIS 41:29–30.

As a dog returns to his vomit, so a fool returns to his folly.

PROVERBS 26:11.

One generation passes away, and another generation comes; but the earth abides forever. The sun also rises, and the sun goes down, and hastens to its place where it arose, The wind goes toward the south, and turns about to the north; it whirls about continually, and the wind returns again according to its circuits. All the rivers run into the sea; yet the sea is not full; to the place from whence the rivers come, there they return again.

ECCLESIASTES 1:4–7.

A time to get, and a time to lose; a time to keep, and a time to cast away; a time to rend, and a time to sew; a time to keep silence, and a time to speak; a time to love, and a time to hate; a time of war, and a time of peace.

ECCLESIASTES 3:1–8.

That which has been is now; and that which is to be has already been; and God requires that which is past.

ECCLESIASTES 3:15.

In the day of prosperity be joyful, but in the day of adversity consider: God also has set the one over against the other, to the end that man should find nothing after him.

ECCLESIASTES 7:14.

Thus were you decked with gold and silver; and your raiment was of fine linen, and silk, and broidered work; you did eat fine flour, and honey, and oil; and you did prosper into a kingdom.

But you did trust in your own beauty, and played the harlot because of your renown, and poured out your fornications on every one that passed by.

And in all your abominations and your whoredoms you have not remembered the days of your youth, when you were naked and bare, and were polluted in your blood.

Because you have not remembered the days of your youth, but have fretted me in all these things; behold, therefore I also will recompense your way upon your head, saith the Lord God: and you shall not commit this lewedness above all your abominations.

Ezekiel 16:13, 15, 22, 43.

It is happened to them according to the true proverb, The dog is turned again to his own vomit; and the sow that was washed to her wallowing in the mire.

2 Peter 2:22.

DAYLIGHT-SAVING TIME

In Jewish reckoning, a day runs from dusk to dusk. Although our days legally commence at midnight, in practice we think of our days running from dawn to dawn; and government wants to manipulate that dawn. In some places people refer to time manipulation as the electric company subsidy law because winter dusk falls by 4:00 P.M. in some northern states, which results in more electricity consumed simply due to normal family routines.

One argument for turning the clocks back in the fall is that people who start work early will have daylight to drive in and thereby reduce accidents. Aren't people more alert after a night's rest and less so after a hard day at work? They must return home after dark. Another argument is that school children have to wait for the bus in the dark. Can't schools begin later in winter? Apparently, only *public* schools have this problem, not private Christian schools. In addition, some dairymen claim that DST throws off the milking rhythm.

On the other hand, some years ago researchers learned that violent crime declined 10 percent when prime mugging hours were reduced. People burned 100,000 fewer barrels of oil per day. There were fewer school bus accidents. Millions of softball players had more time for games on unlighted fields. Florida had more daylight to save than forty-eight other states during the important winter tourist season.

(*See Also:* Communication, Conspiracy, Cycles, Double Standard, Expert, Planned Economy, Power of State)

They change the night into day: the light is short because of darkness.
JOB 17:12.

Woe to those who call evil good and good evil; who put darkness for light, and light for darkness.
ISAIAH 5:20.

DEBTS

"Forgive us our debts, as we forgive our debtors" . . . (LUKE 11:4).

Are debts prohibited in the Bible? No. Can interest be charged on loans? Yes. Does God speak against international lending at a high rate of interest? No.

In the first place, in a free society under the rule of God, free men will contract only for short-term loans, that is, less than seven years. Debtors enslave themselves (PROVERBS 22:7). Debt implies weakness and vulnerability. "Ye are bought with a price; be not ye the servants of men" (1 CORINTHIANS 7:23).

Consumer debt is especially insidious as we gradually replace God with control by man over us. For free men to remain free, "owe no man any thing" (ROMANS 13:8). Nevertheless, God has worked out a solution for debtors to become free again.

Debt contracted for family emergencies must be cancelled at the end of seven years with no future recourse to the debtor's assets. Now that does not mean God encourages wreckless behavior. We are reminded that obligations must be paid (2 KINGS 4:7; ROMANS 13:7–8). This sabbatical release from private or commercial debts serves to remind us to keep our finances in order.

Firms, highly leveraged with long-term debt, are not operating in a godly manner. God encourages us to maintain a sound financial status in personal and business affairs and not recklessly commit resources to an unknowable (to man) future. If businesses would follow that admonition, there would be fewer bankruptcies, more job security, fewer boom-bust cycles, and less concentration of wealth.

In a godly order, liability is unlimited during the seven years, but debt and interest are limited to seven years. Charitable loans, in a category apart, should carry no interest. Request for charitable assistance ought to be honored by persons financially able to assist (DEUTERONOMY 15:7–8).

(*See Also:* Bankruptcy, Charity, Collateral, Contract, Interest, Poverty, Risk Aversion, Self-Discipline)

At the end of every seven years you shall make a cancellation of debts. And this is the manner of the release: Every creditor who lends anything to his neighbor shall cancel the debt; he shall not exact it of his neighbor, or of his brother, because it is called the Lord's release. Of a foreigner you may exact it again; but what is owed by your brother your hand shall release, save when there shall be no poor among you, for the Lord will greatly bless you in the land which the Lord your God gives you for an inheritance to possess: only if you carefully listen to

the voice of the Lord your God, to observe and do all these commandments which I command you this day. For the Lord your God blesses
you, as He promised you; and you shall lend to many nations, but you
shall not borrow; and you shall reign over many nations, but they shall
not reign over you.

Deuteronomy 15:1–6.

If there be among you a poor man of one of your brethren within any of
your gates in your land which the Lord your God gives you, you shall
not harden your heart, nor refrain from helping your poor brother; but
you shall open your hand wide to him, and shall surely lend him
sufficient for his need, in that which he wants.

Deuteronomy 15:7–8.

Then she came and told the man of God. And he said, Go sell the oil,
and pay the debt, and live with your children in rest.

2 Kings 4:7.

The rich rule over the poor, and the borrower is servant to the lender.

Proverbs 22:7.

Be not one of them who strikes hands, or of them who are sureties for
debts.

Proverbs 22:26.

Therefore you ought to have deposited my money with the bankers,
and at my coming I would have received back my own with interest.

Matthew 25:27.

Therefore, brethren, we are debtors, not to the flesh, to live after the
flesh. For if you live after the flesh you shall die; but if you through the
Spirit, do mortify the deeds of the body, you shall live.

Romans 8:12–13.

Render therefore to all their dues: tribute to whom tribute is due;
custom to whom custom; fear to whom fear; honor to whom honor.
Owe no man any thing, but to love one another.

Romans 13:7–8.

If he has wronged you, or owes you, put that on my account; I, Paul,
have written it with my own hand, I will repay it.

Philemon 18–19.

DEFENSE

(*See:* Draft, Military; Military; Military Defense)

DEFICITS

(*See:* Debts, Keynesianism, Welfarism)

DEMAGOGUE

The word *demagogue,* derived from the combination of two Greek words—*demos,* meaning people, and *agogo,* meaning a leader—might be modernized and referred to as ago-go people. This is an apt description of those who allow themselves to be seduced and led by demagogues. Why should Christians avoid demagogues like they would the plague? First, demagogues appeal to the sovereignty of man, not the sovereignty of God. Second, the voice of the demagogue imitates the voice of God. Third, demagogues appeal to rebellious motives, such as power, revenge, sloth, and envy.

Albert Jay Nock wrote,

> According to my observations, mankind are [*sic*] among the most easily tamable and domesticable of all creatures in the animal world. They are readily reducible to submission, so readily conditionable (to coin a word) as to exhibit an almost incredibly enduring patience under restraint and oppression of the most flagrant character. So far are they from displaying any overweening love of freedom that they show a singular contentment with a condition of servitorship, often showing a curious canine pride in it, and again often simply unaware that they are existing in that condition.[1]

This may also explain why demagogues are able to rally so many willing followers. Aristotle said, "Democracies are most commonly corrupted by the insolence of demagogues."[2]

---

[1]Albert Jay Nock, *The Memoirs of a Superfluous Man* (Chicago: Henry Regnery, 1964), p. 314.

[2]Aristotle, *Politics,* Book V, cited in John Bartlett, *Familiar Quotations,* 13th ed. (Boston: Little, Brown, 1955), p. 26.

The dictionary defines a demagogue as "a leader who makes use of popular prejudices and false claims and promises to gain power."[2] This is our usual understanding of the term. In other words, a demagogue is a hypocrite and a liar, whose maledict means are subordinate to questionable ends.

The word *demagogue* sounds too much like demigod. Operating in a demiurgic stratosphere, the demagogue often believes he approaches the Divine, if not supersedes Him. However, the term *demimonde* more appropriately describes demagogues who prostitute the principles of a free society for short-term gains of power and personal prestige and who try to subvert God's long-term plan.

(*See Also:* Crowd Psychology, Demagoguery, Double Standard, Envy, Idolatry, Power, Tinstaafl)

> *For what is the hope of the hypocrite, though he gained, when God takes away his soul?*
> *Job 27:8.*

> *Draw me not away with the wicked, and with the workers of iniquity, who speak peace to their neighbors, but mischief in their hearts.*
> *Psalm 28:3.*

> *The beginning of the words of his mouth is foolishness; and the end of his talk is mischievous madness.*
> *Ecclesiastes 10:13.*

> *The treacherous dealers have dealt treacherously; yea, the treacherous dealers have dealt very treacherously.*
> *Isaiah 24:16.*

> *The chief seats in the synagogues, and the uppermost rooms at feasts, who devour widows' houses, and for a pretense make long prayers.*
> *Mark 12:39–40.*

> *For there are many unruly and vain talkers, whose mouths must be stopped, who subvert whole houses, teaching things which they ought not, for filthy lucre's sake.*
> *Titus 1:10–11.*

> *I saw three unclean spirits like frogs come out of the mouth of the dragon, and out of the mouth of the beasts, and out of the mouth of the false prophet. For they are the spirits of the devils, working miracles,*

[3]*Webster's Seventh New Collegiate Dictionary* (Springfield, Mass.: Merriam, 1976), p. 219.

which go forth unto the kings of the earth and of the whole world, to
gather them to the battle of that great day of God Almighty.

REVELATION *16:13–14.*

DEMAGOGUERY

Demagoguery's success waxes greatest among the ungodly, who lack self-discipline necessary to learn and practice God's ways. Unfortunately, they pass the bill for their stupidity and supineness onto all of us. Practicing believers should not succumb to the delusory promises of evil communicators, who, in their quest for power, speak falsely. Immature minds are attracted by demagoguery, by every wind of doctrine; otherwise it could never succeed. Otherwise Eve would not have believed the arch-demagogue: "Ye shall not surely die. Ye shall be as gods" (GENESIS 3:4–5).

Phineas Taylor Barnum reputedly said, "A sucker is born every minute."[1] John Maynard Keynes, an economist, wrote: "In the United States, it is almost inconceivable what rubbish a public man has to utter if he is to keep respectable."[2]

Both of these gentlemen should know. Both were in the business of selling illusions. Keynes's illusory prosperity, by spending and accumulating debt (as opposed to production and savings), translates into political demagoguery of tax, spend, elect. This demagoguery has given us in recent times high unemployment, high inflation, high prices, and high taxes. Barnum's deceptions were obviously entertainment. They cost only the price of admission; money was spent voluntarily.

"You can free things from alien or accidental laws, but not from the laws of their own nature....Do not go about as a demagogue, encouraging triangles to break out of the prison of their three sides. If a triangle breaks out of its three sides, its life comes to a lamentable end.[3]

(*See Also:* Conspiracy, Corruption, Demagogue, Idolatry, Perjury, Xenophobia)

Wickedness is in the midst thereof: deceit and guile depart not from
her streets.

PSALM *55:11.*

[1]Phineas Taylor Barnum, quoted by Harold L. Ickes, New York *Post,* Nov. 24, 1947, cited in George Seldes, *The Great Quotations* (Secaucus, N.J.: Citadel, 1983), p. 83.

[2]John Maynard Keynes, "The World's Economic Outlook," *Atlantic Monthly,* v. 149 (May 1932), 521-6.

[3]G.K. Chesterton, *Orthodoxy* (Greenwood Press, 1908), chap. 3, p. 91.

Woe to them who call evil good, and good evil; who put darkness for light, and light for darkness; who put bitter for sweet, and sweet for bitter.

ISAIAH 5:20.

Behold you trust in lying words, that cannot profit.

JEREMIAH 7:8.

Be not deceived; evil communications corrupt good manners.

1 CORINTHIANS 15:33.

Let no man deceive you with vain words.

EPHESIANS 5:6.

That we henceforth be no more children, tossed to and fro, and carried about by every wind of doctrine, by the sleight of men, and cunning craftiness, whereby they lie in wait to deceive.

EPHESIANS 4:14.

DEMAND

Buying anything involves a sacrifice (see GENESIS 3:17–19). In order to buy some goods, we cannot acquire other goods because of insufficient income to purchase everything desired. In other words, we always select among alternatives. Intelligent choices mean weighing the cost, or price, of a good against anticipated satisfaction from owning, using, or looking at it.

Trying to satisfy many wants by economizing resources is one of life's recurring decisions. From ECCLESIASTES 1:8, 15, we learn that if human wants are not unlimited, they are expanding without known limits. With "new and improved" products entering the market in a continuous stream, our wants both change and expand, until we find ourselves working overtime or holding two jobs just to satisfy these seemingly insatiable "needs." We enslave ourselves by lack of self-discipline, ever wanting more and more.

When economists speak of demand, they refer to a schedule of quantities of a specific economic good that buyers would purchase at a corresponding schedule of prices in a given market at a given time. Demand does not mean desire. It means that each buyer not only desires something but also has the money and is willing to part with it in exchange for the desired item.

In a free society, people can work as hard as they wish, to earn all they can. They exchange wages for whatever they want, whether the purchase is a foolish one or not. That is, we are free to make our own mistakes. The question of "needs" does not arise. One person's needs may be another person's luxury. In a free society, no one attempts to set priorities on which goods or services to produce to satisfy imaginary "needs." When someone else tells us we do or do not need something, the door opens to a totalitarian dictatorship. Such coercion results in the exchange of one set of circumstances for another usually far worse.

Wanting to live the way of the Lord means sacrificing, or giving up, an unrighteous life for a righteous one—the exchange of one set of circumstances for another. Demand is a bid. It involves a commitment. We can either bid for—or commit our resources of time, energy, and money—to the world or to God. "For what is a man profited, if he gains the whole world, and loses his own soul? Or what will a man give in exchange for his soul?" (MATTHEW 16:26).

(*See Also:* Barter, Demand and Supply, Exchange, Free Market, Price, Value)

When they had eaten up the corn that they had brought out of Egypt, their father said to them, Go again, buy us a little food.
GENESIS 43:2.

All things are full of labor; man cannot express it. The eye is not satisfied with seeing, nor the ear filled with hearing.
ECCLESIASTES 1:8.

That which is wanting cannot be numbered.
ECCLESIASTES 1:15.

All the labor of man is for his mouth, and yet the appetite is not filled.
ECCLESIASTES 6:7.

Seeing there be many things that increase vanity, what is man the better?
ECCLESIASTES 6:11.

Butter and honey shall he eat, that he may know to refuse the evil, and choose the good.
ISAIAH 7:15.

DEMAND AND SUPPLY

Demand, a relation between the quantity of something demanded and its price, in economic terminology, means that a person is ready, willing, and able to buy something. What volume of a certain good will sell in the market depends on its price. When hand-held electronic calculators cost $200 each, relatively few were bought. The price for that same machine dropped to $20, and now many American homes have at least a half dozen scattered and forgotten in various drawers. Supply, on the other hand, means the amount of product suppliers will sell at various prices.

Here is the catch. Buyers want low prices. They will buy relatively few items of the product at high prices. Sellers prefer higher prices. Only a free market can resolve this difference of opinion. No exchange occurs until a price is reached agreeable to buyers and sellers. The interaction of demand and supply determines market price, or what amounts to a peaceful resolution of differences between buyers and sellers.

No government agency with all the computer memory in the world, trying to solve this one single mathematical problem, can ever find the price solution. Yet, the free market, through the division of labor and knowledge and the free functioning of the price system discovers the best price, and business booms. When prices are too high, buyers withdraw. When they are too low, sellers try to find ways to produce more efficiently or else not offer the product or service. The free function of demand and supply guarantees that prices will be set so that there is equality between purchases and sales, maximum production and employment, and the greatest abundance and freedom man can enjoy under God's laws.

(*See Also:* Barter, Contract, Demand, Division of Labor, Equality, Exchange, Market Economy, Price Mechanism, Say's Law)

The famine was over all the face of the earth: and Joseph opened all the storehouses, and sold to the Eygptians; and the famine became severe in the land of Egypt. And all the countries came to Egypt to buy corn.

GENESIS 41:56–57.

I have heard that there is corn in Egypt; get down there, and buy for us from that place, that we may live, and not die.

And the sons of Israel came to buy corn among those who came. And Joseph was the governor over the land, and he it was who sold to all the people of the land.

GENESIS 42:2, 5–6.

According to the number of years after the Jubilee you shall buy from your neighbor, and according to the number of years of crops he shall sell to you. According to the multitude of years you shall increase the price thereof, and according to the fewness of years you shall diminish the price of it, for according to the number of years of the crops does he sell to you.

LEVITICUS 25:15–16.

*There was a great famine in Samaria: and, behold, they besieged it,
until an ass's head was sold for fourscore pieces of silver, and the fourth
part of a cab of dove's dung for five pieces of silver.*

2 KINGS 6:25.

*…Tomorrow about this time shall a measure of fine flour be sold for a
shekel, and two measures of barley for a shekel, in the gate of Samaria.*

2 KINGS 7:1.

*He who withholds corn, the people shall curse him; but blessing shall
be upon the head of him who sells it.*

PROVERBS 11:26.

*The lambs are for your clothing, and the goats are the price of the field.
And you shall have goat's milk enough for your food, for the food of
your household, and for the maintenance of your maidens.*

PROVERBS 27:26–27.

*But by an equality, that now at this time your abundance may be a
supply for their want, that their abundance also may be a supply for
your want: that there may be equality.*

2 CORINTHIANS 8:14.

DEMOCRACY

There is no king saved by the multitude of a host.…

PSALM 33:16.

(*See:* Crowd Psychology, Government, Humanism)

DEPRESSION, ECONOMIC

*The earth also is defiled under the inhabitants thereof, because they
have transgressed the laws, changed the ordinance, broken the
everlasting covenant.*

ISAIAH 24:5.

(*See:* Cycles, Inflation, Statism)

DIRECTED ECONOMY

A directed economy hinders production, for a directed economy is a centrally planned one. We need only look at the Soviet economy and its endless national economic plans. It always falls short of its goals. The economy suffers shortages. Most Russians live worse than our dogs. A few days ago in a shopping center, I saw a parked car with seven yapping poodles, energetically bouncing from glass to glass like highly excited molecules caught in a container. How many Russian people, outside of the Soviet bureaucracy, enjoy that luxury? The failures of centrally directed economies of Cuba, Nicaragua, Ethiopia, East Germany, or Viet Nam are examples of this reality on every continent.

Still, some Americans believe that national planning will provide for a better allocation of resources and production and, hence, higher standards of living. These modern thinkers posit that God (if He exists) created an imperfect world that randomly evolved into chaotic circumstances. It now requires the superior intelligence of man to put things right again. God failed; but men in positions of power, with the aid of technology, have centralized knowledge and become omniscient. God thwarts that quest. Knowledge is decentralized. No man has all the answers.

In a directed economy, central committees decide what to produce, and how much, how to distribute production, and establish local and national priorities. If your personal priorities do not coincide with national ones, you will be raped of your economic freedom. Nevertheless, we still hear the argument that a socialist (i.e., directed) economy operates more efficiently and morally than the free society alternative.

In order for central planning to resemble market efficiency, planners would (1) have complete knowledge of true costs, the market, and alternative production methods, and prices; (2) know everything about supplies and demands for each and every product and service, and then integrate this information into a grand plan; (3) have foresight into future technological changes and how new processes will affect production and the market; and (4) since no one is perfect, errors in foresight must be properly recorded, which means losses and profits—the very things planners say they can avoid.

Central planning almost exclusively focuses on supply. Little is said about demand: the customer-be-damned—quite contrary to the free enterprise approach. For a directed economy to operate efficiently, central planners must be omniscient, and if not omniscient then coercive to iron out demand and supply differences. They deny their mistakes. When Amtrak trains ran more than thirty minutes behind schedule, the definition of lateness was changed. Afterwards, all trains ran on time.

In practice, central planning involves only key industries, not a totally integrated system. In practice, irrational planning results because prices are not openly competitive. In practice, it is an enormous sham, according to Dr. Gary North, who says that planners achieve neither ideological consistency nor economic efficiency.

(*See Also:* Bureaucracy, Elitism, Forecasting, One Worldism, Planned Economy, Rule by Decree, Socialism)

And Pharaoh commanded the same day the taskmasters of the people, and their officers, saying, Ye shall no more give the people straw to make brick, as heretofore.

Exodus 5:6–7.

They gave me also gall for my meat; and in my thirst they gave me vinegar to drink.

Psalm 69:21.

In all labor there is profit; but the talk of the lips tends only to penury.

Proverbs 14:23.

He causes all, both small and great, rich and poor, free and bond, to receive a mark in their right hand, or in their foreheads: and that no man might buy or sell, save he that had the mark, or the name of the beast, or the number of his name.

Revelation 13:16–17.

DISCIPLINE

Is discipline essential during childhood? What does it accomplish? Why is discipline necessary beyond those years? Discipline is a training vehicle necessary to curb excesses. It reminds us we are subordinate to God's laws. Discipline limits evil (Romans 13). Let's consider some examples.

The gold standard, for example, curbs excesses of central bankers. It permits rapid adjustment of international accounts. If a central banker is restricted in paper money creation by the gold content, required to back each unit of paper money, gold is the disciplining mechanism. As long as people can freely shift between gold and paper currency, the central banker would find himself without gold and tons of worthless paper if he ignored gold content limits.

The original, and only, purpose of the U.S. Constitution was to limit governmental exercise of power. Separation of powers in central government, the Bill of Rights, states' rights—these disciplined our republic. The U.S. Constitution carefully establishes what government may do. All residual rights rest with individuals.

Laws concerning contracts and property rights establish parameters for dealing with others. Contracts properly entered into must be fulfilled or a settlement made that is agreeable to the plaintiff. Tangible and intangible property of the owner is carefully protected.

These examples of discipline are essential in the adult world of a free society. As mature individuals and parents, we are responsible for training our children in the ways of discipline, learning the rule of God and civil laws necessary to make a free society function. Employing these same examples, let's see how immature and irresponsible persons function in a humanist society.

Paper currency is issued freely, without discretion or serious thought to future consequences, in a futile, undisciplined attempt to live "higher on the hog" now. Undisciplined politicians find it easier to inflate than eliminate budget deficits. It is an indication of extreme immaturity for a nation's legislators to believe that they can escape monetary discipline and hide their malfeasance behind a maternity skirt of inflated currency. It is an immature populace who believes in free lunches, of something for the price of a printed piece of official paper.

Those who would destroy this great republic have never worked harder than in the past half century to nullify the purpose and intent of the U.S. Constitution. This lack of discipline has reversed powers and rights given to people and their governments. Now all residual powers reside with various governments rather than with the American people. The power of federal government, its bureaucracies, and the judiciary is awesome. It threatens our freedom. For more than forty years the U.S. Supreme Court, no longer concerned with justice and interpretation of the real meaning of the Constitution, either makes law or supports unlegislated regulations of bureaucracies. It has successfully given us a new, unwritten constitution, subject to its own whimsical interpretations; these are additional consequences of lack of discipline.

It is the price we now pay for immature students turned out of public schools, the Spokian child-rearing mentality, and consequences of social revolutionary indoctrination targeted to a public no longer able to reason with sterile minds. Strange as it must at first appear, greater freedom follows from discipline than from undisciplined immaturity and libertinism. The final decision we must make is whether to bear the yoke of the undisciplined rule of man or enjoy the freedom of God's discipline.

(*See Also:* Accountability, Crowd Psychology, Maturity, Self-Discipline, Statism)

If a man has a stubborn and rebellious son, who will not obey the voice of his father, or the voice of his mother, and who when they have chastened him, will not listen to them, then shall his father and his mother lay hold on him, and bring him out to the elders of his city, and to the gate of his place; and they shall say to the elders of his city, this our son is stubborn and rebellious, he will not obey our voice; he is a glutton, and a drunkard. And all the men of his city shall stone him with stones, that he die: so shall you put evil away from you....

DEUTERONOMY 21:18–21.

He also opens their ears to instruction, and commands that they turn from iniquity. If they obey him, they shall spend their days in prosperity, and their years in pleasures. But if they do not obey, they shall perish by the sword, and they shall die without knowledge.

JOB 36:10–12.

Whoever loves instruction loves knowledge; but he who hates reproof is brutish.

PROVERBS 12:1.

Foolishness is bound in the heart of the child; but the rod of correction shall drive it far from him.

PROVERBS 22:15.

Withhold not correction from the child, for if you beat him with the rod, he shall not die. You shall beat him with the rod, and shall deliver his soul from hell.

PROVERBS 23:13–14.

Whoever keeps the law is a wise son; but he who is a companion of riotous men shames his father.

PROVERBS 28:7.

Let every soul be subject to the governing authorities. For there is no authority except from God....

ROMANS 13:1.

Therefore you must be subject, not only because of wrath, but also for conscience sake.

ROMANS 13:5.

For you yourselves know how you ought to follow us, for we were not disorderly among you; nor did we eat anyone's bread free of charge, but worked with labor and toil night and day, that we might not a burden to any of you, not because we do not have authority, but to make ourselves an example of how you should follow us.

2 THESSALONIANS 3:7–10.

Obey those who rule over you, and be submissive, for they watch out for your souls, as those who must give account.

Hebrews 13:17.

DISHONESTY

Dishonesty is unfaithfulness to God's Word and man's word. It is an expression of ethical rebellion in the spheres of business, church, and family. Furthermore, dishonesty distorts the other person's perception of a reality, which translates into the transferring of needless and added costs to the decision maker. We live in a moral universe that points to a final judgment, an accountability for the way we conduct our lives. By conforming our judgment to God's, we reap the preliminary rewards for honesty.

Dishonesty is often manifested in some type of theft (John 12:6). Little thefts like carrying home pens from the office or big thefts like a multimillion-dollar computer theft—both extremes are often ignored, because both are difficult to prosecute.

Then there are hidden thefts often disguised as social justice, where the recipient of public largesse depends on a government, acting on his behalf, to take by force income from friends and neighbors in order for him to enjoy more.

Another frequent and growing form of dishonesty are the half-truths employed to hang someone—the art of intimidation and back-stabbing (*See:* Genesis 12:11–20; 27:6–29; Proverbs 1:10–19.)

Still another form of dishonesty, unpaid wages (*see:* James 5:4), more likely occurs as unpaid debts. For instance, small armies of renters who roam their territories ripping off landlords, yet cry out for stiff regulations over so-called dishonest landlords; and employees who, while not suffering from nonpayment of wages, are often grossly underpaid and seldom receive raises—legal resident immigrants from foreign countries.

In international affairs, the art of diplomacy thrives on deception and dishonesty. However, when treaties are properly agreed to and signed, signatories must be honest in intent or no valid agreement ever exists. Jeremiah 9:8 nevertheless is reminiscent of our disarmament negotiations and treaties with communist countries.

A nation that bases its laws, institutions, and acceptable conduct on acts of dishonesty is a corrupt nation, one that will surely crumble when there is nothing left to sustain it. We cannot escape God's judgment.

(*See Also:* Character, Corruption, Golden Rule, Judgment, Law, Perjury, Rule by Decree, Theft)

…if sinners entice you, do not consent.

Proverbs 1:10.

Getting treasures by a lying tongue is a vanity tossed to and fro of them who seek death.

PROVERBS 21:6.

Confidence in an unfaithful man in time of trouble is like a broken tooth, and a foot out of joint.

PROVERBS 25:19.

Their tongue is an arrow shot out; it speaks deceit. One speaks peaceably to his neighbor with his mouth, but in his heart he lays wait.

JEREMIAH 9:8.

This he said, not that he cared for the poor, but because he was a thief, and had the money box; and he used to take what was put in it.

JOHN 12:6.

Wherefore putting away lying, speak every man truth with his neighbor, for we are members of one another.

EPHESIANS 4:25.

Indeed, the wages of the laborers who mowed your field, which you kept back by fraud, cry out; and the cries of the reapers have reached the ears of the Lord of Sabaoth.

JAMES 5:4.

DISINVESTMENT

For he who has, to him shall be given, and he who has not, from him shall be taken even that which he has.

MARK 4:25.

(*See:* Poor Nations, Taxation)

DIVISION OF LABOR

Each person has the capacity to reason, to establish objectives, and to find means to reach objectives, but not alone. At some point, people discover that cooperation and dividing up work result in greater output and a higher level of material satisfaction. They learn that division of labor multiplies productivity.

Division of labor means specialization: Cain was a farmer, Abel a shepherd. Because of differences among men and differences in geography, there is a need for specialization. By specializing, each of us does one thing well. We become experts. As experts we can produce more in less time than an apprentice. In a free society, if each expert can produce more by expending the same amount of energy, then in the aggregate everyone ends up with more rather than less.

Nevertheless, specialization is risky. If we become proficient and no one wants our services, then, until we become adept in another, more marketable, activity, income is reduced. It is a fragile relationship because we all depend upon one another. Harmony and cooperation are paramount for success of this economic system. It only works efficiently in a free society, because in freedom risks are lowest. In a free society there is greater flow of information, there is greater personal incentive to satisfy consumer needs because of potential gain. A free society is a flexible one. It can react more quickly to new conditions in the business environment. In a free society the division of labor is integrated by market forces: information, prices, profits, and losses. In a statist society, by contrast, if no one wants a particular service, then government must use coercion.

There are three distinct advantages to division of labor:

1. It increases the ability and efficiency of each worker: This one thing I do, and I do it well.
2. It saves time, which frees up time for more prayer and meditation.
3. It multiplies human energy, because with the introduction of machinery and equipment, one person can now do the work of several under more primitive methods.

Division of labor is like using a lever: A little energy expended on one end produces tremendous results on the other end. Every one enjoys more goods and a higher standard of living.

(*See Also:* Exchange, Free Society, Inequality, Specialization, Supply)

Now the Levites were numbered from the age of thirty years and upward: and their number by their polls, man by man, was thirty and eight thousand. Of which, twenty and four thousand were to set forward the work of the house of the Lord; and six thousand were officers and judges: moreover four thousand were porters; and four thousand praised the Lord with the instruments which I made, said David, to praise therewith. And David divided them into courses among the sons of Levi.

1 Chronicles 23:3–6.

Having then gifts, differing according to the grace that is given us, whether prophecy, or ministry, or teaching, or exhortation, he who gives, let him do it with simplicity; he who rules, with diligence; he who shows mercy, with cheerfulness.

                                                              ROMANS 12:6–8.

God has set forth some in the church, first apostles, secondarily prophets, thirdly teachers, after that miracles, the gifts of healing, helps, government, diversities of tongue.

                                                              1 CORINTHIANS 12:28.

But by an equality, that now at this time your abundance may be a supply for their want, that their abundance also may be a supply for your want: that there may be equality.

                                                              2 CORINTHIANS 8:14.

Every man according as he purposes in his heart, so let him give, not grudgingly, or of necessity, for God loves a cheerful giver.

                                                              2 CORINTHIANS 9:7.

He gave some, apostles, and some, prophets, and some, evangelists, and some, pastors, and teachers, for the perfecting of saints, for the work of the ministry, for the edifying of the body of Christ.

                                                              EPHESIANS 4:11–12.

DIVORCE

We have trespassed against our God, and have taken pagan wives....Now, therefore, let us make a covenant with our God to put away all these wives and those who have been born to them.

                                                              EZRA 10:2–3.

(*See:* Idolatry, Family, Marriage)

DOUBLE STANDARD

In a free society there is no place for double standards. In government and legal affairs, everyone is equal before the law. The law applies equally to everyone. There are no special groups, exempt groups, or privileged groups. There is no attempt to remodel society through the work of tax collectors and other redistribution programs or through a system of so-called social laws designed to establish social priorities and privileged sectors. Labor unions no more hold a privileged position in a free society than do automobile manufacturers. Contrary to all this, under humanistic systems, we see a marked deterioration in moral standards and the widespread application of double standards and hypocrisy in political transactions.

In private business transactions, the Bible admonishes vendors to treat all customers alike, not to cheat the buyer with various weights and measures (i.e., keep the thumb off the scale), and not to dilute or adulterate the product. ("Thou shalt not commit adultery.") Honesty in transactions is a rule increasingly less adhered to as we move further away from free society precepts.

Although the following verses are limited to a few instances in government and business dealings, throughout the Bible we read references reproving hypocrites and liars and demagogues. Honesty in all our relationships, including those with the Divine, is the rule of God.

(*See Also:* Demagoguery, Dishonesty, Envy, Law, Moral Principles, Nonalignment, Perjury)

> *You shall have one manner of law, as well for the stranger, as for one of your own country.*
>
> LEVITICUS 24:22.

> *You shall not respect persons in judgment; but he shall hear the small as well as the great.*
>
> DEUTERONOMY 1:17.

> *You shall not have in your bag diverse weights, a great and a small. You shall not have in your house diverse measures, a great and a small.*
>
> DEUTERONOMY 25:13–14.

> *Differing weights and differing measures, both of them alike are an abomination to the Lord.*
>
> PROVERBS 20:10.

DRAFT (MILITARY)

A society under God's laws is kept free by restricting those activities and governmental functions toward which power typically flows and by guarding against the misuse of power. Civil government, by its very nature, is coercive—a legal monopoly of violence. It functions most effectively only by application of force. Therefore, rather than risk temptation put into the hands of unregenerate men, which such a concentration of power allows, freedom's ways can best be served by removing that possibility. The functions of central government are severely restricted.

One of two tasks that falls to civil government is national defense. A conscription system makes possible national defense, but biblical exemptions from military service are many.

According to DEUTERONOMY 20:1–4, the military not only defends, but it also fights God's battles without fear. Notice, however, the draft exemptions allowed in DEUTERONOMY 20:5–8. For instance, cowards and the faint hearted were undesirable conscripts because potentially they could undermine the morale of the army. Newlyweds as well as those who had recently built a house stayed away from war. Although the pastorate often entered battle, they could have invoked exemption. Likewise, the man who had recently planted a vineyard but had not yet enjoyed the fruits of his labor did not go to war. Neither did women nor children!

Rushdoony writes,

> From these exemptions, a general principle appears: *The family has a priority over warfare.* The young bridegroom cannot serve; the new home must come first. The new farmer similarly gains exemption. *Important as defense is, the continuity of life and godly reconstruction are more important.*[1]

(*See Also:* Division of Labor, Family, Liberty, Military Defense, Organization, Responsibility, War)

> *The officers shall speak to the people saying, What man is there who has built a new house and has not dedicated it? Let him go and return to his house, lest he die in the battle, and another man dedicate it. And what man is he who has planted a vineyard, and has not yet eaten of it? Let him also go and return to his house, lest he die in the battle, and another man eat of it. And what man is there who has betrothed a wife, and has not taken her? Let him go and return to his house, lest he die in the battle, and another man take her. What man is there who is fainthearted? Let him go and return to his house, lest his brethren's heart faint as well as his heart.*
>
> DEUTERONOMY 20:5–8.

> *Take the sum of all the congregation of the children of Israel, after their families, by the house of their fathers, with the number of their names, every male by his polls. From twenty years old and upwards, all who are able to go forth to war in Israel; you and Aaron shall number them by their armies.*
>
> NUMBERS 1:2–3.

[1]Rousas John Rushdoony, *The Institutes of Biblical Law* (Nutley, N.J.: The Craig Press, 1973), p. 278.

But the Levites after the tribe of their fathers were not numbered among them. For the Lord had spoken to Moses, saying, Only you shall not number the tribe of Levi, neither take the sum of them among the children of Israel. But you shall appoint the Levites over the tabernacle of testimony, and all the vessels thereof; and they shall minister to it, and shall encamp round about the tabernacle.

NUMBERS *1:47–50.*

From thirty years old and upward until fifty years old shall you number them; all who enter in to perform the service, to do the work in the tabernacle of the congregation.

NUMBERS *4:23.*

From twenty and five years old and upward they shall go in to wait upon the service of the tabernacle of the congregation; and from the age of fifty years they shall cease waiting upon the service thereof, and shall serve no more.

NUMBERS *8:24–25.*

ECONOMICS

(*See:* Demand and Supply, Keynesianism, Market Economy)

ECONOMIC FORECASTS

Forecasting, of course, is not new. Man has always attempted to peer into an unknowable future. Businesspeople must make decisions and plans for the future, regardless of ability to forecast. Since man is not omniscient, unforecasted profits and losses ensue. Businesspeople seek better information about the future in order to reduce waste from incorrect decisions, that is, the losses that result from erroneous forecasts. Economic forecasts concern projections about the economy—those variables that concern all business activity.

Business forecasting often means economic forecasting. Economics began to take on its scientific color after Adam Smith systematically organized what had been known and discussed for centuries preceding the publication of his book in 1776, *The Wealth of Nations*.

The art of contemporary economic forecasting largely has developed from neo-Keynesian macroeconomic models. Its foundations are statist and nonbiblical. It is a wonder this multimillion-dollar business survived. So many models are premised on false assumptions. But voodooism, black and white magic, and endless faith in government policies as a cure-all for government-created economic ills continue to survive—and they are multibillion-dollar businesses.

Nevertheless, economic forecasting is not modern in origin. In the Bible we see, too, that witches and wizards preceded our modern prognosticators by a few thousand years. They did about as well.

(*See Also:* Economic Growth, Expert, Forecasting, Randomness, Risk Aversion, Strategic Planning)

Tomorrow about this time shall a measure of fine flour be sold for a shekel, and two measures of barley for a shekel, in the gate of Samaria.

2 KINGS 7:1.

When I applied my heart to know wisdom, and to see the business that is done upon the earth: then I beheld all the work of God, that a man cannot find out the work that is done under the sun, because though a man labor to seek it out, yet he shall not find it; yea further, though a wise man think to know it, yet shall he not be able to find it.

ECCLESIASTES 8:16–17.

You are wearied in the multitude of your counsels. Let now the astrologers, the stargazers, the monthly prognosticators, stand up, and save you from these things that shall come upon you.

ISAIAH 47:13.

For we know in part, and we prophesy in part. But when that which is perfect is come, then that which is in part shall be done away with.

1 CORINTHIANS 13:9–10.

For now we see through a glass darkly.

1 CORINTHIANS 13:12.

ECONOMIC GROWTH

Some years ago an exchange professor from Bolivia asked, "To what do you attribute the enormous wealth and economic growth of the United States?" In other words, he was asking, why are you so rich and we so poor although both our continents began development around the same period in history?

Economic growth, of course, does not mean simple expansion brought about by erecting a statue in every plaza. Growth alludes to a self-sustaining process. It materializes in higher real income and production levels year after year.

At the time of the professor's question, conventional economic growth wisdom enshrined scattered aphorisms, some of which were: The rivers of the United States flow inward, allowing for easy transportation and settlement, while the great South American rivers flow outward, making cheap river transportation inland nearly impossible; the United States has more natural resources (self-sufficiency), temperate climate, better soil; Europeans brought their wives and families with them and killed the Indian population, while the male Spaniard and Portuguese arrived alone, "married" local Indian women, and put the Indian males to work at forced labor in mines and fields. In other words, these were theories of environmental determinism.

Then someone discovered that North American colonies, and later the United States, were heavily financed with European capital to develop colonial enterprises, while Spain and Portugal drained the South American continent of its gold, silver, and valuable resources.

Too, it was (and still is) widely believed, especially among United Nations elite, that since the United States is a huge common market, the solution to Latin America's slow economic growth rests with the creation of a Latin American Common Market. The same concept has spread to Asian and African countries.

Today, dependency theory supposedly explains poor economic growth in Latin America. This latest theory embraces a blend of Marxism, economic nationalism, the United Nations, and colonialism. Dependency theories all have the following ideas in common:

1. Expansion of capitalism has caused Latin American underdevelopment.
2. Multinational corporations have fragmented domestic markets, and local entrepreneurs have lost their will to lead.
3. Socialism is the only real hope for solving Latin American economic and social problems.

Throughout Latin America (and other countries far less developed), even casual observations affirm that these theories are incomplete or erroneous at best, downright malicious at worst. Latin America, for instance, has ample rich resources; an intelligent population; entrepreneurs with outstanding business perceptions and economic vision; and, especially in recent decades, a substantial inflow of foreign capital.

The answer, of course, to our own success story lies at the very roots of the settling of this land and the founding of our country: One nation, *under God; In God We Trust.* Recurrently, the Old Testament tells the same story: Those nations that prospered and grew adhered to God's laws. When they departed from those tenets of prosperity, they became economically and politically backward. The story is often echoed. With so many historically valid illustrations, it seems impossible to ignore evidence. Still a substantial part of the world, and even Americans, deny this basic, observed truth.

The sampling of biblical verses and quotations reminds us to remember God. He is the Source of all wealth. "The Lord makes poor, and makes rich." "Gold is not made by man but by God. Man only makes the stamp. All things come from God. Not a grain of corn or wheat, or a dollar, is made by man." An erring nation will even lose the ability to make the stamp that marks the gold. To believe otherwise disavows historical evidence.

(*See Also:* Abundance, Capital Formation, Cooperation, Free Society, Liberty, Poor Nations, Prosperity, Zain)

You shall serve the Lord your God, and he shall bless your bread, and your water; and I will take sickness away from the midst of you. There shall nothing cast their young, nor be barren, in your land.

Exodus 23:25–26.

You shall remember the Lord your God, for it is He who gives power to get wealth.

Deuteronomy 8:18.

If you shall listen diligently to the voice of the Lord your God, to observe and do all his commandments, the Lord your God will set you on high above all nations of the earth.

The Lord shall command the blessing upon you in your store-houses, and in all you set your hand to.

The Lord shall make you plenteous in goods, in the fruit of your body, and in the fruits of your cattle, and in the fruit of your ground. The Lord shall open to you his good treasure, the heaven to give the rain to your land in its season, and to bless all the work of your hand; and you shall lend to many nations, and you shall not borrow. And the Lord shall make you the head, and not the tail.

Deuteronomy 28:1, 8, 11–13.

The Lord makes poor, and makes rich. He brings low, and lifts up. He raises up the poor out of dust, and lifts the beggar from the dunghill, to set them among princes, and to make them inherit the throne of glory: for the pillars of the earth are the Lord's, and He has set the world upon them.

1 Samuel 2:7–8.

I have caused you to multiply as the bud of the field, and you have increased and waxed great, and you are come to excellent ornaments: Your breasts are fashioned, and your hair is grown, whereas you were naked and bare. Now when I passed by you, and looked upon you, behold, your time was the time of love; and I spread my skirt over you, and entered into a covenant with you, saith the Lord God, and you became mine.

I clothed you with broider work, and covered you with badgers' skin, and I girded you about with fine linen, and I covered you with silk. I decked you with ornaments, and I put bracelets on your arms, and a chain on your neck. And I put a jewel on the forehead, and earrings in your ears, and a beautiful crown upon your head.... You did eat fine flour, and honey, and oil; and you were exceedingly beautiful, and you did prosper into a kingdom.

But you did trust in your own beauty, and played the harlot because of your renown, and poured out your fornications on everyone who passed by. And of your garments you did take, and decked your high places with various colors, and played the harlct....

Moreover you have taken your sons and daughters, whom you have borne to me, and these you sacrificed to them to be devoured. Is this of your whoredoms a small matter...?

And in all your abominations and your whoredoms you have not remembered the days of your youth, when you were naked and bare, and were polluted in your blood.

Because you have not remembered the days of your youth, but have fretted me in all these things, behold, therefore I also will recompense your way upon your head, saith the Lord God....

EZEKIEL 16:7–8, 10–13, 15, 20, 22, 43.

...the Lord will be the hope of his people, and the strength of the children of Israel.

And it shall come to pass in that day, that the mountains shall drop down new wine, and the hills shall flow with milk, and all the rivers of Judah shall flow with waters, and a fountain shall come forth of the house of the Lord, and shall water the valley of Shittim.

JOEL 3:16, 18.

ECONOMIC SECURITY

Then Jesus said to them, Verily, verily, I say to you, Moses gave you not that bread from heaven; but my Father gives you true bread from heaven. For the bread of God is he who comes down from heaven and gives life to the world. Then they said to him, Lord, evermore give us this bread. And Jesus said to them, I am the bread of life: He who comes to me shall never hunger; and he who believes in me shall never thirst.

JOHN 6:32–35.

(*See:* Savings, Social Security, Work)

ECONOMIST

Economics is what an economist does. But the particular approach to economic analysis and solutions depends upon the philosophical foundation from which economic theory springs. You would not expect much overlap between proposals of a Christian economist and a Marxian economist. Still, very few economists recognize this basic philosophical divergence.

If an economist believes that solutions to economic problems can only be effected through government intervention, he will twist analysis to conform to big government thinking, which includes most economists. Fabian socialist thinking predominates, followed by a growing minority popularly referred to as the Chicago School. A tiny, but rapidly growing, minority adhere to the Austrian School of economic thought, popularly referred to as Free Market Economics.

Christian economics, at least partly Austrian in methodology, does put God first, not the marketplace. Market stability is achieved when we get our priorities right (first verse below). The second verse below is most appropriate for our gaggle of government statisticians (who may call themselves economists), whose predictions and prognostications are often best ignored. Speaking of his economists in 1971, President Nixon said, "They're not always right, but they're always sure." Finally, we note that economics is billed as primarily predictive. The urge to predict is often too great to resist, whether for pay or without (see the third verse below).

(*See Also:* Business, Demand and Supply, Economic Forecasts, Market Economy, Price Mechanism)

> Give to the Lord the glory due His name....Fear before him, all the earth: The world also shall be stable, that it be not moved.
>
> 1 CHRONICLES 16:29–30.

> But you are forgers of lies; you are all physicians of no value.
>
> JOB 13:4.

> I have not sent these prophets, yet they ran; I have not spoken to them, yet they prophesied. But if they had stood in my counsel, and had caused my people to hear my words, then they should have turned from their evil way, and from the evil of their doings.
>
> JEREMIAH 23:21–22.

EDUCATION

In the time of our forefathers, before our great nation reckoned with official blessings of public education, the Federalist papers were circulated, read, and understood by ordinary souls. Meant to be read and comprehended by the butcher, baker, and candlestick maker, they were not circulated as arcane, academic treatises to an elite.

Occasionally a college-level history professor today will assign some Federalist papers. College-level students have difficulty comprehending both the language and the content of these most valuable documents of our heritage.

In *The Communist Manifesto,* we read: "The Communist revolution is the most radical rupture with traditional property relations; no wonder that its development involves the most radical rupture with traditional ideas...Of course, in the beginning, this cannot be effected except by means of despotic inroads on the rights of property; by means of measures, which...necessitate further inroads upon the old social order.... In most advanced countries, the following [measures] will be generally applicable.... Free education for all children in public schools."[1]

After reading only a few lines we have learned that communists are not interested in public education *per se.* They want to make "despotic inroads upon the social order."

What, then, is the social order that Marx and Engels wanted to destroy? Read this.

> Education is the responsibility of the family unit (PROVERBS 22:6). There is a lawful pathway in life, and parents are required by God to impart the details of this law-order to their children. These guidelines are provided by biblical law. Of crucial social significance, then, is the requirement that parents transfer the data of biblical law to their children.
>
> The attempt of secular humanists to transfer this family responsibility to the public school system has to be understood as a direct challenge to a godly social order.[2]

Dr. Paul A. Kienel, executive director of WACS, asks a number of tough questions: "My first question is, would you send or take your children to a government-sponsored and tax-supported church? My second question is, if you would not have anything to do with a government-sponsored church on Sunday, why is it right on Monday to send your children to a government-sponsored nonreligious

---

[1]Marx, Karl and Friedrich Engels, *The Communist Manifesto,* rev. by Samuel H. Beer (New York: Appleton-Century-Crofts, Inc., 1955), pp. 31–32.

[2]Gary North, Ph.D., "An Economic Commentary on the Bible," *Chalcedon Report* (Vallecito, Calif.), April 1978.

secular 'public' school? My third question: What would be your reaction if on Sunday morning you visited your children's Sunday school class and the teacher standing before the students was a non-Christian?"[3]

For his last set of questions, Dr. Kienel asks: "Why do you have different standards for Monday school than you do for Sunday school? Why is it acceptable to have your children taught falsehoods during the week but on Sunday you have a very narrow view as to what they are taught and by whom?"[4]

The debate over education is a debate over the locus of earthly sovereignty. Education is (1) knowledge of God, (2) knowledge of God's works, (3) knowledge of man's responsibilities. (Refer to PROVERBS 1 and PSALM 119.) Through education, there is a transfer of knowledge, such as a program of apprenticeship. This knowledge leads to specialization and division of labor. The end result in a free society is greater production and greater material well-being.

(*See Also:* Character, Children, Crowd Psychology, Educator, Family, Professor, Wisdom)

> *They taught in Judah, and had the book of the law of the Lord with them.*
>
> 2 CHRONICLES 17:9.

> *Man that is in honor, and understands not, is like beasts that perish.*
>
> PSALM 49:20.

> *The fear of the Lord is the beginning of knowledge, but fools despise wisdom and instruction. My son, hear the instruction of your father, and do not forsake the law of your mother.*
>
> PROVERBS 1:7–8.

> *Correction is grievous to him who foresakes the way; and he who hates reproof shall die.*
>
> PROVERBS 15:10.

> *Train up a child in the way he should go; and when he is old, he will not depart from it.*
>
> PROVERBS 22:6.

---

[3]Dr. Paul A. Kienel, "Sunday School vs. Monday School," *The Miletus Epistle* (reprint), (Cross Plains, Texas) p. 166.
[4]Ibid.

*Further, by these, my son, be admonished: of making many books
there is no end; and much study is a weariness of the flesh.*
                                                            ECCLESIASTES 12:12.

*Whom shall he teach knowledge? And whom shall he make to
understand doctrine? those who are weaned from the milk, and drawn
from the breasts. For precept must be built upon precept, precept upon
precept; line upon line, line upon line; here a little, and there a little.*
                                                            ISAIAH 28:9–10.

*Such trust we have through Christ to God-ward: Not that we are
sufficient of ourselves to think any thing as of ourselves; but our
sufficiency is of God, who also has made us able ministers of the new
testament, not of the letter, but of the spirit, for the letter kills, but the
spirit gives life.*
                                                            2 CORINTHIANS 3:4–6.

Prove all things; hold fast that which is good.
                                                            1 THESSALONIANS 5:21.

*Shun profane and vain babblings: for they will increase into more
ungodliness. And their word will eat as does a canker.*
                                                            2 TIMOTHY 2:16–17.

*Foolish and unlearned questions avoid, knowing that they do gender
strifes. And the servant of the Lord must not strive; but be gentle to all
men, apt to teach, patient, in meekness instructing those who oppose
themselves; if God peradventure will give them repentance to the
acknowledging of the truth; and that they may recover themselves out
of the snare of the devil, who are taken captive by him at his will.*
                                                            2 TIMOTHY 2:23–26.

*For the time will come when they will not endure sound doctrine; but
after their own lusts shall they heap to themselves teachers, having
itching ears; and they shall turn away their ears from the truth, and
shall be turned into fables.*
                                                            2 TIMOTHY 4:3–4.

*Wherefore laying aside all malice, and all guile, and hypocrisies, and
envies, and all evil speaking, as newborn babes, desire the sincere
milk of the word, that you may grow thereby.*
                                                            2 PETER 2:1–2.

EDUCATOR

The chief educators of children should be their parents and the pastorate; of women, their husbands and the church; of men, their church leaders. In other words, responsibility for education lies directly on individual family members, supported by leaders of the church organization. Private education is the rule. The educator is a hired tutor of the family. Families reduce costs of tutors by pooling resources, hence, private schools.

Public education, today big business, and public educators represent a powerful force for inculcation of statist dogma. Public educators and state and federal bureaucracies hand-in-hand and by means of coercion (i.e., compulsory public school attendance and compulsory property taxes to support the institution) have moved apparent responsibility for education from the family and church organization to the public domain. In other words, public educators have become agents for pseudo parents—the state.

Public education has brought us new legislation. It requires students to pass a basic literacy test—because many can neither read nor write well after twelve-to-fourteen years of public education—and competency tests for teachers—because many know little either about teaching or about their subject matter even after four to eight years of college-level courses in public education.

For instance, in the state of Florida, public school teachers must pass a twenty-three level competency test, including reading and math. The third year the test was required, out of 14,000 test-takers, 15 percent failed the first time around, which sounds like Florida's teachers must be more competent than New Jersey's. Still, recent high school graduates in Broward County (Florida) bitterly complained about the low level of instruction that left them inadequately prepared for either work or college. Then, a private Christian school gave a test equivalent to the math portion of the teacher competency test to sixth graders. All of them passed with 70 percent or better, some achieving 100 percent. Some of the tougher multiple-guess test questions were on the order of: "Find the sum of 3,905 and 66 and 821."

Such is the state of public education in at least one state. State legislators and uninformed PTA associations, along with influential teachers' labor unions, say the problem can only be resolved with more taxpayers' money. The fact that they have been poor stewards of public money does not deter them from seeking more and more and, no doubt, more. Karl Marx and his coconspirators knew too well what they were up to. Unfortunately American parents and property tax payers have not caught on yet to the hoax.

In virtually all universities the degree Doctor of Education carries scant respect. While we do not judge the relative worth of doctorate degrees, educators, in whatever field, generally rank low in esteem. University business students say; Those who can, do; those who can't, teach; and those who can't teach, teach teachers.

(*See Also:* Children, Education, Expert, Family, Foundation, Professor, Statist)

Be not righteous over much; neither make yourself over wise: why should you destroy yourself?

ECCLESIASTES 7:16.

All this have I proved by wisdom: I said, I will be wise; but it was far from me.

ECCLESIASTES 7:23.

Woe to them who are wise in their own eyes, and prudent in their own right!

ISAIAH 5:21.

They were astonished at his doctrine, for he taught as one who had authority, and not as the scribes.

MARK 1:22.

An instructor of the foolish, a teacher of babes, which has form of knowledge and of the truth in the law. You therefore who teach another, do you not teach yourself? You who preach a man should not steal, do you steal?

ROMANS 2:20–21.

Let no man deceive himself. If any man among you seems wise in this world, let him become a fool, that he may be wise.

1 CORINTHIANS 3:18.

I suffer not a woman to teach, nor to usurp authority over man, but to be in silence.

1 TIMOTHY 2:12.

Ever learning, and never able to come to the knowledge of the truth.

2 TIMOTHY 3:7.

ELITISM

Civil governments of the world, characterized by elitism, govern by and with special privileges. The wealth and privileged life of the bureaucratic elite in the Soviet Union are well documented. The super-rich today include world dictators of communist countries. Former dictator Tito lived in luxury unimaginable by the typical Yugoslavian and unbelieved by the typical American; so does dictator Fidel Castro.

The issue is top-down bureaucracy versus decentralized theocracy. The pyramidal, top-down system is Satan's imitation of God's kingdom—the quest to be as God, i.e., the quest for arbitrary power. Elitism is the possession of monopolistic power, which is exercised over others lawlessly. With decentralization, under God's law, there are multiple hierarchies with the *best* men at the top in *one* organization but who are subordinate to others, such as the church, and ultimately the rule of God. Consequently, there is division of institutional labor, which marks a more efficient system. This advantage is lost with elitism.

Some believe that our own country has followed a course of deterioration from republicanism, to democracy, to representative democracy, to bureaucracy, to elitism, which implies that political representation of the taxpaying public has dwindled and disappeared altogether when our elected "representatives" raise taxes and say, The public be damned.

Naziism, the best popularized example of elitism, considers most other races inferior. Only a superior elite is fit to manage the state machinery. The disabled, elderly, and noncomformist should be exterminated according to some Nazi scientists and university professors.

We practice elitism in the United States. Unwanted babies are destroyed (aborted). Physically undesirable infants are allowed to die without benefit of sustenance or love (infanticide). Increasingly it is suggested that elderly patients be overdrugged (euthanasia) to remove an inconvenience from our midst. Brain implantations and surgery to modify behavior have been employed at least twenty years in the United States. Proposals have been made around the country to eliminate cemeteries so that "wasted land" can be converted to social projects. Nonconformist churches and their schools are harassed and harangued by the IRS, state taxing authorities, public school, health, and welfare agencies, and, in some instances, the local police.

If each of us stands by idly and fails to protest, because always the other fellow bears the burden, not us, we have relinquished responsibility. The time to protest injustice to anyone is when it rears its ugly form, because when will the day come when the powerful state turns its search light on us?—and zap!

Elitism certainly has no place in God's orderly world. Everyone who obeys His commandments are eligible for the rewards. No system of seniority, heredity, or official blessing by the civil government, or the organized church for that matter, sways God's judgment or justice. In a world of elitism, only the Titos and Castros have multimillion-dollar yachts. In a free society, such toys are available for anyone who aspires to acquire them. In a free society functioning in accordance with God's laws, abundance is the rule; in an elitist society, poverty for the majority is the rule.

(*See Also:* Communism, Expropriation, Power of State, Rule by Decree, Slavery, Statism, Theft)

Children in whom was no blemish, but well favored, and skillful in all wisdom, and cunning in knowledge, and understanding science, and such as had ability in them to stand in the king's palace, and whom they might teach the learning and the tongue of the Chaldeans. And the king appointed them a daily provision of the king's meat, and of the wine which he drank, so nourishing them three years, that at the end thereof they might stand before the king.

But Daniel purposed in his heart that he would not defile himself with the portion of the king's meat, nor with the wine which he drank; therefore he requested of the prince of the eunuchs that he might not defile himself.

DANIEL 1:4–5, 8.

For I mean not that other men be eased, and you burdened.

2 CORINTHIANS 8:13.

But if you bite and devour one another, take heed that you be not consumed one of another.

GALATIANS 5:15.

EMINENT DOMAIN

(*See:* Expropriation, Power of State, Private Property)

EMPLOYEE

The Bible says two things about work. Both run contrary to much of contemporary ethics. One is that work we must: No free rides. No reference to endless vacations. No message about retirement—early, late, or otherwise. "Six days shall you labor, and do all your work" (EXODUS 20:9). Second, the Bible does not make reference to job security, or the right to employment (meaning someone else's obligation to meet a payroll). With plenty to do on this earth, we need not sit waiting for someone else to "create" a job.

Let's briefly summarize key verses that directly pertain to employees and their relationships to employers. Duties of employees include, be content (LUKE 3:14), diligent (PROVERBS 22:29), faithful to contractual obligations (MATTHEW 20:1–5), and respectful (1 TIMOTHY 6:1).

On the other hand, employers must compensate employees according to agreement (MATTHEW 10:10), treat them correctly (RUTH 2:4), and pay wages promptly (LEVITICUS 19:13), which meant daily wages for day laborers. (Notice lack of mention of withholding taxes, social security taxes, state income taxes, city income taxes, and miscellaneous taxes.) Further, employers must not oppress employees (GENESIS 31:38–42; DEUTERONOMY 24:14; JAMES 5:4–6).

What types of employees does the Bible mention? All kinds, then, as now: lazy and unworthy ones (JOB 7:1–3; MATTHEW 21:33–41); discontented ones (MATTHEW 20:1–15); and diligent ones (GENESIS 30:27–31).

Good stewardship requires that we make proper use of our talents (and do not bury them). It requires that we do considerably more than the minimum—going the extra mile. Jesus said, "And whosoever shall compel thee to go a mile, go with him two" (MATTHEW 5:41). Whether we work for ourselves or for someone else, we are all working for God. Are you going the extra mile?

(*See Also:* Cooperation, Division of Labor, Productivity, Responsibility, Specialization, Wages, Work)

Tell me what you want for wages, and I will give it. And he said to him, You know how I have served you, and how your cattle were with me. For it was little that you had before I came, and it is now increased into a multitude.

> GENESIS 30:28–30.

You shall not defraud your neighbor, neither rob him: the wages of him that is hired shall not abide with you all night until the morning.

> LEVITICUS 19:13.

You shall not oppress a hired servant who is poor and needy.

> DEUTERONOMY 24:14.

Do you see a man diligent in his business? He shall stand before kings; he shall not stand before mean men.

> PROVERBS 22:29.

…the workman is worthy of his meat.

> MATTHEW 10:10.

For the kingdom of heaven is like a man who is a householder, who went out early in the morning to hire laborers into his vineyard. When he had agreed with the laborers for a penny a day, he sent them into his vineyard. And he went out about the third hour, and saw others standing idle in the marketplace, and said to them, Go also into the vineyard, and whatsoever is right I will give you. And they went their way. Again he went out about the sixth [noon] and the ninth hour, and did likewise. And about the eleventh hour he went out, and found others standing idle, and said to them, Why stand here all the day idle?

They said to him, Because no man has hired us. He said to them, Go also into the vineyard; and whatever is right, that you shall receive. So when evening came, the lord of the vineyard said to his steward, Call the laborers, and give them their hire, beginning from the last to the first. And when they came who were hired about the eleventh hour, they received every man a penny. But when the first came they supposed that they should have received more; and they likewise received every man a penny. And when they had received it, they complained against the landowner, saying, These last have wrought but one hour, and you have made them equal to us, who have borne the burden and heat of the day. But he answered one of them, and said, Friend, I do you no wrong: did you not agree with me for a penny? Take it, and go your way. I will give to this last, even as to you. Is it not lawful for me to do what I will with my own? Is your eye evil, because I am good?

MATTHEW 20:1–15.

…Do violence to no man, neither accuse any falsely; and be content with your wages.

LUKE 3:14.

He who is a hireling, and not the shepherd, whose own the sheep are not, sees the wolf coming, and leaves the sheep, and flees; and the wolf catches them, and scatters the sheep. The hireling flees, because he is a hireling, and cares not for the sheep.

JOHN 10:12–13.

Verily, verily, I say to you, The servant is not greater than his lord; neither he who is sent greater than he who sent him.

JOHN 13:16

Exhort servants to be obedient to their own masters, and to please them well in all things, not answering again; not purloining, but showing all good fidelity; that they may adorn the doctrine of God our Savior in all things.

TITUS 2:9–10.

ENTERPRISE

(*See:* Free Enterprise, Market Economy)

ENVIRONMENTALISM

Because man is not an evolutionary blob in the cosmos, he has a direct mandate from God to subdue the earth and have dominion over all creation, that is, limited sovereignty over nature. Man's purpose here is to honor God by carrying out this mandate.

However, dominion and sovereignty do not equal destruction. Environmentalism pivots on responsibility. Unfortunately, the issues have been obscured with dangerous half-truths overshadowed by a socialist philosophy. Man has been given power over nature. It is also his responsibility to take care of it. Through proper care and management nature gives back to us manifoldly. In other words, we cannot escape judgment of our responsibilities to God.

Private property means that ownership, control of, and responsibility for the land and natural resources are in private hands and not in those of a faceless and vascillating bureaucracy. It means that both benefits and costs accrue to the owner. Consequently, private ownership reduces the exploitation of nature because the owner bears the costs. Harm the environment and you may harm the value of your capital. Furthermore, harm someone else's environment and you bear the cost under the rule of God. Read EXODUS 22:5–6. By contrast, private parties who have been granted special access to so-called public lands have no incentive or responsibility to replace the timber or the land's nutrients or otherwise be good stewards of God's earth.

(*See Also:* Golden Rule, Law of Increase, Natural Resources, Pollution, Risk Aversion, Stewardship)

Then God blessed them, and God said to them, Be fruitful, and multiply, and fill the earth and subdue it; have dominion over the fish of the sea, over the birds of the air, and over every living thing that moves on the earth.

GENESIS 1:28.

Every moving thing that lives shall be food for you. I have given you all things, even as the green herbs.

GENESIS 9:3.

If a man causes a field or vineyard to be grazed, and lets loose his animal, and it feeds in another man's field, he shall make restitution from the best of his own field and the best of his own vineyard. If fire breaks out and catches in thorns, so that stacked grain, standing grain, or the field is consumed, he who kindled the fire shall surely make restitution.

EXODUS 22:5–6.

They have now compassed us in our steps; they have set their eyes bowing down to the earth.

PSALM 17:11.

Fear not therefore, you are of more value than many sparrows.

MATTHEW 10:31.

Even the very hairs of your head are all numbered. Fear not therefore, you are of more value than many sparrows.

LUKE 12:7.

ENVY

Envy and jealousy are not truly synonymous terms. *Jealousy* most commonly expresses discontent regarding love, affections, aims. Although an undesirable trait, jealousy does not carry with it the covetous connotations of envy. *Envy* implies ill will, spite, and hostility toward others, of wanting what others possess (or appear to have). If the object of envy cannot be possessed, it should be destroyed so that no one else can have it either.

If two women claim the same child, the envious one would rather see the child destroyed, so that both claimants lose, than have the other appear to gain. King Solomon said, "Divide the living child in half." The real mother said, "Give her the living child and in no wise slay it." The envious woman said, "Let it be neither mine nor thine, but divide it" (1 Kings 3:25–26). A commodity broker once said to me, "I wouldn't mind socialism if that means nobody else is better off than I am." Those are statements of envy.

Probably the best systematic study of envy appears in a book by Helmut Schoeck.[1] He clearly demonstrates the destructive nature of envy. "The really envious person almost never considers entering into fair competition."[2] "Envy can become more easily institutionalized than, say, desire or joy. As examples of envy manifested in social forms one might perhaps cite instances such as steeply progressive income tax, confiscatory death duties and corresponding customs among primitive peoples, such as the 'muru raid' of the Maoris."[3] "The sociology of power and domination should not overlook the factor of envy."[4] "A notoriously envy

---

[1]Helmut Schoeck, *Envy—A Theory of Social Behavior* (New York: Harcourt, Brace, & World, Inc., 1969).

[2]Ibid., p. 7.

[3]Ibid., p. 8.

[4]Ibid., p. 305.

ridden primitive society is that of the Dobu Islanders, of whom Margaret Mead writes: 'They create situations in which the objectively unlimited supply is redefined as being of fixed and limited quantity. No amount of labor can therefore increase the next year's yam crop, and no man can excel another in the number of his yams without being accused of having stolen (magically) his extra yams from someone's garden.'" Unfortunately, therefore, the actual point of departure for socialist—and for left-wing progressive economic doctrines generally—is identical with that of particularly envy-inhabited primitive peoples."[5]

Statist government types exploit this basic flaw in character of lukewarm believers and of nonbelievers: *envy.* When maids and chauffeurs were recruited by communists in Nicaragua, they were promised the possessions of the very owners for whom they worked. Now that Marxists have taken over Nicaragua, maids and chauffeurs rue the day they ever listened to their Marxist mentors. By any standard they are worse off. Living in the promised (and best) houses are the same Marxist mentors and their Cuban communist advisors.

Regarding the Sixteenth Amendment (income tax), Irwin Schiff writes, "The U.S. electorate was tricked into voting for it because it was presented to them as a 'soak-the-rich' scheme."[6] It really was not a trick. Statists understand the insidious nature of envy. Because of envy the Sixteenth Amendment passed.

Gary North writes, "Envy is loose in the land."[7] He provides several examples of envy in action: terrorism, wealth redistribution schemes, arson, destruction of both property and person. And he wrote a book that is essentially a survival manual in an age of envy. When envy underpins politics, it threatens the whole society. Coeval (today's) politics are the politics of envy.

(*See Also:* Conspiracy, Discipline, Ethics, Freedom, Golden Rule, Inequality, Losses, Maturity)

> For he had possession of flocks, and possession of herds, and great store of servants; and the Philistines envied him. For all the wells that his father's servants had dug in the days of Abraham, the Philistines had stopped them, and filled them with earth.
>
> GENESIS 26:14–15.

> You shall not covet your neighbor's house, you shall not covet your neighbor's wife, nor his manservant, nor his maidservant, nor his ox, nor his ass, nor anything that is your neighbor's.
>
> EXODUS 20:17.

[5]Ibid., p. 305.

[6]Irwin A. Schiff, *The Biggest Con: How the Government Is Fleecing You* (New Rochelle, N.Y.: Arlington House Publishers, 1976), p. 253.

[7]Gary North, *Successful Investing in an Age of Envy,* rev. ed. (Ft. Worth, Tex: Steadman Press, 1982), p. 5.

For wrath kills the foolish man, and envy slays the silly one.

J<small>OB</small> 5:2.

Envy not the oppressor, and choose none of his ways.

P<small>ROVERBS</small> 3:31.

A sound heart is the life of the flesh, but envy the rottenness of the bones.

P<small>ROVERBS</small> 14:30.

Let not your heart envy sinners; but be in the fear of the Lord all the day long.

P<small>ROVERBS</small> 23:17.

Wrath is cruel, and anger is outrageous; but who is able to stand before envy?

P<small>ROVERBS</small> 27:4.

The patriarchs, moved with envy, sold Joseph into Egypt; but God was with him.

A<small>CTS</small> 7:9.

The Jews who believed not, moved with envy, took to them certain lewd fellows of the baser sort, and gathered a company, and set all the city in an uproar, and assaulted the house of Jason, and sought to bring them out to the people.

A<small>CTS</small> 17:5.

Being filled with all unrighteousness, fornication, wickedness, covetousness, maliciousness; full of envy, murder, strife, deceit, malignity; whisperers, backbiters, haters of God, despiteful, haughty, boasters, inventors of evil things, disobedient to parents,...

R<small>OMANS</small> 1:29–30.

Let us walk honestly, as in the day, not in rioting and drunkeness, not in licentiousness and wantonness, not in strife and envying.

R<small>OMANS</small> 13:13.

For I fear, lest, when I come, I shall not find you such as I would, and that I shall be found by you such as you do not wish, lest there be debates, envyings, wraths, strifes, backbitings, whisperings, swellings, tumults.

2 C<small>ORINTHIANS</small> 12:20.

Envyings, murders, drunkenness, revellings, and such like, of the which I tell you before, as I have also told you in time past, that they who do such things shall not inherit the kingdom of God.

GALATIANS 5:21.

He is a fool, knowing nothing, but doting about questions and strifes of words, whereof comes envy, strife, railings, evil surmisings.

1 TIMOTHY 6:4.

If you have bitter envying and strife in your hearts, glory not, and lie not against the truth.

For where envying and strife are, there is confusion and every evil work.

JAMES 3:14, 16.

Wherefore laying aside all malice, and all guile, and hypocrisies, and envies, and all evil speakings, as newborn babes, desire the sincere milk of the word, that you may grow thereby.

1 PETER 2:1–2.

EQUALITY

When a Marxist-trained Sandinista soldier entered an upper-middle-income four-bedroom house in one of the better suburban developments near Managua (the capital of Nicaragua), both his mouth and automatic weapon drooped. His job was to inventory houses for likely expropriation. Awestruck by what to him was a mansion (equivalent to an upper-middle-class abode in the United States), he asked, "How many families live in this house?" The mistress of the house had enough presence of mind, even in the face of a deadly weapon, to say, "There are four families living here." The answer satisfied the young illiterate, since the house had four bedrooms.

Satan wants equality with God. He wants identical outcomes: rebellion versus righteousness. He wants no losers—except God. God offers free men rewards for righteousness (1 CORINTHIANS 3); Satan wants a different set of ethics: different ethics, different rewards. When the state replaces the Rule of Law with laws of statist equality and social justice, outcomes will differ. Under such a regimen, we cannot expect freedom, abundance, or economic growth.

In a March 17, 1980, keynote address before the International Consultation on Simple Lifestyle entitled "Living More Simply for Evangelism and Justice," Ronald

Sider raised the question, "Does the need for 'privacy' and space make it right for one family to occupy a house that...could easily meet the needs of ten or fifteen people?" Of course, under the guise of practical Christianity, Sider advocates equality of wealth and redistribution of income enforced by the coercive power of the state.

Does the Bible support this thesis of economic equality and state intervention to achieve it? The answer is a resounding *no* to both economic equality and state intervention. Such is a denial of the rule of law. Being charitable, helping brethren in times of need, and supporting widows and orphans are duties of regenerate believers. By no stretch of verbal gymnastics does this imply leveling of incomes. Neither do such acts imply destruction of productive capital.

"It is not wealth as such, but wealth gained for itself and by unrighteous means, that God despises. Therefore the mere possession of wealth tells an individual nothing of his standing before God."[1]

Many proponents of economic equality are rarely genuinely interested in helping the poor. Most often, their interests lie in helping themselves to the huge sums of money that bureaucratic administration of poverty requires and the arrogation of power that such forced redistribution of funds carries with it.

Making economic dependents and cripples of the poor is hardly a charitable act by any measure. We learn through struggle and discipline. Saving and investing require extreme sacrifices on the part of those struggling to accumulate wealth. To take wealth away from a person who has for years denied himself the pleasures of the better living that could have resulted through higher consumption levels hardly seems like a just system. It also reduces future productivity.

On the other hand, equality before the law is another issue. Reverend Optiz writes:

> The ideal of equality before the law does not fit either the Platonic or the Aristotelian mold; the metaphysics of Christianity, however, does provide a soil in which personal liberty can take root. Of all the world's great cultures, it is only in Christendom that liberty is taken for granted; personal liberty is the exception everywhere else....
>
> Equality before the law is political liberty viewed from a different perspective; it is also justice, a regime under which no man and no order of men is granted a political license by the State to use other men as their tools or have any other legal advantage over them. Given this framework in a society, the economic order will automatically be free market.[2]

(*See Also:* Capital Formation, Charity, Cradle-to-Grave, Envy, Productivity, Taxation, Tinstaafl)

[1]Gary North, *An Introduction to Christian Economics* (Nutley, N.J.: The Craig Press, 1976), pp. 216–217.

[2]Edmund A. Opitz, *Religion and Capitalism: Allies Not Enemies* (New Rochelle, N.Y.: Arlington House Publishers, 1970), pp. 233, 235.

The rich shall not give more, and the poor shall not give less than half a shekel.

EXODUS 30:15.

Yet you say, The way of the Lord is not equal. Hear now, O house of Israel; Is not My way equal? Are not your ways unequal? When a righteous man turns away from his righteousness, and commits iniquity, and dies in them; for his iniquity that he has done shall he die. Again, when the wicked man turns away from his wickedness that he has committed, and does that which is lawful and right, he shall save his soul alive.

EZEKIEL 18:25–27.

Yet the children of your people say, The way of the Lord is not equal; but as for them, their way is not equal.

EZEKIEL 33:17.

My son, if sinners entice you, consent not. If they say, Come with us, let us lay wait for blood, let us lurk privily for the innocent without cause; let us swallow them up alive as the grave, and whole, as those that go down into the pit; we shall find all precious substance, we shall fill our houses with spoil; cast in your lot among us; let us all have one purse: my son, walk not in the way with them; refrain your foot from their path, for their feet run to evil, and make haste to shed blood.

PROVERBS 1:10–15.

All things come alike to all: there is one event to the righteous, and to the wicked; to the good and to the clean, and to the unclean; to him who sacrifices, and to him who sacrifices not; as is the good, so is the sinner; and he who swears, as he who fears an oath.

ECCLESIASTES 9:2.

For I mean not that other men be eased, and you be burdened; but by an equality, that now at this time your abundance may be a supply for their want, that their abundance also may be a supply for your want, that there may be equality.

2 CORINTHIANS 8:13–14.

ETHICS

Thomas Molnar begins his book, *God and the Knowledge of Reality,* with a discussion of three positions, two of which I will summarize, regarding the God problem.[1] In position A, the removal of God from man's scope renders the world fragile, evil, divided, illusory, and ultimately meaningless because it is unknowable. Best seen in the Kantian system, this position may be identified as moral subjectivisim. Today, we call it situational ethics, meaning that moral choice and behavior depend upon the situation: Is it ever right to steal? Well, that depends—as our children are often taught today in public schools. The human is morally free and is not subject to any external law imposed from the outside.

In position B of Molnar's book, the imminentization of God in man's soul similarly reduces the extramental world to a state of imperfection, porousness, division, and vanity. Since the world is evil, the so-called ethical commands are issued by the demiurgos or lower, anthropomorphic God; hence, they are not to be followed because they further ensnare man in this world, making him a cooperator in the prolongation of an evil state of affairs.[2]

Reverend Rushdoony writes:

> A deeply rooted tradition and faith in Western civilization has [sic] long insisted that love and justice are incompatible. True social order, according to this tradition, must be based on love; all men are brothers, humanity is one family, and mankind must be brought together. In the name of this doctrine of love, and for the unity of mankind, coercion must be applied as necessary to unite and integrate men. . . .
>
> Love and justice, law and liberty, have a common origin in God, and they are not in conflict.
>
> The requirement of God's justice is restitution, . . . not the punishment of the criminal but restitution to the injured party, and, supremely, the restoration of godly order.[3]

Writing on this topic elsewhere, the same author expands on the idea of coercion in a worldly ethical system:

> The goal of this coercive love is brotherhood, human solidarity, unity, and corporateness. [It is] . . . a coerced and enforced requirement by the total state. Corporateness is gained but liberty is lost and tyranny prevails. Christian corporateness and community is [sic] from above in that it is [sic] derived from God's saving grace, but its human manifestation is in free associations. It requires liberty; it runs the risk of tensions, schisms, and divisions, but it is true community and corporateness.[4]

Finally, for a biblical summary of Christian ethics, please read ROMANS 12:1–21; for perversion of ethics, i.e., the guilt of mankind read ROMANS 1:19–32; 2:14–16.

(*See Also:* Character, Freedom, Golden Rule, Justice, Moral Principles, Truth)

[1]Thomas Molnar, *God and the Knowledge of Reality.* (New York: Basic Books, Inc., 1973).

[2]Ibid.

[3]Rousas J. Rushdoony, *Politics of Guilt and Pity* (Fairfax, Va: Thoburn Press, 1978), Chap. 9, pp. 174, 176–77.

[4]Rushdoony, *This Independent Republic* (Nutley, N.J.: The Craig Press, 1964), pp. 84–89.

One law and one manner shall be for you, and for the stranger who sojourns with you.

Numbers 15:16.

You shall not respect persons in judgment; but you shall hear the small as well as the great.

Deuteronomy 1:17.

You shall not do after all the things that we do here this day, every man whatsoever is right in his own eyes. For you are not as yet come to the next and to the inheritance, which the Lord your God gives you.

Deuteronomy 12:8–9.

You shall not have in your bag divers weights.

Deuteronomy 25:13.

A just weight and balance are the Lord's: all the weights of the bag are His work.

Proverbs 16:11.

Be perfect, as your Father in heaven is perfect.

Matthew 5:48.

Be not conformed to this world; but be transformed by the renewing of your mind, that you may demonstrate what is that good, and acceptable, and perfect will of God. For I say, through the grace given to me, to every man who is among you, not to think of himself more highly than he ought to think, but to think soberly, according as God has dealt to every man the measure of faith. For as we have many members in one body, and all members have not the same office, so we, being many, are one body in Christ, and every one members one of another.

...he who gives, let him do it with simplicity; he who rules, with diligence; he who shows mercy, with cheerfulness. Let love be without dissimulation. Abhor that which is evil; cleave to that which is good. Be kindly affectioned one to another with brotherly love; in honor preferring one to another; not slothful in business; fervent in spirit; serving the Lord; rejoicing in hope; patient in tribulation; continuing instant in prayer; giving to the needs of saints; given to hospitality.

If it be possible, as much as lies in you, live peaceably with all men....Avenge not yourselves, but rather give place to wrath: for it is written, Vengeance is mine; I will repay, saith the Lord. Therefore if your enemy hungers, feed him; if he thirsts, give him drink; for in so doing you shall heap coals of fire on his head. Be not overcome of evil, but overcome evil with good.

Romans 12:2–5, 8–13, 18–21.

EVOLUTIONISM

Once upon a long time, during one of those adolescent phases, I decided to become modern and scientific and embrace evolutionism. However, my tainted credentials prevented me subsequently from gaining full membership in that august scientific body: I could not master the basics. For instance, I dared ask, however humbly, for the slimmest shred of proof that all life began when a stray ray of lightning randomly fused hydrogen, oxygen, and carbon atoms to create living cells that subsequently, billions of years later, evolved into George Washington. My timidity prevented me from raising real questions on the origin of the lightning and atoms. If there once was a God, did He really die—burned out from so much creation or perhaps struck by a stray ray of His own lightning?

My great reawakening transpired some years later in one of Washington's famous museums. There was an exhibition on the evolution of man. The first glass cases contained skeletons of monkeys, apes, chimpanzees, and gorillas. Then, in other glass enclosures were skeletons of man evolving over millions and millions of years. Where skeletons could not be pieced together, artistic conceptions of what early man must have looked like (all in accordance with Darwinism) filled in the evolutionary gap.

I stared at the monkey and ape skeletons for a long time. For another long time, I studied the early human skeletons. Something here seemed too familiar. So I returned and studied the apes again. Back and forth I trotted among the various glass enclosures for a couple of hours. You know, I couldn't tell the difference between skeletons of supposedly early men and the apes. I decided then and there that no vague scientific theory would make a monkey out of me.

Touring the rest of the museum, I searched for remnants of flying panthers, walking worms, or any kind of creature that demonstrated, beyond doubt, some intermediate stage of creature development proving the theory of evolution. All I wanted to see was a single piece of hard evidence, no conjecture. I found not one example.

Outside the building, robins clearly remained robins. Chipmunks were chipmunks. Not only did they not mix, they have remained the same unchanging animals for thousands of years. Wasn't there somewhere a groundhog that wanted to be an eagle and sprout wings? (Actually two such flying groundhogs must evolve, a male and female, with the same idea of producing winged groundhogs.) After all, according to evolutionism, any animal from one-celled amoebas to dogs can will itself to a higher evolutionary level. With reason and will, an animal can become what it is not if we follow Darwin's premises to logical ends.

I know that my dog often tried to sing Prince Orlovsky's solo from *Die Fledermaus*. Alas, he was killed by a car, probably driven by a creationist, before he evolved to that stage. When I was a youngster, the neighbor's kid prepared to fly off the roof top of his house in his underwear. Unfortunately, his parents coaxed him from that avian perch before he could sprout wings. Too bad! His parents declined to wait for any drastic evolutionary modifications to his body.

The cartoon strip "Smokey Stover" did offer an artistic conception of an evolutionary hybridization, a goat with an owl's head—labeled "hootenanny." The Smithsonian does not have one yet.

Of course, "scientists" still seek origins of the universe. Especially in academia, they write complex grant proposals. They often end with the elusive suggestion that their research may just throw light on the beginnings of the universe. NSF, NASA, and other Washington agencies then fund these proposals with hundreds of thousands (per grant) of taxpayer's hard-earned dollars. With grant funds, buildings are constructed. Equipment is acquired. Professors and scientists fly around the world on their grant money to meetings.

Finally, the big day arrives. The research is completed and summarized. We will now know the key that will unlock secrets of the universe. The last paragraph always contains the critical phrases: "If we had had more time and money we might have discovered the key to unlock the unknown secrets of the origins of the universe. Ongoing research is highly recommended in the specific areas of..." This is immediately followed by other proposals for money aimed at those "specific areas," and more equipment, conferences, and trips *ad infinitum*.

Of course, you and I know how it all began. Too bad it has been such a closely guarded secret. Such a waste of time, energy, and money, pursuing will-o'-the-wisps!

(*See Also:* Communication, Creation, Education, Family, Foundation, Honesty, Humanism, Idolatry, Randomness)

Saying to a stock, You are my father and to a stone, You have brought me forth: for they have turned their back to Me, and not their face: but in the time of their trouble they will say, Arise, and save us. But where are your gods that you have made? Let them arise, if they can save you in the time of your trouble, for according to the number of your cities are your gods.

JEREMIAH 2:27–28.

The life is more than meat, and the body more than raiment.

Which of you with taking thought can add to his stature one cubit?

If you then be not able to do that thing which is least, why take thought for the rest?

LUKE 12:23, 25, 26.

Professing themselves to be wise, they became fools. And changed the glory of the uncorruptible God into an image made like to corruptible man, and to birds, and fourfooted beasts, and creeping things.

Wherefore God also gave them up to uncleanness through the lusts of their own hearts, to dishonor their own bodies between themselves: who changed the truth of God into a lie, and worshipped and served the creature more than the creator, who is blessed for ever.

ROMANS 1:22–25.

The natural man receives not the things of the Spirit of God: for they are foolishness to him. Neither can he know them, because they are spiritually discerned.

1 CORINTHIANS 2:14.

EXCHANGE

All of life is a series of exchanges—the exchange of one set of circumstances for another. Exchange of goods, real property, services, or ideas may be accomplished: (a) directly via barter, or (b) indirectly through a medium of exchange. Of course, both buyer and seller must have faith in the medium of exchange, something of recognizable value. Bible believers prefer a medium of exchange with an intrinsic value, such as gold, silver, copper, and the like. Believers in humanism put their faith in humanistic governments and pieces of paper inscribed with numbers, pictures, signatures, and fancy engravings, called Federal Reserve Notes.

The Christian who retreats from the benefits of exchange and specialization and places faith entirely in himself and total self-sufficiency does not really build on biblical principles. God tells us to go forth, be fruitful, take dominion over the earth, enjoy God's abundant gifts, and trade our surpluses with others. A talented artist who hides his or her work may express modesty. By not exchanging a production for goods and services produced by others means that we are all just a trifle poorer (see 2 CORINTHIANS 8:15).

Exchange is a voluntary matter. The principle of private property underlies the principle of exchange. If we take property from others without payment, whether by stealth or force (although there may be an exchange such as "we won't harass you for a while if you give us your money"), no voluntary exchange has taken place.

If a prospective buyer says, "I will give you money for the field" (GENESIS 23:13), the owner and seller may decline the offer. If an exchange occurs, then both buyer and seller have gained. Otherwise, one or the other would not have completed the transaction. Through a system of voluntary exchange, always operating within the structure of God's laws, you may well imagine how infinitely rich we all can be.

In an apostate society, exchange does not function in that manner. Let us suppose, by way of a simple example, that through talents of men exercised in a free society, an automobile industry arises. It produces the most economical, dependable, and efficient vehicles in the world. Business booms. All the world wants to own one of these enginering marvels. Many are able to do so as long as no trade barriers are erected.

Over time, however, a group of opportunists and their political representatives seek a way to shift profits from the automobile industry to their own gain. So politicians begin a campaign of "saving us from the automobile industry monopoly." They offer a government-guaranteed program of less work for more pay. The politicians are elected. They pass compulsory unionism laws (to assure their reelection). The automobile companies are outnumbered two to one—unions plus government against the industry. Workers now demand and receive more pay for less work.

Automobile companies complain because costs have risen, and they must raise prices. Now fewer people buy the more expensive automobiles. Profits decline as foreign competition errodes the domestic market.

Then the automobile firms enter into a partnership with unions and government, saying: "If you want to protect these union jobs and this national industry (so vital in war time), you must protect us from those cheap foreign imports." So tariff barriers, along with other restrictions on exchange, are established. The situation now is union, manufacturer, and government against the consumer.

Under governmental protection, automobile concerns substantially raise prices because they no longer face the threat of foreign competition. Unions, in turn, demand more money. Consumers pay higher and higher automobile prices. The average age of cars on the road rises. The industry shrinks because consumers buy fewer autos now than in the days of free exchange. Many auto dealers declare bankruptcy. Foreigners, too, find they can no longer sell in our market, so they stop buying from us because we no longer will exchange products with them.

Eventually, the number of automobiles on the highway diminishes. Car pooling spreads. Finally, government once more steps in; it mandates mass public transportation. Gasoline and other taxes are increased to pay for mass transit. Many major automobile companies have gone bankrupt, except for two or three. Society, now with fewer autos and higher taxes, becomes poorer, more pessimistic, and more depressed about the future.

If serious students of the principles of abundance will put away their prejudices for a time and carefully project results between government by special privilege and a free society under God's laws, they must conclude that while shortcuts may make a few rich, in the long run such ungodly policies destroy the very benefits promised by governmental regulation.

(*See Also:* Market Economy, Price Mechanism, Rule of Law, Savings, Supply, Voluntarism, Wealth, Zain)

I will give you money for the field; take it from me, and I will bury my dead there.

GENESIS 23:13.

Jacob said, Sell me this day your birthright.
GENESIS 25:31.

Jacob loved Rachel, and said, I will serve you seven years for Rachel your younger daughter.
GENESIS 29:18.

You shall dwell with us; and the land shall be before you; dwell and trade therein, and get possessions therein.
GENESIS 34:10.

These men are peaceable with us; therefore let them dwell in the land, and trade therein.
GENESIS 34:21.

We will go by the high way; and if I and my cattle drink of your water, then I will pay for it.
NUMBERS 20:19.

But I will surely buy it of you at a price....So David bought the threshing floor and the oxen for fifty shekels of silver.
2 SAMUEL 24:24.

So David gave to Ornan for the place six hundred shekels of gold by weight.
1 CHRONICLES 21:25.

I bought the field of Hanameel my uncle's son...and weighed him the money, even seventeen shekels of silver.
JEREMIAH 32:9.

Men shall buy fields for money, and subscribe evidences, and seal them, and take witnesses.
JEREMIAH 32:44.

Let not the buyer rejoice, nor the seller mourn...For the seller shall not return to that which is sold.
EZEKIEL 7:12–13.

If you think good, give me my price; and if not, forbear. So they weighed for my price thirty pieces of silver.
ZECHARIAH 11:12.

Are not two sparrows sold for a farthing?
MATTHEW 10:29.

For what is a man profited, if he shall gain the whole world, and lose his own soul? Or what shall a man give in exchange for his own soul?

MATTHEW 16:26.

I beheld, and lo, a black horse; and he who sat on him had a pair of balances on his hand. And I heard a voice in the midst of the four beasts say, A measure of wheat for a penny, and three measures of barley for a penny; and don't hurt the oil and the wine.

REVELATION 6:5–6.

EXPERT

Humanists have not been given the task of discovering what society might be like if God had made it different. It may be a regretable fact that God did not first seek the advice of Woodrow Wilson, Herbert Hoover, John F. Kennedy, Lyndon B. Johnson, and a few others who have sought to impose their New Deal, New Frontier, Great Society, or whatever. God could have amalgamated those lofty ideals and given us the Big Deal Social Order that would not in the remotest resemble the free society of biblical precepts.

Half the fun of being an expert is finding someone who believes you and acts on your expert advice. The other half is getting paid for it. Of course, if you want to establish yourself as an expert, the first step is to leave town. A person must be at least 100 miles (preferably more) from his home base to qualify as an expert.

The "experts" referred to in the first paragraph might have taken consolation in the fact that, even though God is not interested in their advice, Jesus Himself failed to get a ready hearing in His home territory. "For Jesus himself testified, that a prophet has no honor in his own country" (JOHN 4:44).

Certainly, we must carefully choose those whom we regard for expert advice. Personally, I have no difficulty on that issue. The men mentioned in the first paragraph are all dead. Jesus lives.

(*See Also:* Demagogue, Golden Rule, Heroes, Honesty, Randomness, Specialization, Source, Wisdom)

Pharaoh said to Joseph, I have dreamed a dream, and there is none who can interpret it; and I have heard said of you that you can understand a dream to interpret it.

GENESIS 41:15.

A prophet is not without honor, but in his own country, and among his own kin, and in his own house.

MARK 6:4.

You will surely say to me this proverb, Physician, heal yourself: whatsoever we have heard done in Capernaum, do also here in your country. And he said, Verily I say to you, No prophet is accepted in his own country.

Luke 4:23–24.

For Jesus himself testified, that a prophet has no honor in his own country.

John 4:44.

EXPROPRIATION

Expropriation, the confiscation of property, is done in one of two basic ways: (a) the owner is compensated (often not fully or adequately), or (b) the owner is not compensated for property taken.

Compensation, of course, is not simply the fair market value of property. For example, an elderly person forcibly uprooted from familiar surroundings to make way for the new Federal Courthouse suffers psychological and disorientation costs that can never truly be assessed. Or a person, compulsorily dispossessed of family jewelry or silverware (governments do at times make ownership of precious metals illegal) or grave site (because of a new dam and reservoir), places a value on those possessions far greater than any monetary compensation. Usually these family items are just not for sale and well may be intended as an inheritance in accordance with the rule of God.

Property expropriated in the name of "eminent domain," "legislation favoring debtors," "nationalization," or "welfare" is, nevertheless, property that has been taken from some to give to others or to allow others to use and enjoy.

It makes no difference whether that property is for the "public good" or whether the owner was "justly compensated." The state, depriving at sword's point a believer of his rightful possessions, stands by principles of gangsterism, contrary to those tenets of a free society.

Gottfried Dietze writes of the dramatic change in attitude toward private property in the United States.

> After the arrival of the New Deal and its majoritarian pressure, the Supreme Court put up a last fight for the preservation of the traditional rule of law. It was in vain....the Robe capitulated before the popular vogue in 1937. The individual was abandoned to the majority.

Inroads upon property were made not only through new restrictions. Existing restrictions were expanded and more frequently applied. A good example is that of eminent domain. More and more causes were admitted to justify its exercise. Procedural safeguards for the protection of the individual were relaxed. "Full" and "prior" indemnification was replaced by an "adequate" and "latter" one.

The forces that traditionally have been guardians of property failed to halt this development just as they failed to prevent the decline of the law. The United States Supreme Court has been a bulwark for the protection of property ever since its inception. It ceased to be so when it capitulated before the democratic forces in 1937.[1]

(*See Also:* Equality, Inheritance, Power of State, Private Property, Restitution, Statism, Theft)

Abram was very rich in cattle, in silver, and in gold.
    And the Lord said to Abram,... Lift up now your eyes, and look from the place where you are northward, and southward, and eastward, and westward: for all the land which you see, to you will I give it, and to your seed for ever.

GENESIS 13:2, 14–15.

Abram said to the king of Sodom, I have lift up my hand to the Lord, the most high God, the possessor of heaven and earth.

GENESIS 14:22.

You shall not covet your neighbor's house,... nor anything that is your neighbor's.

EXODUS 20:17.

For all manners of trespass, whether it be for ox, for ass, for sheep, for raiment, or for any manner of lost thing, which another challenges to be his, the cause of both parties shall come before the judges; and whom the judges shall condemn, he shall pay double to his neighbor.

EXODUS 22:9.

Remove not the old landmark; and enter not into the fields of the fatherless.

PROVERBS 23:10.

---

[1]Gottfried Dietze, *In Defense of Property* (Baltimore, Md.: John Hopkins University Press, 1971), pp. 159–60.

If it please the king, let it be written that they may be destroyed; and I will pay ten thousand talents of silver to the hands of those who have the charge of the business, to bring it into the king's treasuries.

ESTHER 3:9.

They shall sit every man under his vine and under his fig tree; and none shall make them afraid: for the mouth of the Lord of hosts has spoken it.

MICAH 4:4.

You shall not muzzle the ox that treads out the corn.

TIMOTHY 5:18.

FAMILY

Two themes are prevalent in the verses on family—family unity and family sovereignty. The family is central to the organization and foundation of the Christian social order. Henry Van Til writes, "A people's religion comes to expression in its culture, and Christians can be satisfied with nothing less than a Christian organization of society."[1]

Civilizations rise and fall according to the nature of family life and foundational structures. Humanism is destructive to the family. It ascribes to autonomous man a jurisdiction outside all law and government other than his own. The Bible, on the other hand, has man serve something greater than all creation—God. In the biblical family—the most public of all institutions—treasonous acts (i.e., adultery, homosexuality, etc.) against the family are punishable by death. Notice that treason against the state is not an issue. The family is the core unit of society, not the state.

> The family is the most powerful institution in society, controlling, in terms of biblical law, the three key areas of society, children, property, and inheritance. It is in addition the major welfare agency with its care of old and young, relatives and friends. The family, too, has its place in the tithe....The family is the religious, social, and productive unit; it is also the key institution of society.[2]

Progressive taxation and high church taxes claimed by some sects destroy the family. Heavy taxation represents decapitalization of family and nation. Biblically, both state and church taxes were very modest. As our nation decapitalizes, it crumbles.

---

[1]Henry Van Til, *The Calvinistic Concept of Culture* (Philadelphia: The Presbyterian and Reformed Publishing Company, 1959), p. 245.

[2]Rousas John Rushdoony, *Law and Society,* Vol. II (Vallecito, Calif.: Ross House Books, 1982), p. 131.

The state, in its warfare against society, strikes most emphatically against the family, and then the church. If the integrity and power of the Christian family are destroyed, the church cannot long maintain any strength. The family is the basic community, and thus the primary target of attack, together with Christian faith as such.[3]

(*See Also:* Abortion, Children, Charity, Education, Homosexuality, Inheritance, Marriage)

All the wives shall give to their husbands honor, both to great and small.

> *For he sent letters to all the king's provinces,... and to every people after their language, that every man should bear rule in his own house.*
>
> ESTHER 1:20, 22.

But I would have you know, that the head of every man is Christ, and the head of the woman is the man; and the head of Christ is God.

> 1 CORINTHIANS 11:3.

Have you not read that He who made them at the beginning made them male and female, and said, For this reason a man shall leave his father and mother and be joined to his wife, and the two shall become one flesh? So then, they are no longer two but one flesh. Therefore what God has joined together, let no man separate.

> MATTHEW 19:4–6.

Children, obey your parents in the Lord: for this is right.

> *And, you fathers, provoke not your children to wrath: but bring them up in the nurture and admonition of the Lord.*
>
> EPHESIANS 6:1, 4.

Wives, submit yourselves to your own husbands, as to the Lord, for the husband is the head of the wife, even as Christ is the head of the church.... Therefore as the church is subject to Christ, so let the wives be to their own husbands in everything. Husbands, love your wives, even as Christ also loved the church, and gave himself for it.

> *For this cause shall a man leave his father and mother, and shall be joined to his wife, and they two shall be one flesh.*
>
> EPHESIANS 5:22–25, 31.

[3]Ibid, p. 88.

*Children, obey your parents in the Lord: for this is right. Honor your
father and mother—which is the first commandment with promise—
that it may be well with you, and you may live long on the earth.*

EPHESIANS 6:1–3.

*Let the woman learn in silence with all submission. But I permit not a
woman to teach, nor to usurp authority over the man, but to be in
silence. For Adam was first formed, then Eve. And Adam was not
deceived, but the woman being deceived fell into transgression.*

1 TIMOTHY 2:11–14.

FEDERAL RESERVE SYSTEM

*This image's head was of fine gold, his breast and arms of silver, his
belly and his thighs of brass, his legs of iron, his feet part of iron and
part of clay.*

DANIEL 2:32–33.

(*See:* Exchange, Inflation, Money)

FEMINISM

Despite the demise and resurrection of the ERA, and the host of feminist conferences
financed by the federal government in the 1970s, feminism has been kept alive by
only a handful of activists. Its decline in importance among men and women
everywhere has not made its diminishing number of supporters any less vociferous.
Certainly it is a dead issue among practicing Christian women. Unfortunately, many
real issues underlying the ERA have not been brought to light and openly discussed.
Conflict has been created where before none existed.

The first question is, What do biblical writers say? Calvin clearly held that the
woman's capacities for righteousness, knowledge, and holiness are no less than the
man's. She is fully equal with man on these matters. And these are the important
issues!

However, dominion or government is largely man's domain. Although some knowledge areas appeal more to women, others more to men, this does not imply there should be feminine law or feminine mathematics. Women accomplish some activities naturally better than men, and vice versa, which does not denote that one sex ranks superior to the other. It does mean we have our individual tasks and areas of specialization.

Basil Atkinson writes that human beings, made in the image of God, are essentially moral beings. They were made in two sexes, for two chief purposes. First, God intended reproduction of its kind, a function apparently not shared by angels. It unites the human race in a single bundle of life. The second purpose of creating two sexes reflects the eternal relationship between Christ and His Church (see EPHESIANS 5:25–33).[1]

"Because law is a central manifestation of God's being, a central activity of revolutionary man will be against law," writes Reverend Rushdoony. "The sexual revolution is not content unless it has new laws to break."[2] He goes on to say that such a revolution represents the goal of trying to exclude God from His creation. "To exclude God from His own creation means that everything must be man-made."[3] This translates into test-tube babies; homosexuality; clonal man; and, of course, abortion.

(*See Also:* Abortion, Division of Labor, Draft (Military), Family, Homosexuality, Marriage, Rape, Women)

> *Adam said, This is now bone of my bone, and flesh of my flesh. She shall be called Woman, because she is taken out of man.*
> GENESIS 2:23.

> *To the woman he said, I will greatly multiply your sorrow and your conception; in sorrow you shall bring forth children; and your desire shall be for your husband, and he shall rule over you.*
> GENESIS 3:16.

> *But the queen Vashti refused to come to the king's commandment by his chamberlains; therefore was the king very wroth, and his anger burned in him.*
> ESTHER 1:12.

> *I would have you know, that the head of every man is Christ; and the head of the woman is the man; and the head of Christ is God.*
> 1 CORINTHIANS 11:3.

[1] Basil F. C. Atkinson, *The Book of Genesis*, Part I (Chicago: Moody Press, 1954).
[2] Rousas John Rushdoony, *Revolt Against Maturity* (Fairfax, Va.: Thoburn Press, 1977), p. 132.
[3] Ibid.

For a man indeed ought not to cover his head, forasmuch as he is the image and glory of God; but the woman is the glory of the man.

For the man is not of the woman but the woman of the man.

Neither was the man created for the woman, but the woman for the man.

For as the woman is of the man even so is the man also by the woman; but all things of God.

1 CORINTHIANS 11:7–9, 12.

Let your women keep silence in the churches, for it is not permitted to them to speak; but they are commanded to be under obedience, as also with the law.

1 CORINTHIANS 14:34.

Let the woman learn in silence with all subjection. But I suffer not a woman to teach, nor to usurp authority over the man, but to be in silence.

1 TIMOTHY 2:11–12.

FINANCE

For which of you, intending to build a tower, does not sit down first, and count the cost, whether he has sufficient to finish it? Lest haply, after he has laid the foundation, and is not able to finish it, all who behold it begin to mock him, saying, This man began to build, and was not able to finish.

LUKE 14:28–30.

(*See:* Capital Formation, Investment, Savings)

FISCAL POLICY

(*See:* Redistribution of Income/Wealth, Taxation)

FOOD STORAGE

Storing food represents another form of saving. We save money to meet contingencies; we save food to meet contingencies. Saving gold or food represents good investments in times of inflation, crisis, and civil government failures. The practice of saving is biblically sound. He who does not provide for his family is worse than an infidel.

During the Cuban missile crisis, panic buying in southern Florida set in. Within a few hours, shelves of supermarkets were bare and gasoline pumps were dry as people filled up for a possible quick exit. These supplies were not immediately replenished. A snow blizzard in Colorado closed off supply routes and shortly shelves were emptied of food. Temporary stoppage of supplies, coupled with a panic mentality, can change the local food supply picture in a "twinkling of the eye."

Food shortages can develop due to an adverse change in weather patterns, volcanic destruction of crops, wars, terrorist destruction of storage areas, drought, crop failures, government regulations, union action, while gas shortages can influence both price and availability of food. However, the prepared Christian puts his faith in God and stocks his shelves, rather than depend on the delivery system of an apostate government.

(See Also: Capital Formation, Cycles, Forecasting, Inflation, Risk Aversion, Savings, Strategic Planning)

> Take of all food that is eaten, and you shall gather it to yourself; and it shall be food for you, and for them.
>
> GENESIS 6:21.

> There shall arise seven years of famine.
>
> Let the Pharaoh...appoint officers over the land, and take up the fifth part of the land of Egypt in the seven plenteous years. Let them gather all the food of those good years that come, and lay up corn under the hand of Pharaoh and let them keep food in the cities. And that food shall be for store to the land against the seven years of famine.
>
> GENESIS 41:30, 34–36.

> You shall sow the eighth year, and eat yet of old fruit until the ninth year; until her fruits come in you shall eat of the old store.
>
> LEVITICUS 25:22.

> The Lord shall command the blessing upon you in your storehouses.
>
> DEUTERONOMY 28:8.

All the cities of store that Solomon had,...

1 KINGS 9:19.

He built Tadmoor in the wilderness, and all the store cities, which he built in Hamath.

2 CHRONICLES 8:4.

Hezekiah had exceeding much riches and honor; and he made himself treasuries for silver, and for gold, and for precious stones, and for spices, and for shields, and for all manner of pleasant jewels; storehouses also for the increase of corn, and wine, and oil, and stalls for all manner of beasts, and cotes for flocks.

2 CHRONICLES 32:27–28.

The Lord knows the days of the upright; and their inheritance shall be for ever. They shall not be ashamed in the evil time; and in the days of famine they shall be satisfied. But the wicked shall perish, and the enemies of the Lord shall be as the fat of the lambs; they shall consume; into smoke shall they consume away.

PSALM 37:18–20.

Take, also, wheat, and barley, and beans, and lentiles, and millet, and fitches, and put them into one vessel, and make bread of them for yourself. During the number of the days that you shall lie upon your side, three hundred and ninety days shall you eat thereof. And your meat which you eat shall be by weight, twenty shekels a day: from time to time shall you eat it.

You shall eat it as barley cakes, and you shall bake it using fuel of human waste, in their sight.

EZEKIEL 4:9–10, 12.

Now there came a dearth over all the land of Egypt and Chanaan, and great affliction, and our fathers found no sustenance.

ACTS 7:11.

FORECASTING

Despite many gifts from God to fallen man, the lack of one in particular commands a disproportionately large amount of our attention, that is, the inability to see into the future with any degree of accuracy. Certainly a few forecast better than others, but only very dimly do they see into the future (1 CORINTHIANS 13:12).

In fact, few even observe the present well. Ten witnesses to an auto accident will describe no less than fifteen conflicting versions. (At least half of the persons will diametrically change their story, thereby producing more versions than witnesses.) Hence, if we cannot accurately observe the present, what does that say about our prognostications?

Although most forecasters are wrong most of the time, whether they use stellar or statistical models, these disappointing results do not seem to have harmed the forecasting business or futurology. Of course, anyone who guesses often enough about tomorrows will score an occasional success. Even a blind hog finds an acorn once in a while.

Unbiblically based forecasts will usually prove mistaken. Anyone anticipating a career in forecasting trends, changes, and structural shifts in the economic environment should prepare himself first with a thorough study of the Bible. Forecasting is basically a study in causes and effects. The effects of today result from a multitude of causes that may even link to events decades earlier. Tracing them may prove nearly impossible if your philosophy is not right.

Forecasting is inextricably intertwined with God's order; but none of us has perfect foresight. Consequently, an element of risk resides in every undertaking. We should do well, however, to heed the admonition in PROVERBS 27:1, and consider ECCLESIASTES 10:14 as fair warning before indiscriminately following the mystical chant of the forecasters.

(*See Also:* Economic Forecasts, Experts, Nothing Is Forever, Randomness, Risk Aversion, Strategic Planning)

Boast not of tomorrow, for you know not what a day may bring forth.
PROVERBS 27:1.

A fool is also full of words; a man cannot tell what shall be; and what shall be after him, who can tell him?
ECCLESIASTES 10:14.

As you know not what is the way of the spirit, nor how the bones do grow in the womb of her who is with child, even so you know not the works of God who makes all. In the morning sow your seed, and in the evening withhold not your hand, for you know not whether shall prosper, either this or that, or whether both shall be alike good.
ECCLESIASTES 11:5–6.

Thus saith the Lord God: Woe to the foolish prophets, who follow their own spirit, and have seen nothing! O Israel, your prophets are like the foxes in the deserts.
EZEKIEL 13:3–4.

If the goodman of the house had known what hour the thief would come, he would have watched, and not have suffered his house to be broken into.

LUKE 12:39.

For we know in part, and we prophesy in part.

1 CORINTHIANS 13:9.

Come now, you who say, Today or tomorrow we will go into such a city, and continue there a year, and buy and sell, and make a profit: whereas you know not what shall be on the morrow. For what is your life? It is even a vapor, and that appears for a little time, and then vanishes away.

JAMES 4:13–14.

FOREIGN AID

Contemporary American foreign aid essentially falls into three classifications: military aid, economic aid, and disaster aid. Military aid helps keep friendly nations in power. Economic aid helps keep friendly nations on our side. Disaster aid, a charitable act, may help keep friendly nations friendly and make unfriendly nations less unfriendly. Still other aid flows through international institutions. Foreign aid, then, becomes part and parcel of foreign policy.

This aspect of foreign policy underlies, in part, the quest for internationalization, a one-world order, under the guise of peace, which, for its implementation, results in the transfer of freedom under God's law to a new type of "freedom" under the state's law. "There is a consistent pattern in the social changes that are taking place in this country and all over the world. We witness a trend toward the expansion of the political, coercive sector of the nation, at the expense of the private, voluntary sector."[1]

Reverend Opitz suggests that some contemporary churchmen are preoccupied with the machinery for a worldwide ecclesiastical organization. "The ecumenical movement, like secular internationalism, is based on the idea that the sins of nationalism are virtues when committed by an international body."[2]

Whether we refer to domestic welfarism or internationalism, such programs endorse a planned economy. A planned economy relies on coercion to implement

[1]Edmund A. Opitz, "Painting Government into a Corner," *The Freeman* (February 1964).

[2]Opitz, *Religion and Capitalism: Allies, Not Enemies* (New Rochelle, N.Y.: Arlington House Publishers, 1974), p. 204.

state programs. Therefore, economic growth in less developed countries must be imposed by an outside culture and fed with outside funds (aid); poor countries are so poor they can never make it on their own, or so the argument runs. The omniscient and omnipotent state is our only salvation.

What has resulted from billions and billions of dollars of foreign aid? These transfers, first of all, are government to government, bureaucracy to bureaucracy, resulting in the politically entrenched becoming richer and more powerful. The poor seldom see these funds. Foreign aid promotes slothfulness and irresponsibility. It creates dependence and encourages nonproductivity. When I met with Prime Minister Indira Ghandi in January 1982, her second or third sentence was: "You should give your aid to those countries like us which can make more use of it." For India, dependence on foreign aid had become a staple import.

Foreign aid, not a free gift of nature, magically produced, must be paid for by productive citizens of the donor country, that is, through taxation. Prohibited by Scripture, foreign aid has caused more problems than it has resolved. The chief alternative, of course, for the church organization is the private support of Christian missionary activities. The business alternative calls for private investment of funds in those countries that at least still have some semblance of a free society structure. Private investment keeps funds out of the hands of bureaucrats, creates employment in the local economy, and raises the material standard of living.

(*See Also:* International Trade, One Worldism, Poor Nations, Power of State, Redistribution of Income/Wealth, Xenophobia)

> *Lest you make a covenant with the inhabitants of the land, and they go a whoring after their gods, and sacrifice to their gods, and one of them invites you, and you eat of his sacrifice, and you take of his daughters for your sons, and his daughters go a whoring after their gods, and make your sons play the harlot with their gods.*
>
> EXODUS 34:15–16.

> *The fruit of your land, and all your labors, shall a nation which you know not eat up; and you shall be only oppressed and crushed continually.*
>
> DEUTERONOMY 28:33.

> *There is a league between me and you, as there was between my father and your father. Behold I have sent you silver and gold; go break your league with Baasha, king of Israel, that he may depart from me.*
>
> 2 CHRONICLES 16:3.

> *You have also committed fornication with the Egyptians, your neighbors, great of flesh.*
> *You have also played the whore with the Assyrians, because you were insatiable.*

You have moreover multiplied your fornication in the land of Canaan to Chaldea; and yet you were not satisfied herewith.

As a wife who commits adultery, who takes strangers instead of her husband! Men give gifts to all whores; but you give your gifts to all your lovers, and hire them, that they may come to you on every side for your whoredom.

EZEKIEL 16:26, 28, 29, 32–34.

Herod was highly displeased with them of Tyre and Sidon; but they came with one accord to him, and, having made Blastus the king's chamberlain their friend, desired peace, because their country was nourished by the king's country.

ACTS 12:20.

FOUNDATION

Have you considered that everything we think and do, everything we write, every theory and science or precept depends upon philosophical concepts, much like an inverted pyramid? This kernel of truth underlies our mathematics, social, political, engineering systems; medical treatment; and so on. The structure of our society and its institutions must be consistent and harmonize with the pyramid's pinpoint. Unbalance it with too much weight on one side or another, it will first lean, like the Tower of Pisa, and eventually collapse, like the Roman Empire.

Perhaps you didn't know that mathematics, accounting, astronomy, biology, physics, and many other exact sciences are not very exact at all. Change assumptions and the entire scientific discipline is wiped away, and a new one replaces it.

Suppose we are willing victims of a cruel cosmic hoax: That the lintel, the foundation upon which rests all of our humanly enshrined laws and principles and sciences, is really a lie—a false philosophy. Now it is possible to build an entire system of social organizations and educational systems upon this lie. As long as consistency reigns, the hoax will not be readily discoverable. In the short run it appears to succeed. Satan enjoys an ephemeral victory.

Each, in exercise of his free will, may pick and choose whatever apparent truths appeal at the moment. Over time, each can selectively decide by what truths he will live—something called *situational ethics*—not unlike attaching a parasitic growth to the main pyramid of biblical truth. Some people like warts; they prefer a warty existence.

Traveling by train the other day from Philadelphia to Newark, just before coming into the Trenton station, we passed the back side of rows of houses that residents had transformed into slums. Some back yards had literally been filled with three or more feet of junk. The rabbi sitting next to me said that we must provide these people with education, opportunity, and money, so that they learn to clean up their back yards. Frankly, many people feel more comfortable with junk and warts than with godly order and truth. Junk and warts require less effort to maintain.

I happen to think sound foundations are rather important. A few years ago, following a hurricane in Puerto Rico, I saw many houses slide down a gully or river embankment. They were not built on solid foundations. Mudslides occur in southern California; still people build expensive homes on precarious mountain perches. But to build something enduring, it must be constructed on biblical truths. It's the best foundation we have.

(*See Also:* Ethics, Freedom, Justice, Law, Moral Principles, Nonalignment, Source, Work)

Let the house be built, the place where they offered sacrifices, and let the foundations thereof be strongly laid; the height thereof threescore cubits, and the breadth thereof threescore cubits, with three rows of great stones, and a row of new timber; and let the expenses be given out of the king's house.

EZRA 6:3–4

Can a mortal be more righteous than God? Can a man be more pure than his Maker? If He puts no trust in His servants, if He charges His angels with error, how much less those who dwell in houses of clay, whose foundation is in the dust, which are crushed before the moth? They are destroyed from morning to evening; they perish forever with no one regarding it. Does not their own excellence go away? They die, even without wisdom.

JOB 4:17–21.

Therefore, whoever hears these sayings of mine, and does them, I will liken him to a wise man, who built his house upon a rock; and the rain descended, and the floods came, and the winds blew, and beat upon that house, and it fell not, for it was founded upon a rock.

MATTHEW 7:24–25.

He is like a man who built a house, and dug deep, and laid a foundation on a rock...

But he who hears and does not, is like a man that without a foundation built a house upon the earth, against which the stream did beat vehemently, and immediately it fell; and the ruin of that house was great.

LUKE 6:48–49.

Heaven is my throne, and earth is my footstool. What house will you build me? saith the Lord, Or what is the place of my rest? Has not my hand made all these things?

ACTS 7:49–50.

FREEDOM

A cartoon of a few years ago really says it all about what most people think of freedom. Two sign painters were putting a message on the side of a wall. They had just completed two letters: "FR." One lone man stood on the street below, looking up. By the time the two painters had progressed to "FREE," a sizable crowd had gathered. Finally, the two painters finished their task. The sign painted on the wall read: "FREEDOM." The sidewalk was deserted. The cartoon resounded of something from Turgenev: "My steps echoed dully in the congealing air."

The word *freedom* may be a modern misnomer for freedom, because certainly nothing is free about it. Thomas Paine wrote: "Those who expect to reap the blessings of freedom must undergo the fatigue of supporting it." So fatiguing is it that few carry the burden!

Christians must assume this obligation. We are absolutely prohibited from selling ourselves into bondage. "Ye are bought with a price; be ye not the servants of men" (1 CORINTHIANS 7:23; and see GALATIANS 5:1, 13).

Freedom is not limited to freedom of the press, speech, and assembly. How often we see persons defending one of these freedoms and then just as vigorously oppose economic freedom! Without economic freedom, these other freedoms lose their force, and eventually, they too are lost. The editor who defends freedom of the press and then writes in favor of price controls, deficit spending, or a national health plan is not truly a friend of freedom.

Freedom is not divisible. It is unified and comprehensive. We cannot be free to earn money and not free to spend it. We cannot be half-free or three-quarters free. If our political and economic systems are not created according to, and subject to, God's laws, then we are not living in a free society.

We should resist bondage and personally take on responsibility to promote freedom's ways. Sam Levenson writes, "We are suffering from intellectual truancy at the grass roots level. Men who have been trained to think do not generally offer their ability to do so in their immediate community. Free men should pay for their freedom in time and labor and money."[1] Taylor Caldwell writes, "Freedom imposes obligations to the world. The man who feels he has no obligation knows nothing

[1]Sam Levenson, *Everything About Money* (N.Y.: Pocket Books, 1974), p. 241.

about liberty."[2] And, lastly, Ching Chow proclaimed, "Freedom is important when you don't have it; it should be just as important when you do." Is it important to you?

(*See Also:* Justice, Liberty, Market Economy, Price Mechanism, Private Property, Rule of Law, Self-Discipline, Tinstaafl)

> Then the men of Israel said to Gideon, Rule over us, both you and your son, and your son's son also: for you have delivered us from the hand of Midian. Gideon said to them, I will not rule over you, neither shall my son rule over you: the Lord shall rule over you.
>
> JUDGES 8:22–23.

> The Lord was with him; and he prospered wherever he went; and he rebelled against the king of Assyria, and served him not.
>
> 2 KINGS 18:7.

> The rulers knew not where I had gone, or what I had done.
>
> NEHEMIAH 2:16.

> If you offer a sacrifice of peace offerings to the Lord, you shall offer it at your own will.
>
> LEVITICUS 19:5.

> Arise, go to the wealthy nation, which dwells securely, saith the Lord, which has neither gates nor bars, dwelling alone.
>
> JEREMIAH 49:31.

> The trees of the field shall yield their fruit, and the earth shall yield her increase, and they shall be safe in their land, and shall know that I am the Lord, when I have broken the bands of their yoke, and delivered them out of the hand of those who enslaved them. And they shall no more be prey to the heathen, neither shall the beast of the land devour them; but they shall dwell safely, and none shall make them afraid. I will raise up for them a garden of renown, and they shall be no more consumed with hunger in the land, neither bear the shame of the heathen any more.
>
> EZEKIEL 34:27–29.

> You shall know the truth, and the truth shall make you free.
>
> JOHN 8:32.

> Whosoever commits sin is the servant of sin.
>
> JOHN 8:34.

[2]Taylor Caldwell, *Let Love Come Last* (N.Y.: Jove Pub. Group, 1984), p. 242.

Owe no man anything....
Romans 13:8.

You are bought with a price; be not the servants of men.
1 Corinthians 7:23.

For though I be free from all men, yet have I made myself servant to all, that I might gain more.
1 Corinthians 9:19.

For it is written, that Abraham had two sons, the one by a bondmaid, the other by a freewoman. But he who was of the bondmaid was born of the flesh; but he of the freewoman was by promise. Which things are an allegory: for these are the two covenants; the one from the mount Sinai, which genders bondage, which is Hagar. For this Hagar is mount Sinai in Arabia, and corresponds to Jerusalem which now is, and is in bondage with her children. But Jerusalem above is free, which is the mother of us all.

Nevertheless, what does the scripture say? Cast out the bondwoman and her son: for the son of the bondwoman shall not be heir with the son of the freewoman. So then, brethren, we are not children of the bondwoman, but of the free.
Galatians 4:22–26, 30–31.

Stand fast therefore in the liberty wherewith Christ has made us free, and be not entangled again with the yoke of bondage.
Galatians 5:1.

Let no man defraud you of your reward, taking delight in false humility and worship of angels, intruding into those things which he has not seen, vainly puffed up by his fleshly mind.
Colossians 2:18.

FREE ENTERPRISE

Since the word *capitalism*, popularized by Karl Marx, derogatorily refers to some elements of the free enterprise system, it hardly seems sensible for us to employ a negative term to describe the wealth, prosperity, and economic freedom that grows out of a market economy.

Corporate business comprises only part of the free enterprise world. A philosophical concept, the term *free enterprise* describes a system that uninterruptedly allows individuals to pursue individual ends as long as neither the means nor the ends violates freedoms of anyone else.

Yes, it is true that free enterprise can function in an amoralistic or ethically neutral framework, without reference to race or religion. The underlying principle in a contractual network is that each individual must extend to everyone else those rights he would retain for himself. In other words, if Spencer believes that cheating Jews is acceptable behavior, then Friedman, assuming that same right, feels indifferent in cheating Spencer in transactions. Hence, since Spencer does not like being cheated, he disciplines himself not to cheat others.

However, a free enterprise system is not identical to a free society under God's laws. Free enterprise is a subset of the free society. Actually, it requires some coercion to make a free enterprise system function correctly and advantageously to all participants—rich or poor—in a society.

Two basic elements, a combination of persuasion and coercion, curb excesses of a minority tempted by quick gains to act dishonestly. Most important is the moral framework established by biblical law. Family and friends as well as our church organizations persuade us to act honestly. Believers in the Bible know that disobedience to God's laws brings all kinds of problems. That, too, is a powerful persuader. Finally, a court system, whether privately, church, or government operated, provides the disciplining mechanism.

Civil government plays only a limited role. Hence, limited government is central to a viable free enterprise system. It exists essentially to settle property disputes, enforce terms of private contracts, and punish evil doers, where laws concern crimes against persons and God, not the fiction of crimes against state.

Free enterprise depends on the right to life, liberty, and property. "The 'right' to life must be assumed if the race itself is not to perish. The other rights of the famous triad can be deducted from the first: if one has a 'right' to life, one must be at liberty to work and sustain one's self, and one must have access to the means of production, specifically land and tools. If one can be legally deprived of the right to acquire these, the right to life becomes a permission to be revoked at the politician's or the military man's will."[1]

In 1775, Adam Smith (before publishing his famous *Wealth of Nations*) said, "Little else is required to carry a state to the highest degree of affluence from the lowest barbarism but peace, easy taxes, and a tolerable administration of justice. All governments which thwart the natural course are unnatural, and, to support themselves, are obliged to be oppressive and tyrannical."[2] On restrictions of trade and exchange of goods, Smith spoke of mercantilist regulations as "impertinent badges of slavery imposed by the groundless jealousy of the merchants and manufacturers of the mother country."[3]

Certainly the truth shall make us all free. Freedom's way is the way of the Lord. In a practical, mundane sense, free enterprise is consistent with God's law. All other

[1]John Chamberlin, *The Roots of Capitalism* (Indianapolis, Ind.: Liberty Press, 1976), p. 46.

[2]Quoted in ibid., pp. 40, 42.

[3]Ibid.

systems of coercion and enterprise (socialism, welfarism, etc.) are simply not founded on biblical principles. God is generous; He is a God of abundance. When we disregard those laws—whether willfully or not—we close off the path to peace and prosperity. Free enterprise conducted within God's structure leads to abundance. Consider this example.

The American colonists managed to engage in much free enterprise by ignoring the rules, regulations, and taxes imposed by far-off England. They "had raised smuggling to a fine art. The standard of life rose in North America every time a king's agent was bilked, a tax avoided. Wages were high in New York, money earned good interest, yet the necessities of life were cheap."[4] What is it like today in the Big Apple? Nominal wages are high. Taxes are high. Necessities of life are high.

(*See Also:* Contract, Division of Labor, Free Market, Liberty, Private Property, Prosperity, Voluntarism)

The Lord said, Behold, the people are one;…and now nothing will be restrained from them, which they have imagined to do.
GENESIS 11:6.

The land is worth four hundred shekels of silver; what is that between me and you?…Abraham weighed to Ephron the silver, which he had named in the audience of the sons of Heth, four hundred shekels of silver, current money with the merchant. The field of Ephron …and the cave which was therein, and all the trees that were in the field, that were in all the borders round about, were made sure to Abraham for a possession in the presence of the children of Heth before all that went in at the gate of his city.

The field, and the cave that is therein, were made to Abraham for a possession of a burying place by the sons of Heth.
GENESIS 23:15–18, 20.

These men are peaceable with us; therefore let them dwell in the land, and trade therein.
GENESIS 34:21.

He had much business in the cities of Judah.
2 CHRONICLES 17:13.

For a dream comes through a multitude of business.
ECCLESIASTES 5:3.

He shall judge among many people, and rebuke strong nations afar off; and they shall beat their swords into plowshares, and their spears into

[4] Ibid., p. 18.

pruning hooks: nation shall not lift a sword against nation, neither shall they learn war any more. But they shall sit every man under his vine and under his fig tree; and none shall make them afraid, for the mouth of the Lord of hosts has spoken of it. For all people will walk every one in the name of his god, and we will walk in the name of the Lord our God for ever and ever.

MICAH 4:3–5.

He who reaps receives wages, and gathers fruit for life eternal: that both he who sows and he who reaps may rejoice together.

JOHN 4:36.

Even as I please all men in all things, not seeking my own profit, but the profit of many, that they may be saved.

1 CORINTHIANS 10:33.

Providing for honest things, not only in the sight of the Lord, but also in the sight of men.

2 CORINTHIANS 8:21.

That you study to be quiet, and to do your own business, and to work with your own hands.

1 THESSALONIANS 4:11.

FREE MARKET

By its detractors, the free market is described as an iniquitous den of cutthroat competitors, and the consumer be damned. Even friends of the free market refer to it as orderly chaos or anarchy. For those to whom order translates into an institution presided over and commanded by civil supreme authority, they remain baffled on how anything functions effectively without their intervention. They are the "Give us a king" (1 SAMUEL 8) school of organization.

But in a mysterious way, desires of buyers and sellers are matched, at the right price. When conditions of demand, supply, or cost change, in a perfectly free market a rather rapid adjustment takes place. This led Adam Smith in his book of 1776, *An Inquiry Into the Nature and Causes of the Wealth of Nations,* to refer to "the invisible hand" in the market.[1] Or is it the visible kingdom of God on earth?

[1]Adam Smith, *An Inquiry Into the Nature and Causes of the Wealth of Nations* (New York: The Modern Library, 1937), p. 423.

First, the free market is not really free. There are transaction costs. For instance, if you buy and sell real estate, bonds, or gold, you already know about certain fees and costs—commissions, taxes, legal fees, advertising, and similar costs that put a wedge between prices paid and received. Further, there are information and search costs. Just comparing supermarket advertisements or telephoning a dozen merchants for the best price and service takes time away from other activities.

All of this seemingly insignificant activity molds the market together. It keeps prices competitive. Unreasonably high prices result from, ignorance, not information. Free flow of information—or at least the freedom to seek it—keeps the free market truly responsive.

Second, despite what appears to be shortcomings to the lazy or uninformed, the free market can never be improved through intervention. If a group of sellers collude, consumers can expect fewer goods at higher prices. If someone tries to "corner the market" (assuming that were economically practical), consumers can expect higher prices. If government intervenes with price (or rent) controls, rationing, or restrictions on production, products and housing disappear from the market. If prices are not legally permitted to rise, shortages crop up. New York City rent controls have engendered scarcity of apartment housing, and hundreds of thousands of apartments no longer are available due to abandoned buildings.

Third, a free market is not one of special privilege. Consequently, any attempt at monopoly and high profits will be short lived, as other investors quickly seek out high-profit opportunities and begin producing. An increased supply of goods and services brings prices down. Monopoly and special privilege can only be sustained by police powers of governments. For years the airlines had their Civil Aeronautics Board (CAB) to enforce noncompetitive prices domestically and International Air Transport Association (IATA) to keep passenger air fares high internationally. Your local telephone, electric, and other utility companies use all kinds of arguments to maintain the fiction that free competition would be disastrous; hence, by legislative decree, they have their local monopolies. Similarly, local laws limiting the number of taxicabs, bus services, or whatever drive prices up, the quality of service down. Local governments have attempted to maintain a monopoly on education through laws and Supreme Court decisions. The federal government has a monopoly on the money supply.

In the United States we now have relatively few areas of truly free enterprise. With compulsory unionism, the free market in labor services has diminished. The result? High wages for union workers and higher unemployment among nonunionized ones.

God blesses us with abundance, especially in this great land. If we obey His laws, we prosper. However, production is only part of the picture. Distribution also has its role. The free market provides the most effective delivery system as long as we adhere to God's intentions. With a limited system of government-enforced rules and regulations to keep the dishonest from corrupting the market, we operate in harmony with God's design of a free society. When we lose faith in God and turn to human design, the food will rot in the fields and lumber for housing will remain in its natural forestal state.

After nearly seventy years, have the Soviet socialists solved even these most basic problems with their expropriation of private property and dictatorship of the marketplace? Or compare the standard of living between Taiwan and Communist China. The free market looks good to me! I wouldn't trade it for any humanly contrived alternative that I see, because, frankly, I see no future in poverty for poverty's sake.

(*See Also:* Abundance, Demand, Division of Labor, Economic Growth, Exchange, Freedom, Supply)

> *According to the number of years after the Jubilee, you shall buy from your neighbor, and according to the number of years of crops, he shall sell to you. According to the number of years, you shall increase its price, and according to the fewer number of years, you shall diminish its price, for he sells to you according to the number of years of crops. Therefore, you shall not oppress one another, but you shall fear your God.*
>
> LEVITICUS 25:15–17.

> *Tarshish was your merchant because of your many luxury goods. They gave you silver, iron, tin, and lead for your goods.*
>
> *Syria was your merchant because of the abundance of goods you made. They gave you for your wares emeralds, purple, embroidery, fine linen, corals, and rubies.*
>
> *The merchants of Sheba and Raamah were your merchants. They traded for your wares the choicest spices, all kinds of precious stones and gold.*
>
> EZEKIEL 27:12, 16, 22.

> *Moreover the profit of the earth is for all. The king himself is served by the field.*
>
> ECCLESIASTES 5:9.

> *Neither was there any among them who lacked, for as many as were possessors of lands or houses sold them, and brought the prices of the things that were sold.*
>
> ACTS 4:34.

> *When Jacob heard that there was corn in Egypt, he sent our fathers first.*
>
> ACTS 7:12.

FREE SOCIETY

Freedom is indivisible. A free society is not characterized by selected freedoms—religious worship, economic, political, speech and press. A free market is as inconsistent with socialism as a presumed free press that tilts news and ignores such fundamental losses of freedom as Christian schools and churches being physically invaded or closed by authorities of county, state, or federal governments. If your right arm only is shackled to a tree, while the rest of your body is not restrained, can you truly say you are free?

Our American Constitution brought into existence public acknowledgment of religious freedom. This freedom is vitally important to the existence of a free society under God's law. If the Old Testament bears upon *becoming* free, then the New Testament concerns *being* free. All other freedoms naturally follow spiritual freedom. "Having been set free from sin, you became slaves of righteousness" (ROMANS 6:18).

America's greatest gift to the rest of the world is freedom of religion, the foundation of our economic growth and abundance, freedom of expression, freedom of enterprise, and the extensive political freedom that we have enjoyed during much of our existence as a nation.

For example, compare the United States with France of 1780, before the French Revolution, when French humanism reached its culmination. Four-fifths of the population spent up to 90 percent of its total income on food alone. Imagine that! Around this time in Germany, no more 1,000 people could boast annual earnings of $1,000 or better. In the free society of the new American nation, in service to God, real wages quadrupled between 1800 and 1850, and then they quadrupled again between 1850 and 1900. In other words, a long-lived person earning $1,000 a year in 1800 would be earning $16,000 a year in 1900, after discounting effects of any inflation. Isn't that amazing proof of the viability of a free society working according to God's law?

Unfortunately, over 100 years ago forces were set in motion aimed to destroy our free society. Each decade we became a little less free. However, the effect of this cumulative loss of freedom ripened to high visibility four decades ago. The accelerated decline in freedom these past two decades has reached a critical stage for believers.

Our enemies in this war against Christianity know that with destruction of religious freedom, the remnant of the free society will collapse. This explains the unprecedented attack upon Christian churches and schools these past few years. It is inexplicable why any red-blooded American, whatever his religious beliefs, will passively sit back and, yes, even encourage destruction of a free society that has brought more benefits to him than any other system the world can ever fecundate.

We are still an island of success surrounded by a sea of failures. Courting socialism reminds me of a person descending to the poorest section of town and entering the shack of a fortune teller whom he asks for the secrets of becoming rich and successful. Then not only does he pay for this dubious advice but actually believes it and attempts to implement it. When we let ourselves be bullied into accepting any substitute for the free society—never mind lofty-sounding ideals—then we are an abomination to God and deserve what befalls us.

A free society is either free in its entirety, organized according to Divine mandate, or else it has already embarked on the road to its own destruction. There is no middle of the road. Ludwig Von Mises said the middle of the road leads to socialism.[1] God has made no provision for mixed economies—part godly, part humanistic. God has given us our marching orders—to have dominion, be fruitful, and multiply—as the song says, "Onward Christian Soldiers. . . ."

(*See Also:* Free Market, Private Property, Prosperity, Service, Source, Stewardship, Wealth)

> *In those days there was no king in Israel.*
>
> JUDGES 17:6.

> *When they were but a few in number, yes, very few, and strangers in it; when they went from one nation to another; . . . He suffered no man to do them wrong; yes, He reproved kings for their sakes, saying, Touch not my annointed, and do my prophets no harm.*
>
> PSALM 105:12–15.

> *Let us cast off the works of darkness, and let us put on the armor of light.*
>
> ROMANS 13:12.

> *For one believes that he may eat all things, another who is weak eats herbs. Let not him who eats despise him who eats not; and let not him who eats not judge him who eats, for God has received him.*
>
> ROMANS 14:2–3.

> *For, brothers, you have been called to liberty, only use not liberty for an occasion to the flesh, but by love serve one another.*
>
> GALATIANS 5:13.

> *Beware of dogs, beware of evil workers, beware of the concision, for we are the circumcision, who worship God in the spirit, and rejoice in Jesus Christ, and have no confidence in the flesh.*
>
> PHILIPPIANS 3:2–3.

---

[1]Ludwig von Mises, *Economic Policy: Thoughts for Today* (Chicago: Regnery, 1979), pp. 51–2.

For even when we were with you, this we commanded you, that is any would not work, neither should he eat.

2 THESSALONIANS 3:10.

The husbandman who labors must be first partaker of the fruits.

2 TIMOTHY 2:6.

For this is the will of God, that by doing good you may put to silence the ignorance of foolish men, as free, yet not using your liberty as a cloak for vice, but as servants of God.

1 PETER 2:15–16.

FURY OF A BUREAUCRAT SCORNED

To offer a twist on a time-worn aphorism: Hell hath no fury greater than a bureaucrat scorned! To those readers who have ignored a request for information from some of our better known government agencies, such as Occupational Safety and Health Administration (OSHA), Securities and Exchange Commission (SEC), or various tax collecting agencies, this will have special significance.

The small business operator especially carries the defeating burden of responding to endless questionnaires, often about inane issues or requests for nonexistent data on the business. These form-filling activities take time away from the true purpose of the business, that is, to serve its customers and generate a living for the owner and his or her family. Bureaucrats often do not care what happens to the business as long as precious, job-satisfying forms are filled in properly and returned yesterday.

The owner of a one-person, no-employee shoe repair shop decided to train a part-time apprentice, a high school student, not because he necessarily needed any help running his small operation. Before he could perform his good deed, various bureaucracies required him to fill out forms. Stacked up, they measured nearly five inches high. His choices were either run the business and support his family or spend seventy or eighty hours filling in forms. He put family above state.

Professor Pearson reminds us that "bureaucracies are run for the good and the perpetuation of the bureaucracies, not for the help of those they ostensibly were set up to serve."[1] He also writes "Another bureaucratic law is that power corrupts most people."[2]

[1] Glenn L. Pearson, "Mixed Economies A No-Man's Land," *The Freeman* (August 1982).
[2] Ibid.

For some bureaucrats, even the slightest bit of power is like eating the forbidden fruit. They hear the serpent's words echo in their minds: "For God doth know that in the day you eat thereof, then your eyes shall be opened, and ye shall be as gods, knowing good and evil." (GENESIS 3:5). And what passes for *their* "good" becomes *our* evil.

(*See Also:* Bureaucrat, Demagogue, Envy, Power of State, Rule by Decree, Statist, Tax Collector, World Government, Xenophobia)

It came to pass after these things, that the butler of the king of Egypt and his baker had offended their lord the king of Egypt.

GENESIS 40:1.

All the king's servants, who were in the king's gate, bowed, and reverenced Haman, for the king had so commanded concerning him. But Mordecai bowed not, nor did him reverence.

When Haman saw that Mordecai bowed not, nor did him reverence, then was Haman full of wrath. He thought scorn to lay hands on Mordecai alone; ... but Haman sought to destroy all Jews that were throughout the whole kingdom.

ESTHER 3:2, 5–6.

The wrath of a king is as messengers of death; but a wise man will pacify it.

PROVERBS 16:14.

Then Nebuchadnezzar in his rage and fury commanded to bring Shadrach, Meshach, and Abednego... Nebuchadnezzar spoke and said to them, Is it true, O Shadrach, Meshach, and Abednego, that you do not serve my gods, or worship the golden image which I have set up? Now if you are ready at the time you hear the sound of the cornet, flute, harp, sackbut, psaltery, and dulcimer, and all kinds of music, and you fall down and worship the image which I have made, well; but if you worship not, you shall be cast the same hour into the midst of a burning fiery furnace; and who is that God who shall deliver you out of my hands?

DANIEL 3:13–15.

Then was Nebuchadnezzar full of fury, and the form of his visage was changed against Shadrach, Meshach, and Abednego; Therefore he spoke and commanded that they should heat the furnace seven more times than it was usually heated.

DANIEL 3:19.

GIFTS

(*See:* Bribery, Charity, Inheritance)

GENOCIDE

They have taken crafty counsel against your people, and consulted against your hidden ones. They have said, Come, let us cut them off from being a nation, that the name of Israel may be no more in remembrance.

PSALM 83:3–4.

(*See:* Crowd Psychology, Power of State, Xenophobia)

GOLD

What do you think of people who extol virtues of owning gold instead of saving good old American dollars? Are they oddballs, anti-American, opportunists, or overall biblical?

God commands that we be good stewards over property. To place our faith in apostate governments and not God is idolatry as much as gold worship is idolatrous. However, covenantal Christians who own gold as part of their investment portfolio have taken one of four steps in a hedging strategy. Dr. North refers to this strategy as the four G's: gold, guns, groceries, and God.[1] Interestingly, statists are antigold, antiguns, antifood storage, and anti-God. "And God has given them the spirit of slumber, eyes that they should see not, and ears that they should hear not" (ROMANS 11:8).

People who prefer gold to paper money really say this: I do not believe that government, no matter how benevolent, will act in good faith in the long run. Those in power will be tempted, in an intractable situation, to throw benevolence out the fiscal window and exercise the power of the money presses. Therefore, I put my faith and the future inheritance of my children into hard assets.

Some rank private gold ownership with sin of the highest order. Roosevelt made private gold ownership a criminal act in 1934. Keynes said gold was a barbaric relic. Even when a free market in gold was finally allowed to develop legally in late 1975, the neo-Keynesians said that the price of gold would fall to $20 an ounce.

Governments have argued that paper money will completely replace gold. In 1790, Gabriel Mirabeau, an eighteenth century French revolutionist and statesman, said, "If gold has been hoarded through timidity or malignity, the issue of paper will show that gold is not necessary.[2] They screamed that in the 1960s and 1970s. They whisper it in the 1980s.

In a seminar I attended in Geneva, Switzerland, in 1971, the subject of gold prices arose. Attendees comprised a handful of economists, most with Ph.Ds., from the United States and Europe. Two were consultants with Ministries of Finance in other countries. Gold's price was around $42 an ounce. The concensus of all, except one, was that the gold price had peaked and would surely decline. In that august company I timidly suggested the price of gold might rise as high as $70 or $80 (halving my unspoken sentiments). In the spirit of academic freedom, scoff and spurn were my noble rewards. (Gold subsequently peaked at $800, and in 1985 it has hovered around $300 per ounce.)

(*See Also:* Barter, Exchange, Idolatry, Inflation, Money, Remnant, Stewardship, Value, Wealth)

> *So it was, when the camels had finished drinking, that the man took a golden nose ring weighing half a shekel, and two bracelets for her wrists weighing ten shekels of gold,...*
>
> GENESIS 24:22.

> *Then Moses returned to the Lord and said, Oh, these people have sinned a great sin, and have made for themselves a god of gold.*
>
> EXODUS 32:31.

[1]Gary North, *Successful Investing in an Age of Envy,* rev. ed. (Sheridan, Ind.: Steadman Press, 1982), Chap. 13.

[2]Quoted in Andrew Dickson White, *Fiat Money Inflation in France* (Irvington-on-Hudson, N.Y.: FEE, 1959), p. 45.

They came, both men and women, as many as had a willing heart, and brought earrings and nose rings, rings and necklaces, all jewelry of gold, that is, every man who offered an offering of gold to the Lord.
EXODUS 35:22.

Now the weight of gold that came to Solomon in one year was six hundred and three score and six talents of gold.
2 CHRONICLES 9:13.

I love thy commandments above gold: yea, above fine gold.
PSALM 119:127.

A word fitly spoken is like apples of gold in pictures of silver.
PROVERBS 25:11.

Provide neither gold nor silver nor copper in your moneybelts, . . .
MATTHEW 10:9.

I have coveted no one's silver or gold or apparel.
ACTS 20:33.

GOLDEN RULE

The atheist says, "Do unto others before they do unto you." The agnostic says, "Do unto others, but keep one hand on your wallet—just in case." Believers in the supreme, divine, and absolute laws of God acknowledge accountability, responsibility, and cause and effect. Hence "whatsoever ye would that men should do to you, do ye even so to them" (MATTHEW 7:12).

Years ago, a sales manager said, "Don't take any shortcuts. Keep transactions with your customers above board. Be honest with them and your company. Otherwise, sometime down the road, it will come back to haunt you." Joe Girard, a famous automobile salesman, writes that since each person typically knows 250 others, if he were dishonest with just one, soon a whole football stadium of people would be mad at Joe Girard. He built his successful business on the principle: "With what measure ye mete, it shall be measured to you" (MARK 4:24).

The management of a firm I was associated with some years ago often stressed: "Give full value to your customers for money received." Successful businesspeople know that marketing is not only selling to one-time customers. Profits accrue when people again and again return to buy your product or return to your store. Repeat sales translate into a profitable enterprise. This also means giving full value to your customers. "Give, and it shall be given unto you" (LUKE 6:38).

(*See Also:* Character, Compensation, Double Standard, Ethics, Exchange, Honesty, Law)

Judge not, that you be not judged. For with what judgment you judge, you shall be judged; and with what measure you mete, it shall be measured to you again.
Therefore, all things whatever you would that men should do to you, do you even so to them: for this is the Law and the Prophets.
MATTHEW 7:1–2, 12.

Give, and it shall be given to you: good measure, pressed down, shaken together, and running over will be put into your bosom. For with the same measure that you use, it will be measured back to you.
LUKE 6:38.

GOOD OLD DAYS

Say not, What is the cause that the former days were better than these? For you do not inquire wisely concerning this.
ECCLESIASTES 7:10.

(*See:* Cycles, Nothing Is Forever, Youth Cultism)

GOTHAM CITY

Barron's from time-to-time refers to the foibles and follies of Gotham City. The following verses well describe some excesses of that great city. Whether Babylon, Rome, or Gotham City, an historical continuity looms.

The city, dirty and polluted, an Alsatian den of vice and carnality, reveals both weaknesses and strengths. Yet, when it collapses, the whole world mourns. The federal government answers its distress calls with financial aid; the state government pursues a dual policy—one for its famous city, another for the rest of the state; and its mayors often become famous internationally. It is a city of wealth and the wealthy, yet one of poverty and the impoverished, *in extremis*. Its huge markets and financial centers are a beacon light to the world. Foreign travelers, for social prestige back home, shop its magnificent stores. Who among our country's own inhabitants have not made, or hope to make, the trip to this "Mecca" or at least have money invested in one of its financial institutions or purchased merchandise from its purveyors?

The concentration of wealth tempts those in pursuit of power. With that power comes corruption. Despite the abundance of her delicacies, the city becomes a "habitation of devils and the hold of every foul spirit" (REVELATION 18:2). As with great cities of the past, which have replaced God, a similar end awaits this one: To paraphrase, Gotham City is fallen, is fallen.

(*See Also:* Bankruptcy, Idolatry, Materialism, Nothing Is Forever, Pollution, Power, World Government)

Put yourselves in array against Babylon round about: all you who bend the bow, shoot at her, spare no arrows, for she has sinned against the Lord.

JEREMIAH 50:14.

Woe to her who is filthy and polluted, to the oppressing city! She has not obeyed His voice; she received not correction; she trusted not in the Lord; she drew not near to her God. Her princes within her are roaring lions; her judges are evening wolves who leave not a bone till morning. Her prophets are insolent and treacherous persons; her priests have polluted the sanctuary. They have done violence to the law.

ZEPHANIAH 3:1–4.

There followed another angel, saying, Babylon is fallen, is fallen, that great city, because she made all nations drink of the wine of the wrath of her fornication.

REVELATION 14:8.

...Come, I will show you the judgment of the great whore who sits on many waters, with whom the kings of the earth have committed fornication, and the inhabitants of the earth have been made drunk with the wine of her fornication.

The woman whom you saw is that great city, which reigns over the kings of the earth.

REVELATION 17:1–2, 18.

He cried mightily with a strong voice, saying, Babylon the great is fallen, is fallen, and is become the habitation of devils, and the hold of every foul spirit, and a cage of every unclean and hateful bird. For all nations have drunk of the wine of her fornication, and the kings of the earth have committed fornication with her, and the merchants of the earth are waxed rich through the abundance of her delicacies.

How much she has glorified herself, and lived deliciously, so much torment and sorrow give her: for she says in her heart, I sit a queen, and am no widow, and shall see no sorrow.

The kings of the earth, who have committed fornication and lived deliciously with her, shall bewail her, and lament for her, when they shall see the smoke of her burning.

The merchants of the earth shall weep and mourn over her; for no man buys their merchandise anymore.

For in one hour so great riches come to nothing. Every ship-master, and all the company in ships, and sailors, and as many as trade by sea, stood afar off, and cried, when they saw the smoke of her burning, saying, What city is like this great city!

REVELATION 18:2–3, 7, 9, 11, 17–18.

GOVERNMENT

Reverend Norman Vincent Peale observes with respect to the United States: "Never before had a nation been established on a religious and philosophical base. It was utterly revolutionary. It was unique. But there was a strange power in it all. In a little more than a couple of centuries this fertile soil and intellectual climate has [sic] produced more wealth, more freedom, more human happiness, more human well-being than ever known before in the history of mankind."[1]

Our response should be: And let's keep it that way! But de Montesquieu warned even in 1748, "The deterioration begins with the decay of the principles upon which it was founded."[2] This deterioration and decay the following authors address.

Herbert Quick saw the state as an antisocial institution. He saw that as primarily the arbiter of economic advantage and a potential instrument of exploitation, both its initial intent and function are antisocial.[3] Along the same lines, Albert Jay Nock saw it as "a means of diverting public attention from its flock of uncouth economic chickens on their way home to roost."[4] James Madison was equally pessimistic: "In all cases where a majority are united by common interest or passion, the rights of the minority are in danger. . . . Conscience is known to be inadequate in individuals; in large numbers little is to be expected from it."[5]

[1]Norman Vincent Peale, "Let's Keep America Great," *Creative Help for Daily Living* (July 1982).

[2]Charles de Secondat, Baron de la Brède et de Montesquieu, *Spirit of the Laws.*

[3]Albert Jay Nock, *Memoirs of a Superfluous Man.* (Chicago: Henry Regnesy, 1964), p. 123.

[4]Ibid, p. 247.

[5]James Madison, *The Federalist*, No. 10. (1787).

Since our country did not commence as a democracy, a twentieth-century phenomenon for us, we should seriously heed the warnings of Nock, James Madison, and Alexander Hamilton, who wrote: "It has been observed that a pure democracy, if it were practicable, would be the most perfect government. Experience has proved that no position in politics is more false than this. The ancient democracies, in which the people themselves deliberated, never possessed one feature of good government. Their very character was tyranny."[6]

Finally, Rose Wilder Lane states, "Government has no power but force; it cannot control any man.... To control himself, an individual must control the government that controls him."[7] However, we prefer to find our answer in God's order and His laws. No civil government will be even near perfect. Because of its destructive capabilities, it must be subordinate to the family and the family subordinate to God.

A civil government organized under God's laws has certain, biblically defined characteristics:

1. It is subordinate to individuals, family, and God.
2. Quite limited in authority, it functions to settle disputes and provide protection.
3. Its very limited and highly restricted taxing competence restrains any possibility of exceeding its basic authority, or of supporting the growth and proliferation of bureaucracies.
4. It cannot confiscate property for the common good, for social programs, or to remold society in its likeness; it does not possess power of eminent domain, nor does it have any inherent property rights, for all property belongs to God.
5. Restitution and penalties for wrongful acts are paid to the injured or wronged parties and are not kept by the state; neither does government make restitution out of common (i.e., public) funds. Individuals, not society, respond for their acts.
6. No group (minority or majority) can arrogate special privileges; the law is not a respecter of persons; the rule of law applies.
7. The government enforces penalties (i.e., restitution or capital punishment) for crimes against persons; there are no crimes against the state.

The hierarchy of authority is God, family, and civil government. Without exception, every government in the world has reversed this godly order, placing the state above everyone and above God in very clear opposition to the first commandment: "Thou shalt have no other gods before me." In practice, we find that present-day governments trample each of the Ten Commandments. What consequences can we expect from this reversal of the order of authority? The following verses tell us.

(*See Also:* Bureaucracy, Politicians, Power of State, Rule by Decree, Statism, Taxation, World Government)

[6] Alexander Hamilton, *Works,* Vol. 9.

[7] Rose Wilder Lane, *Discovery of Freedom: Man's Struggle Against Authority,* (Salem, N.H.: Ayer, 1972).

Then the men of Israel said to Gideon, Rule over us, both you and your son, and your son's son also, for you have delivered us from the hand of Midian. And Gideon said to them, I will not rule over you, neither shall my son rule over you: the Lord shall rule over you.

Judges 8:22–23.

But the thing displeased Samuel, when they said, Give us a king to judge us. So Samuel prayed to God. The Lord said to Samuel, Listen to the voice of the people in all that they say to you, for they have not rejected you, but they have rejected me, that I should not reign over them. According to all the works which they have done since the day that I brought them out of Egypt, even to this day, wherewith they have forsaken me, and served other gods, so they do also to you. Now therefore heed their voice. However, you shall solemnly forewarn them, and show them the behavior of the king who will reign over them.

And he said, This will be the manner of the king who shall reign over you: He will take your sons, and appoint them for himself, for his chariots, and to be his horsemen, and some will run before his chariots. And he will appoint captains over thousands, and captains over fifties, and will set some to plow his ground, and to reap his harvest, and to make his weapons of war, and equipment for his chariots. He will take your daughters to be confectionaries, and to be cooks, and to be bakers. He will take the best of your fields, and your vineyards, and your olive groves, and give them to his servants. He will take a tenth of your grain, and your vintage and give it to his officers, and to his servants. He will take your menservants, and your maidservants, and your best young men, and your asses, and put them to his work. He will take a tenth of your sheep: and you will be his servants. You will cry out in that day because of your king which you shall have chosen; and the Lord will not hear you in that day.

Nevertheless, the people refused to obey the voice of Samuel; and they said, Nay, but we will have a king over us, that we also may be like all the nations, and that our king may judge us, and go out before us, and fight our battles.

1 Samuel 8:6–9, 11–20.

When you saw that Nahash the king of the children of Ammon came against you, you said to me, Nay; but a king shall reign over us: when the Lord your God was your king.

1 Samuel 12:12.

The God of Israel said, . . . He who rules over men must be just, ruling in the fear of God.

2 Samuel 23:3.

He trusted in the Lord God of Israel, so that after him was none like him among all the kings of Judah, nor any who were before him. For he held fast to the Lord, and departed not from following him, but kept his commandments, which the Lord commanded Moses. The Lord was with him; and he prospered wherever he went; and he rebelled against the king of Assyria, and served him not.

2 KINGS 18:5–7.

Let the heavens be glad, and let the earth rejoice; and let men say among the nations, The Lord reigns.

1 CHRONICLES 16:31.

So king Rehoboam strengthened himself in Jerusalem, and re-igned...He did evil, because he prepared noi his heart to seek the Lord....There were wars between Rehoboam and Jeroboam continually.

2 CHRONICLES 12:13–15.

Except the Lord build the house, they labor in vain who build it: except the Lord keep the city, the watchman stays awake in vain.

PSALM 127:1.

As a roaring lion, and a raging bear, so is a wicked ruler over the poor people. The prince who lacks understanding is also a great oppressor: but he who hates covetousness shall prolong his days.

PROVERBS 28:15–16.

Woe to you, O land, when your king is a child, and your princes feast in the morning! Blessed are you, O land, when your king is the son of nobles, and your princes feast at the proper time, for strength, and not for drunkenness!

ECCLESIASTES 10:16–17.

Since the day that your fathers came out of the land of Eygpt to this day I have even sent you all my servants the prophets, daily rising up early and sending them; yet they hearkened not to me, nor inclined their ears, but hardened their necks: they did worse than their fathers. Therefore you shall speak all these words to them; but they will not listen to you: you shall also call to them, but they will not answer you. But you shall say to them, This is a nation that obeys not the voice of the Lord their God, nor receives correction: truth is perished, and is cut off from their mouths.

JEREMIAH 7:25–28.

But so shall it not be among you; but whoever shall be great among you, shall be your minister. And whoever of you will be the chiefest, shall be servant of all. For even the Son of man came not to be ministered to, but to minister, and to give his life a ransom for many.

MARK 10:43–45.

Then came also publicans to be baptized, and said to him, Master, what shall we do? And he said to them, Exact no more than that which is appointed you.

LUKE 3:12–13.

Verily, verily, I say to you, The servant is not greater than his lord; neither he who is sent greater than he who sent him.

JOHN 13:16.

We ought to obey God rather than men.

ACTS 5:29.

For in him dwells all the fullness of the Godhead bodily. And you are complete in him, who is the head of all principality and power.

COLOSSIANS 2:9–10.

HARMONY

Individuals, corporations, and organizations essentially operate within two environments: an internal and an external. For example, a business's internal environment includes matters over which it has direct control, such as deciding corporate objectives, deciding products to manufacture, allocating financial resources. Its external environment includes competitors, government regulations, suppliers of raw materials, and matters over which it has only indirect influence, at best.

A successful organization operates harmoniously, or in balance, with its environment. For instance, a business organization may have an outstanding sales team, but if manufacturing, research and development, or financial management have goals distinct from an aggressive sales department, the organization is operating disharmoniously. It will tend toward disintegration. However, when disharmony erupts, forces set in motion tend to bring the organization back into balance, assuming free play of forces.

A free society operates rather effectively as long as harmony reigns, that is, harmony with principles of a free society (internal) and God's laws (external). Resistance to Marxism or socialism or other forms of statism is the expected reaction of a free society protecting itself. The many examples of a free society gone awry in the Bible, resulting in self-destruction and enslavement by totalitarian forces, serve as solid testimony.

(*See Also:* Cooperation, Division of Labor, Free Enterprise, Organization, Price Mechanism, Voluntarism)

> *If a kingdom be divided against itself, that kingdom cannot stand. If a house be divided against itself, that house cannot stand.*
>
> MARK 3:24–25.

...If the salt has lost its saltiness, how will you season with it? Have salt in yourselves, and have peace one with another.

Mark 9:50.

For if the firstfruit is holy, the lump is holy; and if the root is holy, so are the branches. If some branches were broken off, and you, being a wild olive tree, were grafted in among them, and with them became a partaker of the root and fatness of the olive tree, do not boast against the branches. But if you boast, remember that you do not support the root, but the root supports you.

Romans 11:16–18.

...I have said before that you are in our hearts, to die together and to live together.

2 Corinthians 7:3.

That there should be no schism in the body; but that the members should have the same care one for another. Whether one member suffer, all the members suffer with it; or one member be honored, all the members rejoice with it.

1 Corinthians 12:25–26.

If we live in the Spirit, let us also walk in the Spirit. Let us not be desirous of vain glory, provoking one another, envying one another.

Galatians 5:25–26.

HEROES

We have all laughed at comic strip versions of Soviet pseudo-heroes being pinned with huge stellar medals. Their only claim to heroism is worship and support of the state government. Unfortunately, American politics have not been immune to such theatrics.

Soviet- or Nazi-style political hero worship, really a system of control, assures loyalty to the state. In his book, *The Celebration of Heroes: Prestige as a Control System*, Professor William J. Goode writes that prestige is a system of social control. "All people share the universal need to gain the respect or esteem of others, since without it they cannot as easily elicit the help of others, and all individuals and groups give and withhold prestige and approval as a way of rewarding or punishing others."[1] While we need to laugh at our political imaginary heroes, we must also recognize the real purposes behind such manipulations.

We can certainly admire truly heroic individuals. To elevate persons because of their political or bureaucratic roles to near-sainthood (or even attempted sainthood as in the case of Eva Peron) certainly reeks of idolatry. Those in government, as in other professions, are there to serve, not command. "A servant is not greater than his master" (JOHN 15:20).

True heroism, of course, is to be honored, as one man honors another, not as man honors God. Heroism implies superlative courage in achieving some high purpose against odds. We readily recognize those kinds of acts and respect persons doing those gallant deeds. Let's confine the other kind of heroes either to the cartoons or food snack shops where they belong.

(*See Also:* Experts, Fury of a Bureaucrat Scorned, Hippies, Idolatry)

You shall have no other gods before me.
EXODUS 20:3.

Great men are not always wise.
JOB 32:9.

Man who is in honor, and understands not, is like beasts that perish.
PSALM 49:20.

The Lord of hosts has purposed it, to stain the pride of all glory, and to bring into contempt all the honorable of the earth.
ISAIAH 23:9.

He said to them, You are they who justify yourselves before men; but God knows your hearts: for that which is highly esteemed among men is abomination in the sight of God.
LUKE 16:15.

I receive not honor from men.
But I know you, that you have not the love of God in you.
How can you believe, who receives honor one of another, and seek not the honor that comes from God only?
JOHN 5:41–42, 44.

Therefore let no man glory in men. For all things are yours.
1 CORINTHIANS 3:21.

[1]William J. Goode, *The Celebration of Heroes: Prestige as a Social Control System* (Berkely, Calif.: University of California Press, 1978).

...a dumb donkey speaking with a man's voice restrained the madness of the prophet.

2 PETER 2:16.

...by whom a person is overcome, by him also he is brought into bondage.

2 PETER 2:19.

HIPPIES

The Hippie movement of the 1960s was about the most unoriginal event of the era. Hair style, clothes, political philosophies were all imitations of similar past movements. Many Hippie ideas were carbon copies of a nineteenth-century Russian socialist movement.

Nihilists of nineteenth-century Russia, the radical students of their day, professed no beliefs except in revolutionary socialism. Male students wore long hair; females wore theirs short. They stunk. They made themselves as obnoxious and offensive in appearance and conduct as possible. Many wore blue glasses. They particularly attacked Christian morals. About everything you saw or read on Hippies of the 1960s, these Nihilists had already done. Even intellectuals sympathized with these students, then as now.

Before that, *Goliards,* wandering "professional" students of the late Middle Ages, probably saw little of the inside of classrooms. They aimed to destroy civilization, like their communist and socialist imitators of later centuries. They wrote music, too, like modern hippies, and their music expressed hostility toward Christian morals.

Behind these movements lies one central set of objectives: deny the Absolute; there are no absolute laws or morals; whatever is right for the moment is therefore right; there are no restraints on any kind of human behavior. This philosophy is contrary to the foundations that underlie a free society under the rule of God. It only leads to slavery.

(*See Also:* Children, Cycles, Education, Humanism, Nonalignment, Youth Cultism)

There is a generation that curses their father, and does not bless their mother. There is a generation that is pure in their own eyes, and yet is not washed from their filthiness. There is a generation, O how lofty are their eyes! and their eyelids are raised. There is a generation whose teeth are as swords, and their jaws teeth as knives, to devour the poor from off the earth, and the needy from among men.

PROVERBS 30:11–14.

Ah, sinful nation, a people laden with iniquity, a seed of evildoers, children who are corrupters: They have forsaken the Lord…they are gone backward.

ISAIAH 1:4.

Your princes are rebellious, and companions of thieves: every one loves gifts, and follows after rewards. They judge not the fatherless, neither does the cause of the widow come to them.

ISAIAH 1:23.

Does not even nature itself teach you that if a man have long hair, it is a shame to him?

1 CORINTHIANS 11:14.

HOMOSEXUALITY

There are two basic positions on homosexuality. One, paralleling the abortion argument, runs: It is your body and your life to do with what you please. James Kilpatrick sums up the libertarian position on this issue: "Men should be free to pursue their widely varying concepts of happiness so long as they do not encroach upon the rights of their neighbors."[1]

On the other hand, the Bible specifically speaks against this practice. Even the pagan Egyptian *Book of the Dead* required that to become one with heavenly beings man must affirm a confession—"I have not stolen, I have not killed…." etc., one confession of which is, "I have not committed adultery, I have not lain with men."[2]

Some people argue that since God created us with sexual organs, why should He be so concerned with what we do with them. Sex is not the underlying issue here. The basic unit of government under God's law is the family. This organizational hierarchy clearly puts responsibility of education, management, welfare, and accountability squarely on the head of household, the man. This organizational mandate, too, assures freedom from state coercion because the state is subordinate to the family unit.

God condemns any human invention or pursuit that leads to disruption or disintegration of His order. Without restraint of the family as the basic governing block in society, the power of the state is unfettered. In other words, moral anarchy results in totalitarian statism, i.e., coercion, and loss of freedom.

---

[1]James J. Kilpatrick, "Homosexuals and the Law," *Palo Alto Times*, December 15, 1964.

[2]E. A. Wallis Budge (trans.), *The Egyptian Book of the Dead* (New Hyde Park, N.Y.: University Books, 1968), p. 578.

Fundamentally it is a tradeoff: Is the exchange of self-restraint for freedom a better deal than the exchange of a (not so) "new liberty" for a socialist state, whose "object of power is power"?[3]

(*See Also:* Abortion, Capital Punishment, Children, Family, Marriage)

You shall not lie with a male as with a female; it is an abomination.
Leviticus 18:22.

If a man also lie with a male as he lies with a woman, both of them have committed an abomination. They shall surely be put to death; their blood shall be upon them.
Leviticus 20:13.

The woman shall not wear that which pertains to a man, neither shall a man put on a woman's garment: for all who do so are an abomination to the Lord your God.
Deuteronomy 22:5

There shall be no whore of the daughters of Israel, nor a sodomite of the sons of Israel. You shall not bring the hire of a whore, or the price of a dog, into the house of the Lord your God for any vow: for even both of these are an abomination to the Lord your God.
Deuteronomy 23:17–18.

God gave them up to uncleanness through the lusts of their own hearts, to dishonor their own bodies between themselves: who changed the truth of God into a lie, and worshipped and served the creature more than the Creator.... For this cause God gave them up to vile affections: for even their women did change their natural use into that which is against nature: and likewise also the men, leaving the natural use of the woman, burned in their lust one toward another; men with men committing what is shameful, and receiving in themselves the penalty of their error which was due.
Romans 1:24–27.

Know you not that the unrighteous shall not inherit the kingdom of God? Be not deceived: neither fornicators, nor idolators, nor adulterers, nor effeminate, nor abusers of themselves with mankind, nor thieves, nor covetous, nor drunkards, nor revilers, nor extortioners, shall inherit the kingdom of God.
1 Corinthians 6:9–10.

[3]George Orwell, *1984* (New York: Signet Books, 1983), p. 84.

HONESTY

Without honesty in transactions, a free society cannot long survive. Religion and morals and a system of law and godly order constrain any group of persons or businesses who seek special privileges. Those who pursue unfair advantages and special privileges, lacking coercive power of government to do it for them, would have to resort to other forms of coercion (such as highway robbery, whether done in the name of Robin Hood or Jesse James). In other words, dishonesty in transactions is a denial of godly order.

Word soon gets around that an individual or business is dishonest and cannot be trusted. Still some people take shortcuts. They try to achieve gain at the expense of others. In an honest transaction, both parties gain because both parties are free to enter or not enter into a contract. Unless both parties believe beforehand they will be better off after transacting than before, there would be no voluntary exchange.

Dishonesty means that someone loses in the transaction. With some dishonest gainers and many losers, the free society deteriorates. However, with honesty in transactions, everyone can potentially gain. Those who steal and engage in shoddy dealings or rely on coercion have no place in a free society.

Of course, that may sound naive in the 1980s. Cynicism, probably reaching a climax in the 1960s and 1970s, has turned us away from honesty as being the best policy. Given our present environment, the strictly honest person really stands out in the community. For instance, one well-known religious organization has so well indoctrinated its members on this principle of honesty, that a bank loan officer granted a personal loan solely on the basis of a person belonging to that organization: They have the reputation for being honest. Is striving for a reputation like that naive?

(*See Also:* Character, Contract, Golden Rule, Harmony, Private Property, Responsibility, Self-Discipline)

You shall not commit adultery.

Exodus 20:14.

You shall not have in your bag differing weights, a great and a small.
You shall not have in your house differing weights, a great and a small.

Deuteronomy 25:13–14.

The Lord rewarded me according to my righteousness; according to the cleanness of my hands has He recompensed me.

Psalm 18:20.

Differing weights and differing measures, both of them alike are an abomination to the Lord.

PROVERBS 20:10.

A good name is better than precious ointment....

ECCLESIASTES 7:1.

He who is faithful in that which is least is faithful also in much; and he who is unjust in the least is unjust also in much. If therefore you have not been faithful in the unrighteous mammon, who will commit to your trust the true riches?

And if you have not been faithful in that which is another man's, who shall give you that which is your own? No servant can serve two masters: for either he will hate the one, and love the other, or else he will hold to the one and despise the other. You cannot serve God and mammon.

LUKE 16:10–13.

...He who enters not by the door into the sheepfold, but climbs up some other way, the same is a thief and a robber. But he who enters in by the door is the shepherd of the sheep.

JOHN 10:1–2.

Jesus answered him, I spoke openly to the world; I ever taught in the synagogue, and in the temple, wherever the Jews always resort; and in secret have I sold nothing.

JOHN 18:20.

Let us walk honestly, as in the day, not in rioting and drunkenness, not in licentiousness and lewdness, not in strife and envy.

ROMANS 13:13.

Wherefore putting away lying, speak every man truth with his neighbor, for we are members of one another.

EPHESIANS 4:25

Lie not one to another, seeing that you have put off the old man with his deeds, and have put on the new man, which is renewed in knowledge after the image of him who created him.

COLOSSIANS 3:9–10.

That you may walk honestly toward them who are without, and that you may lack nothing.

1 THESSALONIANS 4:12.

HUMANISM

Humanism, a frightfully deceptive word, may, to some, convey compassion, charity, and love toward fellow humans. This describes Christian behavior. Humanism, in fact, means quite the opposite.

Humanists count humanism as a fourth religion, along with Protestant, Catholic, and Jewish religions. The American Humanist Association, under the authorship of Edwin H. Wilson, has prepared a booklet, *Humanism, The Fourth Faith,* in which several characteristics of humanism are identified:

1. The Humanist lives as if this world were all and enough. He is not other-worldly. He holds that time spent in contemplation of a possible afterlife is time wasted. He fears no hell and seeks no heaven, save those which he and other men create on this earth.
2. He believes in people.
3. He believes in human equality.
4. Freedom of thought and action is a necessary part of the Humanist's way of life.
5. The Humanist accepts the world view of science and the scientific method of testing truth.
6. He seeks the cooperation of all men of good will to end poverty, war, disease, and prejudice.... The Humanist knows he is not outside nature and that he must study and conform to nature's laws.... Humanists also realize that man must work with and attempt to control nature on a planetary scale under some sort of democratic federation for the salvation of all men.[1]

From this we learn that humanists believe that man is a product of his environment; the salvation of mankind is through the sole efforts of man himself; no higher authority exists than man himself, who is the source of all law and morals; morals are the product of each generation and do not derive from any absolute principles; only science and the scientific method are competent to test propositions and derive truths; evolutionism explains human existence; war, disease, and poverty are not the fault of man but must be overcome by his political action; only Socialism can accomplish these aims; and these lofty goals will not be achieved until a world government determines production and use of goods. God has been replaced. His laws have no place in the humanist universe.

More specifically, what will humanism lead to in practice? Francis Schaeffer states: "As in our country, humanism leads to abortion, infanticide, euthanasia, and a loss of compassion; this view of final reality does so more totally in the communist bloc because it is totally committed to this view. There is a total emphasis that there are no fixed values. Therefore, there is a total emphasis that there is only arbitrary

[1]Cited in Edmund A. Opitz, *Religion and Capitalism: Allies, Not Enemies* (New Rochelle, N.Y.: Arlington House, 1974), p. 156.

law." He also says, "...in the more total expression in the Soviet system humanism leads to internal oppression and external expansion and oppression."[2]

That seems a little strong, doesn't it? Still, after careful study, we cannot conclude otherwise. Alert Jews and Christians recognize that they are on an irreconcilable collision course with humanism. Some even speak of it as *war.*

> One good proof of that war is the exclusivity of government schools. Their absurd attempt to exclude the Lord is an expression of the hostility one religion has for another. In this case the religion is Satanic and calls itself Humanism. We know that Humanism is a religion, not just because the United States Supreme Court says so, but because the Humanists say so themselves, in their own publications.
>
> What kind of religion is it? Karl Marx—in one of the few places we can be sure he knew what he was talking about—said that his system and Humanism are the same thing.[3]

Humanism, in other words, is another fancy name for totalitarianism. We may sympathize with some of their charitable *objectives*, but we, as Christians, can never accept their tenets or *humanist means* to achieve those objectives.

(*See Also:* Communism, Elitism, Evolutionism, Nonalignment, One Worldism, Rule by Decree)

> The earth also was corrupt before God, and the earth was filled with violence. God looked upon the earth and behold, it was corrupt; for all flesh had corrupted his way upon the earth.
>
> Genesis 6:11–12.

> You shall not go after other gods, of the gods of the people.
>
> Deuteronomy 6:14.

> ...Let us fall now into the hands of the Lord; for His mercies are great: and let me not fall into the hand of man.
>
> Samuel 24:14.

> What is man, that you should magnify him? And that you should set your heart upon him? And that you should visit him every morning, and try him every moment?
>
> Job 7:17–18.

---

[2]Francis A. Schaeffer, "The Secular Humanistic World View versus the Christian World View and the Biblical Perspectives on Military Preparedness," a speech given at the Mayflower Hotel, Washington, D.C., June 22, 1982. Copyright 1982 by Francis A. Schaeffer.

[3]Alan Stang, "What the War Is Really About," *Christianity & Civilization*, 2 (Winter 1983), 24–39.

Man that is born of woman is of few days, and full of trouble.

JOB 14:1.

How much more abominable and filthy is man who drinks iniquity like water?

JOB 15:16.

Be merciful to me, O God: for man would swallow me up; he fighting daily oppresses me.
    In God have I put my trust: I will not be afraid what man can do unto me.

PSALM 56:1, 11.

The Lord is on my side, I will not fear. What can man do to me?
    It is better to trust in the Lord than to put confidence in man.

PSALM 118:6, 8.

There is a way that seems right to man, but the end thereof are the ways of death.

PROVERBS 16:25.

Man's goings are of the Lord; how can a man then understand his own way?

PROVERBS 20:24.

...For a piece of bread a man will transgress.

PROVERBS 28:21.

I said in my heart concerning the estate of the sons of men, that God might manifest them, and that they might see that they themselves are beasts.

ECCLESIASTES 3:18.

Cease from man, whose breath is in his nostrils: for wherein is he to be accounted of?

ISAIAH 2:22.

O Lord, I know that the way of man is not in himself; it is not in man who walks to direct his steps.

JEREMIAH 10:23.

...They make you vain. They speak a vision of their own heart, and not out of the mouth of the Lord.

JEREMIAH 23:16.

*Yet the children of your people say, The way of the Lord is not equal;
but as for them, their way is not equal.*

EZEKIEL 33:17.

*You have plowed wickedness, you have reaped iniquity; you have
eaten the fruit of lies because you did trust in your way, in the multitude
of your mighty men.*

HOSEA 10:13.

*He turned and said to Peter, Get behind me, Satan: you are an offense
to me, for you savor not the things that are of God but those that are of
men.*

MATTHEW 16:23.

*Howbeit in vain do they worship me, teaching for doctrines the
commandments of men. For laying aside the commandment of God,
you hold the tradition of men, as the washing of pots and cups, and
many other such like things you do.*

MARK 7:7–8.

*There is nothing from without a man, that entering into him can defile
him; but the things which come out of him, those are they that defile
the man.*

MARK 7:15.

*Jesus looking upon them says, With men it is impossible, but not with
God: for with God all things are possible.*

MARK 10:27.

*That which is born of the flesh is flesh; and that which is born of the
Spirit is spirit.*
    *And this is the condemnation, that light is come into the world,
and men loved darkness rather than light because their deeds were
evil. For everyone who does evil hates the light, neither comes to the
light, lest his deeds should be reproved.*

JOHN 3:6, 19–20.

*... Refrain from these men, and let them alone: for if this counsel or this
work be of men, it will come to nothing; but if it be of God, you cannot
overthrow it: unless you be found even to fight against God.*

ACTS 5:38–39.

...After my departing shall grievous wolves enter in among you, not sparing the flock. Also of your own selves shall men arise, speaking perverse things, to draw away disciples after them.

Acts 20:29–30.

Professing themselves to be wise, they became fools.

And changed the glory of the uncorruptible God into an image made like to corruptible man, and to birds, and fourfooted beasts, and creeping things.

Wherefore God also gave them up to uncleanness through the lusts of their own hearts, to dishonor their own bodies between themselves: who changed the truth of God into a lie, and worshipped and revered the creature more than the Creator, who is blessed for ever.

Romans 1:22–25.

...Let God be true, but every man a liar....

Romans 3:4.

For they, being ignorant of God's righteousness, and going about to establish their own righteousness, have not submitted themselves to the righteousness of God.

Romans 10:3.

...Be not conformed to this world.

Romans 12:2.

...Let no man glory in man....

1 Corinthians 3:21.

Now the works of the flesh are manifest, which are these: adultery, fornication, uncleanness, lasciviousness, idolatry, witchcraft, hatred, variance, emulations, wrath, strife, seditions, heresies, envyings, murders, drunkenness, revellings, and such like, of which I have told you before ... that they who do such things shall not inherit the kingdom of God. But the fruit of the Spirit is love, joy, peace, longsuffering, gentleness, goodness, faith, meekness, temperance, against such there is no law.

Galatians 5:19–23.

Beware lest any man spoil you through philosophy and vain deceit, after the tradition of men, after the rudiments of the world, and not after Christ.

Colossians 2:8.

Not giving heed to Jewish fables, and commandments of men, that turn from the truth.

Titus 1:14.

For all flesh is as grass, and all the glory of man as the flower of the grass. The grass withers, and the flower thereof falls away; but the word of the Lord endures forever.

1 Peter 1:24–25.

HYPOCRISY

…For we have made lies our refuge, and under falsehood have we hid ourselves.

Isaiah 28:15.

(*See:* Demagoguery, Double Standard, Liberalism)

IDOLATRY

Idols that see not; hear not; and speak not; that are made of wood, metal, plaster of Paris, or whatever material; and that are easiest to recognize are the easiest to avoid. However, idolatry includes any system outside of God's order that is sought to resolve problems. Consequently, idols can be institutions, persons (living or dead), nature, or rituals.

In answer to my comment that the world was under God's control, a humanist said, "It doesn't look like He's doing a very good job of it." His prescription was for man to straighten out the chaotic mess God had got us into with a strong, centralized federal government to implement his ideas. His idol was the monolithic state.

His remedy is not an uncommonly desired one in the United States, as "golden calves" (i.e., government agencies) appear to resolve energy problems, jobless problems, inflation problems, high interest problems, education problems, economic growth problems, all caused by the government in the first place. "There ought to be a law (meaning, we need another state institution)..." is too often on the tips of tongues.

This escape from responsibility, a sign of immaturity, carries with it the most dangerous implications. Think, for a moment, why someone else should eagerly take over your cares and concerns. For money? control? power? Certainly it takes money to run any organization. Guess who supplies the money (via taxation)? If you do not take charge of your own life and accept its challenges, not only do you forgo the learning experience, but you forfeit control over your own decision making. The accumulation of power in the hands of an elite leads to some form of enslavement for the many. That power is surrendered in bits and pieces every time we say, "Here, Sam, you do it."

The fabricated gods are dead, inert, incapable of creating one single job, one dollar of income, or one piece of machinery, or even of carrying you to xhat far-off land where wars and strife and hunger and man's inhumanity to man do not exist. Only one system has ever given us freedom, an abundance of material goods, long periods of peace: only the free society under God's laws. Those who return from

Cuba, the Soviet Union, or Red China and praise those governments are either blind or liars. The case for freedom is a simple one: Open your eyes and look around the world. Then leave idolatry to the heathens.

(*See Also:* Elitism, Humanism, Maturity, Slavery, Subsidies, Tinstaafl, Welfarism)

He who sacrifices to any god, save the Lord only, shall surely be utterly destroyed.

Exodus 22:20.

The Lord was angry with Solomon, because his heart was turned from the Lord God of Israel, who had appeared to him twice, and had commanded him concerning this thing, that he should not go after other gods; but he kept not that which the Lord commanded. Wherefore the Lord said to Solomon, Forasmuch as this is done of you, and you have not kept My covenant and My statutes, which I have commanded you, I will surely rend the kingdom from you, and will give it to your servant. Notwithstanding in your days I will not do it for David you father's sake, but I will rend it out of the hand of your son.

1 Kings 11:9–12.

...After that Amaziah was come from the slaughter of the Edomites, that he brought the gods of the children of Seir, and set them up to be his gods, and bowed before them, and burned incense under them. Wherefore the anger of the Lord was kindled against Amaziah, and he sent him a prophet, who said to him, Why have you sought after the gods of the people, which could not deliver their own people out of your hand?

2 Chronicles 25:14–15.

What profit is the image that the maker should carve it, the molten image, a teacher of lies, that the maker of his work trusts in it, to make dumb idols? Woe to him who says to the wood, Awake! To the dumb stone, Arise! It shall teach! Behold it is laid over with gold and silver, and there is no breath at all in the midst of it. But the Lord is in His holy temple; let all the earth keep silence before him.

Habakkuk 2:18–20.

...When you did not know God, you served those who by nature are not gods. But now after you have known God, or rather are known by God, how is it that you turn again to the weak and beggarly elements, to which you desire again to be in bondage?

Galatians 4:8–9.

Outside are dogs and sorcerers and sexually immoral and murderers and idolaters, and whoever loves and practices a lie.

REVELATION 22:15.

IMPORTS

Imports are goods and services that flow across international borders. Obviously, their measurement of quantity or value, as well as crossing an arbitrarily defined geographical boundary, are artificial concepts—the creation of man. In a broader sense, immigration is the import of human labor and talent, although international trade accounting ignores persons.

Is it moral or immoral to purchase imports? Organized labor says that it is immoral to buy from foreigners because it reduces job availability for nationals. Others say, Buy American (or Canadian, Mexican) because that is the patriotic thing to do.

If the objective is to increase the number of jobs, exporting is better than importing. If the objective is to obtain a higher material standard of living, importing is better, because we use their labor and their tools, but we get to enjoy the fruits of their work, making them, in a sense, our servants. Typically, of course, imports are paid for with exports, so that international trade benefits all parties involved.

Why do some persons want to prohibit or reduce imports? Those persons and businesses protected from foreign competition often earn more wages and profits than they could in a competitive situation. In order to assure continuance of these high incomes, the consumer is led to believe he errs in getting the most value for his money. Also, those who object to imports say that exporters and the people they employ, who depend on a foreign market, are less valuable. Remember that if we no longer import, foreigners will not have the means to buy our goods. Hence, our own export industries would fail. A system of special privileges and protection denies God's laws.

(*See Also:* Demand and Supply, Free Market, International Trade, Productivity, Specialization)

Solomon numbered all the strangers in the land of Israel, after numbering wherewith David his father had numbered them; and they found a hundred and fifty thousand [150,000] and three thousand and six hundred [3,600].

2 CHRONICLES 2:17.

Now the weight of gold that came to Solomon in one year was six hundred and three score and six [666] talents of gold, beside that which traders and merchants brought. All the kings of Arabia and governors of the country brought gold and silver to Solomon.

2 CHRONICLES *9:13–14.*

For the king's ships went to Tarshish with the servants of Huram: every three years once came the ships of Tarshish bringing gold, and silver, ivory, and apes, and peacocks.

2 CHRONICLES *9:21.*

INDEBTEDNESS

(*See:* Bankruptcy, Debt, Interest)

INDIVIDUALISM

In a Christian free society, individuals are important. They do count. They do not matter in totalitarian societies. According to Marxist theology, the individual has no inherent right to his own personal goals. These are subordinated to the state's whims. In despotic regimes of ancient Egypt, Far East Empires, and parts of South America, it was believed that the ruler had become deified, taking charge of human affairs, the combination of Church and state so carefully avoided in the formation of our own country. Later this idea became diluted in the form of the divine rights of kings and caesars.

Individualism did not prevail. The individual was locked into the state mechanism—heart and soul. However, writers of our own Declaration of Independence dealt with the idea of God-given rights, which to them, were self-evident truths. Now the intrinsic value of the individual was no longer discounted.

Reverend Opitz writes:

The West was Christian in its assumptions about man and his destiny; its aspirations were Christian.

But now there is widespread confusions as to what it means to be a human being, and uncertainty as regards the individual's relation to God.

Balloting of sorts goes on in all modern states, and therefore most countries call themselves "democracies," merely because men are counted. The individual in mass societies doesn't count.

Our ancestors believed that each man counted because they knew that each man was accountable. In the religious faith they professed, the individual had to render an account of his life before God, and therefore he was, in his own and in his fellow's eyes, a responsible being. These are the convictions we must recover; that each of us counts, that each of us is responsible.[1]

From the Bible we learn that man is exempt from the deterministic parameters that strictly constrain nature. When he forgets his God-given gifts, he soon creates societal institutions that deliberately deny liberties of mind and conscience.

(*See Also:* Accountability, Character, Inequality, Liberty, Remnant, Self-Discipline)

You shall not follow a multitude to do evil; neither shall you testify in a cause so as to turn aside after many to pervert justice.

EXODUS 23:2.

Be not conformed to this world, but be transformed by the renewing of your mind.

ROMANS 12:2.

There is one glory of the sun, and another glory of the moon, and another glory of the stars, for one star differs from another star in glory.

1 CORINTHIANS 15:41.

INEQUALITY

Suppose that in some country all wealth of the nation is distributed absolutely equally among inhabitants. Will that achieve either an equal or an equitable distribution of wealth?

In some countries under plant-closing laws, workers receive severance pay. For instance, with the 1981 British steel plant closings, some workers collected severance pay equivalent to $15,000 to $20,000 in one lump sum. Now picture this. Workers have just lost their employment with no future prospects of reemployment either in the same industry or a related industry, but they have in hand a big chunk of dough. What would you do? Frankly, I would be alarmed with my situation. I would pay off debts and save the remainder at interest. The local English merchants enjoyed an unusual business boom as the unemployed rushed to squander their last paycheck and severance pay.

[1] Edmund A. Optiz, *Religion and Capitalism: Allies, Not Enemies* (New Rochelle, N.Y.: Arlington House Publishers, 1974), pp. 210-11.

Someone once estimated that if all wealth in the United States were equally redistributed, within a few years much would be concentrated in the hands of about 2 percent of the population. Some people like to spend, others save, and still others invest to accumulate wealth. Each has different goals. Saving involves a sacrifice; few will submit themselves to such self-discipline. Puerto Rico, for example, as an island economy, spends more than it earns in income. Negative savers, they depend on welfare transfers from the Continent to pay for this high consumption rate. Puerto Rico, also, is typically a poor area.

Government agencies do much to achieve this mythical equality with various programs. These programs represent forced redistribution of wealth and income. They contribute to another kind of inequality—political inequality. Every type of coercive redistribution scheme widens political power differentials in our society. However, we notice that bureaucrats do not subject themselves to this same criterion of economic and political equality. They have used their political power to enhance the economic well-being of friends and associates and in the process enjoy an abundance of fringe benefits themselves.

No one is even created equal in the sense of sameness: our fingerprints differ; our body organs are of different sizes and are not located in precisely the same location in each person; even inherited wealth differs tremendously. We have neither identical goals or aspirations nor the same self-disipline necessary to achieve aims. Some will pay a high price for financial success, others will not. This competition encourages us to sharpen skills, test ideas in the real world, and serve our fellow humans in a number of ways.

On the other hand, we are or should be equal before the law, in matters of principle. We stand equal before God to be judged according to our deeds and misdeeds.

(*See Also:* Accountability, Envy, Equality, Freedom, Redistribution of Income/Wealth)

Having then gifts, differing according to the grace that is given us,...
ROMANS 12:6.

...Every man has his proper gift of God, one after this manner, and another after that.
1 CORINTHIANS 7:7.

Now there are diversities of gifts, but the same spirit.
1 CORINTHIANS 12:4.

There is one glory of the sun, and another glory of the moon, and another glory of the stars, for one star differs from another star in glory.
1 CORINTHIANS 15:41.

Therefore let no one judge you in food or in drink, ... Let no one defraud you of your reward, taking delight in false humility...inflated without cause by his fleshly mind.

COLOSSIANS 2:16, 18.

INFLATION

"What used to cost $5 to buy, now costs $10 to repair" (Anonymous).

Inflation is typically described as a rise in the price level. This is not really correct. We should identify inflation in order to determine proper corrective prescriptions for its cure—a separation of causes and effects.

A rise in the price level often results from monetary inflation. However, it is possible to inflate the money supply without any noticeable rise in the price level. In fact, under certain conditions, for short periods, inflation combined with a *fall* in the price level can occur.

To inflate means to increase. Monetary inflation, or just inflation, signals an increase in the supply of money, the medium of exchange. Money is exchanged for goods or services, for convenience in transactions, or for preserving wealth in the form of a monetary asset.

Paper currency offers the advantage of exchanging something that costs little to produce (our Federal Reserve Notes) for things of much greater value. Hence, creating more paper money brings greater profit to the originator of the paper currency; but the more paper money there is in circulation, the less each monetary unit is worth. Consequently, the original printer of the currency must create larger and larger amounts in order to buy the same volume of goods and services. Printing costs rise too. So, in order to keep currency production costs down, the money maker adds more zeroes. A former $1 then becomes $10, then $100, and so on. Only the inflationist can keep his costs under control and in the process of inflating earn enormous profits.

Obviously, such a system is profitable if only a few catch on to the scam. If government retains the money-printing monopoly, they object to any competition and force "counterfeiters" out of business.

So, increasing the money supply inflates it. Whether it has been inflated by creation of ten pieces of paper or a million is immaterial, since both represent an increase in the money supply. Therefore, inflation can only be stopped by *not* printing more money. Crude oil prices, labor unions, foreign trade, big business—none of these directly *cause* inflation. They may pressure government to inflate, or they may raise the prices of raw materials, finished products, or labor, but inflation only results from an increase in the money supply.

Is inflating dishonest? Currency debasement is the oldest form of monetary inflation. By clipping or sweating coins (which reduces the amount of precious metal in each circulating coin) new coins are minted from the residuals, which circulate with the debased currency. The theft occurs by reducing the metalic value of coins in tiny amounts. Notice that Isaiah mentions both money inflation and lowering of wine quality. Quality of merchandise deteriorates as inflation progresses: hamburgers get smaller; plastic substitutes for metal; articles disappear from the marketplace; and personal services disappear as we pump our own gasoline, carry our own luggage, and lines get longer at the supermarket or bank.

Inflation supposedly creates employment. Yet, we see that unemployment has always been highest where inflation has been highest, in any country in any age. Because inflation distorts price signals, too many goods of one kind are produced and not enough of another are produced. As the economic system becomes more chaotic, investment strategy becomes one of preserving wealth rather than necessarily channeling it into more productive endeavors. Therefore, jobs melt away due to lack of new investment; low-profit products disappear from the market; and the government usually responds with controls that only exacerbate an already distorted market. The only expansion occurring in the economy is the government's increase of the money supply.

Inflation is the only tax from which there is no escape, although some better avoid its impact than others. For example, owners of private retirement funds, savings accounts, fixed-income annuities, and similar monetary assets have lost an unknown amount of wealth in the trillions. A rise in the general price level of goods and services signals taxation, or confiscation, of income. As companies attempt to remain competitive, they lower the quality of their products, and thereby are unwitting accomplices with the government in this deceptive process. The inflation tax alone is an awesome tax burden on the American public; but that is the price for wanting a king to judge us, to fight our battles, to take over our responsibilities, and to supplant our decisions. (see 1 SAMUEL 8).

(*See Also:* Inflationist, Keynesianism, Money, Pollution, Power of State, Savings, Taxation)

Take away the dross from the silver, and it will go to the silversmith for jewelry. Take away the wicked from before the king, and his throne will be established in righteousness.

PROVERBS 25:4–5.

Your silver has become dross, your wine mixed with water; your princes are rebellious, and companions of thieves.... Therefore, saith the Lord.... I will ease Me of My adversaries, and avenge Me of My enemies; and I will turn My hand upon you, and purely purge away your dross, and take away your tin; and I will restore your judges as at the first, and your counsellors as at the beginning....

ISAIAH 1:22–26.

Son of man, the house of Israel has become dross to Me; they are all bronze, tin, iron, and lead, in the midst of a furnace; they have become dross from silver. Therefore saith the Lord God: Because you have all become dross, behold therefore, I will gather you into the midst of Jerusalem. As men gather silver, bronze, iron, lead, and tin into the midst of a furnace, to blow fire on it, to melt it; so will I gather you in my anger and in my fury, and I will leave you there and melt you. Yea, I will gather you and blow on you with the fire of my wrath, and you shall be melted in its midst. As silver is melted in the midst of a furnace, so shall you be melted in its midst; then you shall know that I, the Lord, have poured out my fury on you.

EZEKIEL 22:18–22.

...When will the new moon be gone, that we may sell corn? and the sabbath, that we may set forth wheat, making the ephah small, and the shekel great, and falsifying balances by deceit? That we may buy the poor for silver, and the needy for a pair of shoes; yea, and sell the refuse of the wheat?

AMOS 8:5–6

Let him who stole steal no more; but rather let him labor, working with his hands the things which are good, that he may have to give to him who needs.

EPHESIANS 4:28.

That no man go beyond and defraud his brother in any matter....

1 THESSALONIANS 4:6.

INFLATIONIST

Many believe in the false doctrine of inflationism. Inflation, probably the most misunderstood part of economic theory, has provided fertile ground for germination of inflationist seeds. Chief among famous economists has been the Fabian socialist, John Maynard Keynes, who proposed that wars be financed with the inflation tax rather than direct taxes because a hidden tax is more palatable to the unwary. A good part of World War II was financed by means of inflating the money supply and then hiding the dastardly deed with a combination of price controls and substitute money, such as coupons, tokens, and rationing books.

The scam worked so well and the American public was so thoroughly confused that a host of social welfare programs were financed with this method beginning in the mid-1960s. The inflationists in our legislatures know no better way to finance ever-expanding government expenditures while the antiinflationists are unable to extricate the economy from this monetary entanglement. We now have an entire generation who has had no other experience than inflationism.

Inflationists are as dishonest as any other kind of robber who forcefully wrenches our hard-earned savings from our gnarled hands. They have committed adultery; they have adulterated our money supply and polluted our savings. As our incomes buy less and less, wives are forced into the work force and away from the home and rearing of their children. The head of the household spends less time in his proper role, as he is forced to seek second employment. The family unit becomes a center for governments to loot, now servants of the state, and Christians surrender their God-granted freedom for brummagems of the inflationists. Must we continue singing "*Backward* Christian Soldiers"?

(*See Also:* Expropriation, Inflation, Interest, Keynesianism, Money, Private Property, Tax Collector)

> The tabernacles of robbers prosper, and they who provoke God are secure, into whose hand God brings abundantly.
>
> Job 12:6.

> But you are forgers of lies, you are all physicians of no value.
>
> Job 13:4.

> Though wickedness be sweet in his mouth, though he hide it under his tongue, though he spare it, and forsake it not, and keep it still within his mouth, yet his meat in his bowels is turned; it is the gall of asps within him. He has swallowed down riches, and he shall vomit them up again. God shall cast them out of his belly.
>
> Job 20:12–15.

INHERITANCE

Two goals of Karl Marx were (1) abolition of private property, and (2) abolition of inheritance. Inheritance consists of more than material goods and real estate. Marxists are least concerned about real property. That can be easily expropriated or confiscated through property or inheritance taxes. Other forms of socialism may allow for some private ownership, but in the end, inherited wealth is confiscated through heavy taxation. They strive to weaken the family and want the family to look stateward for guidance and assistance, not Godward.

When God speaks of inheritance, He refers also to moral, spiritual, and social landmarks guarded and passed on by the family. Marxists want to destroy the family as keeper of moral percepts and want to substitute the state as both originator and keeper of statist principles. Marxists most fear the inheritance of God's laws.

The landmark concept also carries with it the symbolic meaning of stability, the continuity of the rule of God, the family, the Judeo-Christian society, and the integrity of private property. (Actually the word *private* is redundant since all property under God's law is private in the sense of stewardship.) Any attempt to separate persons from honestly gained wealth is ungodly. Ill-gotten wealth, on the other hand, does not belong to the state either. Wrongfully acquired property is returned to rightful owners. Even persons who lost property through mismanagement can still reclaim it.

Hence, under God's laws, strict adherence to matters of private property, inheritance, freedom to buy and sell is basic and practical in the operation and maintenance of a free society. Those who study and understand God's plan know that private property and inheritance underpin God's system.

(*See Also:* Capital Formation, Children, Free Enterprise, Private Property, Savings, Source, Wealth)

He said, Lord God, whereby shall I know that I will inherit it?

GENESIS 15:8.

And Jacob said, Sell me this day your birthright.

GENESIS 25:31.

And Rachel and Leah answered and said to him, Is there yet any portion or inheritance for us in our father's house? Are we not counted of him strangers? for he has sold us, and has quite devoured also our money. For all the riches which God has taken from our father, that is ours, and our children's....

GENESIS 31:14–16.

...If a man die, and have no son, then you shall cause his inheritance to pass to his daughter. And if he have no daughter, then you shall give his inheritance to his brothers. And if he have no brothers, then you shall give his inheritance to his father's brothers. And if his father have no brothers, then you shall give his inheritance to his kinsman that is next to him of his family, and he shall possess it....

NUMBERS 27:8–11.

You shall not remove your neighbor's landmark, which they of old time have set in your inheritance, which you shall inherit in the land that the Lord your God gives you to possess.

DEUTERONOMY 19:14.

...That you may be strong, and eat the good of the land and leave it for an inheritance to your children for ever.

EZRA 9:12.

A good man leaves an inheritance to his children's children, and the wealth of the sinner is laid up for the just.

Proverbs 13:22.

House and riches are the inheritance of fathers, and a prudent wife is from the Lord.

Proverbs 19:14.

Yea, I hated all my labor which I had taken under the sun, because I should leave it to the man who shall be after me.

Ecclesiastes 2:18.

... The prince shall not take of the people's inheritance by oppression, to thrust them out of their possession; but he shall give his sons inheritance out of his own possession, that my people be not scattered every man from his possession.

Ezekiel 46:18.

And one of the company said to him, Master, speak to my brother, that he divide the inheritance with me.

Luke 12:13.

And the younger of them said to his father, Father, give me the portion of goods that falls to me....

Luke 15:12.

And he gave him no inheritance in it, no, not so much as to set his foot on.

Acts 7:5.

INSTITUTIONALISM

Their idols are silver and gold, the work of men's hands. ... They who make them are like them; so is everyone who trusts in them.

Pslam 115:4, 8.

(See: Bureaucracy, Idolatry, Statism)

INTEREST

Benjamin Franklin said, "'Tis against some men's principles to pay interest, and seems against others' interest to pay the principal."

Payment of interest for money borrowed actually represents at least three separate costs: time, inflation, and risk. Lumped together, these are called *interest*.

While we cannot alter *time*, we can affect its use by borrowing. Borrowing allows a business to construct a plant today instead of waiting. It allows a consumer to spend now instead of later. But there is a cost for rearranging the use of time. Borrowing can only be achieved if someone else has refrained from current consumption or from expanding a business, that is, has performed an act of saving. A lender gives up purchasing power today. In a sense a lender may say he has lent time to borrowers—and he expects to be paid for it. Hence, one element of interest is payment for the use of time, the time value of money. The more people want to live in the now, and not the future, the higher will be the time value of money—a question of demand and supply.

The second element of interest refers to *inflation*. A thousand dollars lent today should have the same purchasing power when the loan is repaid. If inflation affects money's purchasing power, the lender, while receiving the same number of dollars when the loan is repaid finds that those dollars buy less than before and must be compensated for the loss.

Risk means that there is a chance that the borrower cannot or will not repay part or all of the loan. A higher risk premium is assigned to riskier clients. Obviously, a certain amount of estimation and guess work is involved in forecasting the ravaging effects of inflation and the character and credit-worthiness of borrowers; but there is a restraint on interest rates. The free market puts a cap on interest charges. A lender who charges too high interest, too far above the market rate, will attract the worst and riskiest clients; and one who charges too much below the market rate will have more clients than money to lend.

This ends the minicourse on interest rate determination. "But," you say, "the Bible prohibits charging interest, so this discussion is a moot issue." If a brother is in need and requires a loan to buy food or meet an emergency, you may not charge interest on that loan. Interest means payment for time and risk. If you lend an unbeliever funds, you may charge interest. Similarly, business loans and loans to foreigners can bear interest. The only prohibition on interest concerns charitable loans to other believers.

(*See Also:* Business, Charity, Contract, Debts, Inflation, Pledge, Price, Risk Aversion, Savings)

> If you lend money to any of my people who are poor among you, you shall not be like a moneylender to him; you shall not charge him interest.
>
> *EXODUS 22:25.*

You shall not charge interest to your brother—interest on money or food or anything that is lent out at interest. To a foreigner you may charge interest, but to your brother you shall not charge interest.
DEUTERONOMY 23:19–20.

Why then did you not put my money in the bank, that at my coming I might have collected it with interest?
LUKE 19:23.

INTERNATIONAL TRADE

The fundamentals underlying buying and selling of goods and services internationally are no different from those for domestic trade. Deciding to buy a Plymouth or a Datsun usually has little to do with place of manufacture. Creation of national boundaries is a political act, not an economic one.

Although most economists agree on benefits of international trade, few can make the intellectual leap to extend similar free market concepts to domestic exchange. When political and economic barriers to trade are least, more exchanges occur. As barriers to trade increase, the volume of trade declines.

Why should we buy from foreigners? Why should they buy from us? One time a group of persons from a less developed country complained that the United States was robbing them of their natural resources. I complained that they were robbing us of our Chevrolets and Fords. They had missed the whole point of trade. Exchanges take place when both parties to the trade are better off after trading than before; otherwise, no peaceful exchange can occur.

We import coffee, cocoa, tea, and bananas because we cannot produce any significant quantity of these products. We also import wine and shirts even though we produce both in abundance. If imports satisfy tastes of a class of consumers, or if goods can be manufactured elsewhere more cheaply, it pays to import those items for which we have a comparative disadvantage, while we gain by concentrating energies on what we do best: high technology and agricultural commodities, for example.

However, if clothing manufacturers and their labor unions can convince Congress to pass protective tariffs to raise the price of apparel goods to the consumer, several outcomes arise: (a) international trade will decline; (b) the domestic price of clothing will rise; (c) the variety of goods will tend to diminish; (d))corporate profits of clothing manufacturers will rise; (e) union employees will get more money; and (f) the consumer will be worse off.

God's way is one of abundance and freedom. The other way is one of shortages, high prices, and loss of economic freedom.

(*See Also:* Cooperation, Demand and Supply, Imports, Price Mechanism, Say's Law, Specialization)

The Lord shall open to you his good treasure, the heaven to give the rain to your land in his season, and to bless all the work of your hand; and you shall lend to many nations, and you shall not borrow.
D<small>EUTERONOMY</small> 28:12.

So Hiram gave Solomon cedar trees and fir trees according to all his desire. Solomon gave Hiram twenty thousand measures of wheat for food to his household, and twenty measures of pure oil: thus gave Solomon to Hiram year by year.
1 K<small>INGS</small> 5:10–11.

And Solomon had horses brought out of Egypt, and linen yarn; the king's merchants received the linen yarn at a price. And a chariot came up and went out of Egypt for six hundred shekels of silver, and a horse for a hundred and fifty; and so for all the kings of the Hittites, and for the kings of Syria, did they bring them out by their means.
1 K<small>INGS</small> 10:28–29.

Jehoshaphat made ships of Tharshish to go to Ophir for gold…
1 K<small>INGS</small> 22:48.

And Solomon sent to Huram, the king of Tyre, saying, As you dealt with David, my father, and sent him cedars to build a house to dwell in, even so deal with me.
2 C<small>HRONICLES</small> 2:3.

Silver spread into plates is brought from Tarshish, and gold from Uphaz, the work of the workman, and of the hands of the founder: blue and purple is their clothing; they are all the work of cunning men.
J<small>EREMIAH</small> 10:9.

They have made all your ship boards of fir trees of Senir; they have taken cedars from Lebanon to make masts for you. Of the oaks of Bashan have they made your oars; the company of the Ashurites have made your benches of ivory, brought out of the isles of Chittim. Fine linen with broidered work from Egypt was that which you spread forth to be your sail; blue and purple from the isles of Elishah was that which covered you.
E<small>ZEKIEL</small> 27:5–7.

Judah, and the land of Israel, they were your merchants. They traded in your market wheat of Minnith, and Pannag, and honey, and oil, and balm. Damascus was your merchant in the multitude of the wares of your making, for the multitude of all riches, in the wine of Helbon, and white wool. Dan also and Javan going to and from occupied in your fairs: bright iron, cassia, and calamus, were in your market. Dedan was your merchant in precious clothes for chariots. Arabia, and all the princes of Kedar, they traded with you in lambs, and rams, and goats; in these were they your merchants. The merchants of Sheba and Raamah, they were your merchants. They traded in your fairs with the best of all spices, and with precious stones, and gold. Haran, and Canneh, and Eden, the merchants of Sheba, Asshur, and Chilmad, were your merchants. These were your merchants in all sorts of things, in blue clothes, and embroidered work, and in chests of rich apparel, bound with cords, and made of cedar, among your merchandise.

EZEKIEL *27:17–24.*

INTERNATIONALISM

(*See:* Communism, One Worldism, United Nations)

INVESTMENTS

Investment complements saving. Essentially we make one of two decisions over income: to consume or not consume. To consume means spending for consumption goods, i.e., goods that may bring satisfaction during use but produce no further income. To save is not to consume. Investing means to put savings into productive employment.

Saving must precede investing. Productive investments yield a return. However, not all of us are adept at placing savings in profitable endeavors. Hence, we use financial intermediaries, such as banks and insurance companies, which, in turn, lend our savings to investors. We can also lend directly to businesses by purchasing bonds and notes; or we can participate in business ownership by buying stocks or partnerships, even though we are not active in the management of those enterprises.

What is the real force behind investment decisions? The real power in a free market system lies with consumers. Consumers demand. Entrepreneurs organize the business activity and gather funds. Producers produce and sell to consumers who want those goods and services. Ludwig von Mises writes; "No matter what the financial structure of the firm or company may be, the entrepreneur who operates with other people's money depends no less on the market, that is, the consumers, than the entrepreneur who fully owns his own outfit."[1]

What would happen in an economy that operated in strict accordance with God's laws? No inflation, minimal taxes, no taxes on savings or investments, free market for goods and services and no coercive elements preventing downward price flexibility. Consumers demand, profits accrue, investment follows profits, technology lowers costs, and through experience and learning business assets are used with greater efficiency. The result is an ever-increasing demand prompted by falling prices accompanied with rising supplies as a result of increased investment in capital.

In our humanistic society, we now have quite the opposite: falling real after-tax incomes, products of declining quality accompanied with rising prices, shortages, decreasing amounts of savings available for capital investment, and goods produced in response to the artificial stimulus of inflation and government direction.

(*See Also*: Capital Formation, Management, Production, Return on Investment, Savings, Say's Law)

Also, he built towers in the desert, and dug many wells, for he had many cattle, both in the low country, and in the plains....
2 CHRONICLES 26:10.

A good man shows favor, and lends; he will guide his affairs with discretion.
PSALM 112:5.

That our storehouses may be full, affording all manner of store: that our sheep may bring forth thousands and ten thousands in our streets. That our oxen may be strong to labor; that there be no breaking in, nor going out; that there be no complaining in our streets.
PSALM 144:13–14.

Where no wood is, there the fire goes out....
PROVERBS 26:20.

For he who has, to him shall be given; and he who has not, from him shall be taken even that which he has.
MARK 4:25.

[1]Ludwig von Mises, "The Economic Role of Saving and Capital Goods," *The Freeman* (August 1963).

No man puts new wine into old bottles, else the new wine will burst the bottles, and be spilled, and the bottles shall perish. But new wine must be put into new bottles, and both are preserved.

LUKE 5:37–38.

Then came the first, saying, Lord, your pound has gained ten pounds. And he said to him, Well, you good servant; because you have been faithful in a very little, you have authority over ten cities.

LUKE 19:16–17.

But this I say, He who sows sparingly shall reap also sparingly; and he who sows bountifully shall reap also bountifully.

2 CORINTHIANS 9:6.

JEALOUSY

...If any man's wife go aside, and commit a trespass against him, and a man lie with her carnally, and it be hid from the eyes of her husband, and be kept close, and she be defiled, and there be no witness against her, neither she be taken with the manner; and the spirit of jealousy come upon him, and he be jealous of his wife, and she be defiled, or if the spirit of jealousy come upon him, and he be jealous of his wife, and she be not defiled, then shall the man bring his wife to a priest and he shall bring her offering for her, the tenth part of an ephah of barley meal...for it is an offering of jealousy, an offering of memorial, bringing iniquity to remembrance.

NUMBERS 5:12–15.

(*See:* Envy, Family; Golden Rule)

JUDGMENT

One point clearly arises in the following verses: judgment comes from God, not man. We are responsible to the final Authority, God, the Judge, to whom we answer. Judgment is an ongoing process; God curses and blesses according to man's behavior.

The individual is judged. The family is judged. The nation is judged. When God judges a nation, He gives power to another nation to defeat it and enslave it. How often that happened to Israel! Families may disappear when no male heirs are born into it—once again the judgment of God.

The key point is that God, not man, judges. Standards, i.e., our laws, must operate on God's principles, not humanistic ones. "For if we would judge ourselves, we should not be judged" (1 CORINTHIANS 11:31). This responsibility cannot be eluded. The problem with human judgment is sometimes it's wrong (GENESIS 39:10–20), vengeful (1 SAMUEL 25:20–35), circumstantial (JOSHUA 22:10–34), or prejudicial (LUKE 7:38–50).

God's judgment on the other hand, punishes evil (EXODUS 20:5), chastises and corrects (2 SAMUEL 7:14; HABAKKUK 1:12), or warns others (LUKE 13:3). God judges us because of disobedience to the rule of God (2 CHRONICLES 7:19–22); sins of rulers (2 CHRONICLES 21:1–7); rejection of God's warnings (2 CHRONICLES 36:16–17); and idolatry, *inter alia.*

How can we avoid the wrath of God? Well, here are a few ways: by turning to God (DEUTERONOMY 28:15–68); by prayer (2 KINGS 19:14–26); by turning away from sin (JEREMIAH 7:3–7). Avoidance of problems, of course, begins with self-judgment, which begins with self-discipline and forbearance from hypocrisy (MATTHEW 7:1–6), and ends in the final judgment (ROMANS 14:10).

(*See Also:* Accountability, Honesty, Justice, Law, Restitution, Self-Discipline, Stewardship)

For all manner of trespass, whether it be for ox, for ass, for sheep, for raiment, or for any manner of lost thing, which another challenges to be his, the cause of both parties shall come before the judges, and whom the judges shall condemn, he shall pay double to his neighbor.
EXODUS 22:9.

And they shall be for you cities for refuge from the avenger, that the manslayer die not, until he stand before the congregation in judgment.
NUMBERS 35:12.

Judge not, that you be not judged, for with what judgment you judge, you shall be judged; and with the same measure you use, it will be measured to you. Why do you look at the speck in your brother's eye, but do not consider the plank in your own eye? Or how can you say to your brother, Let me remove the speck out of your eye; and a plank is in your own eye? Hypocrite! First remove the plank from you own eye, and then you will see clearly to remove the speck out of your brother's eye. Do not give what is holy to the dogs; nor cast your pearls before swine, lest they trample them under their feet, and turn and tear you in pieces.
MATTHEW 7:1–6.

But I say to you that for every idle word men may speak, they will account of it in the day of judgment.
MATTHEW 12:36.

We know that the judgment of God is according to truth against those who practice such things. Do you think this, O man, you who judge those practicing such things, and doing the same, that you will escape the judgment of God?

ROMANS 2:2–3.

Why do you judge your brother? Or why do you show contempt for your brother? For we shall all stand before the judgment seat of Christ. For it is written, As I live, saith the Lord, every knee shall bow to me, and every tongue shall confess to God. So then every one of us shall give account of himself to God. Let us therefore not judge one another any more; but rather judge this, that no man put a stumbling-block or an occasion to fall on his brother's way.

ROMANS 14:10–13.

He who is spiritual judges all things, yet he himself is judged of no man.

1 CORINTHIANS 2:15.

Behold, the Lord comes with 10,000 of his saints, to execute judgment on all, to convict all who are ungodly among them of all their ungodly deeds which they have committed in an ungodly way, and of all the harsh things which ungodly sinners have spoken against Him.

JUDE 15.

For in one hour your judgment has come.

REVELATION 18:10.

I saw the dead, small and great, stand before God; and the books were opened; and another book was opened, which was the book of life. The dead were judged out of those things which were written in the books, according to their works.

REVELATION 20:12.

JUSTICE

A society that is not grounded on the triune God and His law is a society destined to reveal its basic hostility to justice.

Without justice, the law becomes a form of theft. Stripped of justice, the law becomes an instrument of extortion and oppression in the hands of whatever group of men control it. If men of wealth control the state, the law becomes their tool to subjugate the poor and to make them poorer. If poor men control the state, the law then is used to rob the rich and all hard-working men to support those who want to live on the proceeds of robbery. In the one case it is called the maintenance of social order, and in the other it is called social justice and social welfare, but in both cases it is robbery.[1]

Social justice is dispensed according to the social economics of justice, as though there were a fixed supply of it coupled with unlimited demand for it. Social engineers, of course, trust only themselves and their agencies to distribute this so-called justice in agreement with statist priorities.

Social justice, really another name for welfarist economics, boils down to reallocation of wealth and income according to state-divinized principles that change with the wind. Justice and righteousness in the Bible are identical. Social justice, a humanist creation, covertly takes from many to give to some. Saint Augustine, in *The City of God*, likens this kind of justice to a band of robbers. "Justice being taken away, then what are kingdoms but great robberies? For what are robberies themselves, but little kingdoms?"[2]

Social justice becomes marked by serious punishment for crimes against the state. Notice the stiff jail sentences and fines of tax evaders or license evaders or similar crimes against the state, compared with those of real criminals. Restitution, equality before the law, and judgment of the criminal underscore real justice.

Justice is marked by the application of God's righteousness. It means the godly administration of judgment. In the Bible there is only one kind of justice—that established by God's law. While social justice is abstract, abstruse, and arbitrary, divine justice is practical, fully developed with concrete examples and specific acts, based on never-changing principles.

(*See Also:* Capital Punishment, Ethics, Judgment, Liberty, Perjury, Responsibility, Rule of Law)

> *The Lord said to him, Therefore, whoever slays Cain, vengeance shall be taken on him sevenfold.... If Cain shall be avenged sevenfold, truly Lamech seventy and sevenfold.*
>
> GENESIS *4:15, 24.*

> *Whoso sheds man's blood, by man shall his blood be shed.*
>
> GENESIS *9:6.*

> *Just balances, just weights, a just ephah, and a just hin, shall you have....*
>
> LEVITICUS *19:36.*

[1]Rousas J. Rushdoony, *Law and Liberty* (Fairfax, Va.: Thoburn Press, 1971), pp. 90–91.

[2]Saint Augustine, *The City of God* (Trans. by Marcus Dods) (N.Y.: The Modern Library, 1950), p. 112.

You shall have one manner of law, as well for the stranger, as for one of your own country....

LEVITICUS *24:22.*

The Lord is longsuffering, and of great mercy, forgiving iniquity and transgression, and by no means clearing the guilty, visiting the iniquity of the fathers upon the children to the third and fourth generation.

NUMBERS *14:18.*

When the king asked the woman, she told him. So the king appointed to her a certain officer, saying, Restore all that was hers, and all the fruits of the field since the day that she left the land, even until now.

2 KINGS *8:6.*

Shall mortal man be more just than God? Shall a man be more pure than His Maker?

JOB *4:17.*

Does God pervert judgment? Or does the Almighty pervert justice?

JOB *8:3.*

Touching the Almighty, we cannot find Him out. He is excellent in power, and in judgment, and in plenty of justice. He will not afflict.

JOB *37:23.*

The path of the just is as the shining light, that shines more and more unto the perfect day. The way of the wicked is as darkness. They, know not at what they stumble.

PROVERBS *4:18–19.*

A false balance is an abomination to the Lord; but a just weight is his delight.... A hypocrite with his mouth destroys his neighbor; but through knowledge shall the just be delivered.

PROVERBS *11:1,9.*

To do justice and judgment is more acceptable to the Lord than sacrifice.

PROVERBS *21:3.*

For there is not a just man on the earth, who does good, and sins not.... For oftentimes also your own heart knows that you yourself likewise have cursed others.

ECCLESIASTES *7:20, 22.*

Because sentence against an evil work is not executed speedily, therefore the heart of the sons of men is fully set in them to do evil.

ECCLESIASTES 8:11.

According to their deeds, accordingly He will repay, fury to His adversaries, recompense to His enemies.

ISAIAH 59:18.

All who found them have devoured them; and their adversaries said, We offend not, because they have sinned against the Lord, the habitation of justice, even the Lord, the hope of their fathers.

JEREMIAH 50:7.

He who is faithful in that which is least is faithful also in much; and he who is unjust in the least is unjust also in much. If therefore you have not been faithful in the unrighteous mammon, who will commit to your trust the true riches?

LUKE 16:10–11.

For it seems to me unreasonable to send a prisoner, and not withal to signify the crimes laid against him.

ACTS 25:27.

Who shall lay anything to the charge of God's elect? It is God who justifies.

ROMANS 8:33.

That no man is justified by the law in the sight of God, it is evident; for the just shall live by faith. The law is not of faith; but the man who does them shall live in them.

GALATIANS 3:11–12.

Alexander the coppersmith did me much evil. The Lord reward him according to his works.

2 TIMOTHY 4:14.

He who is unjust, let him be unjust still; and he who is filthy, let him be filthy still; and he who is righteous, let him be righteous still; and he who is holy, let him be holy still. Behold, I come quickly, and My reward is with Me, to give every man according as his work shall be. I am Alpha and Omega, the beginning and the end, the first and the last.

REVELATION 22:11–13.

KEYNESIANISM

One form of economic thinking, Keynesianism, has dominated national policies for decades. Lord John Maynard Keynes, commissioned by Fabian Socialists, organized and wrote in 1935 a new general theory of economics.[1] Unlike Karl Marx, whose fuzzy and confused economic theories led nowhere, Keynes had a thorough grasp of economic history.

Consequently, Keynes put together an argument plausible to left-leaning economists. Keynes wove a mixture of acceptable economic theory, untested ideas, and wishful thinking into a general theory praised by American and British socialists. Neo-Keynesians have further compounded their ignorance of economic reality with mathematical models built on highly restrictive assumptions that abstract from the real world. They rely on government intervention in the marketplace to make them work. Students are still fed this polluted philosophy.

For Keynesians, economic growth occurs because demand precedes production. As a matter of policy, government must increase demand by inflating the currency supply. By consuming more, according to the argument, more goods will be produced. Let's reduce this argument to simplest terms and see if it will indeed produce economic growth and prosperity. Remember, now, the theory says that by decapitalizing, by spending our savings, we become richer.

Let's assume that as a farmer you have reserved seed corn for next year's planting. No seed, no crop next year! Logic and experience tell you that larger crops result from more seed corn planted each year. However, in order to have more seed available next spring, you must reduce consumption of corn during the winter—an act of saving prior to investment. You know, too, that if you eat your seed corn during the winter, come spring, some gigantic problems will arise.

Keynesianism essentially posits the opposite. First we need to consume more— eat the seed corn—run down savings, and then magically (never explained by

[1]John Maynard Keynes. *The General Theory of Employment, Interest and Money.* N.Y.: Macmillan, 1961.

economists) we will have more corn in future years. This theorizing promotes government deficit spending. Government deficits are supported by a combination of higher taxes, inflation, and public borrowing.

Keynesianism is predicated on extensive governmental intervention. What better way than with deficits? If people eat their seed corn and are in debt, the unregenerate must look to the omnipotent state for sustenance. Puerto Rico, for instance, as an economy, spends more than it earns in income. It generates no savings. All deficits must be financed. Through collection of taxes the American people support the island with so-called transfer payments (a nice term meaning to take forcefully wealth from some to give to others).

Franklin Delano Roosevelt, as you will recall, put some of these economic theories into bizarre practice. Roosevelt believed one source of our (government-induced) economic woes was low agricultural prices. So he proposed raising the price level of farm products by reducing their supply. According to economic theory, if demand remains constant, but supply is reduced, prices will rise. So far, correct. Roosevelt twisted good theory by destroying agricultural crops. He ordered new-born pigs slaughtered, crops plowed under, and storage grains destroyed in order to reduce supply. If a limited food supply is such a glorious idea, then certainly countries like Bangladesh, Haiti, Sri Lanka, and many others must be paradises on earth!

Neo-Keynesians favor inflation as a policy tool, especially to reduce unemployment and increase economic growth. If inflation cures all, why did it destroy the economies of Germany, China, Russia, and France? Why are Argentina and Mexico in financial trouble today? Such are the monuments to man's efforts to replace God by separating liberty and truth from government.

(See Also: Capital Formation, Economic Forecasts, Inflationist, Planned Economy, Redistribution of Income/Wealth)

> The fool folds his hands together, and eats his own flesh.
> ECCLESIASTES 4:5.

> The Lord will enter into judgment with the ancients of His people, and the princes thereof; for you have eaten up the vineyard; the spoil of the poor is in your houses.
> ISAIAH 3:14.

> Behold joy and gladness, slaying oxen, and killing sheep, eating flesh, and drinking wine. Let us eat and drink, for tomorrow we shall die.
> ISAIAH 22:13.

> Many false prophets shall rise, and shall deceive many.
> MATTHEW 24:11.

Every man who strives for the mastery is temperate in all things. Now they do it to obtain a corruptible crown, but we an incorruptible.

1 Corinthians 9:25.

KIDNAPPING

Kidnapping, terrorism, holding hostages, and hijacking are all prohibited by the Bible. The penalty for stealing another person, i.e., kidnapping, is death. Kidnapping, of course, is another form of enslavement. Hence, anyone, whether in organized crime, organized bureaucracy, or organized government, and whether he kidnaps the person or his wealth, exposes himself to the same penalty—death.

The eighth commandment reads: "You shall not steal" (Exodus 20:15). Specifically, we learn from Bible study that it means you shall not steal people, wealth, or freedom of others by forcibly enslaving their persons or property. Kidnapping, certainly, robs a person of freedom.

Kidnapping has become a lucrative business, especially for terrorist gangs, who use collected ransoms to finance more terrorism. However, few kidnappers are severely punished, even if caught. Capital punishment is the exception rather than the rule.

In a free society, those who would invert God's order are punished not only for the act committed but also because they threaten the peace and prosperity of the free society. Keep in mind that in biblical law there were no prison sentences. Criminals were either executed, or they made restitution.

In a humanist society, criminals are exonerated, even revered: "And they cried out all at once, saying, Away with this Man, and release to us Barabbas, who for a certain sedition made in the city and for murder, was cast into prison" (Luke 23:18–19). Often in a statist society, criminals and their ilk rise to key positions. Therefore, undue sympathy for criminals leads to our own self-destruction and enslavement.

(*See Also:* Capital Punishment, Inflation, Justice, Rule of Law, Taxation, Theft)

He who steals a man, and sells him, or if he is found in his hand, he shall surely be put to death.

Exodus 21:16.

If a man is found stealing any of his brethren of the children of Israel, and makes merchandise of him, or sells him, then that thief shall die; and you shall put evil away from among you.

Deuteronomy 24:7.

LABOR

The harvest is truly great, but the laborers are few. Pray, therefore, to the Lord of the harvest, that He would send forth laborers into His harvest.
LUKE 10:2.

(*See:* Labor Market, Wages, Work)

LABOR MARKET

Wages in a free society depend largely upon demand for and supply of labor skills, not necessarily the number of workers. Consequently, unskilled labor, always abundant in supply, commands the lowest wages in the labor market. They are the least productive workers. Therefore the employer can never pay workers more than they are worth—i.e., more than their productivity—and still remain in business. An individual worker can raise his own wages in two basic ways: (1) either become more productive, usually by application of capital equipment (which requires greater investment on the part of the businessperson); or (2) raise his skill levels.

In a controlled market, wages can be raised by force. When government makes unionism compulsory and backs up labor unions with the force of law, both employees and employer have lost some of their freedom to the union bosses. If unions raise the contract wage above the market rate, then someone has to pay the difference. Studies have proven that high union wages produce lower overall wages for nonunionized workers, increase the level of unemployment nationally, and decrease total productive activities of the nation.

Once again we learn that a free society operating under God's laws is not only just but produces a higher level of material well-being as well.

(*See Also:* Contract, Division of Labor, Employees, Exchange, Productivity, Technology, Wages.)

There are workmen with you in abundance: hewers and workers of stone and timber, and all types of skillful men for every kind of work.

1 CHRONICLES 22:15.

The king and Jehoiada gave it to those who did the work of the service of the house of the Lord, and hired masons and carpenters to repair the house of the Lord, and also such as wrought iron and brass to mend the house of the Lord.

2 CHRONICLES 24:12.

He hired also one hundred thousand mighty men of valor out of Israel for a hundred talents of silver.

2 CHRONICLES 25:6.

LAW

Signs throughout the state of Connecticut read: "Drive 55—It's not only a good idea, *it's the law!*" Suppose the signs read: "All Christians must deny God as the absolute Power—It's not only a good idea, *It's the law!*" Ridiculous, you say. But in America: (1) The Bible is religiously barred from public schools; (2) courts no longer recognize Christianity as the common law foundation; (3) governments have padlocked church buildings and Christian schools and have confiscated church property, because they will not deny God, the Supreme Law Giver; (4) humanism, without competitors, is the sole religion permitted in public schools. Remember, *it's the law!*

"The modern state is increasingly prone to legislate envy. Since it derives its law from man, not God, its law and 'social justice' become revelations of the nature of man, not God."[1]

"In the United States, there is a steady movement by regulation and by law to enforce a 'public social policy' doctrine on all churches. This would give the federal government the power to regulate, control, or eliminate any and all groups whose stands conflict with 'public policy.' Such a trend spells the death of freedom."[2]

---

[1]Rousas John Rushdoony, "What Is Law?" *Chalcedon Report,* no. 216 (Vallecito, Calif.), July 1983.

[2]Rushdoony, "The Law, the State, and the People," *Chalcedon Position Paper,* no. 40 (Vallecito, Calif.: Chalcedon).

God's law is not identified with public social policy or state interest. His law is not identified with any class, race, or nation. It is above particular human interests. Civil government does not belong in the realm of God's providential rule. The right of kings and politicians to rule is far from divine. What is law then?

All law is religious in its presuppositions. It expresses basic and ultimate values. It rests on morality. Morality rests on religion. Weaken the religious foundations, and morality, and the legal foundations likewise erode.

> Biblical law gives us freedom from men and from the state, but not from God. The social order created by Biblical law distrusts man as a sinner and thus minimizes his controls while stressing his responsibility. This means that Biblical law leads to a minimal state.
> Those who despise God's law are thus railing against responsibility, justice, and responsible freedom. Freedom under God makes us members of, not lords over, one another. It delivers us from bondage into a calling under God. The law of God is justice; man's law-making leads to injustice."[3]

"The purpose of Biblical law is to punish and restrain evil, and to protect life and property, to provide justice for all people.... Humanistic law aims at saving man and remaking society. For humanism, salvation is an act of state."[4] The next time someone says, *It's the law!*, ask, whose law? "Whenever and wherever law has been seen as the voice of the people or the voice of the state, this totalitarian faith has prevailed. Either law is transcendental, or it's the product of some human agency."[5]

(*See Also:* Discipline, Family, Foundation, Justice, Law and Order, Moral Principles, Rule of Law)

You shall teach them ordinances and laws, and shall show them the way in which they must walk, and the work they must do.
                                                                                   EXODUS 18:20.

Let your heart therefore be perfect with the Lord our God, to walk in His statutes, and to keep His commandments, as at this day.
                                                                                   1 KINGS 8:61.

The statutes, and the ordinances, and the law, and the commandment, which He wrote for you; you shall observe to do forever; and you shall not fear other gods.
                                                                                   2 KINGS 17:37.

[3]Ibid.

[4]Rushdoony, *Law and Liberty* (Fairfax, Va.: Thoburn Press, 1977), p. 3.

[5]Rushdoony, "The Law, the State, and the People," *Chalcedon Position Paper*, no. 40 (Vallecito, Calif.: Chalcedon).

The law of the Lord is perfect, converting the soul: the testimony of the Lord is sure, making the wise simple. The statutes of the Lord are right, rejoicing the heart: the commandment of the Lord is pure, enlightening the eyes.

PSALM 19:7–8.

The mouth of the righteous speaks wisdom, and his tongue talks of judgment. The law of his God is in his heart; none of his steps shall slide.

PSALM 37:30–31.

Blessed are the undefiled in the way, who walk in the law of the Lord.

PSALM 119:1.

Blessed are you, O Lord: teach me Your statutes. . . . I will delight myself in your statutes: I will not forget Your word.

PSALM 119:12, 16.

The proud have had me greatly in derision; yet have I not declined from Your law. ... Horror has taken hold upon me because of the wicked who forsake Your law. ... The proud have dug pits for me, which are not after Your law.

PSALM 119:51, 53, 85.

They who forsake the law praise the wicked; but such as keep the law contend with them.

PROVERBS 28:4.

For the Lord is our judge, the Lord is our lawgiver, the Lord is our king; He will save us.

ISAIAH 33:22.

I have written to him the great things of My law, but they were counted as a strange thing.

HOSEA 8:12.

A certain lawyer stood up, and tempted him, saying Master, what shall I do to inherit eternal life? He said to him, What is written in the law? How do you read it? He, answering, said, You shall love the Lord your God with all your heart, and with all your soul, and with all your strength, and with all your mind, and your neighbor as yourself. And He said to him, You have answered right: do this, and you shall live.

LUKE 10:25–28.

This people who know not the law are cursed. ... Does our law judge any man, before it hears him, and knows what he does?

JOHN 7:49, 51.

For as many as have sinned without law shall also perish without law; and as many as have sinned in the law shall be judged by the law. For not the hearers of the law are just before God, but the doers of the law shall be justified.

ROMANS 2:12–13.

Do we then make void the law through faith? God forbid; yea, we establish the law.

ROMANS 3:31.

For we know that the law is spiritual....

ROMANS 7:14.

So then with the mind I myself serve the law of God; but with the flesh the law of sin.

ROMANS 7:25.

If you fulfill the royal law according to the Scripture, You shall love your neighbor as yourself, you do well; but if you have respect to persons, you commit sin, and are convinced of the law as transgressors. .For whoever shall keep the whole law, and yet offend in one point, he is guilty of all.

JAMES 2:8–10.

LAW AND ORDER

For political candidates, the buzz phrase, "law and order," provides a handy shorthand label for identifying a candidate's position. It's clever because it means different things to different persons. The Christian will ask: Whose law? Whose order?

In these days of powerful competing religious forces, we must scrutinize the moral law and moral order being espoused. Marxian Communism represents a potent religious doctrine. Particularly wide-spread among Third World countries, they have not yet experienced the full weight of its yoke as have slaves of communist countries. The second most powerful religious force is humanism and the modern technological state, offering still another facet of world socialism. In another part of the world militant Islam has become a force to be reckoned with.

In all of these religious movements, leaders believe that an elite cadre can control external affairs. They all believe in the dynamic force of history, a kind of fatalism. To put it in our terms, we observe that all of these religions have a proselytizing wing, whose recruitment tactics and persistence should be noted. These, as well as other competing religions, favor one worldism, especially if they are the elite in charge of the "new world order." In fact, these religions are more similar than different, all really being variants of socialism, or statism, a better label.

If we compare these religions with all others, whose names are legion, it comes down to an *us* versus *them*. The "them" all appear with the same drab grayness. No society's structure of law and order can claim neutrality. Laws are predicated on the presupposition that certain acts are wrong in keeping with the moral and religious order of that society. Consequently, laws cannot be neutral for they cannot be separated from a moral and religious system of law and order.

Therefore, when we speak of law, we must speak of the whole law of God. God's law is comprehensive. When we speak of order, we speak of the rule of God, God's way to organize our earthly activities. God's kingdom is comprehensive. The issue of law and order, then, is God's sovereignty versus man's sovereignty.

(*See Also:* Communism, Foundation, Government, Humanism, Judgment, Law, One Worldism)

> *The Lord says, Because they have forsaken My law, which I set before them, and have not obeyed My voice, neither walked therein, but have walked after the imagination of their own heart, and after Baalim, which their fathers taught them; therefore, thus says the Lord of hosts, the God of Israel; Behold, I will feed them, even this people, with wormwood, and give them water of gall to drink. I will scatter them also among the heathen, whom neither they nor their fathers have known, and I will send a sword after them, till I have consumed them.*
> JEREMIAH 9:13–16.

> *...that you yourself walk orderly, and keep the law.*
> ACTS 21:24.

> *If any man defile the temple of God, him shall God destroy, for the temple of God is holy, which temple you are.*
> 1 CORINTHIANS 3:17.

> *Let all things be done decently and in order.*
> 1 CORINTHIANS 14:40.

> *All things are lawful for me, but all things are not expedient; all things are lawful for me, but I will not be brought under the power of any.*
> 1 CORINTHIANS 6:12.

But we know that the law is good, if a man uses it lawfully; knowing this, that the law is not made for a righteous man, but for the lawless and disobedient, for the ungodly and for sinners, for unholy and profane, for murderers of fathers and murderers of mothers, for manslayers, for whoremongers, for them who defile themselves with mankind, for kidnappers, for liars, for perjured persons, and if there be any other thing that is contrary to sound doctrine.

1 TIMOTHY 1:8–10.

For whoever shall keep the whole law, and yet offend in one point, he is guilty of all.

JAMES 2:10.

LAW OF INCREASE

I had read PMA (positive mental attitude) books by Napoleon Hill, Norman Vincent Peale, and many others, and intellectually understood the oft-mentioned concept of the law of increase. Never had I met anyone like a chiropractor who told of a boy scout seeking a $2.50 donation for some project. The chiropractor answered him, "Sure, I'd like to have $25." That chiropractor believed that his bread upon the waters came back to him tenfold. Ten was the magic number. He spoke as though he really believed and experienced this multiplication. Others say that the multiplier may be a hundred, or fifty, or even less than ten.

Does the principle of increase really work? We know it does. Observation convinces us. Plant a seed and thousands of seeds from a single plant may result in some instances, only a few in others. Some persons save and sacrifice and then lose everything in an economic crash or poor business venture. Others save and save, and their money barely multiplies at the low interest rate paid by the bank. Some invest a few dollars in a risky venture, and almost effortlessly, it returns ten thousand-fold.

If the principle applies in nature and finance, is it not reasonable to assume that it works for health, happiness, peace, love, and the many more important matters in life? "I will multiply the fruit of the trees...." (EZEKIEL 36:30).

(*See Also:* Abundance, Discipline, Foundation, Inequality, Optimism, Prosperity, Source).

Then the angel of the Lord said to her, I will multiply your descendants exceedingly, so that they shall not be counted for the multitude.

GENESIS 16:10.

But the children of Israel were fruitful and increased abundantly, multiplied and grew exceedingly mighty.

EXODUS 1:7.

And when your herds and your flocks multiply, and your silver and your gold are multiplied, and all that you have is multiplied; then your heart is lifted up, and you forget [that it was] the Lord, thy God who brought you forth out of the land of Egypt, from the house of bondage.

DEUTERONOMY 8:13–14.

Eastward he settled as far as the entrance to the wilderness this side of the river Euphrates, because their cattle had multiplied in the land of Gilead.

1 CHRONICLES 5:9.

Their sorrows shall be multiplied who hasten after another god.

PSALM 16:4.

He who loves silver will not be satisfied with silver; nor he who loves abundance, with increase. This is also vanity.

ECCLESIASTES 5:10.

Cast your bread upon the waters, for you will find it after many days. Give a serving to seven, and also to eight for you do not know what evil shall be upon the earth.

ECCLESIASTES 11:1–2.

You have multiplied the nation and not increased its joy; they rejoice before You according to the joy of harvest, as men rejoice when they divide the spoil. For You have broken the yoke of his burden and the staff of his shoulder, the rod of his oppressor....

ISAIAH 9:3–4.

For our transgressions are multiplied before You, and our sins testify against us....

ISAIAH 59:12.

I will multiply the fruit of the tree and the increase of the field, so that you need never again bear the reproach of famine among the heathen.

EZEKIEL 36:30.

You have multiplied your merchants more than the stars of heaven: the cankerworm spoils and flies away.

NAHUM 3:16.

These are they which are sown on good ground; such as hear the word, and receive it, and bring forth fruit, some thirtyfold, some sixty, some a hundred.

MARK 4:20.

Take heed what you hear: with what measure you mete, it shall be measured to you; and to you who hear shall more be given. For he who has, to him shall be given....

MARK 4:24–25.

Mercy, peace, and love be multiplied to you.

JUDE 2.

LAW OF OPPOSITES

When I began formal university study of (Keynesian) economics after some years in business, I experienced difficulty analyzing some of the strange precepts that passed for economic theory. For instance, I learned that a budget deficit was good but a budget surplus was bad, that jobs are created via inflation, that progressive taxation made us all richer, and other strange concepts. But who was I to question the sages? So, to pass test questions that defied logic and required a credibility-stretching answer, I applied the law of opposites. Too often the answer preferred by the professor was opposite of the one that seemed logical and consistent from a Christian viewpoint.

We learn today that the criminals are the oppressed of society, that failures are victims of their environment, that evil is good and good is evil, and the list goes on. It is not surprising that some speak of the world of illusion. This world, according to human invention, indeed offers illusory charms, a world filled with the inverted logic of man, while truth always reigns in God's order and laws for the governance of a free society.

(*See Also:* Conspiracy, Demagoguery, Double Standard, Envy, Expert, Idolatry.)

False witnesses did rise up. They laid to my charge that I knew not. They rewarded me evil, for good, to the spoiling of my soul.

PSALM 35:11–12.

He who justifies the wicked, and he who condemns the just, both of them alike are an abomination to the Lord. Why is there in the hand of a fool the purchase price of wisdom, since he has no heart for it?

PROVERBS 17:15–16.

Woe to those who call evil good, and good evil; who put darkness for light, and light for darkness; who put bitter for sweet, and sweet for bitter! Woe to those who are wise in their own eyes, and prudent in their own sight!

ISAIAH 5:20–21.

Every good tree bears good fruit, but a bad tree bears bad fruit. A good tree cannot bear bad fruit, nor can a bad tree bear good fruit. Every tree that does not bear good fruit is cut down and thrown into the fire. Therefore, by their fruits you will know them.

MATTHEW 7:17–20.

Brood of vipers! How can you, being evil, speak good things?...

MATTHEW 12:34.

But God has chosen the foolish things of the world to confound the wise; and God has chosen the weak things of the world to confound the things that are mighty.

1 CORINTHIANS 1:27.

Test all things; hold fast what is good. Abstain from all appearance of evil.

1 THESSALONIANS 5:21–22.

LAWYERS

He said, Woe to you also, you lawyers, for you lay men with burdens grievous to be borne, and you yourselves touch not the burdens with one of your fingers....Woe to you, lawyers! For you have taken away *the key of knowledge; you entered not in yourselves, and those who were entering in you hindered.*

LUKE 11:46, 52.

(*See:* Court System, Law, Law and Order)

LEADERSHIP

You shall provide out of all the people able men, such as fear God, men of truth, hating covetousness, and place such over them, to be rulers of thousands, and rulers of hundreds, rulers of fifties, and rulers of tens.

EXODUS 18:21.

(*See:* Character, Management, Organization)

LEASE

A certain man planted a vineyard, and set a hedge about it, and dug a place for the winefat, and built a tower, and let it out to husbandmen, and went to a far country.

MARK 12:1.

(*See:* Rent, Return on Investment)

LENDER

A good man shows favor, and lends. He will guide his affairs with discretion.

PSALM 112:5.

(*See:* Debt, Savings)

LEVERAGE, FINANCIAL

(*See:* Debt, Investment, Risk Aversion)

LIABILITY

The Bible speaks out on liability. Through descriptions, termed case law today, the Bible provides clear examples on the type and extent of liability.

Several things can be gleaned from these sample verses. First, liability under biblical law is limited: an eye for an eye, tooth for a tooth. Compare this to the outrageously high court awards in liability cases in our modern society. Second, an injured man can be compensated for loss of time, which places a value on time. Third, man is obligated to keep his home safe for guests and visitors, but that liability does not extend to trespassers. Fourth, he is responsible for pets he keeps around the house, whether bull or bulldog. If he keeps his bull or bulldog fenced, he is not responsible for injury to the trespasser.

The key word is *responsibility*. Man is responsible for his actions and carelessness. He is responsible to God; God is not responsible. In our modern society, the key words are escape from responsibility, called passing the buck. Even in states where a system of restitution operates, usually the state (i.e., taxpayers) pays restitution, not the criminal. Under His law, God imposes restraints on man, making him liable according to damages inflicted or losses sustained; man makes restitution to man in obedience to God.

(*See Also:* Discipline, Golden Rule, Judgment, Law, Losses, Private Property, Responsibility, Surety)

If men contend with each other, and one strikes the other with a stone or with his fist, and he does not die but is confined to his bed, if he rises again and walks about outside with his staff, then he who struck him shall be acquitted. He shall only pay for the loss of his time, and shall provide for him to be thoroughly healed. If a man beats his servant or his maidservant with a rod, so that he dies under his hand, he shall surely be punished. Notwithstanding, if he remains alive a day or two, he shall not be punished, for he is his property. If men fight, and hurt a woman with child, so that her fruit departs from her, yet no lasting harm follows, he shall surely be punished accordingly as the woman's husband imposes on him; and he shall pay as the judges determine.

But if any lasting harm follows, then you shall give life for life, eye for eye, tooth for tooth, hand for hand, foot for foot, burn for burn, wound for wound, stripe for stripe.

                                                                    EXODUS 21:18–25.

If an ox gore a man or a woman, that they die, then the ox shall be surely stoned, and his flesh not be eaten; but the owner of the ox shall be quit. But if the ox were wont to push with his horn in the past, and it had been testified to his owner, and he has not kept him in, but that he has killed a man or a woman, the ox shall be stoned, and his owner also shall be put to death.

                                                                    EXODUS 21:28–29.

If a man shall open a pit, or if a man shall dig a pit, and not cover it, and an ox or ass fall into it, the owner of the pit shall make it good, and give money to the owner of them; and the dead beast shall be his.

                                                                    EXODUS 21:33–34.

If a man shall cause a field or vineyard to be eaten, and lets loose his beast, and it feeds in another man's field, of the best of his own field, and of the best of his own vineyard, shall he make restitution.

                                                                    EXODUS 22:5.

When you build a new house, then you shall make a battlement for your roof, that you bring not blood upon your house, if any man· fall from there.

                                                                    DEUTERONOMY 22:8.

LIBERAL

Nineteenth-century economic liberals believed in the free market system as the means to greater freedom for producer and consumer alike. Twentieth-century liberals—economic and political—look upon the free market system as the cause of economic and political woes, and propose more government control over our incomes and lives. One person has defined a modern liberal as someone liberal with other people's money. Another person has described them as humanitarians with guillotines. Still another has likened liberals to penguins: The penguin flies backward because he doesn't care to see where he's going, but wants to see where he's been.

Many people who call themselves liberals may not be. Others who call themselves liberals are closet socialists. Americans are confused on this issue as some studies have shown: Americans tend to talk conservative but vote liberal. For example, in one Northeast state, the majority of people talk like dyed-in-the-wool conservatives. Yet, throughout the state they voted for liberals who were rated by one organization as the most anti–free enterprise politicians in the country based on their congressional voting record.

> Avoid the man or woman whose tenderness pours out in an extravagant flood upon the children and animals. These are dangerous people. For they can justify the atrocities of war, the burning of cities, by some vague and specious explanation; they can, in silence, or with vague dissent, look upon injustice, and feel only indifference, or, worse, some perverted pleasure.[1]

We all know a few people who fit that description, and a few who fit Alexander Herzen's statement from a *Critique of Dostoyevsky*: "Compassionate love may be very strong. It sobs, it burns, then it wipes away its tears—and it does nothing."

Discussion is difficult with a liberal; argumentation is impossible. Often a liberal argues from the perspective of legalism, whereas believers speak of justice. For a liberal, justice means social justice, a remaking of society in a socialist image. Notice, too, that a liberal sprinkles language with metaphoric descriptions. For example, a Massachusetts senator described energy problems as trying to swim upstream against a strong current, yards away from a dam. (Certainly his description was more colorful than my recap of it.) Yet, if a believer employs figures of speech, metaphors, and the like, the liberal will immediately accuse him of exaggeration.

We must be careful with labels, especially with those that apply to ourselves, for we may find that some of our friends who think exactly as we do carry quite opposite labels. We live in a period in which language has been deliberately confused and definitions perverted. What hidden objectives underlie this tyranny of words?

(*See Also:* Communication, Demagogue, Law of Opposites, Liberalism, Maturity, Nonalignment)

> *Woe to them who are wise in their own eyes, and prudent in their own sight!*
>
> ISAIAH 5:21.

> *Behold, a king shall reign in righteousness, and princes shall rule in judgment....The vile person shall be no more called liberal, nor the churl said to be bountiful. For the vile person will speak villany, and his heart will work iniquity, to practice hypocrisy, and to utter error against the Lord, to make empty the soul of the hungry, and he will cause the drink of the thirsty to fail. The instruments of the churl are evil. He*

---

[1]Taylor Caldwell, *Let Love Come Last* (New York: Jově, 1981), p. 58.

devises wicked devices to destroy the poor with lying words, even when the needy speaks right. But the liberal devises liberal things; and by liberal things shall he stand.

ISAIAH 32:1, 5–8.

Desiring to be teachers of the law, understanding neither what they say nor whereof they affirm.

1 TIMOTHY 1:7.

LIBERALISM

Liberalism in the 1980s differs little, if at all, in principle from socialism, humanism, welfarism, Keynesianism, statism, or Marxism. Its language may differ, but its goals are essentially identical: power, control over incomes and wealth, and establishment of the state as the supreme entity, the maker and giver of all law.

Liberals may weep over the poor in public or wax eloquently over the disadvantaged, criminals, or darter snails (but not over unborn babies being aborted), but to finance their causes, they insist on expropriated funds (i.e., tax money) administered by public institutions under their control. Like communism, liberalism relies on hypocrisy, crisis situations, and phony issues to centralize power in the hands of the state (as long as liberals control it).

Liberalism offers a dangerous doctrine because despite apparently convincing arguments, it aims for no less than complete control over our lives and incomes from before birth to after death. Innocent sounding phrases such as mixed economy, incomes policies, federal assistance programs, and national health care betray the real intent of liberalism. Each and every program amounts to a high degree of government intervention and centralization of political and economic power.

Although prompted by good intentions, such a program [of liberalism] is usually the outgrowth of egomania fanned by self-hypnotism. "I am right. Those who disagree are wrong. If they can't be forced into line, they must be destroyed."[1]

Those who believe that liberals are fair, open-minded, and compromising have never really locked horns with them. Everything they accuse their conservative opponents of more appropriately describes liberals and their doctrine of liberalism. For instance, a liberal acquaintance of mine was in charge of some government program (as they so often are). To be "fair," he created a panel of economists consisting of three Keynesian economists, a Marxist economist, and then as an

---

[1]Henry Grady Weaver, *Mainspring of Human Progress* (Irvington-on-Hudson, N.Y.: Foundation for Economic Education, 1972), p. 40.

afterthought, he added a Chicago School monetarist. To him that was balance and fairness. The panel was loaded four-to-one, decidedly left, or statist, on most issues, and five-to-zero on some issues. Rather than worry over political labels, Christians must resist a common enemy—secular humanism—and see the relationships between what the Bible says and events in the world around us.

(*See Also:* Bureaucracy, Cradle-to-Grave, Demagoguery, Envy, Law of Opposites, Liberal)

> Then there arose certain of the synagogue, which is called the synagogue of the Libertines, and Cyrenians, and Alexandrians, and of them of Cilicia and of Asia, disputing with Stephen. They were not able to resist the wisdom and the spirit by which he spoke. Then they bribed men, who said, We have heard him speak blasphemous words against Moses, and against God. They stirred up the people, and the elders, and the scribes, and came upon him, and caught him, and brought him to the council. And set up false witnesses, who said, This man ceases not to speak blasphemous words against this holy place, and the law; for we have heard him say that this Jesus of Nazareth shall destroy this place, and shall change the customs which Moses delivered us.
>
> ACTS 6:9–14.

> Even as they did not like to retain God in their knowledge, God gave them over to a reprobate mind, to do those things which are not convenient; being filled with unrighteousness, fornication, wickedness, covetousness, maliciousness; full of envy, murder, deceit, malignity; whisperers, backbiters, haters of God, despiteful, proud, boasters, inventors of evil things, disobedient to parents, without understanding, covenant breakers, without natural affection, implacable, unmerciful, who knowing the judgment of God, that they who commit such things are worthy of death, not only do the same, but have pleasure in them who do them.
>
> ROMANS 1:28–32.

LIBERTARIANISM

Libertarianism may be described as freedom without essential reference to God, often Kantian in logic. That, however, does not mean that libertarians are necessarily atheistic; a great many believers are counted among their ranks. Occasional socialists also appear in their memberships, or those who espouse Social Christian doctrine.

Libertarianism is grounded on ethically neutral principles. The great moral principle underlying the logic of libertarianism may be summarized as: Each person may do whatever he or she wishes as long as each does not infringe on the rights of any other. In areas where interests overlap, then courts will decide.

Although there is a strong position with respect to fulfillment of contracts in libertarianism, fundamental moral principles found in the Judeo-Christian precepts may be absent. On the question of moral issues, the libertarian falls into a bottomless trap or bedpartnership with socialism.

For example, in the political platform of the Libertarian Party, government is defined as an institution extremely limited in powers. However, even though many libertarians may agree to the necessity of national defense, just as many will argue against stockpiling weapons. Peaceful trade, not war, is the battle cry.

Libertarians strongly support religious freedom, economic freedom, and all other freedoms. However, they extend that same contractual relationship into areas in which Christians are uncomfortable or to which they object. Libertarians are particularly vociferous on victimless crimes. What a community may call criminal activity, some libertarians may describe as two adults consummating a contractual agreement, such as prostitution, drug purchases and sales, homosexuality, or pornography.

Believers, of course, can find much in common with many ideas propounded by libertarians: limited civil government; an efficient court system; elimination of federal income taxation and central banking; return to the gold standard; spiritual freedom; peace; enforcement of contracts; free market system; and many other similar institutional arrangements of a free society. If they tied that bundle with the rule of God, it would be a handsome package.

(*See Also:* Contract, Exchange, Freedom, Individualism, Private Property, Rule of Law, Tinstaafl, Voluntarism)

Give none offense, neither to the Jews, nor to the Gentiles, nor to the church of God.

1 CORINTHIANS 10:32.

Let no man therefore judge you in meat, or in drink, or in respect of a holy day, or of the new moon, or of the Sabbath days.

COLOSSIANS 2:16.

Wherefore, if you be dead with Christ from the rudiments of the world, why, as though living in the world, are you subject to ordinances, ... after the commandments and doctrines of men?

COLOSSIANS 2:20, 22.

LIBERTY

"...with liberty and justice for all." No one can explain liberty without reference to God, our Creator and Source. Justice does not mean social justice, the molding of society and man's behavior according to ephemeral human objectives. Justice makes sense only with reference to divine law and order. Throughout the entire Bible, God tells us how to achieve liberty and maintain that liberty by practicing His laws daily, which hardly implies that liberty and justice come without work and discipline.

Liberty is not unrestricted freedom. Unlimited freedom is destructive. Anarchy would reign, followed by implementation of a totalitarian system. Unlimited freedom is libertinism, which was so forcefully advocated during the Hippie movement.

God, being the Absolute, is the only One absolutely free. We, on the other hand, are subject to the rule of God. Freedom from this law, so widely advocated today by our humanists, will always end in freedom *from* liberty. Liberty is destroyed. Liberty is maximized under discipline, especially self-discipline. We become rich by disciplining ourselves not to spend. Our country becomes wealthy by not squandering resources through heavy taxation and inflation. We gain liberty by not being libertine. In other words, all comes at a cost.

"The something we call the free society does not come out of nothing. Such institutions as the free market and limited government are not among the marks of homo sapiens wherever he appears; these manifestations are rare events in human history...." There are things seen and things not seen. We see the institutions of our common life—free or collectivized—but we do not see the fundamental assumptions and premises about life, the universe, and man, which give rise to these institutions, and support them in both our sentiments and intellect."[1]

Justice and liberty for all come about because of those who sacrifice their lives and fight to retain liberty, those who accept the responsibility and mandate God has given us, and those who realize that a continuing price must be paid by everyone and every generation if we sell our freedom and birthright for a few government subsidies (see James 1:25).

Very frankly, most Americans who have come through the public education system in recent decades have only a foggy notion of liberty or its costs. They will fight hard and complain bitterly for and about their government handouts—subsidies, welfare, public schooling, and so forth, and they react in knee-jerk fashion, the way they have been taught, to government-created problems, always demanding more government. Will they get what they want and deserve and drag the rest of us along into human bondage?

---

[1]Edmund A. Opitz, *Religion and Capitalism: Allies, Not Enemies* (New Rochelle, N.Y.: Arlington House Press, 1974), p. 174.

(*See Also:* Foundation, Freedom, Free Society, Justice, Law, Libertarianism, Responsibility)

The rulers knew not whether I went, or what I did.

NEHEMIAH *2:16.*

So shall I keep Your law continually for ever and ever. And I will walk at liberty, for I seek Your precepts. I will speak of Your testimonies also before kings, and will not be ashamed.

PSALM *119:44–46.*

Be not conformed to this world: but be transformed by the renewing of your mind....

ROMANS *12:2.*

Conscience, I say, not your own, but of the other; for why is my liberty judged of another man's conscience? For if I by grace be a partaker, why am I evil spoken of for that for which I give thanks?

1 CORINTHIANS *10:29–30.*

Now the Lord is that Spirit; and where the Spirit of the Lord is, there is liberty.

2 CORINTHIANS *3:17.*

Because of false brothers unawares brought in, who came in privily to spy out our liberty which we have in Christ Jesus, that they might bring us into bondage.

GALATIANS *2:4.*

Stand fast therefore in the liberty wherewith Christ has made us free, and be not entangled again with the yoke of bondage.

GALATIANS *5:1.*

For, brothers, you have been called to liberty; only use not liberty for an occasion to the flesh, but by love serve one another.

GALATIANS *5:13.*

Whoever looks into the perfect law of liberty, and continues therein, he being not a forgetful hearer, but a doer of the work, this man shall be blessed in his deed.

JAMES *1:25.*

LONG-RANGE PLANNING

(*See:* Economic Forecasts, Forecasting, Strategic Planning)

LOSSES

In any type of society losses arise. In a free society, the risk of erring and losing falls to the one who has responsibility for the erroneous decisions. In a controlled society, losses are passed on to the weakest segment of that society. For example, many states as well as the federal government carry risk pools for medical malpractice, political risks in overseas investment, disaster risks, and so on. Well, we know that the governments do not, and cannot, absorb risks because they produce no income, nor do they in most instances charge a sufficiently high risk premium. Who bears the losses? We, the taxpayer, carry the risks and bear the losses.

A free society provides us with learning experiences. If we err, do not obey God's commandments, then only those who are responsible carry losses. If we subvert God's laws, then we bear the losses. What a just way to learn! What discipline! How careful we become when we cannot pass the bill to others!

(*See Also:* Compensation, Liability, Risk Aversion, Self-Discipline, Strategic Planning)

A curse, if you will not obey the commandments of the Lord your God, but turn aside out of the way ... to go after other gods, which you have not known.

DEUTERONOMY 11:28.

Woe to the wicked! It shall be ill with him, for the reward of his hands shall be given him.

ISAIAH 3:11.

...He who has not, from him shall be taken even that which he has.

MARK 4:25.

MAJORITY RULE

You shall not follow a multitude to do evil; neither shall you testify in a dispute so as to turn aside after many to pervert justice.

Exodus 23:2.

(*See:* Crowd Psychology, Remnant, Rule by Decree)

MANAGEMENT

Managers control, direct, organize, plan, challenge, and perform administrative functions necessary to successful leadership. Managers are neither superior nor inferior to organizational subordinates. Each has duties. Through specialization and cooperation, each can accomplish more and lighten the physical burden of everyone. Moses learned the advantages of delegation of authority and responsibility. Rather than reduce his power and prestige, delegation of authority actually enhanced his sphere of influence and ability to lead.

Management organization in the Bible is both pyramidal—with power and responsibility radiating outward and downward from a vertex of authority—as well as horizontal, i.e., individual responsibility to other organizations such as the Church. In modern management terminology, we see elements of both Theory X and Theory Y, that is, of centralized authority and participatory management.

Centralization of power establishes constraints and discipline in contractual relationships with others. However, decisions are essentially decentralized, resting primarily with the family who has basic responsibilities for the education, welfare, security, health, and so on of its members. Business organizations profit through similar organizational structures that allow for individual responsibility while still protecting the integrity of the organization, providing direction from the top to accomplish its mission.

Management has a particularly difficult task. Not everyone is suited for it. Certainly we admire excellence of a rare poet or artist. When our vehicles break down, we appreciate skills of an outstanding mechanic. But we hardly notice an outstanding security guard, lawn maintenance person, or an assistant manager's assistant, let alone properly reward superior performance. Such elitism represents poor management, certainly not consistent with the Word. A successful manager knows that "God will bring every work into judgment" (ECCLESIASTES 12:14).

(*See Also:* Contract, Cooperation, Productivity, Responsibility, Self-Discipline, Work)

Joseph found grace in his sight, and he served him. He made him overseer of his house, and all that he had put into his hand.
                                                                              GENESIS 39:4.

When Moses' father-in-law saw all that he did to the people, he said, What is this thing that you are doing to the people? Why do you sit alone, and all the people stand by you from morning until evening? ... You will surely wear away, both you and this people who are with you, for this thing is too heavy for you; you are not able to perform it yourself alone.
                                                                           EXODUS 18:14, 18.

You shall provide out of all people able men, such as fear God, men of truth, hating covetousness; and place such over them, to be rulers of thousands, and rulers of hundreds, rulers of fifties, and rulers of tens. ... So it shall be easier for yourself, and they shall bear the burden with you.
                                                                         EXODUS 18:21–22.

David numbered the people who were with him, and set captains of thousands and captains of hundreds over them.... But the people answered, You shall not go forth, for if we flee, they will not care for us; neither if half of us die will they care for us; but now you are worth ten thousand of us. Therefore now you are of more help to us in the city.
                                                                         2 SAMUEL 18:1, 3.

He becomes poor who deals with a slack hand; but the hand of the diligent makes rich.
                                                                         PROVERBS 10:4.

Be diligent to know the state of your flocks, and look well to your herds. For riches are not for ever, and does the crown endure to every generation?

                                                                    PROVERBS 27:23–24.

Jesus called them to Him, and said, You know that the princes of the Gentiles exercise dominion over them, and they who are great exercise authority over them. But it shall not be so among you; but whoever shall be great among you, let him be your minister; and whoever will be chief among you, let him be your servant; even as the Son of man came not to be ministered to, but to minister, and to give His life a ransom for many.

                                                                    MATTHEW 20:25–28.

Which of you, having a servant plowing or feeding cattle, will say to him by and by, when he is come from the field, Go and sit down to meat? And will not rather say to him, Make ready wherewith I may sup, and gird yourself, and serve me, till I have eaten and drunk, and afterward you shall eat and drink? Does he thank the servant because he did the things that were commanded him? I think not.

                                                                    LUKE 17:7–9.

MANAGEMENT BY OBJECTIVES

For we are saved by hope; but hope that is seen is not hope; for what a man sees, why does he yet hope for?

                                                                    ROMANS 8:24.

(*See:* Business, Management, Strategic Planning)

MARKET ECONOMY

In a pure market economy, all prices are determined and all transactions occur when buyers and sellers freely contract and when information is available. Market imperfections creep in when groups of buyers and/or sellers collude, withhold products from the market, or when information is unavailable or expensive to acquire. Market imperfections result in prices different from those found in a perfectly free market.

For instance, if citrus growers destroy part of their orange crop to drive up prices, many potential buyers will consume fewer or no oranges. If a group of buyers purchases and hoards large quantities of silver, the near-term price will rise rather precipitously. In the long run, however, aberrations will disappear in a free market.

Sometimes an erroneous argument is advanced, because of these usually short-lived imperfections, that the free market fosters monopolies. In a free market no monopoly can sustain itself for long. A firm retains monopolistic powers only with government help. Suppose, for instance, that a firm, due to technological superiority, acquires some high degree of market power. First, what price will the monopolist seek? High or low? Conventional street wisdom says high,, on the assumption that a monopolist can sell any volume at any price and generate huge profits.

Assume this were possible. In a market economy, no special privileges, such as patent rights or protection (by legislative fiat) from competitors prevail. In a market economy, entrepreneurs continually seek profit opportunities. Therefore, a high-profit enterprise will attract competitors or imitators who cut prices and erode profits of a budding monopolist. Consequently, the monopolist may well opt for a strategy of low price and large market (high volume), rather than high price and small market to forestall potential competition.

Without coercion a producer cannot maintain monopolistic power. Coercion requires force. But buyers would protest and resist a monopolist who employed a private army to restrain trade. Therefore, those who refuse to obey the rules of freedom and the market economy seek government intervention. They let government, the third party, supply the force. Hence, we have situations such as single-firm utility companies—privately or publicly owned water, gas, sewage, telephone, and electric companies from which the consumer must buy or do without.

Other companies support government licensing or rules (e.g., banking prior to 1984, or airlines before 1978) to limit domestic competitors or impose high tariffs or quotas to limit foreign imports (e.g., motorcycles, baseball gloves), or create federal market boards (e.g., citrus fruits, milk, walnuts), promulgate legislation to enforce a labor monopoly in certain skills and geographical areas (e.g., physicians).

For the consumer, the Lord's way is best. The free flow of products in a market economy results in the largest quantity, highest quality, and most diverse selection of goods and services at lowest prices. Before the communist takeovers in Cuba and Nicaragua, fruits and vegetables were cheap, plentiful, and exported. Under communist rule, food and other agricultural products have become scarce, even rationed, high priced, and imported. Those who hate the free market hate both humanity and God; their rhetoric is best ignored.

(*See Also:* Abundance, Business, Demand and Supply, Free Society, Golden Rule, Prosperity)

> *He bought a parcel of a field...for a hundred pieces of money.*
> Genesis 33:19.

You shall not steal, neither deal falsely, neither lie to one another.
                                                                    LEVITICUS *19:11.*

You shall do no unrighteousness in measurement of length, weight, or volume. Just balances, just weights, ... shall you have: I am the Lord your God, which brought you out of the land of Egypt.
                                                                    LEVITICUS *19:35–36.*

If you sell anything to your neighbor, or buy anything of your neighbor's hand, you shall not oppress one another.
                                                                    LEVITICUS *25:14.*

You shall buy meat of them for money, that you may eat; and you shall also buy water of them for money, that you may drink.
                                                                    DEUTERONOMY *2:6.*

For the Lord your God brings you into a good land, a land of brooks of water, of fountains and depths that spring out of valleys and hills; a land of wheat and barley, and vines, and fig trees, and pomegranates, a land of olive oil, and honey; a land wherein you shall eat bread without scarceness, you shall not lack any thing in it; a land where stones are iron, and out of whose hills you may dig brass.
                                                                    DEUTERONOMY *8:7–9.*

King David said to Ornan, Nay; but I will verily buy it for the full price, for I will not take that which is yours for the Lord, nor offer burnt offerings without cost. So David gave to Ornan for the place six hundred shekels of gold by weight.
                                                                    1 CHRONICLES *21:24–25.*

That you may buy speedily with this money bullocks, rams, lambs, with their meat offerings, and their drink offerings, and offer them upon the altar of the house of your God which is in Jerusalem.
                                                                    EZRA *7:17.*

He who withholds corn, the people shall curse him; but blessing shall be upon the head of him who sells it.
                                                                    PROVERBS *11:26.*

It is good for nothing, it is good for nothing, says the buyer but when he has gone his way, then he boasts.
                                                                    PROVERBS *20:14.*

The profit of the earth is for all: the king himself is served by the field.... When goods increase, they are increased who eat them; and what good is there to the owners, saving the beholding of them in their eyes?

ECCLESIASTES *5:9, 11.*

Butter and honey shall he eat, that he may know to refuse the evil, and choose the good.

ISAIAH *7:15.*

Judah, and the land of Israel, they were your merchants. They traded in your market wheat of Minnith, and Pannag, and honey, and oil, and balm. Damascus was your merchant in the multitude of the wares of your making, for the multitude of all riches, in the wine of Helbon, and white wool. Dan also and Javan going to and fro occupied your fairs: bright iron, cassia, and calamus were in your market. Dedan was your merchant in precious clothes for chariots. Arabia, and all the princes of Kedar, they occupied with you in lambs, and rams, and goats: in these were they your merchants. The merchants of Sheba and Raamah, they were your merchants; they occupied in your fairs with chief of all spices, and with all precious stones, and gold. Haran, and Canneh, and Eden, the merchants of Sheba, Asshur, and Chilmad, were your merchants. These were your merchants in all sorts of things, in blue clothes, and broidered work, and in chests of rich apparel, bound with cords, and made of cedar, among your merchandise.

EZEKIEL *27:17–24.*

The foolish said to the wise, Give us of your oil, for our lamps are gone out. But the wise answered saying, Not so, lest there be not enough for us and you; but go rather to them who sell, and buy for yourselves.

MATTHEW *25:8–9.*

Now there is at Jerusalem by the sheep market a pool....

JOHN *5:2.*

MARRIAGE

With the family as the basic building block in God's free society, the endurance of the institution of marriage should come as no surprise. Although Islam allows for a maximum of four wives, should wealth and circumstance permit, in practice, most

Muslims find that one suffices. Wisely, Christianity counsels monogamy. However, many "Christian" Americans act like Muslims, who, while not keeping four wives at once, may indeed have four wives, one at a time. The difference seems more semantical than real. Stories of harem intrigues and discontent should discourage any potential polygamist. Keeping a paramour has driven more than one man to bankruptcy and despair.

Since marriage is a contract between husband and wife, before God, it should neither be entered into cavalierly nor readily broken. Certainly the Bible permits divorce; it particularly discourages pairing with an unbeliever. Marriage with a believer not only allows for perpetuation of the human race in a godly state but for passing along Christian ideals, precepts, and laws to succeeding generations.

Two key messages appear in the verses: One is that marriage is a serious matter and that choosing a bride or a groom (whether by self or family) is not a Saturday night special. Contrary to the cry of feminists, marriage partners have an exceedingly important role to play, and not just in the bedroom. The woman is a helpmeet for her husband and a cornerstone of the family. The husband is the head of the wife and the family, himself under the headship of Jesus Christ.

(*See Also:* Children, Family, Feminism, Maturity, Responsibility, Women, Work)

...For Adam there was not found a help meet for him.

Genesis 2:20.

They [the priests, the sons of Aaron] shall not take a wife who is a whore, or profane....

Leviticus 21:7.

He [the high priest] shall take a wife in her virginity. A widow, or a divorced woman, or profane, or a harlot, these shall he not take; but he shall take a virgin of his own people to wife.

Leviticus 21:13–14.

This is the thing that the Lord commands concerning the daughters of Zelophe—had, saying, let them marry to whom they think best, only to the family of the tribe of their father shall they marry .... Every daughter, who possesses an inheritance in any tribe of the children of Israel, shall be wife to one of the family of the tribe of her father, that the children of Israel may enjoy every man the inheritance of his fathers.

Numbers 36:6, 8.

Let your fountain be blessed, and rejoice with the wife of your youth. Let her be as the loving hind and pleasant roe; let her breasts satisfy you at all times; and be ravished always with her love.

PROVERBS 5:18–9.

A virtuous woman is a crown to her husband; but she who makes ashamed is as rottenness in his bones.

PROVERBS 12:4.

It is better to dwell in a corner of the housetop than with a brawling woman in a wide house.

PROVERBS 21:9.

A continual dropping on a very rainy day and a contentious woman are alike.

PROVERBS 27:15.

Who can find a virtuous woman? For her price is far above rubies.

PROVERBS 31:10.

Have you not read, that He who made them at the beginning made them male and female, and said, For this cause shall a man leave father and mother, and shall cleave to his wife, and the two shall be one flesh? Wherefore they are no more twain, but one flesh. What therefore God has joined together, let no man put asunder.

MATTHEW 19:4–6.

Whoever puts away his wife and marries another commits adultery; and whoever marries her who is put away from her husband commits adultery.

LUKE 16:18.

Wives, submit yourselves to your own husbands, as to the Lord. For the husband is the head of the wife, even as Christ is the head of the church; and He is the savior of the body. Therefore as the church is subject to Christ, so let wives be to their own husbands in everything. Husbands, love your wives, even as Christ also loved the church, and gave Himself for it.... So ought men to love their wives as their own bodies. He who loves his wife loves himself.

EPHESIANS 5:22–25, 28.

Marriage is honorable in all, and the bed undefiled; but whoremongers and adulterers God will judge.

HEBREWS 13:4.

MARXIST

You shall make no covenant with them, or with their gods. They shall not dwell in your land, lest they make you sin against Me, for if you serve their gods, it will surely be a snare to you.

EXODUS 23:32–33.

(*See:* Communist, Statist, World Government)

MATERIALISM

I well remember a discussion I once had with several foreign college classmates who had concluded that the people in their (less-developed and poorer) countries were more spiritual than materialistic Americans. What struck me as incongruous, if not hypocritical, was that these students coveted American wealth, took economic development courses to learn how to make their countries materially rich (which often boiled down to some scheme to transfer American wealth to them), and discussed get-rich-quick possibilities in their own countries or how to live in the United States without working. In conversations with foreign presidents or prime ministers, economic ministers, and diplomats, I do not recall one conversation that was even remotely spiritual.

Perhaps a have-not can readily claim spirituality. But when all communications are devoid of it, it is hardly convincing. In fact, a more defendable position is to argue that America is materially wealthy because of its spiritual origins, its practicing faith, and its generosity throughout the world.

The rich man's difficulty of entry into heaven does not arise from his material acquisitions but total preoccupation with that wealth. Materialism means putting trust in goods and wealth and gold and money—in other words, idolatry. It excludes God. It openly denies God, the Source of every material thing, whether we own it (for a while) or not. Put God first and our needs will be met. Those who put God last—if at all—have a real problem. Materialism is not the exclusive domain of the rich. It may be more pervasive among the poor.

(*See Also:* Communism, Economic Growth, Elitism, Envy, Foreign Aid, Welfarism)

If I have made gold my hope, or have said to the fine gold, You are my confidence; If I rejoiced because my wealth was great, and because my hand had gotten much ... this also was an iniquity to be punished by the judge: for I should have denied the God who is above.

JOB 31:24–25, 28.

Some trust in chariots, and some in horses; but we will remember the name of the Lord our God.

PSALM 20:7.

They who trust in their wealth, and boast themselves in the multitude of their riches, none of them can by any means redeem his brother, nor give to God a ransom for him.

PSALM 49:6–7.

All the labor of man is for his mouth, and yet the appetite is not filled.

ECCLESIASTES 6:7.

They shall cast their silver in the streets, and their gold shall be removed. Their silver and their gold shall not be able to deliver them in the day of the wrath of the Lord. They shall not satisfy their souls, neither fill their bowels, because it is the stumbling block of their iniquity.

EZEKIEL 7:19.

They drank wine, and praised the gods of gold, and of silver, of brass, of iron, of wood, and of stone.

DANIEL 5:4.

The cares of this world, and the deceitfulness of riches, and the lusts of other things entering in, choke the word, and it becomes unfruitful.

MARK 4:19.

...How hard is it for them who trust in riches to enter into the kingdom of God!

MARK 10:24.

When Simon saw that through laying on of the apostles' hands the Holy Ghost was given, he offered them money, saying, Give me also this power, that on whomever I lay hands he may receive the Holy Ghost. But Peter said to him, Your money perish with you, because you have thought that the gift of God may be purchased with money. You have neither part nor lot in this matter, for your heart is not right in the sight of God. Repent, therefore, of this your wickedness, and pray God, if

*perhaps the thought of your heart may be forgiven you, for I perceive
that you are in the gall of bitterness, and in the bond of iniquity.*

ACTS 8:18–23.

MATURITY

Being children of God does not mean we should remain forever children, forsaking responsibility and the wonderful experiences that accompany maturity. God expects us to be mature, responsible adults; whereas statist governments encourage us to remain immature, irresponsible children forever dependent upon the state. We cannot expect to be simultaneously wards of the state and good Christians.

Dr. Hobart Mowrer, a well-known psychiatrist, explains childish behavior this way: "A child can operate in either of two ways: (a) of his own free will or (b) under parental compulsion."[1] Before reading more of Dr. Mowrer's remarks, let's substitute the word *person* for child, and *state* for parental; now reread the preceding statement. "By acting maturely and responsibly, the child enjoys many privileges and is indeed 'free.'"[2] He says that if the child forgets or ignores first principles, he loses freedom and self-direction. Ignore God's laws, and we surrender freedom and control over our affairs to some human authority.

Dr. Mowrer has a further word on maturity. "Historically, in both literate and non-literate societies, human beings are supposed to have reached the age of discretion by early adolescence; yet here [in the United States] we have the spectacle of grown men and women soberly insisting that, in effect, they cannot tell right from wrong—and that no one else can."[3]

(*See Also:* Accountability, Cradle-to-Grave, Crowd Psychology, Self-Discipline, Youth Cultism)

*His parents answered them and said, We know that this is our son, and
that he was born blind; but by what means he now sees, we know not,
or who has opened his eyes, we know not; he is of age, ask him; he
shall speak for himself.*

JOHN 9:20–21.

*When I was a child, I spoke as a child, I understood as a child, I
thought as a child; but when I became a man, I put away childish*

[1]O. Hobart Mowrer. *The Crisis in Psychiatry and Religion* (New York: D. Van Nostrand, 1961), p. 30.

[2]Ibid., p. 33.

[3]Ibid., p. 41.

things. For now we see through a glass darkly, but then face-to-face; now I know in part, but then shall I know even as also I am known.

1 CORINTHIANS 13:11–12.

Brothers, be not children in understanding; however, in malice be babes, but in understanding be men.

1 CORINTHIANS 14:20.

Flee also youthful lusts: but follow righteousness, faith, charity, peace, with them who call on the Lord out of a pure heart. But foolish and unlearned questions avoid, knowing that they do gender strifes.

2 TIMOTHY 2:22–23.

That the aged man be sober, grave, temperate, sound in faith, in charity, in patience. The aged women likewise, that they be in behavior as becomes holiness, not slanderers, not given to much wine, teachers of good things, that they may teach the young women to be sober, to love their husbands, to love their children, to be discreet, chaste, keepers at home, good, obedient to their own husbands, that the Word of God be not blasphemed.

TITUS 2:2–5.

MILITARY

War is ugly. Good Christians prefer peace and trade to war. Wars fought in biblical times were for defense of justice and the nation and for suppression of evil.

In a television comedy, two opposing generals prayed their separate, but identical prayers to the same God, asking for victory. This hypocrisy evinces in today's vicious political wars fought for world domination and economic advantages.

Biblical wars, fought in the name of God, were, first, to destroy evil, and then to restore godly order. For instance, the Canaanites were under judicial sentence by God; they were engaged in every kind of perverse and degenerate activity. "Virtually every kind of perversion was a religious act: and large classes of sacred male and female prostitutes were a routine part of the holy places. Thus, God ordered all the Canaanites to be killed (DEUTERONOMY 2:34; 3:6; 20:16–18; JOSHUA 11:14), both because they were under God's death sentence, and to avoid the contamination of Israel."[1]

---

[1]Rousas John Rushdoony, *The Institutes of Biblical Law* (Nutley, N.J.: The Craig Press, 1973), p. 279.

Rules of war are well outlined in the Bible. Above all, wars were not elevated to the high priority they have been in this century. There was a draft system (discussed elsewhere); but the continuity of family and life took preference over soldiering. Wars were primarily defensive. Where offensive actions were undertaken, they were against other men and their institutions, and not against the earth. But the best of all worlds is peace in a free society reconstructed under the rule of God.

(*See Also:* Draft, Family, Law and Order, Military Defense, War)

Every man of the children of Israel shall pitch by his own standard, with the ensign of their father's house, far off about the tabernacle of the congregation shall they pitch.

NUMBERS 2:2.

So there were delivered out of the thousands of Israel, a thousand of every tribe, twelve thousand armed for war.

NUMBERS 31:5.

When you besiege a city for a long time, while making war against it to take it, you shall not destroy its trees by wielding an axe against them; if you can eat of them, do not cut them down to use in the siege, for the tree of the field is man's food.

DEUTERONOMY 20:19.

When the army goes out against your enemies, then keep yourself from every wicked thing. If there is any man among you who becomes unclean by some occurrence in the night, then he shall go outside the camp; he shall not come inside the camp. But it shall be, when evening comes, that he shall wash himself with water; and when the sun sets, he may come into the camp again. Also you shall have a place outside the camp, where you may go out; and you shall have an implement among your equipment, and when you sit down outside, you shall dig with it and turn and cover your refuse. For the Lord your God walks in the midst of your camp, to deliver you and give your enemies over to you; therefore your camp shall be holy, that He may see no unclean thing among you, and turn away from you.

DEUTERONOMY 23:9–14.

...For he had nine hundred chariots of iron; and twenty years he mightily oppressed the children of Israel.

JUDGES 4:3.

Rebuke the company of spearmen, the multitude of the bulls, with the calves of the people, till every one submit himself with pieces of silver; scatter the people who delight in war.

PSALM *68:30.*

The soldiers likewise demanded of him saying, And what shall we do? And he said to them, Do violence to no man, neither accuse any falsely; and be content with your wages.

LUKE *3:14.*

MILITARY DEFENSE

During the past two decades, the United States has steadily turned from a defensive arsenal to an offensive one. Not only is this a suicidal policy, it is not a Christian one. When wars must be fought, they are primarily defensive. Notice, for example, in DEUTERONOMY 17:16 the restriction on maintaining a large supply of horses. In modern terminology, horses are offensive weapons. It is difficult to justify war on biblical grounds when the arsenal largely comprises offensive weapons.

Were Christ and His followers pacifists? No one can possibly conclude that either from the language or actions of either Christ or His disciples. His apostles did not spend so much time in jail because they were pacifists.

When Jesus was asked if it is lawful to give tribute to Caesar, He asked to see a penny. "Whose image and superscription has it?" He asked. They answered, "Caesar's." "Render therefore unto Caesar the things that are Caesar's, and to God the things that are God's" (LUKE 20:25). This is a defensive statement, not a pacifying one. When Caesar begins claiming God's things for his own, it's time for military defense, for it is a serious matter.

On one hand, except for those exempt from the draft, men have every obligation to defend an ungodly attack on their nation and a moral responsibility to support military defense with time, effort, and money. On the other hand, if Caesar drafts young men for an ungodly war, then, I believe, they have a moral right to refuse to fight or even support it.

(*See Also:* Accountability, Discipline, Draft, Family, Freedom, Law, Military, One Worldism, Private Property)

When Abram heard that his brother was taken captive, he armed his trained servants, born in his own house, three hundred and eighteen, and pursued them into Dan.

GENESIS *14:14.*

He shall not multiply horses for himself, nor cause the people to return to Egypt to multiply horses, for the Lord has said to you, You shall not return to that way again.

DEUTERONOMY 17:16.

Rehoboam dwelled in Jerusalem, and built cities for defense in Judah....He fortified the strongholds, and put captains in them, and store of food, and of oil and wine. In several cities he put shields and spears, and made them exceedingly strong, having Judah and Benjamin on his side.

2 CHRONICLES 11:5, 11–12.

He placed forces in all the fenced cities of Judah, and set garrisons in the land of Judah, and in the cities of Ephraim, which Asa his father had taken. The Lord was with Jehoshaphat, because he walked in the first ways of his father David, and sought not Baalim, but sought the Lord God of his father, and walked in His commandments, and not after the doings of Israel.

2 CHRONICLES 17:2–4.

Proclaim this among the Gentiles; Prepare war, wake up the mighty men, let all the men of war draw near; let them come up; beat your plowshares into swords, and your pruninghooks into spears; let the weak say, I am strong. Assemble yourselves, and come, all you heathen, and gather yourselves together round about: there cause your mighty ones to come down, O Lord....The Lord will be the hope of His people, and the strength of the children of Israel.

JOEL 3:9–11, 16.

When a strong man, fully armed, keeps his own palace, his goods are in peace; but when a stronger than he shall come upon him, and overcome him, he takes from him all his armor wherein he trusted, and divides his spoils.

LUKE 11:21–22.

MONEY

Money serves several roles: (a) a medium of exchange to facilitate transactions; (b) a store of value to maintain wealth in the form of monetary savings; (c) a way of keeping score, a *numéraire*, so that the value of everything else can be expressed relative to a common denominator. Actually, the existence of money and financial institutions permit a society to operate more freely and efficiently.

The problem arises when greedy persons subvert and exploit the monetary system for personal advantage or power with theft by inflation. When humanistic governments pollute (i.e., inflate) the money supply, they disrupt or destroy all of the functions that money in a godly society should serve.

Instead of facilitating transactions, an inflated money supply encourages less efficient bartering, the rush to get rid of depreciating money as rapidly as possible, and, under extreme cases, refusal of sellers to even accept worthless paper money for goods. Inflation destroys savings. Further, with inflation, we have no accurate means of measuring relative incomes or prices as the value of money continually changes.

Hence, inflation is dysfunctional. It destroys a free society. Under God's laws, we do not steal; *ergo*, inflation is prohibited. Values must be sustained. Prices should reflect fairly reasonable relationships between demand and supply, not of government power and deception. Inaccurate price signals trigger inappropriate investments and incorrect production of goods and services. Society becomes poorer when money has been misused and savings taxed away via the cruelest of all taxes—inflation.

Consequently, gold has often served as money because it removes certain controls and influences from greedy and dishonest persons. Electronic transfers of funds may be more efficient and convenient, but can we trust apostate and corrupt men, the unbelievers, with our money? Would we not be better off to use Christian money for God's purposes than squander it on ones designed by and for humanist governments?

(*See Also:* Barter, Capital Formation, Exchange, Gold, Inflation, Price Mechanism, Savings, Value)

> *When money failed in the land of Egypt and in the land of Canaan, all the Egyptians came to Joseph and said, Give us bread, for why should we die in your presence?...*
>
> GENESIS 47:15.

> *So Ahab spoke to Naboth, saying, Give me your vineyard, that I may have it for a garden of herbs, because it is next to my house; and for it I will give you a vineyard better than it, or, if it seems good to you, I will give you its worth in money.*
>
> 1 KINGS 21:2.

> *They also gave money to the masons and the carpenters, and food, drink, and oil to the people of Sidon and Tyre to bring cedar logs from Lebanon to the sea at Joppa....*
>
> EZRA 3:7.

Be careful to buy with this money bulls, rams, and lambs, with their grain offerings and their drink offerings, and offer them on the altar of the house of your God in Jerusalem.

EZRA 7:17.

He has taken a bag of money with him, and will come home on the appointed day.

PROVERBS 7:20.

For wisdom is a defense, and money is a defense; but the excellence of knowledge is that wisdom gives life to those who have it.

ECCLESIASTES 7:12.

A feast is made for laughter, and wine makes merry; but money answers all things.

ECCLESIASTES 10:19.

Why do you spend money for what is not bread, and your wages for what does not satisfy?

ISAIAH 55:2.

Now Jesus sat opposite the treasury and saw how the people put money into the treasury. Many who were rich put in much.

MARK 12:41.

For the love of money is the root of all evil, which while some coveted after they have erred from the faith, and pierced themselves through with many sorrows.

1 TIMOTHY 6:10.

MONOPOLY

Therefore let him who thinks he stands take heed lest he fall.

1 CORINTHIANS 10:12.

(See: Exchange, Free Market, Market Economy)

MONUMENT BUILDING

Then the princes, the governors, and captains, the judges, the trea-surers, the counsellors, the sheriffs, and all the rulers of the provinces, were gathered together for the dedication of the image that Nebuchad-nezzar had set up.

DANIEL 3:3.

(*See:* Economic Growth, Foreign Aid, Poor Nations)

MORAL PRINCIPLES

A recurring theme throughout this volume is that our actions must be bound by limits, by a discipline outside of man that defines boundaries within which man must operate: absolute principles, or, in other words, moral absolutes. But aren't there exceptions? According to the circumstances? We do tell little white lies, don't we?

Professor Joseph Fletcher, famed author of *Situation Ethics*, says, "Whether we ought to follow a moral principle or not would, I contend, always depend upon the situation.... If we are, as I would reason, obliged in conscience sometimes to tell white lies, as we often call them, then in conscience we might be obliged sometimes to engage in white thefts and white fornications and white killings and white breakings of promises and the like."[1]

Professor Fletcher's moral foundations are as shifty as the weather in Rhode Island. He said that it was all right sometimes to lie, or steal, or kill. Others have asked whether Professor Fletcher lied when he wrote his book, or when he lectured. Since Fletcher has no absolutes, can we believe him?

Once moral foundations are discarded, standards disappear. For instance, when does a little white lie become a medium white lie? At what point does it turn into a full-fledged lie? Can you tell with any certainty based on Fletcher's statements? Do you have any difficulty defining that difference when applying moral principles of the Bible?

Fletcher and other humanists believe that a little murder now and then is fine—a "white killing," like abortion. "A little killing periodically, depending on circum-

---

[1] Cited in a sermon by Dr. D. James Kennedy, "Moral Absolutes: Yes or No?" given at Coral Ridge Presbyterian Church, Ft. Lauderdale, Florida, on October 11, 1981.

stances, is great for everyone." Well, my neighbor has had her mother in a nursing home for seventeen years, and during the entire period the mother has been a vegetable, apparently recognizing no one. Her costs approach $2,000 a month—quite a bit for this middle-income family. Moral relativists would quickly agree that overdosing the mother with drugs would be best for everyone—with the exception, possibly, of the profitable life-support industry.

Moral absolutes translate into no exceptions to the rule. If you receive public welfare, education, or some other subsidy, it is no less stealing because Robin Hood did it for you. Taking wealth and income by direct or indirect force, threat, or intimidation is no less theft.

Moral principles are that which people ought to do, not necessarily what they are doing. If, by majority vote, the American populace approves euthanasia or public education, this does not make it morally right. What do the principles say? Do they prohibit killing or stealing? If First Principles make an act wrong, then no amount of public voting or verbal gymnastics will make it right.

(*See Also:* Discipline, Ethics, Foundation, Judgment, Justice, Nonalignment)

> *They who forsake the law praise the wicked; but such as keep the law contend with them.*
>
> PROVERBS 28:4.

> *While we look not at the things which are seen, but at the things which are not seen, for the things which are seen are temporal; but the things which are not seen are eternal.*
>
> CORINTHIANS 4:18.

> *Beware lest any man spoil you through philosophy and vain deceit, after the tradition of men, after the rudiments of the world, and not after Christ.*
>
> COLOSSIANS 2:8.

> *That no man go beyond and defraud his brother in any matter....*
>
> 1 THESSALONIANS 4:6.

> *That you walk honestly toward them who are without, and that you may lack nothing.*
>
> 1 THESSALONIANS 4:12.

> *If a man also strive for masteries, yet is he not crowned, except he strive lawfully.*
>
> 2 TIMOTHY 2:5.

MORTGAGE

Some also there were who said, We have mortgaged our lands, vineyards, and houses, that we might buy corn, because of the dearth. There were also those who said, We have borrowed money for the king's tribute, and that upon our lands and vineyards.

NEHEMIAH 5:3–4.

(*See:* Bankruptcy, Debt, Taxation)

MURDER

(*See:* Abortion, Capital Punishment, Family)

NATIONALISM

We found this fellow perverting the nation, and forbidding to pay taxes to Caesar, saying that he himself is Christ, a King.

Luke 23:2.

(*See:* Power of State, Statism, Xenophobia)

NATURAL RESOURCES

Oh to return to the pristine state of nature: sparkling brooks, huge forests, kingly animals befriending man, food spontaneously appearing! It sounds like someone's imaginary heaven, not reality. As I fly over Florida swamps or glide past mangroves in their natural state, I ask, Who would want to live here? Through man's effort and his domination of nature, parts of Florida have been transformed into beauty spots, as Phoenix has been recast into a veritable oasis surrounded by a sea of Arizona aridity.

God, the Creator of all, divulges a hierarchical order within the creation plan. Man, subordinate to God, has dominion over nature. Dominion does not license destruction or waste, although some have exercised extremely poor stewardship. There is order. Nature is fulfilled through the exercise of human dominion.

Natural resources are often labeled renewable and nonrenewable. First, heavy demand on a natural resource changes. Less than 100 years ago, crude oil's principal refined product was kerosene. If lengthy geological processes form crude oil, then this process must run continuously, not something that ceased eons ago. Whether we use it at a rate faster than its creation, no one knows. We do know, however, that shortages result from political intervention. We know, too, that left to the free market the price of crude would probably drop by 90 percent, a good indication of its plentifulness. Then again, in another 100 years, dandelions and crab grass may become our most precious natural resources.

The only truly nonrenewable resource seems to be man, especially in his human existence. The time of our earthly existence is our most precious resource. Using it wisely by dedicating our services to God is the best use we can make of our "natural" resource.

(*See Also:* Creation, Division of Labor, Environmentalism, Productivity, Source, Technology)

> God said, Let Us make man in Our image, after Our likeness; and let them have dominion over the fish of the sea, and over the fowl of the air, and over the cattle, and over all the earth, and over every creeping thing that creeps upon the earth.
>
> GENESIS 1:26.

> God blessed Noah and his sons, and said unto them, Be fruitful, multiply, and replenish the earth. And the fear of you and the dread of you shall be upon every beast of the earth, and upon every fowl of the air, upon all that moves upon the earth, and upon all the fishes of the sea, into your hands are they delivered.
>
> GENESIS 9:1–2.

> You shall command the children of Israel, that they may bring you pure olive oil beaten for the light, to cause the lamp to burn always.
>
> EXODUS 27:20.

> O Lord, how manifold are Your works! In wisdom have You made them all; the earth is full of Your riches. So is this great and wide sea wherein all things creep innumerable, both small and great beasts.
>
> PSALM 104:24–25.

NEW SOLUTIONS TO MONUMENTAL PROBLEMS

> For My thoughts are not your thoughts, neither are your ways My ways, saith the Lord.
>
> ISAIAH 55:8.

(*See:* Demagoguery, Expert, Keynesianism)

NO FREE LUNCH

…If anyone will not work, neither shall he eat.
                                    2 THESSALONIANS 3:10.

(*See:* Cradle-to-Grave, Tinstaafl, Work)

NONALIGNMENT

Nonalignment, a middle-of-the-road philosophy allegedly pursued by most Third World countries, initially meant, "We'll combine the best of the communist world with the best of the capitalist world into our own special mixture—the best of both worlds." Then why not take the best God has to offer, and the best of Satan, and combine them into our own worldly, nonaligned system and call it *humanism?*
    Libor Brom says that our choices are commitment or holocaust.

> We ask ourselves who has caused the protracted holocaust in the world. Could it be that for evil to win only one thing is necessary—good people who do nothing? Or that the hottest places in Hell are reserved for those who, at the time of moral crisis, retain their neutrality?[1]

Middle-of-the-roaders, a popular position, are also called *mainstreamers.* Once they were characterized as indecisive and whimsical persons. Over the years, we have been conditioned to respond to tough questions with noncommittal answers. Remember in your (public) school days, when the teacher presented a series of propositions: This is right; this is left; which do you think, children, is best? Many of us were guided right into the middle position and soon learned that middle-of-the-road answers brought approval.
    With God, we cannot be nonaligned. Break one of God's laws, and we have broken them all. We cannot be halfway with God. Melding the "best" of both worlds means rejecting God for the world. Commitment takes courage, sacrifice, and work; but so do most things that are worthwhile.
    (*See Also:* Accountability, Discipline, Double Standard, Foundation, Wisdom)

[1] Libor Brom, "Where Is Your America?" *Imprimis* (August 1982) (published by Hillsdale College, Hillsdale, Mich.).

Either make the tree good, and its fruit good; or else make the tree corrupt, and its fruit corrupt, for the tree is known by its fruit.

MATTHEW 12:33.

You cannot drink the cup of the Lord, and the cup of devils; you cannot be partakers of the Lord's table, and of the table of devils.

1 CORINTHIANS 10:21.

As God is true, our word toward you was not yea and nay. For the Son of God, Jesus Christ, who was preached among you by us, even by me and Silvonus and Timotheus, was not yea and nay, but in Him was yea. For all the promises of God in Him are yea....

2 CORINTHIANS 1:18–20.

But let him ask in faith, nothing wavering. For he who wavers is like a wave of the sea driven with the wind and tossed.

JAMES 1:6.

The tongue can make no man tame; it is an unruly evil, full of deadly poison. Therewith bless we God, even the Father; and therewith curse we men, which are made after the similitude of God. Out of the same mouth proceed blessing and cursing. My brothers, these things ought not to be so. Does a fountain send forth at the same place sweet water and bitter? Can the fig tree, my brothers, bear olive berries? Either a vine, figs? So can no fountain both yield salt water and fresh.

JAMES 3:8–12.

Draw near to God, and He will draw near to you. Cleanse your hands, you sinners; and purify your hearts, you double minded.

JAMES 4:8.

Above all things, my brothers, swear not, neither by heaven, neither by the earth, neither by any other oath; but let your yea be yea, and your nay, nay, lest you fall into condemnation.

JAMES 5:12.

I know your works, that you are neither cold nor hot. I wish you were cold or hot. So then because you are lukewarm, and neither cold nor hot, I will spew you out of My mouth. Because you say, I am rich, and wealthy with goods, and have need of nothing, and know not that you are wretched, and miserable, and poor, and blind, and naked; I counsel you to buy of Me gold tried in the fire, that you may be rich,

*and white raiment, that you may be clothed, and that the shame of your
nakedness does not appear; and annoint your eyes with eyesalve, that
you may see.*

REVELATION 3:15–18.

NOTHING IS FOREVER

Many years ago my department head attempted to extract a promise of eternal
servitude, apparently forgetting (despite his expertise in American economic history)
that even indentured servants had better contract terms. A vow of 'til death do us part
never passed my lips. Instead, I repeatedly reminded him that nothing was forever.
And it wasn't. I left. His subsequent sudden death at age fifty reminded me that our
earthly residence is brief and temporary.

How quickly we can be destroyed! An earthquake in Southern California, a riot
in Miami, a hurricane in Louisiana, a tornado in Illinois, or blackbirds in North
Dakota can wipe out a lifetime of work and savings. Disobedience to God brought
destruction of cities and empires: Sodom and Gomorrah, Babylon and Medo-Persia!
How quickly, too, can God raise us up if we follow His ways! He maketh poor; but
He maketh rich, too.

Are we immune to the will of God? Even the Titanic, "unsinkable by God
Himself," sank as though God stood ready to illustrate the principle that nothing,
except Him, is forever. To place faith in human values, institutions, and physical
structures is a losing strategy. The winning strategy, the only permanent victory,
builds on putting our faith and work in the only viable game around. God holds all
the aces.

(*See Also:* Cycles, Food Storage, Nonalignment, Private Property, Remnant,
Risk Aversion)

*For we are strangers before You, and sojourners, as were all our fathers;
our days on the earth are as a shadow, and there is none abiding.*

1 CHRONICLES 29:15.

*Is there not an appointed time to man upon the earth? Are not his days
also like the days of a hireling? As a servant earnestly desires the
shadow, and as a hireling looks for the reward of his work, so am I
made to possess months of vanity, and wearisome nights are appointed
to me....My days are swifter than a weaver's shuttle, and are spent
without hope. O remember that my life is wind; my eye shall no more
see good.*

JOB 7:1–2, 6–7.

He sees that wise men die, likewise the fool and the brutish person perish, and leave their wealth to others. Their inward thought is, that their houses shall continue for ever, and their dwelling places to all generations; they call their lands after their own names. Nevertheless, man being in honor abides not; he is like the beasts that perish.

PSALM 49:10–12.

Man is like to vanity: his days are as a shadow that passes away.

PSALM 144:4.

Riches are not for ever; and does the crown endure to every generation?

PROVERBS 27:24.

Then shall the dust return to the earth as it was; and the spirit return to God who gave it.

ECCLESIASTES 12:7.

Thorns shall come up in her palaces, nettles and brambles in the fortresses thereof; and it shall be a habitation of dragons, and a court for owls.

ISAIAH 34:13.

The grass withers, the flower fades but the word of our God shall stand forever.

ISAIAH 40:8.

You, Lord, in the beginning have laid the foundation of the earth; and the heavens are the works of Your hands. They shall perish; but you remain; and they all shall wax old as does a garment; and as a vesture shall you fold them up, and they shall be changed; but You are the same, and Your years shall not fail.

HEBREWS 1:10–12.

Let the brother of low degree rejoice in that he is exalted; but the rich, in that he is made low, because as the flower of the grass he shall pass away.

JAMES 1:9–10.

Whereas you know not what shall be tomorrow. For what is your life? It is even a vapor, that appears for a little time, and then vanishes away.

JAMES 4:14.

OBLIGATION

(*See:* Bankruptcy, Debt, Interest)

OCCUPATION

(*See:* Division of Labor, Specialization, Work)

ONE WORLDISM

Pursuit of world order and a one-world government is as old as Satan's demagoguery in the Garden of Eden. The concept appeals to nonbelievers, who recognize the need for a higher order but refuse to accept God as the supreme Authority. It appeals to those unwilling to accept the responsibilities of freedom.

Assume you live in a small town run by a corrupt elite. It's appealing to look to a strong *state government* to put the rascals in their place and yank the political power rug from under their financial empire. Corrupt state officials and representatives who pass higher and higher taxes are so well entrenched, it appears, that only a powerful *federal government* can step in and break the power mosaic into its smaller parts. But what do you do with an oppressive central government, short of civil war or revolution? Wouldn't it be nice to appeal to a "super daddy," a benevolent *world government* and world police force to eradicate the dictators and bureaucrats? Appealing, isn't it? Peace and safety the world over!

But suppose this benevolent super government turns malevolent? After all, it is run by men who may see a golden opportunity for world dictatorship. The world government will be headed by atheists, socialists, taoists, and others who may be quite unfriendly to Christianity, the free society, and the American way of life. Now who will you appeal to? Caesar? There are no higher Caesars in power. There will be "peace," all right, if by peace you mean lack of large-scale wars, but probably not the peace you have in mind. "For when they shall say, Peace and Safety; then sudden destruction comes upon them...." (1 THESSALONIANS 5:3).

One world under the rule of God is truly His mandate. Christians have an obligation to implement God's free society. That obligation begins with each individual and his family to learn and study God's way and then discipline himself accordingly.

One world under the rule of man presents a bleak picture of poverty and oppressiveness with a fancy label. The U.N. General Assembly's 1974 declaration on the Establishment of a New International Economic Order sounds innocuous enough when they deal with international inequalities of resources and manufactured wealth. The U.N. Assembly states that no sovereign state shall be subject to any external "economic, political, or other types of coercion." But how will our new masters achieve their egalitarianism, the global redistribution of income and wealth? By force? I know of no other way to coerce even our liberal intellectuals to reduce themselves to poverty levels, except to confiscate our vast wealth, accumulated by hard work and decades of sacrifice, at gun point. One worldism—do you favor it?

(*See Also:* Communism, Elitism, Slavery, Taxation, Terrorism, United Nations, World Government)

...If you will not listen to the voice of the Lord your God, to observe and do all His commandments and His statutes which I command you this day....The fruit of your land, and all your labors, shall a nation which you know not eat up; and you shall be only oppressed and crushed always.... The Lord shall bring you, and your king which you shall set over you, to a nation which neither you nor your fathers have known; and there you shall serve other gods, wood and stone. ... You shall beget sons and daughters, but you shall not enjoy them, for they shall go into captivity...The stranger who is within you shall get up above you very high; and you shall come down very low....The Lord shall bring a nation against you from afar, from the end of the earth, as swift as the eagle flies, a nation whose tongue you shall not understand.

DEUTERONOMY 28:15, 33, 36, 41, 43, 49.

The children of Israel dwelt among the Canaanites, Hittites, and Amorites, and Perizzites, and Hivites, and Jebusites; and they took their daughters to be their wives, and gave their daughters to their sons, and served their gods. The children of Israel did evil in the sight of the Lord, and forgot the Lord their God, and served Baalim and the groves.

JUDGES 3:5–7.

You are no more strangers and foreigners, but fellow citizens with the saints, and of the household of God, and are built upon the foundation of the apostles and prophets, Jesus Christ Himself being the chief cornerstone, in whom all the building fitly framed together grows into a holy temple in the Lord, in whom you are also build together for a habitation of God through the Spirit.

EPHESIANS 2:19–22.

For when they shall say, Peace and safety; then sudden destruction comes upon them, as labor pains upon a woman with child; and they shall not escape.

1 THESSALONIANS 5:3.

OPTIMISM

Who's in charge? Conspirators? La Costra Nostra? The IRS? Evolutionists? Communists? Terrorists? Big government? The bureaucracy? Giant corporations? Doomsdayers and end-of-the-worlders? They? Nature? Aliens? Planets and stars and mysterious cosmic influences? That radio preacher? *Nobody?*

If you picked any of the above, you live in a hopeless world, where there's a good chance that if things can get worse, they will. If man, or nature (which may include the neighbor's cat), is in charge, we have every right to be pessimistic. Unregenerate men have run affairs terribly for several thousand years. If you know who really commands this world, you need no artificial stimulus to live one day to the next.

An optimist knows that God is in charge. As long as God is in our lives, and we live according to His rules, how can we be anything less than optimistic about the future? If man has the power of decision to live righteously, then he must also have the power to live in evil. Job learned that to think evil brings evil upon us. To think right thoughts will result in right deeds.

In other words, think positively, but not like the college professor who told his students: "When you take my tests, don't come in with a negative frame of mind, thinking, 'I might not pass this test.' Think positively! Say, 'I *will* fail.'" Did the Lord create namby-pamby Christians, who wipe noses on sleeves and wring hands, cluck tongues, and proclaim their own virtues?

If you truly believe that God reigns and that He performed the miracles in the Bible, and that if God has brought His servants out of seemingly impossible situations, then why cannot practicing believers wrench control from corrupt and unregenerate men and establish order under God's law? "The Lord is my Helper, and I will not fear what man shall do to me" (HEBREWS 13:6). Isn't it about time that Christians put some of that optimism into practice and stand up and be counted the other six days of the week as well?

(*See Also:* Accountability, Foundation, Free Society, Individualism, Nonalignment, Prosperity)

The thing which I greatly feared is come upon me, and that which I was afraid of is come to me.

JOB 3:25.

Eat not the bread of him who has an evil eye, neither desire his dainty meat: For as he thinks in his heart, so is he. Eat and drink, he says to you; but his heart is not with you.

PROVERBS 23:6–7.

For the just man falls seven times, and rises up again; but the wicked shall fall into mischief.

PROVERBS 24:16

Be not hasty in your spirit to be angry; for anger rests in the bosom of fools.

ECCLESIASTES 7:9.

If your right eye offend you, pluck it out, and cast it from you, for it is profitable for you that one of your members shall perish, and not your whole body should be cast into hell.

MATTHEW 5:29.

All things, whatever you shall ask in prayer, believing, you shall receive.

MATTHEW 21:22.

Why should it be thought a thing incredible with you, that God should raise the dead?

ACTS 26:8.

Purge out therefore the old leaven, that you may be a new lump, as you are unleavened. For even Christ our passover is sacrificed for us. Therefore, let us keep the feast, not with old leaven, neither with the leaven of malice and wickedness, but with unleavened bread of sincerity and truth.

1 CORINTHIANS 5:7–8.

Let your speech be always with grace, seasoned with salt, that you may know how you ought to answer every man.

COLOSSIANS 4:6.

…The Lord is my helper, and I will not fear what man shall do to me.
HEBREWS 13:6.

ORGANIZATION

Organizations are created and designed to carry out missions and achieve objectives. Management, of course, provides direction and planning and moves an organization along in some direction. The organizational structure itself provides the vehicle for communication links among its various parts.

Organizational structure depends upon size, i.e., the number of individuals involved, and the purposes for which the enterprise was established. Vertical separations along functional lines (sales, finance, production) in companies are often called *divisions*. Horizontal separations (from top management to the lowest level of subordinates) can be accomplished in a pyramidal structure. Matrix organizational structures, sometimes created for specific projects, are smaller business units that combine technical skills (horizontally) under the direction of a project manager.

Typically, operations requiring a great deal of professionalism and independence and individual responsibility will function best in a more informal structure (e.g., an association of architects, or engineers, or physicians). Operations that require considerable uniformity, such as assembly line production, best accomplish objectives in a formal structure under a strict set of management rules.

In other words, a Christian who truly practices his religion and adheres to God's law will be freer and more independent as long as he accepts his responsibilities and fulfills his duties to God and family. As we shift this responsibility more to others and demand our rights from a state authority to provide us jobs, subsidies, and freedom from worry and self-discipline, then the more rigid and strict the organizational structure with a corresponding decline in freedom. A free society may require work, but it's worth it.

(*See Also:* Business, Free Enterprise, Harmony, Management, Specialization, Strategic Planning)

> *You shall provide out of all the people able men, who fear God, men of truth, hating covetousness, and place such over them, to be rulers of thousands, and rulers of hundreds, rulers of fifties, and rulers of tens.*
> *EXODUS 18:21.*

> *David numbered the people who were with him, and set captains of thousands and captains of hundreds over them.*
> *SAMUEL 18:1.*

It pleased Darius to set over the kingdom a hundred and twenty princes, who should be over the whole kingdom; and over these three presidents, of whom Daniel was the first: that the princes might give account to them, and the king should have no damage. Then this Daniel was preferred above the presidents and princes, because an excellent spirit was in him; and the king thought to set him over the whole realm.

DANIEL 6:1–3.

For the body is not one member, but many. If the foot shall say, Because I am not the hand, I am not of the body, is it therefore not of the body? If the ear shall say, Because I am not the eye, I am not of the body, is it therefore not of the body? If the whole body were an eye, where were the hearing? If the whole were hearing, where were the smelling? But now has God set the members every one of them in the body as it has pleased Him. And if they were all one member, where were the body? But now are they many members yet but one body. The eye cannot say to the hand, I have no need of you; nor again the head to the feet, I have no need of you. Nay, much more those members of the body, which seem to be more feeble, are necessary.

1 CORINTHIANS 12:14–22.

POSITIVE MENTAL ATTITUDE

Better is the end of a thing than the beginning; and the patient in spirit is better than the proud in spirit.

ECCLESIASTES 7:8.

(*See:* Individualism, Optimism, Prosperity)

PAWN

If your brother be very poor, and has sold some of his possessions, and if any of his kin come to redeem it, then shall he redeem that which his brother sold.

LEVITICUS 25:25.

(*See:* Collateral, Debt, Pledge)

PAYROLL

(*See:* Exchange, Wages, Work)

PEACE TREATY

When we read press stories of youngsters writing to Soviet leaders asking when will we have peace and Soviet leaders answer that their only desire is peace, or they mention U.S. defensive weapons buildup, the press cries "war mongers" and ranks Soviet leadership alongside the Pope in prayers for peace. Peace treaties may make good political fodder. They are worthless if (a) peace is not defined and (b) both sides do not have sincere intentions.

To communists, peace means a world of slavery under communist domination after all dissenters have been silenced. America's definition of peace means freedom from coercion, threat, fear of the enemy, and so forth. Communist signatories do not intend to keep either the spirit or letter of treaties. To them, treaties are made to be broken, useful only if they further the cause of communism. Of more than sixty treaties with the Soviets, they have broken all but one. Americans, respecting contractual relationships, a basic element of a free society, foolishly expect the Soviets to have the same ethics.

Our SALT agreements are as sturdy as the wall in EZEKIEL 13. EXODUS 34:12 warns against making agreements with unbelievers. The Lord tells us that His ways are not our ways. Saint Paul warns us not to yoke ourselves with unbelievers. Their standards cannot be identical to ours. Otherwise, either they are not unbelievers or we are not believers. Treaties made on earth are also bound in heaven, but only among righteous people. Although we should continue peace efforts, it should be a Christian peace, not a communist one.

(*See Also:* Communication, Contract, Freedom, Nonalignment, Statism, United Nations)

> *Take heed to yourself, lest you make a covenant with the inhabitants of the land where you go, lest it be a snare in the midst of you.*
> *EXODUS 34:12.*

> *Give to the Lord the glory due His name; bring an offering, and come before Him; worship the Lord in the beauty of holiness. Fear before Him, all the earth; the world also shall be stable, that it be not moved.*
> *1 CHRONICLES 16:29–30.*

> *The work of righteousness shall be peace; and the effect of righteousness quietness and assurance for ever.*
> *ISAIAH 32:17.*

> *Because, even because they have seduced My people, saying, Peace, and there was no peace, and one built up a wall, and, lo, others*

daubed it with untempered mortar; say to them who daub it with untempered mortar, that it shall fall; there shall be an overflowing shower; and you, O great hailstones, shall fall, and a stormy wind shall rend it. Lo, when the wall is fallen, shall it not be said to you, Where is the daubing with which you have daubed it? . . . So I will break down the wall that you have daubed with untempered mortar, and bring it down to the ground, so that the foundation thereof shall be discovered, and it shall fall, and you shall be consumed in the midst thereof; and you shall know that I am the Lord.

EZEKIEL 13:10–12, 14.

PERJURY

Perjury is no longer a heavy in modern society. So heinous is perjury in biblical law, the perjurer endures a penalty equal with the criminal. For instance, a person guilty of perjury in a capital felony case would suffer the death penalty. Do unto others. . . . The court system depends upon honest testimony. The justice system breaks down without it. In our envy-ridden society, calumny and perjury not only increase but such behavior is normalized. Gangsterism is championed over righteousness and justice. The honest remnant is anomalous. The rest of society feels uncomfortable with such honesty and discounts it.

Perjury is not restricted to witnesses. Police and prosecutors who knowingly alter evidence or introduce false evidence or bribe witnesses are no less immune and should, according to biblical law, be subject to the same penalties. Shouldn't this principle be reinstated into American law?

(*See Also:* Accountability, Capital Punishment, Communication, Court System, Dishonesty, Testimony)

You shall not bear false witness against your neighbor.

EXODUS 20:16.

You shall not raise a false report; put not your hand with the wicked to be an unrighteous witness.

EXODUS 23:1.

One witness shall not rise up against a man for any iniquity. . . . If a false witness rise up against any man to testify against him that which is wrong, then both the men, between whom the controversy is, shall stand before the Lord, before the priests and the judges, who shall be in those days; and the judges shall make diligent inquisition; and, behold, if the witness be a false witness and has testified falsely against his brother, then you shall do to him, as he thought to have done to his brother: so shall you put evil away from among you. Those who remain shall hear, and fear, and shall henceforth commit no more any such evil among you. Your eye shall not pity, but life shall go for life, eye for eye, tooth for tooth, hand for hand, foot for foot.

DEUTERONOMY 19:15–21.

False witnesses did rise up; they laid to my charge things I knew not. They rewarded me evil for good to the spoiling of my soul.

PSALM 35:11–12.

Remove from me the way of lying, and grant me Your law graciously.

PSALM 119:29.

A false witness shall not be unpunished, and he who speaks lies shall not escape.

PROVERBS 19:5.

…For we have made lies our refuge, and under falsehood have we hid ourselves.

ISAIAH 28:15.

PERSUASION

To cause someone to do what we want boils down to coercion or persuasion. Coercion, of course, means the use or threat of force. Persuasion means convincing. Persons agree quickest when there is mutual gain. For instance, a company selling ultralight aircraft convinces the buyer he will benefit more with an aircraft than by keeping his money. The prospective purchaser learns that an ultralight craft is cheaper to operate than conventional craft, there is considerable freedom from government regulation, it costs a fraction of conventional airplanes, he can enjoy freedom of flight. In other words, the company sells benefits. On the other hand, the pilot's spouse enumerates the dangers of flying, consequences of leaving a family spouseless, and may even threaten divorce.

The prospective buyer of an aircraft must also weigh the disadvantages of not buying a new automobile or room addition against the cost of the aircraft. However, this appraisal depends upon honest information. If the seller lies or hides important facts, this dishonesty is not truly persuasion.

A free society relies on persuasion, with one important exception—government. By its very nature and purpose of existence, government operates on a principle of force. As long as this coercive power restrains true criminals for the protection of society, and its powers are strictly limited, it functions according to divine principles. When people in government decide to remake society along some human-devised plan and force people to conform to statist logic, then government has exceeded its bounds. Freedom depends upon voluntary acts, i.e., persuasion, not coercion.

(*See Also:* Contract, Cooperation, Exchange, Free Market, Golden Rule, Libertarianism, Voluntarism)

A soft answer turns away wrath, but grievous words stir up anger.
PROVERBS 15:1.

Pleasant words are as a honeycomb, sweet to the soul, and health to the bones.
PROVERBS 16:24.

Better is the end of a thing than the beginning thereof; and the patient in spirit is better than the proud in spirit.
ECCLESIASTES 7:8.

One man esteems one day above another; another esteems every day alike. Let every man be fully persuaded in his own mind.
ROMANS 14:5.

PLANNED ECONOMY

Managers of organizations plan, direct, and control. They establish missions and goals. They formulate plans. They direct subordinates to carry out means for moving the organization in the desired direction. They monitor actions of people, evaluate their performance, control costs and operations, and generally keep a tight rein on operations.

Since businesses and other organizations operate successfully by planning and controlling, why not expand this concept to an entire economy? Let the federal government decide objectives of society, formulate plans for carrying them out, and then move people around in different tasks—from each according to his needs? Just think how efficient everything would be! Would it not be a marvelous society: no waste; every need taken care of; everyone doing some useful, meaningful, and beneficial task for society?

Quite honestly, would you really want to live in such a society, even if such efficiency were possible? In the first place, we see how inept our own bureaucracies operate. Why should they do any better with full control than they do with partial control? In the second place, to plan the dawn-to-dawn activities of an entire society requires an omniscience equal to God's. In the third place, aren't you mature enough to decide what is best for you and your family? Are you ready to exchange freedom from decision making—to do what you want, to go where you want, and to say what you want—for life-long security (assuming it were even possible)?

Business planning is a voluntary relationship. You may put up with the wrong end of a horse for a while because the job pays well, but whenever you are ready to reclaim any lost freedom, you can leave. When government plans, they discourage emigration. Communist countries operate with planned economies. They are inefficient, coercive, and poor in material benefits as well as in freedom. Hardly a worker's paradise!

When we want everything planned, we become like dumb animals, unable to make intelligent decisions. We grope along the wall like the blind. Decision making and responsibility require exercise, as do our muscles, or else they atrophy and we become swallowed up by the state. State planning is not God's planning. Statists substitute their law for God's law; they are pagans. The Lord brings the advice of heathens to a dead end; and we're at a dead end if we go against God's order.

(*See Also:* Directed Economy, Elitism, Equality, Expert, Power of State, Rule by Decree)

We grope for the wall like the blind, and we grope as if we had no eyes. We stumble at noon day as in the night; we are desolate places as dead men. We roar all like bears, and mourn sore like doves. We look for judgment, but there is none; for salvation, but it is far off from us.

ISAIAH 59:10–11.

You have forsaken Me, says the Lord, you have gone backward; therefore, will I stretch out My hand against you, and destroy you; I am weary with repenting.

JEREMIAH 15:6.

Be not as the horse, or as the mule, which have no understanding: whose mouth must be held in with bit and bridle, lest they come near to you.

PSALM 32:9.

The Lord brings the counsel of the heathen to nothing; He makes the devices of the people of no effect. The counsel of the Lord stands for ever, the thoughts of His heart to all generations. Blessed is the nation whose God is the Lord; and the people whom he has chosen for His own inheritance.

PSALM 33:10–12.

Let them not say in their hearts, Ah, so we would have it; let them not say, We have swallowed him up.

PSALM 35:25.

PLEDGE

A pledge is like a security deposit. A pledge relates to property given as security for a debt. A landlord, creditor, or lender has every right to expect some type of security. Any lender knows that character is more important than capacity to repay a debt. In these modern times, when lying prevails and the game is to cheat and when the law favors criminals, dishonest renters, and so forth, a pledge, or security, is indispensable, for the honest are becoming fewer.

However, we do read that certain types of pledges were forbidden, such as tools of trade necessary to make a living. Even a garment taken from a poor person must be returned by nightfall. It can only be pledged diurnally. Being poor, of course, excuses no one from debts. Obligations must be paid. On the other hand, failure to restore a pledge is an abominable act, one subject to the severest penalty.

In our modern socialist society, it is quite acceptable to take from those who have, no matter how hard they have worked to save. In many states, renters are encouraged and supported by laws to rip off landlords. They can steal property, destroy it, fail to pay rent for extended periods, run up huge utility bills, and then seek the free service of a public defender to sue for the likely return of their pledge, i.e., security deposit. Statism legislates against God's law and order, against freedom, and for enslavement of all.

(*See Also:* Character, Collateral, Contract, Debts, Law and Order, Private Property, Surety)

He said, I will send you a kid from the flock. And she said, Will you give me a pledge until you send it? He said, What pledge shall I give you? And she said, Your signet, and your bracelets, and your staff that is in your hand.

GENESIS 38:17–18.

I will be surety for him; of my hand shall you require him. If I bring him not to you, and set him before you, then let me bear the blame for ever.

GENESIS 43:9.

No man shall take the nether or the upper millstone to pledge, for he takes a man's life to pledge.

DEUTERONOMY 24:6.

When you lend to your neighbor any manner of loan, you shall not go into his house to fetch his pledge. You shall stand without, and the man to whom you do lend shall bring forth the pledge without to you. If he be a poor man, you shall not sleep with his pledge; you shall surely restore to him the pledge when the sun goes down, that he may sleep in his garmet and bless you, and it shall be righteousness to you before the Lord your God.

DEUTERONOMY 24:10–13.

Lay down now, put me in a surety with you. Who is he who will strike hands with me?

JOB 17:3.

If he begets a son who is a robber, a shedder of blood, and who does any one of these things, and who does not any of these duties, but even has eaten upon the mountains, and defiled his neighbor's wife, has wronged the poor and needy, has taken by violence, has not restored the pledge, and has lifted up his eyes to the idols, has committed abomination, has given forth upon interest, and has taken increase, shall he then live? He shall not live; he has done all these abominations; he shall surely die; his blood shall be upon him.

EZEKIEL 18:10–13.

POLITICIAN

It's amazing how many biblical verses relate to those who run civil governments—politicians and bureaucrats. There are too many to reproduce here. Of course, the Bible refers to princes and kings, titles we do not employ in the United States. Nevertheless, they make laws, run branches of government, and are its visible representatives. Most of these verses reflect the less desirable faces of politicians, for power corrupted long before Lord Acton said it.[1] Of course, there are good politicians. Any politician reading these verses knows that they do not apply to him but to his opponent or to those of the other party. We quite agree.

(*See Also:* Crowd Psychology, Demagogue, Government, Power of State, Rule by Decree)

---

[1]In a letter to Bishop Mandell (Creighton, 1887) Lord John Acton wrote, "Power tends to corrupt; absolute power corrupts absolutely."

You shall in any wise set him king over you, whom the Lord your God will choose: one from among your brothers shall you set king over you; you may not set a stranger over you, which is not your brother. But he shall not multiply horses to himself nor cause the people to return to Egypt. ... Neither shall he multiply wives to himself, that his heart turn not away; neither shall he greatly multiply to himself silver and gold. It shall be, when he sits upon the throne of his kingdom, that he shall write him a copy of this law in a book out of that which is before the priests, the Levites. It shall be with him, and he shall read therein all the days of his life, that he may learn to fear the Lord his God, to keep all the words of this law and these statutes, to do them.

DEUTERONOMY 17:15–20.

The God of Israel said, the Rock of Israel spoke to Me. He who rules over men must be just, ruling in the fear of God.

2 SAMUEL 23:3.

Though his excellency mount up to the heavens, and his head reach to the clouds; yet he shall perish for ever like his own dung. They who have seen him shall say, Where is he? He shall fly away as a dream, and shall not be found, yea, he shall be chased away as a vision of the night. The eye also which saw him shall see him no more; neither shall his place any more behold him.

JOB 20:6–9.

The kings of the earth set themselves, and the rulers take counsel together, against the Lord, and against His Annointed, saying, Let Us break their bands asunder, and cast away their cords from Us. ... Be wise now therefore, O ye kings; be instructed, ye judges of the earth. Serve the Lord with fear, and rejoice with trembling.

PSALM 2:2–3, 10–11.

There is no king saved by the multitude of a host; a mighty man is not delivered by much strength.

PSALM 33:16.

Their inward thought is, that their houses shall continue for ever, and their dwelling places to all generations; they call their lands after their own names. Nevertheless, man being in honor abides not; he is like the beasts that perish. This their way is their folly; yet their posterity approves their sayings. ... Like sheep they are laid in the grave; death shall feed on them; and the upright shall have dominion over them in the morning; and their beauty shall consume in the grave from their dwelling.

PSALM 49:11–14.

The words of his mouth were smoother than butter, but war was in his heart; his words were softer than oil, yet were they drawn swords.
PSALM 55:21.

Let his days be few; and let another take his office.
PSALM 109:8.

It is better to trust in the Lord than to put confidence in princes.
PSALM 118:9.

Put not your trust in princes, nor in the son of man, in whom there is no help. His breath goes forth, he returns to his earth; in that very day his thoughts perish.
PSALM 146:3–4.

The Lord takes pleasure in His people; He will beautify the meek with salvation....Let the high praises of God be in their mouth, and a two-edged sword in their hand; ... to bind their kings with chains, and their nobles with fetters of iron; to execute upon them the judgment written: this honor have all His saints.
PSALM 149:4, 6, 8–9.

Confidence in an unfaithful man in time of trouble is like a broken tooth, and a foot out of joint.
PROVERBS 25:19.

...A fool's voice is known by multitude of words.
ECCLESIASTES 5:3.

The words of wise men are heard in quiet more than the cry of him who rules among fools. Wisdom is better than weapons of war; but one sinner destroys much good.
ECCLESIASTES 9:17–18.

The beginning of the words of his mouth is foolishness; and the end of his talk is mischievous madness.
ECCLESIASTES 10:13.

For the leaders of this people cause them to err; and they who are led of them are destroyed.
ISAIAH 9:16.

Woe to them who decree unrighteous decrees, and who write grievousness which they have prescribed.
ISAIAH 10:1.

O Lord our God, other lords beside You have had dominion over us; but by You only will we make mention of Your name. They are dead, they shall not live; they are deceased, they shall not rise; therefore, you have visited and destroyed them, and made all their memory to perish.

ISAIAH 26:13–14.

They bend their tongues like their bow for lies; but they are not valiant for the truth upon the earth, for they proceed from evil to evil, and they know not Me, says the Lord.... They will deceive every one his neighbor, and will not speak the truth; they have taught their tongue to speak lies, and weary themselves to commit iniquity. Your habitation is in the midst of deceit; through deceit they refuse to know Me, says the Lord.

JEREMIAH 9:3, 5–6.

Nebuchadnezzar the king of Babylon has devoured me; he has crushed me; he has made me an empty vessel; he has swallowed me up like a dragon; he has filled his belly with my delicates; he has cast me out.

JEREMIAH 51:34.

The prince shall not take of the people's inheritance by oppression, to thrust them out of their possession; but he shall give his sons inheritance out of his own possession, that My people be not scattered every man from his possession.

EZEKIEL 46:18.

Though you exalt yourself as the eagle, and though you set your nest among the stars, thence will I bring you down, says the Lord.

OBADIAH 1:4.

That they may do evil with both hands earnestly, the prince asks, and the judge asks for a reward; and the great man, he utters his mischievous desire: so they wrap it up.

MICAH 7:3.

Woe to you, scribes and Pharisees, hypocrites! For you pay tithe of mint and anise and cummin, and have omitted the weightier matters of the law, judgment, mercy, and faith: these you ought to have done, and not to leave the other undone....

Woe to you...! For you make clean the outside of the cup and of the platter, but within they are full of extortion and excess....

Woe to you...! For you are like whited sepulchres, which indeed appear beautiful outward, but are within full of dead men's bones, and of all uncleanness. Even so you also outwardly appear righteous to men, but within you are full of hypocrisy and iniquity. Woe to you, scribes and Pharisees, hypocrites! Because you build the tombs of the prophets, and garnish the sepulchres of the righteous.

MATTHEW 23:23, 25, 27–29.

POLITICS

A whip for the horse, a bridle for the ass, and a rod for the fool's back.

PROVERBS 26:3.

(*See:* Crowd Psychology, Expert, Politician)

POLL TAX

You shall even take five shekels a piece by the poll, after the shekel of the sanctuary....

NUMBERS 3:47.

(*See:* Government, Taxation)

POLLUTION

The word *pollution* immediately brings to mind contamination of nature or of the physical environment, such as rivers, air, and mountains. However, our environment comprises more than these physical areas. First of all, we should not pollute the land (see NUMBERS 35:33). Many environmentalists would alter that verse and say, "You shall not *use* the land." Throwing beer cans in rivers and parks and tossing fast-food paper products out the car window reveal not only uncultivated manners but unchristian behavior. When Christianity and respect for private property were taught in schools, these types of pollution were not a major problem. Environmentalism, now taught in public educational institutions, does little to reinstill these basic principles. Consequently, pollution problems have worsened.

Industrial pollution refers to manufacturers' use of air and water and other elements without paying for or returning them to their original clean state. Such externalities tend to benefit consumers of that product everywhere (because of lower manufacturing costs), and employees and stockholders of the firm (because of greater profits), but an essential cost has been ignored, one that is passed along to anyone who wants to use clean water or air.

Far worse than these—ignored by environmentalists—is pollution of God's Word and His laws. Penalties for dirtying up water and air are minor compared with God's penalties for muddying up His rule in a free society. Prosperity, peace, abundance, harmony, and freedom are God's promises for adhering to His rules. Quite opposite is the price we pay for pollution.

(*See Also:* Compensation, Environmentalism, Gotham City, Idolatry, Source, Technology)

You shall not pollute the land wherein you are: for blood it defiles the land: and the land cannot be cleansed of the blood that is shed therein, but by the blood of him that shed it.
NUMBERS 35:33.

Lift up your eyes to the desolate heights and see: Where have you not lain with men? By the road you have sat for them, as the Arabian in the wilderness; and you have polluted the land with your whoredoms and with your wickedness. Therefore, the showers have been withheld, and there has been no latter rain; and you had a whore's forehead; you refused to be ashamed.
JEREMIAH 3:2–3.

For the children of Judah have done evil in my sight, says the Lord; they have set their abominations in the house which is called by My name, to pollute it.
JEREMIAH 7:30.

Then said I, Ah, Lord God! behold my soul has not been polluted, for from my youth until now have I not eaten of that which dies of itself, or is torn in pieces; neither came these abominable flesh into my mouth.
EZEKIEL 4:14.

I will do these things to you, because you have gone a whoring after the heathen, and because you are polluted with their idols.
EZEKIEL 23:30.

Arise, and depart, for this is not your rest; because it is polluted, it shall destroy you, even with a sore destruction.
MICAH 2:10.

Known to God from the beginning of the world are all His works. Wherefore my sentence is, that we trouble them not, which from among the Gentiles are turned to God; but that we write to them, that they abstain from pollution of idols, and from fornication, and from things strangled, and from blood.

ACTS 15:18–20.

The second angel poured out his vial upon the sea; and it became as the blood of a dead man; and every living soul died in the sea.

REVELATION 16:3.

POOR NATIONS

As the United Nations economic policies change, labels change. Poorer countries have been called havenots, periphery, undeveloped, underdeveloped, less developed, monoculture economies, the lower hemisphere, the colored peoples, Third World countries, and similar labels, but all are not equally poor. With few exceptions, Latin American countries are several times richer than many African and Asian countries: hence, the emerging or industrializing economies. Economic development conferences have aroused excitement on (a) common markets; (b) industrialization; (c) obtaining high (above-market) prices for exports; (d) wealth-transfer schemes including grants, untied aid, interest-free loans, and subsidies.

Poor nations, with their U.N. bloc vote, mostly blame North America for their plight (ignoring that the United States and Canada not many decades ago were as "poor" as some of these nations are today. The poor countries say that they are poor because we, in North America, are rich. Too, they claim we consume the world's natural resources at an alarming rate. For example, in the 1950s, they pointed out that 6 percent (United States and Canada) of the world's population consumed 40 percent of the world's total production of goods and services. (That 40 percent has now dropped well below 30 percent.) They ignored the fact that 6 percent of the world produced—with their labor and machinery—more than 45 percent of total output, and that American enterprises supported jobs and growth in many poor nations.

To rectify matters, they proposed that all rich countries give 1 percent of their Gross National Products to poor countries. That goal still exists. However, by the early 1970s, it was voted the world would soon end, that it would run out of natural resources. The objective was to bring the United States to its industrial knees by denying it access to imported raw materials. In other words, they would use the envy approach: "By golly, if we can't have it, neither will they." But they surely loved our gifts of equipment, power plants, roads, and manufactured "luxuries" that they imported.

Always their governments sought the quick fix: instant wealth. Mostly, they lamented their poverty stemmed from concentration on agricultural production, except when coffee and cotton prices were very high in the early 1950s. Now, many are industrialized. They still indict us. They discovered that industry alone does not make a country rich. The secret now lies in technology. Once again, they accuse, *culpa nostra,* because we will not freely give away hard-won technology. No doubt, as famines multiply, they will one day discover that agriculture is the answer and will say capitalist deception forced them to industrialize. Of course, the United States has two great production and trade advantages: agriculture and technology.

They've missed the whole point, chasing phantoms. They still haven't discovered the secret to American wealth lies *not* in America. All comes from our Father, who art in heaven....

(*See Also:* Capital Formation, Economic Growth, Envy, Free Society, Poverty, U.S.A.)

> ...*If you will not listen to the voice of the Lord your God, to observe to do all His commandments and His statutes:...Cursed shall you be in the city, and cursed shall you be in the field. Cursed shall be your basket and your store. Cursed shall be the fruit of your body, and the fruit of your land, the increase of your kine, and the flocks of your sheep....*
>
> *The Lord shall make the pestilence cleave to you....*
>
> *The Lord shall make the rain of your land powder and dust....*
>
> *The Lord shall cause you to be smitten before your enemies.... The Lord shall smite you with madness, and blindness, and astonishment of heart....*
>
> *You shall betroth a wife, and another man shall lie with her....*
>
> *The fruit of your land, and all your labors, shall a nation which you know not eat up....*
>
> D<small>EUTERONOMY</small> 28:15–18, 21, 24–26, 28, 30, 33.

> *If you will not obey the voice of the Lord, but rebel against the commandment of the Lord, then shall the hand of the Lord be against you, as it was against your fathers.*
>
> 1 S<small>AMUEL</small> 12:15.

> *The word of the Lord that came to Jeremiah concerning the dearth. Judah mourns, and the gates thereof languish; they are black unto the ground, and the cry of Jerusalem is gone up. Their nobles have sent their little ones to the waters; they came to the pits, and found no water; they returned with their vessels empty; they were ashamed and confounded, and covered their heads. Because the ground is parched, for there was no rain on the earth; the plowmen were ashamed, they*

covered their heads. Yea, the hind also calved in the field, and forsook it, because there was no grass. The wild asses did stand in the high places; they sniffed at the wind like jackals; their eyes did fail because there was no grass. O Lord, though our iniquities testify against us, do it for Your name's sake, for our backslidings are many; we have sinned against You.

JEREMIAH 14:1–7.

She has changed My judgments into wickedness more than the nations, and My statutes more than the countries that are round about her; for they have refused My judgments and My statutes, they have not walked in them....

A third part of you shall die with the pestilence, and with famine shall they be consumed in the midst of thee; and a third part shall fall by the sword round about you; and I will scatter a third part into all the winds, and I will draw out a sword after them.

EZEKIEL 5:6, 12.

Egypt shall be a desolation, and Edom shall be a desolate wilderness, for the violence against the children of Judah, because they have shed innocent blood in their land.

JOEL 3:19.

Therefore I say to you, The kingdom of God shall be taken from you, and given to a nation bringing forth the fruits thereof.

MATTHEW 21:43.

POVERTY

Poverty has no macro definition, measurability, or solutions. Governments demarcate a poverty level and then shower families with aid to dependent children, rent subsidies, legal assistance, abortions, free schooling, food stamps, and so on. But these families must live irresponsibly: in debt, no savings, no investments or property, no inheritance put aside for their children—people who barely survive from paycheck to paycheck. Another family, with identical income but Christian ethics, through continuous vigilance and exercise of self-discipline, manages to buy a house and put funds aside for emergencies. The second family not only is disqualified from subsidies (which they'd not even accept) but is taxed onerously because they have acted responsibly.

My own experiences convince me that real poverty is an attitudinal, not a financial, condition. In fact, I define poverty as wanting, no, craving, more than is possible to acquire at present. By that definition, poverty can strike at any income level—and it does. I distinctly remember a young couple with two children. He was laid off from construction employment. He spent his time bemoaning his fate to relatives and whining to whoever would listen. His only significant debt was his house mortgage, and unemployment compensation sufficiently covered that and other essentials. Still he managed to sponge from a sister-in-law, who owned nothing, had heavy debts, and could not even maintain herself. Finally, a brother-in-law employed him temporarily, but he complained bitterly and constantly about him and the work. This family definitely had a poverty mentality. They will always be poor in heart and materially as long as they harbor this attitude.

Material poverty pales in significance to the burden of spiritual poverty. Poor health, unhappiness, being out of step with the Lord's way—no government can solve these poverty problems. Humanists believe that poverty and the poverty mentality result from environmental conditions: Change a family's surroundings and poverty automatically disappears. In other words, if the poverty problem cannot be resolved with $500 billion of government expenditures, then we need to spend $900 billion. Believers know that the poverty mentality dissolves when there is a decision, a commitment to Christ, and a followthrough, living each day according to the rule of God.

(*See Also:* Debts, Law of Increase, Liberty, Poor Nations)

If you do not obey Me, and do not do all these commandments, and if you despise My statutes, or if your soul abhors My judgments, so that you do not perform all My commandments, but break My covenant, I also will do this to you: I will even appoint terror over you, wasting disease and fever, which shall consume the eyes and cause sorrow of heart. And you shall sow your seed in vain, for your enemies shall eat it. I will set My face against you, and you shall be slain before your enemies. Those who hate you shall reign over you, and you shall flee when no one pursues you. After all this, if you do not obey Me, then I will punish you seven times more for your sins. I will break the pride of your power; I will make your heavens like iron and your earth like bronze. Your strength shall be spent in vain, for your land shall not yield its output, nor shall the trees of the land yield their fruit. Then, if you walk contrary to Me, and are not willing to obey Me, I will bring on you seven times more plagues, according to your sins. I will also send wild beasts among you, which shall rob you of your children, destroy your livestock, and make you few in number; and your highways shall be desolate....

When I have cut off your supply of bread, ten women shall bake your bread in one oven, and they shall bring it back to you your bread by weight, and you shall eat and not be satisfied....

You shall eat the flesh of your sons, and you shall eat the flesh of your daughters. I will destroy your high places, cut down your incense altars, and cast your carcasses on the lifeless forms of your idols; and My soul shall abhor you. I will lay waste your cities and bring your sanctuaries to desolation, and I will not smell the fragrance of your sweet aromas. I will bring the land to desolation, and your enemies who dwell in it shall be astonished at it.

LEVITICUS *26:14–22, 26, 29–32.*

Behold I set before you this day a blessing and a curse; a blessing if you obey the commandments of the Lord your God; and a curse if you will not obey the commandments of the Lord your God....

DEUTERONOMY *11:26–28.*

... If you will not hearken to the voice of the Lord your God, to observe to do all His commandments and His statutes:... Cursed shall you be in the city, and cursed shall you be in the field. Cursed shall be your basket and your store. Cursed shall be the fruit of your body, and the fruit of your land, the increase of your kine, and the flocks of your sheep.... The Lord shall make the pestilence cleave to you. ...The Lord shall smite you with a consumption, and with a fever, and with an inflammation, and with extreme burning, and with the sword....

The Lord shall make the rain of your land powder and dust....

You shall plant a vineyard, and shall not gather the grapes from it. Your ox shall be slain before your eyes, and you shall not eat thereof....

You shall carry much seed into the field, and shall gather but little in....

Because you served not the Lord your God with joyfulness, and with gladness of heart, for the abundance of all things.

DEUTERONOMY *28:15–18, 21–22, 24, 30–31, 38, 47.*

There is he who makes himself rich, yet has nothing; there is he who makes himself poor, yet has great riches.

PROVERBS *13:7.*

The poor is hated even of his own neighbor; but the rich has many friends.

PROVERBS *14:20.*

The poor uses entreaties; but the rich answers roughly.

PROVERBS *18:23.*

He who loves pleasure shall be a poor man; he who loves wine and oil shall not be rich.

PROVERBS *21:17.*

Yet a little sleep, a little slumber, a little folding of the hands to sleep: so shall your poverty come as one who prowls, and your want as an armed man.

PROVERBS 24:33–34.

He who tills his land shall have plenty of bread; but he who follows after vain persons shall have poverty enough.

PROVERBS 28:19.

When his disciples saw it, they had indignation, saying, To what purpose is this waste? For this ointment might have been sold for much, and given to the poor. When Jesus understood it, He said to them, Why trouble the woman, for she has wrought a good work upon Me. For you have the poor always with you; but Me you have not always.

MATTHEW 26:8–11.

POWER

Commenting on a politician, a colleague said to me, "I think Senator _____ is an honest man. Look how wealthy he is. What can he possibly gain by staying in the Senate? I think the only reason he does it is to serve the people." Yes, that senator certainly votes to do good for and to us, whether we want public largesse or not: national health care, federal education, elimination of right-to-work laws, federal jobs program, higher income taxes.... I think you get the picture. Let's see what Dr. George Roche (president of Hillsdale College and one-time candidate for the United States Senate) has to say about this:

> Unlike the Greeks, who had seen the state as the central feature of society, the early Christians saw the state as an institution in and of a sinful world. While the state was needed to exercise power to protect men from other men in this flawed world, the Christian saw the state itself as a flawed and potentially dangerous wielder of power....
>
> Wielders of power are destroying the world in the mistaken belief that they are improving it. Many men have experienced the temptation to remake the world.
>
> One of the worst features of the planned society is its incorporation of religious zeal in the service of repressive ends.
>
> The increasing spread of the planned society has tended to sweep aside such institutional guarantees as religion and private property, and has tended to override the traditional political bulwarks against such unchecked exercise of power....
>
> So long as government is viewed as an agency through which virtue and happiness for the individual may be attained, so long as governments are viewed as

causes rather than effects, so long as individuals believe that self-responsibility may be escaped through retreat to the collective ethic, power will be rampant in our society.[1]

Recall the Salem (Massachusetts) witch hunts? They began when undisciplined girls, of undisciplining parents, hid behind witchcraft to conceal their own indolence. Adults, duped by the fallacious premise of the "innocence of children," lent respectability to the tale. Finally, opportunists used the crisis for their own gains. Anyone acknowledging witchcraft forfeited property rights. Cruel tortures were devised to elicit such "confessions." Many lost property. (The accused were killed anyway, only quicker.) But there were strong men, too, who endured long days of continuous torture so that their families could retain property rights. Thus power, in the hands of a few ungodly men, can completely destroy a society, as it did Salem!
(*See Also:* Corruption, Demagogue, Envy, Expropriation, Power of State, World Government)

God has spoken once, twice have I heard this: that power belongs to God.

PSALM 62:11.

He [God] rules by His power forever; His eyes behold the nations; let not the rebellious exalt themselves.

PSALM 66:7.

Where the word of the king is, there is power; and who may say to him, What are you doing?

ECCLESIASTES 8:4.

There is no man who has power over the spirit to retain the spirit; neither has he power in the day of death; neither shall wickedness deliver those who are given to it.

ECCLESIASTES 8:8.

For what is a man advantaged, if he gain the whole world, and lose himself, or be cast away?

LUKE 9:25.

Jesus answered, You could have no power at all against me, except it were given you from above; therefore, he who delivered Me to you has the greater sin.

JOHN 19:11.

[1]George C. Roche, III, *Power* (Irvington-on-Hudson, N.Y.: Foundation for Economic Education, circa 1968), pp. 4, 39, 50.

Let every soul be subject to the higher powers. For there is no power but of God: the powers that be are ordained of God. Whoever resists the power, resists the ordinance of God; and they who resist shall receive to themselves damnation.

ROMANS 13:1–2.

POWER OF STATE

Despite centers of influence and trend-setters, the only *power structure* is government. Only civil government can mobilize resources, draft men into the military, confiscate property, tax, and grant monopolistic privileges. Throughout this volume we have referred to the state as an entity having this power to do to others.

> Power obeys its own laws, and one of its basic laws ... is *the use of political power to enhance the economic well-being of officeholders and their friends,* at the expense of the rest of the nation. Albert Jay Nock designated this perversion of government as The State, a two-headed monster comprising, on one hand, those who wield political power—officeholders—and on the other, their friends who derive economic advantages for themselves from a wrongful exercise of political power. "Votes and taxes for all; subsidies for us and our friends," is the rationale.[1]

Dr. D. James Kennedy delivered a sermon on "Government: A Fearful Master." He said, "In the past year we have seen church schools closed, churches padlocked, and pastors thrown into jail." (By the way, he was referring to the United States of America.) "This portends great evil for our society. In time, government might arrogate to itself the power to obliterate the freedom we have known." He continued, "The Church has its own master. He is Christ, not Caesar. The Church is not subject to the powers of the state. God has ordained both and God is over both."[2]

Power of state leads to government by privilege. For a few to enslave many they must either apply pervasive force, such as military occupation, or rely on lies and deceit. J. Edgar Hoover referred to communists as masters of deceit. By deceit and demagoguery, deluded masses vote themselves into slavery on the mere promise of something for nothing. Americans voted for the Sixteenth (Income Tax) Amendment, elect legislators who promise higher taxes, and accept statist and humanistic propaganda above the Word of God. In *Newsweek* George Will called for more

---

[1] Edmund A. Opitz, *Religion and Capitalism: Allies, Not Enemies* (New Rochelle, N.Y.: Arlington House Publishers, 1974), p. 243.

[2] D. James Kennedy, "Government: A Fearful Master," sermon delivered at Coral Ridge Presbyterian Church, Fort Lauderdale, Florida, on February 14, 1982.

taxes to support government spending.[3] DeTocqueville, in 1835, predicted this "democratic despotism," in *Reflections of America.*[4] Rev. Optiz calls it "despotism by consent."[5]

Christians who read, study and believe the Bible and daily practice biblical precepts will not permit such tampering. Reportedly there are fifty million active Christians. Why do they whisper and not shout against the power of State? William Perkins (1558-1602), an English Puritan, wrote: "If it should fall out that men's law be made of things evil, and forbidden by God, then there is no bond of conscience at all; but contrariwise men are bound in conscience not to obey."

(*See Also:* Demagoguery, Law, Power, Rule by Decree, Statism, World Government)

The king answered and said to the Chaldeans, The thing is gone from me. If you will not make known to me the dream, with its interpretation, you shall be cut in pieces, and your houses shall be made a dunghill. But if you show the dream, and its interpretation, you shall receive of me gifts and rewards and great honor....

DANIEL 2:5–6.

For this cause the king was angry and very furious, and commanded to destroy all the wise men of Babylon.

DANIEL 2:12.

...To you it is commanded, O people, nations, and languages, that at that time you hear the sound of the cornet, flute, harp, sackbut, psaltery, dulcimer, and all kinds of music, you fall down and worship the golden image that Nebuchadnezzar the king has set up. Whoever does not fall down and worship shall the same hour be cast into the midst of a burning fiery furnace.

DANIEL 3:4–6.

The king shall do according to his will; and he shall exalt himself and magnify himself above every god....

DANIEL 11:36.

Woe to him who covets evil gain for his house, that he may set his nest on high, that he may be delivered from the power of disaster!

HABAKKUK 2:9.

[3]George F. Will, "On Revenues and Ronald Reagan," *Newsweek,* July 15, 1983, p. 80.

[4]Alexis de Tocqueville, *Democracy in America* (New York: New American Library, 1956), pp. 301-14.

[5]Opitz, *op. cit.,* Chapter 14.

The coming of the lawless one is according to the working of Satan, with all power, signs, and lying wonders, and with all unrighteous deception among those who perish, because they did not receive the love of the truth, that they might be saved.

2 Thessalonians 2:9–10.

They had tails like scorpions, and there were stings in their tails. Their power was to hurt men five months.

Revelation 9:10.

PRECUT BUILDINGS

The house, when it was in building, was built of stone made ready before it was brought there, so that there was neither hammer nor ax nor any tool of iron heard in the house while it was in building.

1 Kings 6:7.

(*See:* Business, Technology)

PRESS, FREEDOM OF

(*See:* Communication, Free Society, Libertarianism)

PRICE

As long as more people want a thing than the amount of it available (i.e., relative scarcity), a price must be paid to acquire it. This underlies all economic theory. It began when Adam and company got tossed out of the garden: "In the sweat of your face shall you eat bread" (Genesis 3:19). Henceforth everything had to be paid for with the price of labor.

Some things carry a zero price. Someone who lives on or near an ocean beach would not pay for sand or salt water. However, an Upper Arlington, Ohio, family may pay a good price for sand in the sandbox, or bottled saltwater to cure dandruff. Other things carry a negative price; those that can't even be given away. Consequently, you pay someone to take away garbage and trash.

In the free market, price fairly accurately reflects this relative scarcity. In a controlled market, price is not an accurate indicator. To producers, price provides some clue on what buyers want; it directs investment and production accordingly. To consumers, price affords the buyer information, to compare sellers, and whether they should buy now or later, or at all. The socialist guarantee of everything free for everybody is a fallacious and unattainable promise, demagoguery that started in GENESIS 3:4; "You shall not surely die." It denies the sovereignty of God. Christians should not walk in the counsel of such people.

(*See Also:* Demand and Supply, Exchange, Interest, Market Economy, Price Mechanism, Wages)

...They drew and lifted up Joseph out of the pit, and sold Joseph to the Ishmaelites for twenty pieces of silver....

GENESIS 37:28.

Take double money in your hand; and the money that was brought again in the mouth of your sacks, carry it again in your hand: peradventure it was an oversight.

GENESIS 43:12.

...We will go by the highway; and if I and my cattle drink of your water, then I will pay for it....

NUMBERS 20:19.

...But I will surely buy it of you at a price. Neither will I offer burnt offerings unto the Lord my God of that which costs me nothing. So David bought the threshing floor and the oxen for fifty shekels of silver.

2 SAMUEL 24:24.

A chariot came up and went out of Egypt for six hundred shekels of silver, and a horse for a hundred and fifty; and so for all the kings of the Hittites, and for the kings of Syria, did they bring them out by their means.

1 KINGS 10:29.

David said to Ornan, Grant me the place of this threshing floor, that I may build an altar there to the Lord; you shall grant it to me for the full price....

1 CHRONICLES 21:22.

...The king's merchants received the linen yarn at a price.
2 CHRONICLES 1:16.

...If you think good, give me my price; and if not, forbear....
ZECHARIAH 11:12.

Who, when he had found one pearl of great price, went and sold all
that he had, and bought it.
MATTHEW 13:46.

PRICE MECHANISM

Imagine arousing from a Van Winklean sleep of twenty years. Your first task is to assign prices to everything. Half of the products you've never seen before. How would you decide prices? Communist societies must also price every good, relative to all other goods. Is a pair of shoes worth ten pairs of socks, forty pounds of bananas, or one-third of a new jacket? How do you know? The communists, of course, cheat. Prices cannot be arbitrarily assigned, so they use free market prices as a guideline for their own corrupt systems.

Why are prices so important? They bring demand and supply together. In a free market, they are an important signaling device. In a free market, prices result from millions of transactions and express, in summary fashion, actual desires of buyers and sellers. Uncontrolled prices are a mark of economic freedom. Rising prices signal to manufacturers that demand is strong and that it may be the time to expand productive facilities and employ more persons. Falling prices may suggest a declining market opportunity, so that investors shift funds from producing what buyers want less of into production of things buyers want more of. Buyers, by comparing prices, both among the same product and across products, keep sellers on their toes, assuring competition and getting their money's worth.

Fool around with the price mechanism, and false signals emanate. For instance, if government imposes price controls on certain products, causing them to be priced below their market rate, what happens? If something is abundantly available, like dead leaves in the fall, you would expect the price to be zero. No one wants them. Price appears when something is widely demanded but not abundantly supplied. Price acts as a rationing mechanism. As price rises, some buyers cool their desires or buy less of the product. As price falls, then more of the product is consumed. If government arbitrarily assigns a price below the market price, then demand for that item will rise; but sellers do not willingly take losses, so production slows down.

When government intervenes in the marketplace, shortages arise. Assume that the government imposes rent controls in your city. It rolls back rent prices by ten years. People would prefer to rent than own. Landlords, on the other hand, would first try to cut corners, discontinuing repair and other services and then let buildings deteriorate until they were condemned for back taxes. Soon abandoned buildings mark the skyline. A shortage of decent housing prevails. The government solved nothing. They created a problem that can only be resolved by a return to the free market, which establishes the rate of exchange on the basis of what free men and women want.

(*See Also:* Exchange, Free Market, International Trade, Labor Market, Price, Return on Investment)

> ...The land is worth four hundred shekels of silver; what is that between me and you? Bury your dead.
>
> GENESIS 23:15.

> He bought a parcel of a field, where he had spread his tent, at the hand of the children of Hamor, Shechem's father, for one hundred pieces of money.
>
> GENESIS 33:19.

> ...I have heard there is corn in Egypt; get down there, and buy for us from there, that we may live, and not die.... The sons of Israel came to buy corn among those who came.... And Joseph...sold to all the people of the land....
>
> GENESIS 42:2, 5–6.

> According to the multitude of years you shall increase the price thereof, and according to the fewness of years you shall diminish the price of it, for according to the number of the years of the fruits does he sell to you.
>
> LEVITICUS 25:16.

> Moreover he said to me, Son of man, behold I will break the staff of bread in Jerusalem; and they shall eat bread by weight, and with care; and they shall drink water by measure, and with astonishment.
>
> EZEKIEL 4:16.

> But by an equality, that now at this time your abundance may be a supply for their want, that their abundance also may be a supply for your want: that there may be equality.
>
> 2 CORINTHIANS 8:14.

PRIVATE PROPERTY

Biblical faith builds on a foundation of possession of land and ownership of private property. Statists put their faith in state ownership of property and communal interests in all other property. More specifically, in a biblical sense, ownership means private use of that property. Socialism, for example, may allow for titling of property in individual names and even temporary possession of it, but the state controls its use: zoning regulations, type and number of occupants, what may or may not be grown on the land and how much, a heavy inheritance tax, and restrictions on transfers of title. In other words, the state not only limits and restricts property use but also may charge a rental fee, commonly called "property taxes." In other words, the positions of believers and unbelievers are incompatible and irreconcilable. Let's look at some of these differences.

Basic to private property is freedom. Freedoms are inseparable. Freedom must have some external guarantee. In the case of human freedom, it is property. "A man is free on the inside because he can call his soul his own; he is free on the outside because he can call something he has his own." When Man belongs to the state, he uses it only with permission. My uncle, who spent ten years of a thirty-year sentence in Siberia, returned to his native Lithuania. The state allowed him, in old age, to live on the family farm, which they had confiscated, in the original house, along with a modest state pension and a small radio. The state let him know it was the great giver of sustenance and freedom. What freedoms? The state taketh, and the state giveth but not as much as it taketh.

Biblical law protects the family—the fundamental governing unit—with safeguards. Private property and the right of inheritance are key defenses, the family's protection from the state. Communism replaces the family. It wants no other gods between the individual (who is state property) and the state. Abolition of private property destroys the family. Under biblical law, property is protected from taxation, confiscation, and eminent domain. Even the father cannot squander his children's inheritance.

If we own or are responsible for something, we likely will take care of it. One time I had rented two furnished units to closely related persons. In one case, the electric was paid for by the renter, in the other case, I carried the obligation. The one responsible for electricity very rarely used air conditioners, even when the temperature stayed in the 90s. The other person operated the air conditioner with doors and windows opened and with total disregard to cost and workload on the unit, because I, not she, paid the electricity bill. Similarly, environmentalists would have little to protest if land, the one-third of the United States now held hostage by governments, were returned to private ownership. Loggers, cattle ranchers, miners, campers, and other users of public property have less concern over it than they would their own private property.

Voting and freedom have often been linked to property ownership. Among our early statesmen, James Madison, for example, expressed considerable concern over allowing nonlanded interests to vote, because "the rights of property and the public liberty will not be secure in their hands."[1] Governor Morris predicted that the vote of property-less men would be controlled by the great and rich and an oligarchic rule would ensue.[2] I recall a friend who worked many years ago for the Democratic party in West Virginia. During elections, his job was to drive poor people to and from the polls to vote Democratic, to whom he paid each $1 in cash. If you and I and Joe all have equal vote on whether to put a tax on Joe's property, he's outnumbered. When our country was founded, about 90 percent of the people owned property. Today, cities swing the vote. The urban vote can include a goodly number of welfarers and government employees, who, living off the state, have an interest in raising taxes on others' property.

How have predictions worked out? Our federal government is ruled by an elite corps, an oligarchy that, if not serving in office, controls those in public office and even the bureaucracy. We agree, therefore, with Reverend Rushdoony that private property and moral order are closely linked and that every attack on private property is an attack on God's order.[3]

(*See Also:* Exchange, Free Society, Inequality, Moral Principles, Pledge, Property Taxes, Stewardship, U.S.A.)

> *In the same day the Lord made a covenant with Abram, saying, To your seed have I given this land....*
>
> GENESIS 15:18.

> *He bought a parcel of a field, where he had spread his tent, at the hand of the children of Hamor, Shechem's father, for a hundred pieces of money.*
>
> GENESIS 33:19.

> *You shall dwell with us; and the land shall be before you; dwell and trade therein, and get your possessions therein.*
>
> GENESIS 34:10.

> *You shall not steal.*
>
> EXODUS 20:15.

---

[1] James Madison, *The Federalist* (1787-88), No. 10.

[2] Charles C. Tansill (ed.), *Documents Illustrative of the Formation of the Union of the American States*, 69th Congress, 1st Session, House Document No. 398 (Washington, D.C.: G.P.O., 1927), p. 488-89.

[3] Rousas John Rushdoony, *Law and Society* (Vallecito, Calif.: Ross House Books, 1982), "God's Property Rights," pp. 534–38.

If you meet your enemy's ox or his ass going astray, you shall surely bring it back to him again.

EXODUS 23:4.

If a man sell a dwelling house in a walled city, then he may redeem it within a whole year after it is sold....

LEVITICUS 25:29.

You shall not remove your neighbor's landmark, which they of old time have set in your inheritance....

DEUTERONOMY 19:14.

...The Lord your God has given you rest, and has given you this land.

JOSHUA 1:13.

...That you may be strong, and eat the good of the land, and leave it for an inheritance to your children for ever.

EZRA 9:12.

His substance also was seven thousand sheep, and three thousand camels, and five hundred yoke of oxen, and five hundred she asses, and a very great household, so that this man was the greatest of all the men of the east.

JOB 1:3.

The heavens are yours, the earth also is yours, as for the world and the fulness thereof, You have founded them.

PSALM 89:11.

Whoever keeps the fig tree shall eat the fruit of it, so he who waits on his master shall be honored.

PROVERBS 27:18.

That every man should eat and drink, and enjoy the good of his labor, it is the gift of God.

ECCLESIASTES 3:13.

The people also shall be all righteous: they shall inherit the land forever, the branch of My planting, the work of My hands, that I may be glorified.

ISAIAH 60:21.

They shall build houses and inhabit them; and they shall plant vineyards, and eat the fruit of them.

ISAIAH 65:21.

Men shall buy fields for money, and subscribe evidences, and seal them, and take witnesses....

JEREMIAH 32:44.

The prince shall not take of the people's inheritance by oppression, to thrust them out of their possessions; but he shall give his sons inheritance out of his own possessions, that My people be not scattered every man from his possessions.

EZEKIEL 46:18.

Is it not lawful for me to do what I will with my own? Is your eye evil, because I am good?

MATTHEW 20:15.

He who is a hireling, and not the shepherd, whose own the sheep are not, sees the wolf coming, and leaves the sheep, and flees; and the wolf catches them, and scatters the sheep. The hireling flees because he is a hireling, and cares not for the sheep.

JOHN 10:12–13.

A certain man named Ananias, with Sapphira his wife, sold a possession.... While it remained, was the land not your own? And after it was sold, was it not in your own power?...

ACTS 5:1, 4.

...He who plows should plow in hope; and he who threshes in hope should be partaker of his hope.

1 CORINTHIANS 9:10.

Charge them who are rich in this world, that they be not highminded, nor trust in uncertain riches, but in the living God, who gives us richly all things to enjoy. That they do good, that they be rich in good works, ready to distribute, willing to communicate.

1 TIMOTHY 6:17–18.

The husbandman who labors must be first partaker of the fruits.

2 TIMOTHY 2:6.

PRODUCTION

Production results from the proper combination of natural resources and time and the application of human energies. This immutable law is set forth in Genesis. We can increase production through more efficient use of time and human energies. By withholding present consumption, we can produce intermediate, or capital goods, i.e., tools and equipment. The use of capital multiplies output possibilities with the same expenditure of human energies—an increase in *productivity*.

Many express concern over the United State's diminishing productivity, declining output, and aging capital. The solution proposed is a formalized national strategic plan to mobilize and organize the industrial sector. Can the United States effectively compete in world markets without such national economic planning?

> To a growing number of Americans, the answer is no. In a recent survey conducted by The Garth Group, 83 percent of our citizens believe that we need a national plan to mobilize our resources and to make American business more competitive with the rest of the world. Among those in industry who strongly support national economic planning are such prominent board chairmen as W. Michael Blumenthal of Burroughs, Fletcher Byron of Koppers, and Thornton Bradshaw of RCA, who says: "I advocate...national planning as a means of saving the very market system so often considered to be inconsistent with it."[1]

Franklin Delano Roosevelt said something along those lines in the 1930s as he instituted socialistic policies in a purported effort to save "capitalism." Many economic text books of the 1950s to 1970s parroted that message.

Think on this: How did America become great, the world's industrial leader? With a series of national economic plans beginning in 1776? By controlling the market with red tape, restrictions, taxation, and national policies that encouraged some industries and discouraged others? By protecting and subsidizing high-cost, inefficient producers? By legislating compulsory unionism? *No!* If we control the economy through national planning, then we have not saved the market system but have contributed to its further destruction. By definition, the market system depends upon freely contracting parties, not government intervention.

Companies providing employment, inventions, new technology, and innovative ideas are small ones, often with fewer than fifty employees. Most small organizations eagerly compete in the marketplace. They do so without national planning. Large firms seeking government interference want to insulate themselves from competitive forces. Certainly many have become entangled in governmental red tape—here and abroad. We sympathize with their plight; but the "hair of the dog that bit them" is a foolish remedy, and a very selfish one.

We need to control civil government, not production, and remove those obstacles to living in a free society under the rule of God. "The fact that our free individual enterprise system enabled our people to save and invest and buy and own the tools of production has resulted in this nation being able to achieve the greatest material well-being for more people than ever before in the history of mankind. Thus it is obvious our material fruits had spiritual roots! *Free men, under God, produce*

[1]Quoted in David A. Heenan, *The Re-United States of America* (Reading, Mass.: Addison-Wesley, 1983), p. 185.

better.... But, Caesar is chewing up our resources and competing for that which is available in the money market."[2]

We are subjected to national planning. In 1947, civil governments confiscated less than 20 percent of the Gross National Product (GNP). It now reaches 50 percent, by conservative accounting. In 1947, governments employed fewer than 6 million persons. They employ close to 15 million today. The number of control and planning agencies has multiplied. We have to look long and hard to find remnants of the free enterprise system at work (usually in the underground economy). In less than two decades we have tumbled from a first-class nation under God to an unrespected world position under humanism. We became number one in the world through hard work, in freedom. We can again, not through government national planning but in obedience to God's laws.

(*See Also:* Business, International Trade, Market Economy, Productivity, Strategic Planning, Work)

> *Yea, the Lord shall give that which is good; and our land shall yield her increase.*
>
> PSALM 85:12.

> *That our garners may be full, affording all manner of store; that our sheep may bring forth thousands and ten thousands in our streets; that our oxen may be strong to labor; that there be no breaking in, nor going out; that there be no complaining in our streets.*
>
> PSALM 144:13–14.

> *He who tills his land shall have plenty of bread; but he who follows after vain persons shall have poverty enough.*
>
> PROVERBS 28:19.

> *For a dream comes through a multitude of business.*
>
> ECCLESIASTES 5:3.

> *Blessed are you who sow beside all waters, who send forth there the feet of the ox and the ass.*
>
> ISAIAH 32:20.

> *These are they which are sown on good ground; such as hear the Word, and receive it, and bring forth fruit, some thirtyfold, some sixty, some a hundred.*
>
> MARK 4:20.

---

[2]Rus Walton, *One Nation Under God* (Old Tappan, N.J.: Fleming H. Revell, 1975), pp. 166–67.

Now he who ministers seed to the sower both minister bread for your food, and multiply your seed sown, and increase the fruits of your righteousness.

                                                                                2 CORINTHIANS 9:10.

Let him who stole steal no more; but rather let him labor, working with his hands the thing which is good, that he may have to give to him who needs.

                                                                                EPHESIANS 4:28.

The husbandman who labors must be first partaker of the fruits.

                                                                                2 TIMOTHY 2:6.

For the earth which drinks in the rain that comes often upon it, and brings forth herbs useful for those who cultivate it, receives blessing from God. But that which bears thorns and briars is rejected, and is nigh to cursing, whose end is to be burned.

                                                                                HEBREWS 6:7–8.

PRODUCTIVITY

Productivity, a test of efficiency, appropriately focuses on how much output can be achieved at any given level of expenditure of human energy. Production of goods is the result of a combination of human energy applied to natural resources, to capital (tools and equipment), and to efficient use of time.

Higher wages depend on higher productivity. We cannot earn more unless we produce more. The key is *time*. Rising productivity depends, as well, on technology and its application in the form of better tools and equipment. A typical employee in the United States will have the use of $30,000 or more of capital equipment, and in some industries as high as $300,000 per worker. The greater efficiency results in greater production for a given level of energy expenditure, and we all enjoy more material goods and higher wages. Suppress savings and investment, tie the inventors up with red tape and government regulations, discourage workers by taxing away their increased earnings, and we end up with a nation of declining productivity. We may have bigger government in such a system, about the only activity growing, but nothing is better.

Through the harmonious cooperation of American workers and American companies, productivity has increased several times since World War II days. Still, after-tax, after-inflation paychecks for most people do not reflect this growth. Someone computed that a person earning $10,000 annually in 1963 would have to earn $70,000 in 1983 *just to stay even*. Rising prices, rising taxes, rising social security taxes, and declining product quality mark the difference.

What happened? Men in government discovered that if increased productivity, resulting from technological efficiencies, were progressively taxed away, people would not complain or even realize it until it was too late. Then government got carried away beginning in the mid-1960s with a tax-spend-elect program that even exceeded productivity changes. In recent years we have had periods of declining real incomes.

Productivity did not keep pace with the taxing programs because of excessive government controls over the remnant of the free market. Government policies have discouraged entrepreneurship, the source of much new technology and innovations; and have steadily raised direct and indirect taxes on the American people, driving some to an underground economy.

The many books and seminars on productivity emphasize secondary causes. Productivity is not fractional but depends on organizational activity. If substantial private resources are diverted to handling government red tape, persons employed in those activities decrease output of the enterprise. In other words, to support some in unproductive endeavors, others must work harder and be paid less. The more government interferes, the more organizational productivity will decline. If the government did nothing more than remove 50 percent of business requirements, regulations, and taxes, our jump in productivity would far exceed Japan's, or whatever standard. If we add our current productivity crisis to all other crises of three decades—the dollar, food, pollution, energy, stagflation—we can summarize the trend as follows: controlled citizens and uncontrolled government. Certainly not God's way!

(*See Also:* Free Enterprise, Labor Market, Management, Organization, Production)

> Take it of them, that they may be to do the service of the tabernacle of the congregation; and you shall give them to the Levites, to every man according to his service.
>
> NUMBERS 7:5.

> The thoughts of the diligent tend only to plenteousness; but of everyone who is hasty only to want.
>
> PROVERBS 21:5.

> Do you see a man diligent in his business? He shall stand before kings; he shall not stand before mean men.
>
> PROVERBS 22:29.

> If the iron be blunt, and he do not whet the edge, then must he put to more strength....
>
> ECCLESIASTES 10:10.

Ten acres of vineyard shall yield one bath, and the seed of a homer shall yield an ephah.

                                                                          ISAIAH 5:10.

To one he gave five talents, to another two, and to another one: to every man according to his own ability, and immediately went on a journey. Then he who had received the five talents went and traded with them, and made another five talents. And likewise he who had received two gained two more also.

                                                                          MATTHEW 25:15–17.

Every branch in Me that bears not fruit He takes away; and every branch that bears fruit, He purges it, that it may bring forth more fruit.

                                                                          JOHN 15:2.

Be not deceived; God is not mocked, for whatsoever a man sows, that shall he also reap.

                                                                          GALATIANS 6:7.

PROFESSIONALISM

…What is the chaff to the wheat? says the Lord.

                                                                          JEREMIAH 23:28.

(*See:* Quality, Service, Specialization)

PROFESSOR

Since most universities are run like bureaucracies, it is not surprising that professors often act like bureaucrats. Especially among the larger universities, education is seldom part of their mission. Obtaining state and federal grants, filing grant proposals to acquire research funds, lobbying, sustaining a national and international reputation, and tapping rich alumni for money occupy more energies than any other activities.

The promotion and tenure process often has little to do with academic excellence. Professors, often appointed because of the number of public grants they received while in graduate school, are promoted and tenured if they can obtain funds from government agencies and liberal foundations. In other words, the professional beggar achieves more status in the university system than the serious academician.

Retention is decided by a series of committees who, more often than not, vote yea or nay based on a person's politics than on his or her credentials. Hence, because a coalition of liberals, socialists, and marxists tends to dominate many major universities, no true academic freedom prevails. Similarly, promotion depends, in part, on the number and quality of academic journal articles written by the professor. Quality means publishing in those journals acceptable to the committees. Since such articles are usually refereed by liberals in other universities, still another door is closed to the Christian professor missionary in pagan universities (and even in some so-called Christian ones as well).

While innovative concepts are ostensibly encouraged in these universities, in truth, acceptable innovations must fall within the liberal mainstream. Let someone suggest a Christian viewpoint, whether at an informal luncheon or formal presentation of a paper, and every effort is made to discredit that individual and to exclude him both socially and academically.

The arrogant superiority demonstrated by these intellectuals makes a thinking person shudder, knowing that so many of them spend considerable time in Washington, D.C., providing counsel and advice, which, almost without exception, produces more government intervention. For them, government is the *sine qua non*. They may attend their churches and synagogues, but God is rarely a part of their academic lives and is pointedly excluded from the classroom. The following verses, as well as the next three quotes, are appropriate enough.

"The eagle never lost so much time as when he submitted to learn of the crow." —William Blake.

"I've known countless people who were reservoirs of learning yet never had a thought." —Wilson Mizner.

"Tim was so learned that he could name a horse in nine languages. So ignorant that he bought a cow to ride on." —Benjamin Franklin.

(*See Also:* Educator, Elitism, Envy, Expert, Idolatry, Truth, Wisdom)

Does not their excellency which is in them go away? They die, even without wisdom.

Job 4:21.

Should a wise man utter vain knowledge, and fill his belly with the east wind? Should he reason with unprofitable talk? Or with speeches wherewith he can do no good?

Job 15:2–3.

The beginning of the words of his mouth is foolishness; and the end of his talk is mischievous madness.... The labor of the foolish wearies every one of them, because he knows not how to go to the city.

Ecclesiastes 10:13, 15.

Beware of the scribes, who desire to walk in long robes, and love greetings in the markets, and the highest seats in the synagogues, and the chief rooms at feasts.

LUKE 20:46.

Professing themselves to be wise, they became fools.

ROMANS 1:22.

Where is the wise? Where is the scribe? Where is the disputer of this world? Has not God made foolish the wisdom of this world?

1 CORINTHIANS 1:20.

…Knowledge puffs up, but charity edifies. If any man think that he knows any thing, he knows nothing yet as he ought to know.

1 CORINTHIANS 8:1–2.

For you suffer fools gladly, seeing you yourselves are wise.

2 CORINTHIANS 11:19.

…from which [faith unfeigned] some, having strayed, have turned aside to idle talk, desiring to be teachers of the law, understanding neither what they say nor the things which they affirm.

1 TIMOTHY 1:6–7.

If any man teach otherwise, and consent not to wholesome words, even the words of our Lord Jesus Christ, and to the doctrine which is according to godliness, he is proud, knowing nothing, but doting about questions and strifes of words, whereof comes envy, of men of corrupt minds, and destitute of the truth, supposing that gain is godliness; from such withdraw yourself.

1 TIMOTHY 6:3–5.

Ever learning, and never able to come to the knowledge of the truth.

2 TIMOTHY 3:7.

Who is a wise man and endowed with knowledge among you? Let him show out of a good conversation his works with meekness of wisdom. But if you have bitter envying and strife in your hearts, glory not, and lie not against the truth. This wisdom descends not from above, but is earthly, sensual, devilish.

JAMES 3:13–15.

There were false prophets also among the people, even as there shall be false teachers among you, who privily shall bring in damnable heresies, even denying the Lord that brought them, and bring upon themselves swift destruction.

2 Peter 2:1.

PROFIT

A Russian proverb—Without profit, a man has no pants—was the response of a Soviet diplomat after conclusion of the 1972–1973 Soviet-American wheat deal. The Soviets had directly sold, at twice the price in Southeast Asia, some wheat bought from us cheaply. The Soviets garnered huge profits—both economic and political.

What the IRS and big labor call profits differs from the economist's definition. To them profits abide *before* investors are rewarded for their risks and investments. When automobile companies generate some "profits," organized labor immediately screams that they will renegotiate their contract before the previous one has expired. The IRS taxes away so-called corporate profits. Dividends are paid to investors out of what survives, and some is retained in the corporation for reinvestment. No wonder that productivity has declined in the United States. With big labor and governments grabbing "profits," little remains for reinvestment to increase capital, expand, and create more jobs.

Economists often consider profits residual—what remains after *everyone* else is paid. In other words, after suppliers are paid, laborers and management receive their market (not union) rate, interest charges are paid, and finally investors receive an appropriate return on investment, then if anything remains, it may be profit. By the economist's definition, most businesses do not earn profits.

Profits can also be likened to those amounts received over and above the market rate. For instance, if investors are paid a 25 percent return on an investment that would normally yield 18 percent, certainly they are earning a 7 percent profit. The same is true of exorbitant management compensation. What about organized labor? If organized labor extracts from a company more than they would earn in a free market, laborers and union management are receiving unearned profits. More often than not, unionized labor may be the only ones accumulating profits in an organization.

Finally, profits are sometimes mistaken for return on risk. Suppose that you invest in a very risky venture, like a gold mine in Norfolk, Virginia. If you lose your investment, no one comes to your aid with either offers of sympathy or money. If a productive gold mine materializes and you earn 500 percent return on your investment, then everyone cries unfair, unearned income, exorbitant profits, and both the union and the IRS will confiscate as much of your profits as you've not shielded from them. That high return is hardly a profit, but payment for risk taking. On the other hand, if you opened a bank in Virginia Beach and generated that kind of return on investment, those are indeed profits, possibly obscene ones at that.

(See Also: Forecasting, Inequality, Interest, Return on Investment, Strategic Planning)

Treasures of wickedness profit nothing; but righteousness delivers from death.

PROVERBS 10:2.

The thoughts of the diligent tend only to plenteousness; but of every one who is hasty only to want.

PROVERBS 21:5.

What profit has a man of all his labor which he takes under the sun? One generation passes away, and another generation comes, but the earth abides forever.

ECCLESIASTES 1:3–4.

Say to the righteous, that it shall be well with him, for they shall eat the fruit of their doings.

ISAIAH 3:10.

For whoever has, to him shall be given, and he shall have more abundance; but whoever has not, from him shall be taken away even that he has.

MATTHEW 13:12.

For what is a man profited, if he shall gain the whole world, and lose his own soul? Or what shall a man give in exchange for his own soul?

MATTHEW 16:26.

He who has received five talents came and brought another five talents saying, Lord, you delivered to me five talents; behold, I have gained beside them five talents more.

MATTHEW 25:20.

Cast the unprofitable servant into outer darkness; there shall be weeping and the gnashing of teeth.

MATTHEW 25:30.

These are they who are sown on good ground; such as hear the word, and receive it, and bring forth fruit, some thirtyfold, some sixty, some a hundred.

MARK 4:20.

...Take heed what you hear; with what measure you mete, it shall be measured to you; and unto you who hear shall more be given. For he who has, to him shall be given....

MARK 4:24–25.

He called his ten servants, and delivered them ten pounds, and said to them, Occupy till I come.... It came to pass, that when he was returned, having received the kingdom, then he commanded these servants to be called to him, to whom he had given the money, that he might know how much every man had gained by trading. Then came the first, saying, Lord, your pound has gained ten pounds.

LUKE 19:13, 15–16.

It is the spirit that quickens; the flesh profits nothing; the words that I speak to you, they are spirit, and they are life.

JOHN 6:63.

Avoiding this, that no man should blame us in this abundance which is administered by us.

2 CORINTHIANS 8:20.

He who ministers seed to the sower both ministers bread for your food, and multiplies your seed sown, and increases the fruits of your righteousness.

2 CORINTHIANS 9:10.

PROLETARIANISM

Delight is not seemly for a fool, much less for a servant to have rule over princes.

PROVERBS 19:10.

(*See:* Communism, One Worldism, Welfarism)

PROPERTY TAXES

If you rent a house and pay a monthly sum to the landlord, who owns the house? As a tenant, you acquire certain rights, and as a lessor, you surrender temporarily certain rights to the lessee. However, there is no doubt who owns the property.

Property taxes are like paying rent. If we do not pay them, we can be evicted the same as a lessee. Failure to pay personal property taxes can result in expropriation of our possessions to be disposed of at the will of the state. Who, then, really owns our property?

Typically, about three-fourths of real property taxes support the public school system, the lucrative salaries of administrators, union wages for teachers, books, toys, athletic equipment, musical instruments, swimming pools, public transportation, coffee and donuts, subsidized meals, and all items subsumed under "public education." For many school districts, these costs add up to around $2,000 per student per academic year. If property taxes typically run $1,000 a year per residence, then families with school-aged children in public schools receive a subsidy, a grant of money forcibly taken from their neighbors. For parents with children in private schools, they not only must contribute to the support of their unbelieving neighbors but bear the double burden of private school tuition.

The other one-fourth of property taxes supports local governments, libraries, parks, and other activities. There is little quarrel with the need to run local civil government—courts and police. However, libraries, for example, should charge a user fee, not a public tax. Few people use them but every property owner (absentee or not) pays for them.

Biblical law prohibits property taxes because they destroy the family and the liberty of man. Property and inheritance taxes are the state's way of destroying the family, undermining the rule of God and usurping everyone's freedom. Property must be left intact for future generations to assure family stability and continuity of the Christian society.

(*See Also:* Expropriation, Power of State, Private Property, Taxation, Theft)

> *If a soul sin, and commit a trespass against the Lord, and lie unto his neighbor in that which was delivered him to keep, or in fellowship, or in a thing taken away by violence, or has deceived his neighbor, ... then it shall be, because he has sinned, and is guilty, that he shall restore that which he took violently away, or the thing which he had deceitfully gotten....*
>
> LEVITICUS 6:2, 4.

> *You shall not defraud your neighbor, neither rob him....*
>
> LEVITICUS 19:13.

> *Jehoiakim gave the silver and the gold to Pharaoh; but he taxed the land to give the money according to the commandment of Pharaoh. He exacted the silver and the gold of the people of the land, of every one according to his taxation, to give it to Pharaoh-necho.... He did that which was evil in the sight of the Lord, according to all that his fathers had done.*
>
> 2 KINGS 23:35, 37.

...and the chief seats in the synagogues, and the uppermost rooms at feasts, who devour widows' houses....

MARK 12:39–40.

PROSPERITY

Reverend Norman Vincent Peale's oft-repeated verse for problem-solving and prosperity is: "I can do all things through Christ who strengthens me" (PHILIPPIANS 4:13). This implies many things. First, there must be desire and a goal firmly established in the mind of the believer. Second, there must be action, for without action even the world would not have been created. Third, one must select the right means and call upon Christ to guide and carry through the means to the ends. Fourth, there must be faith to carry us through periods of adversity; and if we believe that verse, we have the faith.

There are all kinds of prosperity, not just material prosperity (discussed elsewhere). Whatever prosperity we seek, it pours out abundantly when we are partners with God; this is the only enduring prosperity. While you ruminate on your own riches, think of greater ones such as the prosperity of health, happiness, peace, and all other types of wealth that derive from the establishment of a free society under the rule of God.

We can do it, because we "can do all things through Christ who strengthens" us. First, visualize in your mind's eye what this world would be like if we lived in a Christian society obeying God's laws. Think about this in some detail. No doubt you will want to study this subject further. This book will help. Second, for every decision, ask yourself whether it falls within biblical guidelines. Third, think carefully how you can bring about this wonderful prosperity to your family and friends. Fourth, take action and for every action, consider whether you are personally living within God's laws every day. Finally, carry the message to your local community by right action; and why not run for public office? Prosperity? It's ours if we can live up to the standards! God has promised it!

(*See Also:* Abundance, Economic Growth, Free Market, Law of Increase, Self-Discipline, Stewardship, Work)

For he clave to the Lord, and departed not from following Him, but kept His commandments, which the Lord commanded Moses. The Lord was with him; and he prospered wherever he went; and he rebelled against the king of Assyria, and served him not.

2 KINGS 18:6–7.

Then you shall prosper, if you take heed to fulfill the statutes and judgments which the Lord charged Moses with concerning Israel: be strong, and of good courage; dread not, nor be dismayed.

1 CHRONICLES 22:13.

...As long as he sought the Lord, God made him to prosper.

2 CHRONICLES 26:5.

...That you may be strong, and eat the good of the land, and leave it for an inheritance to your children for ever.

EZRA 9:12.

If they obey and serve Him, they shall spend their days in prosperity, and their years in pleasures. But if they obey not, they shall perish by the sword, and they shall die without knowledge.

JOB 36:11–12.

Blessed is the man who walks not in the counsel of the ungodly, nor stands in the way of sinners, nor sits in the seat of the scornful. But his delight is in the law of the Lord; and in His law does he meditate day and night. He shall be like a tree planted by the rivers of water, that brings forth his fruit in his season; his leaf also shall not wither; and whatever he does shall prosper.

PSALM 1:1–3.

Learn to do well; seek judgment, relieve the oppressed, judge the fatherless, plead for the widow. Come now, and let us reason together, says the Lord: though your sins be as scarlet, they shall be as white as snow; though they be red like crimson, they shall be as wool. If you are willing and obedient, you shall eat the good of the land; but if you refuse and rebel, you shall be devoured with the sword, for the mouth of the Lord has spoken it.

ISAIAH 1:17–20.

You have removed my soul far off from peace; I forgot prosperity. I said, My strength and my hope is perished from the Lord.

LAMENTATIONS 3:17–18.

PROSTITUTE

Some libertarians postulate that crimes consist of those acts where one human harms others. These acts do not include contractual relationships that adults enter voluntarily. Hence, prostitution, drug sales and purchases, pornography, and homosexuality may not be prosecutable under a libertarian system of laws. Libertarianism is founded on principles of contractual relationships rather than on biblical precepts. Of course, in many instances there is positional overlap. Let's consider one that does not overlap—prostitution. Prostitution is condemned by the Bible. Aside from that, do libertarians have a tenable position? A prostitute offers a personal service, negotiates an exchange price with a client, and off they go to complete the transaction. Where's the harm?

One, either the prostitute or the client may have an undisclosed communicable disease, which can spread rapidly through prostitution and can harm innocent parties, even months later. Unborn babies and donated blood recipients are two examples.

Two, prostitution contributes to the destruction of the family, the very foundation of God's order on earth.

Three, the libertarian arguing against victimless crimes probably envisions the prostitute operating in another part of town or hidden away from the public eye, not in front of his own home or in sight of his own wife and children. The value of commercial or residential property in a decent neighborhood can quickly decline when prostitutes begin working the streets. Would you want to purchase a home for your family in an area frequented by prostitutes or sit on your front porch in the sight of such contracts being negotiated?

Four, some suggest that rape would decline if prostitution laws were liberalized. As our society became "liberated" *from* discipline and obedience to God's laws, as sexual promiscuity rose in incidence, both rape and prostitution *increased*. Prostitution, therefore, is neither victimless nor harmless.

(*See Also:* Abortion, Ethics, Family, Law and Order, Libertarianism, Rape)

There shall be no ritual harlot of the daughters of Israel, nor a sodomite of the sons of Israel. You shall not bring the hire of a harlot or the price of a dog to the house of the Lord your God for any avowed offering, for both of these are an abomination to the Lord your God.
DEUTERONOMY 23:17–18.

The lips of a strange woman drop as a honeycomb, and her mouth is smoother than oil; but her end is bitter as wormwood, sharp as a two-edged sword. Her feet go down to death; her steps take hold on hell.
PROVERBS 5:3–5.

To keep you away from the evil woman, from the flattery of the tongue of a strange woman. Lust not after her beauty in your heart; neither let her take you with her eyelids. For by means of a whorish woman a man is brought to a piece of bread; and the adulteress will hunt for the

precious life. Can a man take fire in his bosom, and his clothes not be burned? Can one go upon hot coals, and his feet not be burned?
PROVERBS 6:24–28.

For a whore is a deep ditch; and a strange woman is a narrow pit. She also lies in wait as for a prey, and increases the transgressors among men.
PROVERBS 23:27–28.

PROTECTIONISM

(*See:* Bribery, Imports, International Trade)

PUBLIC EDUCATION

Children in whom was no blemish, but well favored, and skillful in all wisdom, and cunning in knowledge, and understanding science, and such as had ability in them to stand in the king's palace, and whom they might teach the learning and the tongue of the Chaldeans. And the king appointed them a daily provision of the king's meat....
DANIEL 1:4–5.

(*See:* Education, Educator, Professor)

PUNITIVE DAMAGES

Or all that which he has sworn falsely, he shall even restore it in the principal, and shall add the fifth part more to it, and give it to him to whom it appertains, in the day of his trespass offering.
LEVITICUS 6:5.

(*See:* Court System, Law, Restitution)

QUALITY

REVELATION 21:9–27 describes the New Jerusalem. Only the most valuable materials form its foundations and structures: precious stones, and pearls, and streets of pure gold. No mention of soft plastics, discount store imitations, or pot-holed thoroughfares. We read of a first-class city. God speaks of the best, first fruits, unblemished animals in sacrifice—only quality products and labor. When Jesus handed out talents for investment, who received the greatest reward? He who did a quality job of investing!

Quality marks a free society under God's laws. God talks of abundance, prosperity, first-rate production, craftsmanship, happiness, health, and freedom. What are the major topics of discussion in a statist or humanist society? Scarcity and shortages, poverty and income redistribution, falling productivity and quality of product, state-planned happiness, national health care, taxes, and more taxes! You can easily verify those statements. Read the Bible objectively to confirm the first. Read and listen to the media and politicians, and you will document the second.

Quality in thinking precedes quality in production and in life. "Without a demand for virtue and talents, there can be no excellence, no exemplars."[1] Even agnostics agree that we are what we think. "For as he thinketh in his heart, so is he" (PROVERBS 23:7). We can still produce in mass quantities, but workmanship, pride, and corporate responsibility surely reduce recalls and the number of trips to the store for exchanges. The apprenticeship system still results in the best and most knowledgeable workers. We learn better by working under the guidance of a master, whether we repair a furnace or repair our souls with Bible study.

(*See Also:* Character, Free Enterprise, Golden Rule, Honesty, Service, Specialization, Value)

---

[1]Leonard Read, *Who's Listening* (Irvington-on-Hudson, N.Y.: Foundation for Economic Education, 1973), p. 166.

Do not give what is holy to the dogs; nor cast your pearls before swine, lest they trample them under their feet. ...

MATTHEW 7:6.

The kingdom of heaven is like a merchant seeking beautiful pearls, who, when he had found one pearl of great price, went and sold all that he had and bought it.

MATTHEW 13:45–46.

According to the grace of God, which is given me, as a wise masterbuilder, I have laid the foundation, and another builds on it. But let every man take heed how he builds thereupon.

1 CORINTHIANS 3:10.

If any man's work abide which he has built thereupon, he shall receive a reward. If any man's work shall be burned, he shall suffer loss....

1 CORINTHIANS 3:14–15.

I counsel you to buy of me gold tried in the fire, that you may be rich, and white raiment, that you may be clothed, and that the shame of your nakedness does not appear; and annoint your eyes with eyesalve, that you may see.

REVELATION 3:18.

QUALITY CIRCLES

(*See:* Productivity, Service, Specialization)

RANDOMNESS

Certainty means without doubt you know an event will happen. *Uncertainty* means that you haven't the foggiest notion whether an event will occur or not. *Risk* states the statistical probability of an occurrence. You plan a picnic; meteorologists forecast a 60 percent chance of rain. Will it rain or not? Will it rain where you will picnic? The odds of six out of ten that it will rain is supposed to be a step up from complete uncertainty.

Randomness presents one crucial difference between believers and non-believers. Evolutionists believe that *by chance* planets and stars come into existence; *by chance* organic life (carbon-hydrogen-oxygen) sprang up. Further, by a whole series of random events, man evolved. Once rational man arrived, randomness disappeared. Man now controls the creation process. He can mold his environment and universe any way he pleases; and he pleases himself by forming an institution, an idol, to whom he ascribes ultimate power and authority—the state.

Believers know that nothing occurs by chance. By examining the order of the universe, the smallest discernible particles, they see design and planning and purpose. Engineering on the tiniest insect is no less perfect than on the largest animal. God pays attention to details. If man randomly arose, then he has no purpose greater than random existence. If God created man, then he has purpose within the larger design. Randomness leads to hopelessness and pessimism. Belief in creation by a Supreme Power leads to optimism and purposeful action of man.

(*See Also:* Creation, Evolutionism, Foundation, Individualism, Law, Risk Aversion)

> *Watch: if it [the ark of the Lord] goes up the road to its own territory, to Beth Shemesh, then He has done us this great evil. But if not, then we shall know that it is not His hand that struck us; it was by chance that it happened to us.*
>
> 1 SAMUEL 6:9.

...As I happened by chance to be on Mount Gilboa, there was Saul, leaning on his spear; and indeed the chariots and horsemen followed hard after him.

2 SAMUEL 1:6.

I returned and saw under the sun, that the race is not to the swift, not the battle to the strong, neither yet bread to the wise, nor yet riches to men of understanding, nor yet favor to men of skill; but time and chance happen to them all.

ECCLESIASTES 9:11.

In the morning sow your seed, and in the evening withhold not your hand, for you know not whether shall prosper, either this or that, or whether they both shall be alike.

ECCLESIASTES 11:6.

RAPE

Under biblical law, the death penalty awaits those who commit violent crimes, incorrigibles, even delinquent children, and rape of a married or betrothed woman. The rape test is whether the attacked woman cries out and, in an urban or populated setting, is heard. In other words, there must be testimony or corroboration. Seduction is a slightly different matter. If a betrothed virgin is seduced and does not appeal for help, then the death penalty applies to both: to her because she did not scream for help; to him because he violated his neighbor's wife.

Preservation of family presides above all. Destroy the family, and God's order is under attack. For that reason law treats the unbetrothed virgin, who is raped or seduced, differently. Since she has lost her virginity, she is less desirable as a wife. Therefore, the man must pay her (a dowry). If the man is acceptable to the father, he must marry her, without right of divorce. If he is not acceptable, at least the former virgin has received some money to make her attractive to a suitable marriage partner.

(*See Also:* Abortion, Family, Feminism, Justice, Marriage, Restitution, Women)

When Shechem, the son of Hamor the Hivite, prince of the country, saw her, he took her, and lay with her, and defiled her.... Two of the sons of Jacob, Simeon and Levi, Dinah's brothers took each man his sword and came upon the city boldly, and slew all the males. And they slew Hamor and Shechem his son with the edge of the sword, and took Dinah out of Shechem's house....

GENESIS 34:2, 25–26.

If a man entices a virgin who is not betrothed, and lies with her, he shall surely pay the bride-price for her to be his wife. If her father utterly refuses to give her to him, he shall pay money according to the bride-price of virgins.

EXODUS 22:16–17.

If a young woman who is a virgin is betrothed to a husband, and a man finds her in the city, and lies with her, then you shall bring them both out to the gate of that city, and you shall stone them to death with stones; the young woman because she did not cry out in the city, and the man because he humbled his neighbor's wife; so you shall put away the evil person from among you. But if a man finds a betrothed young woman in the countryside, and the man forces and lies with her, then only the man who lay with her shall die. But you shall do nothing to the young woman; there is in the young woman no sin worthy of death, for just as a man rises against his neighbor and kills him, even so is this matter; for he found her in the countryside, and the betrothed young woman cried out, but there was no one to save her. If a man finds a young woman who is a virgin, who is not betrothed, and he seizes her and lies with her, and they are found out, then the man who lay with her shall give to the young woman's father fifty shekels of silver, and she shall be his wife because he has humbled her; he shall not be permitted to divorce her in all his days.

DEUTERONOMY 22:23–29.

RED TAPE

[The king said]...if you show the dream and its interpretation, you shall receive of me gifts and rewards and great honor.... They said, Let the king tell his servants the dream.... The king answered, I know of certainty that you would gain time, because you see the thing is gone from me.

DANIEL 2:6–8.

(See: Bureaucracy, Directed Economy, Fury of a Bureaucrat Scorned)

REDISTRIBUTION OF INCOME/WEALTH

Late in 1974, the ministerial association of Washington, D.C., conducted a survey to check on the needs of the poor within that city. That survey indicated that there were some pressing needs. Need for food, need for housing, need for clothing and medical assistance. This in a district that has a higher per capita income than any state in the union.

Spokesmen for the ministerial association called a press conference to announce their plan of action to relieve the needs revealed by the survey: *they would call upon government to provide the assistance required.*

One cannot fault the clergymen for their concern. But, one can fault them for their course of action. Caesar was their answer. They belittled God.[1]

Reinhold Niebuhr, founder of the Fellowship of Socialist Christians (like saying the Satanic-Christian Fellowship), said we should employ Marxist methodology to achieve Christian objectives.[2] Redistribution of income applies Marxist means to apparently Christian goals. A Christian does not take his neighbor's property by stealth or force. All redistribution schemes rely on stealth (hidden taxes, inflation) and force (income and property taxes). Ostensibly these expropriated assets alleviate the poor and suffering. But as more money is channeled into welfare and egalitarian programs, the number of "poor" grows even faster.

Of course, believers know that welfarism, a giant scam, bilks us of fruits of our labor. Slavery and elitism, never new, must rely on increasingly ingenious ploys to confiscate wealth with minimum protest and the safest environment for our "do-gooders," who do quite "good" for themselves. Too, willing "innocents" in this scam, the shills—often liberal intellectuals enjoying comfortable salaries and positions of influence—tout egalitarianism under labels like transfer payments, incomes policy, and bribing the poor so they will not destroy us, along with elegant mathematical models and lofty language.

Obviously, for social ministers, welfarists, and the like, their god is indeed dead. Since God has not done His job properly, it's time for Socialist Christians and the government to straighten out the mess. I heard that message often enough from clergy and others in El Salvador and in Nicaragua. We know what they did to Nicaragua. Intelligent believers know what they intend for El Salvador. Redistribution of income and wealth means confiscation, i.e., taking property by force without compensation. We used to call it theft. Who lives in those expropriated homes in Nicaragua? The Marxist governing elite and their Cuban advisors! Once a principle of theft becomes an established norm, or right, then where does theft stop?

[1]Russ Walton, *One Nation Under God* (Old Tappan, N.J.: Fleming H. Revell, 1975), pp. 178–79.
[2]Ibid., p. 181.

(*See Also:* Demagoguery, Equality, One Worldism, Planned Economy, Statism, Taxation, Welfarism)

Then it shall be, because he has sinned, and is guilty, that he should restore that which he took violently away, or the thing which he has deceitfully gotten, or that which was delivered him to keep, or the lost thing which he found.

LEVITICUS 6:4.

You shall do no unrighteousness in judgment; you shall not respect the person of the poor, nor honor the person of the mighty....

LEVITICUS 19:15.

They shall not build, and another inhabit; they shall not plant, and another eat.... They shall not labor in vain....

ISAIAH 65:22–23.

After the league made with him, he shall work deceitfully, for he shall come up, and shall become strong with a small people. He shall enter peaceably even upon the fattest places of the province; and he shall do that which his fathers have not done, nor his fathers' fathers; he shall scatter among them the prey, and spoil, and riches; yea, and he shall forecast his devices against the strongholds, even for a time.

DANIEL 11:23–24.

RELIGIOUS FREEDOM

If you offer a sacrifice of peace offerings to the Lord, you shall offer it at your own will.

LEVITICUS 19:5.

(*See:* Freedom, Source)

REMNANT

A Hindu mystic said that of many called few will come. Of those who come few will get into heaven. A Christian religious sect says that of billions who have passed through the earth, very few are righteous enough to enter heaven, except for the

144,000 (REVELATION 14:3). Apparently the forbidden fruit—the lawlessness of Satan—has greater appeal. Still, through every trial and tribulation a remnant remains to preserve the Word, the law of God, for future generations. Noah's family, a remnant, carried aboard a remnant of animals. Lot's family, a remnant, were refugees from that ancient human paradise of corruption. The task of restoration of godly rule rests on the remnant. Dr. Gary North speaks to today's remnant and publishes *Remnant Review*. He writes:

> Chapters 8–10 and 12–14 of the book of Zechariah are deeply imbued with the spirit and language of external victory over evil. The restoration of godly rule is prophesied in all of its force and clarity. Restoration shall be in time and on earth.... Restoration is the promise of the prophetic vision.
>
> How does God intend to bring this about? Not by some discontinuous political event, or some miraculous intervention into the daily processes of the world, but by steady spiritual progress.[1]

(*See Also:* Creation, Free Society, Judgment, Law, Liberty, Source, Truth)

... Lift up your prayer for the remnant who are left.

> 2 KINGS 19:4.

Haman said to king Ahasuerus, There is a certain people scattered abroad and dispersed among the people in all the provinces of your kingdom; and their laws are different from all people; neither do they keep the king's laws: therefore it is not for the king's profit to suffer them.

> ESTHER 3:8.

Except the Lord of hosts had left to us a very small remnant, we should have been as Sodom, and we should have been like Gomorrah.

> ISAIAH 1:9.

The remnant shall return, even the remnant of Jacob, to the mighty God. For though your people Israel be as the sand of the sea, yet a remnant of them shall return....

> ISAIAH 10:21–22.

It shall come to pass in that day that the Lord shall set his hand again the second time to recover the remnant of His people.

> ISAIAH 11:11.

[1]Gary North, *The Dominion Covenant: Genesis* (Tyler, Tex.: Institute for Christian Economics, 1982), p. 448.

...The remnant shall be very small and feeble.

ISAIAH 16:14.

The remnant that is escaped of the house of Judah shall again take root downward, and bear fruit upward. For out of Jerusalem shall go forth a remnant....

ISAIAH 37:31–32.

Yet will I leave a remnant, that you may have some who shall escape the sword among the nations, when you are scattered through the countries. They who escape of you shall remember Me among the nations where they shall be carried captives, because I am broken with their whorish heart, which has departed from Me, and with their eyes, which go a whoring after their idols; and they shall lothe themselves for the evils which they have committed in all their abominations. And they shall know that I am the Lord, and that I have not said in vain that I would do this evil to them.

EZEKIEL 6:8–10.

I will surely assemble, O Jacob, all of you; I will surely gather the remnant of Israel....

MICAH 2:12.

But what says the answer of God to him [Elisha]? I have reserved to myself seven thousand men, who have not bowed the knee to the image of Baal. Even so then at this present time also there is a remnant according to the election of grace.

ROMANS 11:4–5.

RENT

When someone rents or leases property from another, the renter acquires a bundle of rights. These rights do not include ownership but only the right to use the property, within limitations. If rented property is damaged, lost, or stolen, then the renter must restore it to original condition. In other words, with those acquired rights also tags along responsibility.. Otherwise, it makes little sense for the owner to lend or rent.

Laws today, especially on real property rental, are decidedly against the landlord. A lawyer in Hollywood, Florida, who has processed more than 30,000 evictions over a decade said, "Landlords are definitely second-class citizens before the court." To sue in small claims court, for example, costs $2.50 for any suit except for rent, which costs the landlord $46.50. The landlord must pay for legal representation, if any. The renter receives free legal advice from a public defender, paid by the landlord's taxes. The law enforcement and judicial systems offer no assistance to landlords, but legislators are quick to impose higher taxes on the unorganized landlords, whether they own one rental unit or thousands. Hardly biblical in practice!

(*See Also:* Accountability, Law and Order, Liability, Private Property, Property Taxes, Restitution)

> It shall come to pass in the increase, that you give the fifth part to Pharaoh, and four parts shall be your own, for seed in the field, and for your food, and for them of your households, and for food for your little ones.
>
> GENESIS 47:24.

> If a man borrows anything from his neighbor, and it becomes injured or dies, the owner of it not being with it, he shall surely make it good. But if its owner was with it, he shall not make it good; if it was hired, it came for its hire.
>
> EXODUS 22:14–15.

> And He began to speak unto them by parables. A certain man planted a vineyard, set a hedge about it, and dug a place for the winefat, and built a tower, and let it out to husbandmen, and went to a far country. At the season he sent to the husbandmen a servant, to receive from the husbandmen of the fruit of the vineyard.
>
> MARK 12:1–2.

REPUTATION

(*See:* Character, Remnant)

RESPONSIBILITY

One crucial difference between the free society under the rule of God and human-devised institutions of government is *responsibility*. Under God's system, responsibility falls upon the individual and his family, as well as his society. Responsibility implies a cause-and-effect relationship. Things happen because someone caused events. We cannot blame fate, our horoscope, or some mysterious sideral waves undulating over the planet for fortunes and misfortunes.

As a commodity trader, I concluded that some people want to lose. I have interviewed thousands of small business owners. Many barely eke out a living. Through a series of decisions, they put themselves into situations that guarantee losses. When guilt peddlers blame opulent America for the world's woes, notice how many Americans accept it and readily cave in to unrealistic demands. Of course, if you receive public education, food stamps, farm subsidies, protection from foreign competition, low-interest education loans, or whatever subsidy or welfare, then you are not guiltless.

Ungodly systems remove responsibility. Consequently, Marxists speak of the dictates of history as though an animate history responds for the march of world communism. Welfarists speak of environmental causes of poverty or success: Environment, not the individual, is responsible. A demagogue warns of impending disaster and riots unless demanded conditions change, and then organizes the riots. A murderer disclaims responsibility for a killing. Merely experimenting, taking a blood sample, he fulfilled a frustrated ambition of wanting to be a surgeon but could not because he was born in the ghettos. And the bleeding hearts say, "He's right. He's not responsible for the crime. Society is."

In their hearts, most people do know better. What matters is God's law. Simply stated, a person is responsible for thoughts and deeds, whether intentional or accidental. The buck stops right there.

(*See Also:* Accountability, Character, Judgment, Law and Order, Maturity, Responsibility, Tinstaafl)

> *I will be surety for him; of my hand shall you require him. If I bring him not to you, and set him before you, then let me bear the blame forever.*
> GENESIS *43:9.*

> *If one man's ox hurt another's, that it dies, then they shall sell the live ox, and divide the money of it; and the dead ox also they shall divide. Or if it be known that the ox used to push in times past, and his owner has not kept him in, he shall surely pay ox for ox; and the dead ox shall be his own.*
> EXODUS *21:35–36.*

> *If a man shall deliver to his neighbor money or stuff to keep, and it is stolen out of the man's house, if the thief be found, let him pay double. If the thief be not found, then the master of the house shall be brought to the judges, to see whether he has put his hand on his neighbor's goods.*
> EXODUS *22:7–8.*

If a man borrows anything of his neighbor, and it is hurt or dies, the owner thereof being not with it, he shall surely make it good. But if the owner thereof be with it, he shall not make it good; if it be a hired thing, it came for his hire.

EXODUS 22:14–15.

If a soul sins, and commits any of these things which are forbidden to be done by the commandments of the Lord, though he knew it not, yet he is guilty, and shall bear his iniquity.

LEVITICUS 5:17.

You shall have one law for him who sins through ignorance....whether he be born in the land, or a stranger....

NUMBERS 15:29–31.

When you build a new house, then you shall make a battlement [railing] for your roof, that you bring not blood upon your house, if any man fall from there.

DEUTERONOMY 22:8.

The fathers shall not be put to death for the children, neither shall the children be put to death for the fathers: every man shall be put to death for his own sin.

DEUTERONOMY 24:16.

Even a child is known by his doings, whether his work be pure and whether it be right.

PROVERBS 20:11.

Suffer not your mouth to cause your flesh to sin; neither say before the angel, that it was an error....

ECCLESIASTES 5:6.

He who digs a pit shall fall into it; and whoever breaks a hedge, a serpent shall bite him.

ECCLESIASTES 10:8.

Woe is me for my hurt! My wound is grievous; but I said, Truly this is a grief, and I must bear it.

JEREMIAH 10:19.

Every one shall die for his own iniquity; every man who eats the sour grape, his teeth shall be set on edge.

JEREMIAH 31:30.

When I say to the wicked, You shall surely die, and you give him not warning, nor speak to warn the wicked from his wicked way, to save his life, the same wicked man shall die in his iniquity; but his blood will I require at your hand. Yet if you warn the wicked, and he turn not from his wickedness, nor from his wicked way, he shall die in his iniquity; but you have delivered your soul.

EZEKIEL 3:18–19.

So then every one of us shall give account of himself to God.

ROMANS 14:12.

If any provide not for his own, and especially for those of his own house, he has denied the faith, and is worse than an infidel.

1 TIMOTHY 5:8.

RESTITUTION

"Restitution and restoration are the essence of justice. The prison system as an answer to the problem of crime is a modern and anti-Biblical scheme: it does nothing to further either restitution or restoration.... It does not remedy the crime, nor does it remedy the criminal...."[1] In many jurisdictions, the legal system no longer even makes a pretense to justice. Often its mission is geared to enlarge the tax gathering mechanism, i.e., a revenue-producing profit center. Some states purport to have reinstituted restitution, but the criminal does not make restitution; the state pays restituted claims as well as supports the criminal in prison with tax money.

Restitution means returning property or restoring it to its original state, plus a fine often equal to its value. Without amercement thieves are encouraged because at worst they only have to return stolen property. Meanwhile, they use it, and if they return property well used or partially destroyed, then what has the thief lost? The fine is not paid to the state. The robbed has been harmed. The robbed should be recompensed. In biblical law, the injured party receives the fine or its value. In serious crimes, capital punishment is the form of restitution. In other words, in biblical law, *criminals* are punished and victims are compensated for losses, and such compensation is paid by the criminal.

In our humanistic society, the *victim* endures penalty by his losses, court costs, legal fees, inconvenience since trials are usually established for the convenience of the criminal. To add insult to injury, not only is the victim not compensated in criminal cases, but he must pay taxes for keeping the criminal, for his legal counsel,

[1]Rousas John Rushdoony, *Law and Society,* Vol. II (Vallecito, Calif.: Ross House Books, 1982), p. 32.

and welfare to support the criminal's family. Our society is antithetical to God's plan. It is destructive of God's order. It makes heroes of criminals, who may even be elected to public office. Such is social justice.

(*See Also:* Capital Punishment, Compensation, Justice, Law and Order, Responsibility, Rule of Law)

If men strive together, and one smite another with a stone, or with his fist, and he die not, but keeps to his bed: If he rises again, and walks abroad upon his staff, then shall he who smote him be quit; only he shall pay for the loss of his time, and shall cause him to be thoroughly healed.

EXODUS 21:18–19.

If men strive, and hurt a woman with child, so that her fruit depart from her, and yet no mischief follow, he shall be surely punished, according as the woman's husband will lay upon him; and he shall pay as the judges determine. And if mischief follow, then you shall give life for life.

EXODUS 21:22–23.

If an ox gore a man or woman, that they die, then the ox shall be surely stoned, and his flesh shall not be eaten; but the owner of the ox shall be quit. But if the ox were wont to push with his horn in times past, and it has been testified to his owner, and he has not kept him in, but that it has killed a man or woman, the ox shall be stoned, and its owner also shall be put to death. If there be laid on him a sum of money, then he shall give for the ransom of his life whatever is laid upon him.... If the ox shall push a manservant or a maidservant, he shall give to their master thirty shekels of silver, and the ox shall be stoned.

EXODUS 21:28–30, 32.

If a man shall steal an ox or a sheep, and kill it, or sell it, he shall restore five oxen for an ox, and four sheep for a sheep. If a thief be found breaking in, and he is smitten so that he dies, there shall be no blood shed for him. If the sun has risen on him, there shall be blood shed for him, for he should make full restitution: if he have nothing, then he shall be sold for his theft. If the theft be certainly found in his hands alive, ... he shall restore double. If a man shall cause a field or vineyard to be eaten, and shall put in his beast, and shall feed in another man's field, of the best of his own field, and of the best of his own vineyard, shall he make restitution. If fire breaks out, and catch in thorns, so that the stacks of corn, or the standing corn, or the field, be consumed, he who kindled the fire shall surely make restitution. If a man delivers to his neighbor money or stuff to keep, and it be stolen out of the man's house, if the thief be found, let him pay double. If the thief be not found, then the master of the house shall be brought to the judges, to see whether he has put his hand unto his neighbor's goods.

EXODUS 22:1–8.

If a soul commits a trespass, and sin through ignorance, in the holy things of the Lord, then he shall bring for his trespass unto the Lord a ram without blemish out of the flocks, with your valuation in shekels of silver, after the shekel of the sanctuary, for a trespass offering; and he shall make amends for the harm that he has done in the holy thing, and shall add the fifth part to it....

LEVITICUS 5:15–16.

...Because he has sinned, and is guilty, he shall restore that which he took violently away, or the thing which he has deceitfully gotten, or that which was delivered him to keep, or the lost thing which he found, or all that about which he has sworn falsely, he shall even restore it in the principal, and shall add the fifth part more thereto, and give it to him to whom it pertains....

LEVITICUS 6:4–5.

...When a man or woman shall commit any sin that men commit, to do a trespass against the Lord, and that person be guilty, then they shall confess their sin which they have done, and he shall recompense his trespass with the principal thereof, and add to it a fifth part, and give it to him against whom he has trespassed.

NUMBERS 5:6–7.

Men do not despise a thief, if he steals to satisfy his soul when he is hungry; but when he is found, he shall restore sevenfold; he shall give all the substance of his house.

PROVERBS 6:30–31.

When I say to the wicked, You shall surely die, if he turn from his sin, and do that which is lawful and right; if the wicked restore the pledge, give again what he had robbed, walk in the statutes of life, without commiting iniquity; he shall surely live; he shall not die.

EZEKIEL 33:14–15.

Whom the heaven must receive until the times of restitution of all things, which God has spoken by the mouth of all His holy prophets since the world began.

ACTS 3:21.

RETURN ON INVESTMENT

If you place money in a savings account or an annuity fund, upon withdrawal you expect in return something additional to the principal. Why? First, you probably have a contract calling for payment of interest. Second, by saving today you give up something—the right to enjoy spending the money for things now—and by lending, someone else's enjoyment is your sacrifice. You must wait for return of your money, so you expect compensation for waiting.

Suppose you invest money in a business venture without guarantee of return—only risk. Why do you buy stock in a corporation or invest in a business? Because you expect to participate in future profits, if any, a payment for risk. Would you invest in a business which, by covenant, could never pay you a cent in dividends? If you cannot receive a return on investment, why part with savings? Hence, a return induces you to invest.

Contrast an interest-bearing contract with a business investment. With one you have a guaranteed fixed return. In the second case, you have no guarantees. If the venture fails, you lose all or part of your investment. If it barely succeeds, your return will be low. If it is very successful, your return may be large. Are you entitled to it? You took the risk of loss. Are you not equally entitled to rewards?

God operates on a plan of abundance. Throw a seed into the ground, it returns hundreds. Crops and cattle multiply, investments profit, because God created a system of multiplication. Therefore, God's people receive a return on investments, one not confiscated by the state for redistribution to the indolent or taxed away to build up the state's treasuries.

(*See Also:* Abundance, Interest, Investment, Law of Increase, Private Property, Risk Aversion)

> Then Isaac sowed in that land, and received in the same year a hundredfold; and the Lord blessed him.
>
> GENESIS 26:12.

> The man increased exceedingly, and had much cattle, and maidservants, and menservants, and camels, and asses.
>
> GENESIS 30:43.

> If your brother be waxen poor, and has sold away some of his possession, and if any of his kin come to redeem it, then shall he redeem that which his brother sold. If the man has none to redeem it, and himself be able to redeem it, then let him count the years of the sale thereof, and restore the surplus to the man to whom he sold it, that he may return to his possession.
>
> LEVITICUS 25:25–27.

Yea, the Lord shall give that which is good; and our land shall yield her increase.

PSALM 85:12.

Then came the first, saying, Lord, your pound has gained ten pounds.... I say to you, That to every one who has shall be given; and from him who has not, even that he has shall be taken away from him.

LUKE 19:16, 26.

I have planted, Apollos watered; but God gave the increase. So then neither is he who plants any thing, neither he who waters; but God gives the increase. Now he who plants and he who waters are one; and every man shall receive his own reward according to his own labor.

1 CORINTHIANS 3:6–8.

...Thrust in your sharp sickle, and gather the clusters of the vine of the earth; for her grapes are fully ripe.

REVELATION 14:18.

RICHES

Better is a handful with quietness, than both hands full with travail and vexation of spirit.

ECCLESIASTES 4:6.

(*See:* Abundance, Return on Investment, Wealth)

RISK AVERSION

To add a pedagogical dimension to risk analysis, financial analysts speak of risk lovers, risk averters, and risk neutrals. Anyone completely immune to risk must be dead, and risk neutrality is not germane to the discussion. Gamblers are referred to as risk lovers, because the chance of loss far exceeds possibilities of gain. Professional gamblers believe they can beat the odds; otherwise they would not play, which really makes them risk averters. Others may be unaware or disbelieve the odds of losing. Still others gamble for fun and excitement, setting aside a fixed sum to lose at the tables. These are not risk lovers.

This leaves us with risk averters. We have an imperfect knowledge of the future. Hence, risk resides in any undertaking. Risk means the chance that future projected outcomes will differ from actual future results, a statistical measure.

Risk deals in probabilities. If we can reduce an outcome to a probabilistic statement, then we can incorporate risk costs into decisions. For instance, an insurance company knows that in Norman, Oklahoma, a certain number of fires will occur each year based on historical data. What they cannot predict is precisely which building will burn; but it does not matter. Based on projected losses, according to statistical probability, they incorporate future anticipated losses into costs of operations and claims and then assign a premium on *all* fire insurance policies in Norman sufficiently high to cover anticipated costs and losses.

If we anticipate an investment opportunity, then we should consider the risk of partial loss of investment as well as risk of business failure, and then decide if projected return on investment covers these risks. Is it worthwhile? Personally, I prefer sure things. That's why I bet on God's order.

(*See Also:* Forecasting, Losses, Profit, Return on Investment, Source)

> ... *Behold, if the Lord would make windows in heaven, might this thing be? He said, Behold, you shall see it with your eyes, but shall not eat thereof.*
> 2 KINGS 7:2.

> *For to him who is joined to all the living there is hope, for a living dog is better than a dead lion.*
> ECCLESIASTES 9:4.

> *Cast your bread upon the waters, for you shall find it after many days.*
> ECCLESIASTES 11:1.

> *Boast not yourself of tomorrow, for you know not what a day may bring forth.*
> PROVERBS 27:1.

RULE BY DECREE

To rule by decree introduces arbitrariness, uncertainty, and abuse in a society. Recall the surprise of liberal psychologists, who, listening to a generation of nihilists raised on moral relativism, changing values, and flexible rules, heard their progeny decry their uncertain and unstable environments. Children from happy homes mature with a set of reasonable rules, known beforehand and equitably enforced, without exception. Unhappy homes are often ones where parents rule by decree, inventing rules for one moment, rescinding them another.

Administrative decrees of bureaucracies, based on arbitrary and capricious decisions, destabilize our environment. Business, for instance, never knowing whether the government will vote today yea on one thing, and nay on the same thing another day, operates in a high-risk environment. Higher risks raise costs. If businesses account for these costs, then the consumer pays more for goods. If investors decide that risks are too great and the government too unpredictable, they will postpone investment decisions. Less investment means fewer jobs.

Civil government should contribute to a stable, predictable environment. Enough uncertainty already exists. Business people must cope with business risk and financial risk. Employees must invest in education, spend time in apprenticeship, and make long-term commitments. Governments and their agencies need not enlarge risk. If we know the rules in advance, and that rich and poor alike are equal before the law, then we become more productive Christians.

(*See Also:* Forecasting, Fury of a Bureaucrat Scorned, Law and Order, Risk Aversion)

> *[The king said]…but if you show the dream and its interpretation, you shall receive of me gifts and rewards and great honor…. But if you will not make known to me the dream, there is but one decree for you….*
> DANIEL 2:6, 9.

> *For this cause the king was angry and very furious, and commanded to destroy all the wise men of Babylon. The decree went forth that the wise men should be slain….*
> DANIEL 2:12–13.

> *You, O king, have made a decree, that every man who shall hear the sound of the cornet, flute, harp, sackbut, psaltery, and dulcimer, and all kinds of music, shall fall down and worship the golden image. And whoever falls not down and worships, that he be cast into the midst of a burning fiery furnace.*
> DANIEL 3:10–11.

> *…Know, O king, that the law of the Medes and Persians is that no decree nor statute which the king establishes may be changed.*
> DANIEL 6:15.

RULE OF LAW

When the Rule of Law prevails, justice reigns. When disputes and cases are decided according to the person or his wealth or influence, circumstances, public mood, press coverage, racial origins, religious beliefs, political expediency, legal technicalities, or for any reason other than law, then a system of privilege exists. Then tyranny is just around the corner.

First of all, the Rule of Law derives from principles. If these principles are based on anything other than God's laws, then a system of Rule by Decree has replaced the Rule of God.

A society may also promulgate certain rules for greater freedom through order. An example of this is traffic laws that require everyone to drive on the right side. Without these rules, less freedom arises. Driving to work would be infarctic. You may think driving around the *glorietas* in Mexico City or through the streets of Naples, Italy, is harrowing, but the nearest to cheap thrills from a chaotic system exists in India. An Indian friend of mine said that if he were to return to New Delhi, where he grew up, he would not drive for the first six months until he became reaccustomed to the system.

Second, the rule of law grants no special privileges to either majorities or minorities. That confuses majoritarian thinkers. Let's suppose that the majority of voters in Jessup, Georgia, votes for a city law that requires every citizen to own a handgun. How do you handle the minority who refuses? Frankly, every person at his own discretion may own or not own a handgun. Such a law cannot ethically carry any force. It can, at best, only amount to a resolution or suggestion. If a majority wants a minority to move out of town, about all they can do is offer to buy their properties and pay moving expenses, and the minority need not accept. By the same token, the minority may not dictate to the majority.

Third, rules and penalties are known beforehand. With court cases, the objective is to establish guilt and require appropriate restitution, not engage in philosophical treatises on reconstituting society. Since capital crimes carry the death penalty, the potential criminal knows the consequence of his acts beforehand. Full responsibility for the crime falls on him alone. Courts do not exist to make law, get involved with social justice, or change the law or circumstances of the crime.

Ignorance of the law is no excuse—and no major problem either. We all know the essential do's and don'ts of the Bible. At one time our own laws were equally simple and straightforward. They did not require a legal genius to know basic law and interpret it for clients. There were not so many laws that myriad interpretations could arise either. In contrast to God's way, we have rule by decree, situational ethics, and criminals supported by tax money.

(*See Also:* Capital Punishment, Court System, Law, Private Property, Restitution, Self-Discipline)

You shall neither vex a stranger, nor oppress him, for you were strangers in the land of Egypt.

EXODUS 22:21.

You shall have one manner of law, as well as for the stranger, as for one of your own country.

LEVITICUS 24:22.

You shall not respect persons in judgment; but you shall hear the small as well as the great....

DEUTERONOMY 1:17.

Behold, a king shall reign in righteousness, and princes shall rule in judgment.... The work of righteousness shall be peace; and the effect of righteousness quietness and assurance for ever.

ISAIAH 32:1, 17.

All things whatsoever you would do that men should do to you, do you even so to them, for this is the law and the prophets.

MATTHEW 7:12.

It is easier for heaven and earth to pass, than one tittle of the law to fail.

LUKE 16:17.

Is the law then against the promises of God? God forbid; for if there had been a law given that could have given life, verily righteousness should have been by the law.

GALATIANS 4:21.

But if you bite and devour one another, take heed that you be not consumed one of another.

GALATIANS 5:15.

But he who does wrong shall receive for the wrong which he has done; and there is no respect of persons.

COLOSSIANS 3:25.

But we know that the law is good if a man uses it lawfully.

1 TIMOTHY 1:8.

I charge you before God, and the Lord Jesus Christ, and the elect angels, that you observe these things without preferring one before another, doing nothing by partiality.

1 TIMOTHY 5:21.

SALE

A certain man named Ananias, with Sapphira his wife, sold a possession.

ACTS 5:1.

(*See:* Exchange, Price Mechanism, Private Property)

SAVINGS

Why save? Why not eat, drink, and be merry, borrow heavily, run up unpaid bills, enjoy life, for tomorrow you may be dead? You cannot both spend and save. One act precludes the other. Believers tend toward financial conservatism. Family continuity depends on sound finances and inheritance. Both require savings. Saving suggests foregone consumption. If we spend a couple of federal reserve notes for a bag of candy, both money and soon the candy disappear. Purchases, such as refrigerators, automobiles, and lawn mowers last for several years; these, too, are consumption goods or durables.

Saving translates into investing, such as income property, financial securities, or a grove of walnut trees. Although businesses are typically investments, a hobby or plaything called a business is probably consumption. Homes represent a mixed bag. On one side, a house represents a consumer purchase since it yields no financial income. On the other hand, it provides a place for rearing children, a retreat from the world, a sanctuary for meditation, and an inheritance.

A believer provides for an inheritance to children and grandchildren. Through the family, God's Word is learned, the Law practiced, and principles of liberty are passed to succeeding generations. During our earthly sojourn, we generate a certain income. Therefore, time influences earnings. By not consuming, we save, in effect, time, a gift for the future.

Savings make possible the stock of capital equipment (tools and machinery). People have used some of their time to invent and their savings to construct prototypes. However, technology alone is insufficient. For instance, Egyptians had developed an early steam engine several thousand years ago. A Swiss reinvented it a couple hundred years before James Watt invented a commercial application. Our enjoyment of products and lighter burdens today are the inheritance left us by generations of men and women who saved and invested.

(*See Also:* Capital Formation, Economic Growth, Food Storage, Self-Discipline, Wealth)

> *Behold, there will come seven years of great plenty throughout all the land of Egypt. There shall arise after them seven years of famine.... Let Pharaoh... appoint officers over the land, and take up the fifth part of the land in the seven plenteous years.*
>
> GENESIS 41:29–30, 34.

> *Give a portion to seven, and also to eight, for you know not what evil shall be upon the earth.*
>
> ECCLESIASTES 11:2.

> *If a man lives many years, and rejoices in them all; yet let him remember the days of darkness, for they shall be many.*
>
> ECCLESIASTES 11:8.

> *You ought, therefore, to have put my money to the exchangers, and then at my coming I should have received my own with usury.*
>
> MATTHEW 25:27.

> *Charge them who are rich in this world, that they be not highminded, nor trust in uncertain riches, but in the living God, who gives us richly all things to enjoy, that they do good, that they be rich in good works, ready to distribute, willing to communicate, laying up in store for themselves a good foundation against the time to come, that they may lay hold on eternal life.*
>
> 1 TIMOTHY 6:17–19.

SAY'S LAW

Developed in the nineteenth century by Jean Baptiste Say, the most simplified statement of Say's Law of Markets is: Supply creates its own demand. The supply of computers gives rise to demand for paper, furniture, and metal boxes. The supply of chocolate-drop cookies gives rise to demand for T-shirts, tennis balls, gasoline, and other things cookie sellers want. Under conditions of market equilibrium, supply and demand not only equate, but are identical, since every product may be looked upon as either supply of its own kind or demand for other things.

Here are three versions of Say's Law:

1. Supply creates its own demand; hence, aggregate overproduction is impossible.
2. Partial overproduction implies a balancing of underproduction elsewhere in the economy; hence, equilibrium is restored by competition, that is, by the price mechanism and the mobility of capital.
3. Because aggregate demand and aggregate supply are necessarily equal, and because of the equilibrating mechanism, production can be increased indefinitely and the accumulation of capital (tools and equipment) can proceed without limit.

John Maynard Keynes claimed to have successfully refuted Say, substituting his own theories. New Dealism and inflation are two products of Keynesianism. The results of fifty years of these policies are high unemployment, high taxation, growing government, burgeoning bureaucracy, and ever-deepening recessions. Keynesianism focuses on consumption: full employment results from governmental expenditures and deficit financing.

The Christian view is that jobs are created when factories produce. The biblical equivalent of Say's law of markets appears in 2 CORINTHIANS 8:14, supported by 2 CORINTHIANS 9:6.

(*See Also:* Market Economy, Price Mechanism, Production, Savings, Supply)

All things are full of labor; man cannot utter it; the eye is not satisfied with seeing, nor the ear filled with hearing.

ECCLESIASTES *1:8.*

When goods increase, they are increased who eat them; and what good is there to the owners thereof, saving the beholding of them with their eyes?

ECCLESIASTES *5:11.*

...You shall eat this year such as grows of itself; and the second year that which springs of the same; and in the third year sow, and reap, and plant vineyards and eat the fruit thereof.

ISAIAH *37:30.*

But by an equality, that now at this time your abundance may be a supply for their want, that their abundance also may be a supply for your want, that there may be equality.

2 CORINTHIANS *8:14.*

But this I say, He who sows sparingly shall reap also sparingly; and he who sows bountifully shall also reap bountifully.

2 CORINTHIANS 9:6.

SELF-DISCIPLINE

Self-discipline, a study in contradictions, deserves our most resolute consideration. Self-discipline means that less transforms into more. If you want material wealth, do you squander every penny you receive, or do you restrict spending? Saving means not spending. The more we save now, the fewer things we enjoy and use now. At some point, through wise stewardship of savings, we will have even more.

Suppose you generate $20,000 a year. Spending it all each year, you can only acquire a $50,000 house (at stable prices), assuming a long-term mortgage. Although you will have bought that house three times over (including interest on a forty-year loan), you will still live in a $50,000 house. But if you save $7,000 per year at 10 percent, compounded, in twenty years you will have more than $400,000. From interest on accumulated savings plus income of $20,000, you can now afford several times the house of twenty years earlier. Nothing has changed except your attitude toward saving plus self-discipline to carry it through.

How do we become acquainted with God's Word and His order? Certainly not with boob tube entertainment! By giving *less* to dubious pleasures, we end up with *more.*

Does self-discipline apply in civil government? Civil governments legislate, regulate, and entangle society in red tape in pursuit of elusive social justice and power. Therefore, as a basic premise, let's assume that the more civil government the less freedom (economic, political, and religious) we have. Every enduring law and order system rests firmly on self-government. The first step in effective government is commandment-abiding self-government. This means adherence to the biblical pattern under the law, with God's rule at the top, self-disciplined men at the bottom, and a system of appeals courts in between. By denying our lower nature its uncontrolled direction in taking, debauching, corrupting, and entering into immoral arrangements, we give ourselves, through self-discipline, greater freedom. The more we ask governments to do for us, the more regulations government imposes and the higher the price paid in lost freedom. More civil government equals less freedom. But through less we have more.

(*See Also:* Abundance, Compensation, Discipline, Free Society, Return on Investment, Prosperity, Savings)

He who is slow to anger is better than the mighty; and he who rules his spirit than he who takes a city.

PROVERBS 16:32.

*Better is a dry morsel, and quietness therewith, than a house full of
sacrifices with strife.*

PROVERBS 17:1.

*The spirit of a man will sustain his infirmity; but a wounded spirit who
can bear?*

PROVERBS 18:14.

*My brothers, count it all joy, when you fall into various temptations;
knowing this, that the trying of your faith works patience.... Blessed is
he who endures temptation, for when he is tried, he shall receive the
crown of life, which the Lord has promised to them who love Him. Let
no man say when he is tempted, I am tempted of God, for God cannot
be tempted with evil, neither does He tempt any man; but every man is
tempted, when he is drawn away of his own lust, and enticed. Then
when lust is conceived, it brings forth sin; and sin, when it is finished,
brings forth death.*

JAMES 1:2–3, 12–15.

*Wherefore, my beloved brothers, let every man be swift to hear, slow to
speak, slow to wrath; for the wrath of man works not the righteousness
of God.*

JAMES 1:19–20.

SERVICE

Service is the life of a believer. We are created to serve. We can choose what kind of
service and whom to serve. Our greatest freedom comes when we serve God and His
ways. The greatest potential for slavery comes when we serve sin, the pleasure of
man, and the ways of humanism and powers of darkness. If you are not certain
whom or what you serve, analyze your goals. What do you usually think about? And
the acid test is How do you spend your time? In what activities? Once you've chosen
whom you want to serve, what *kind* of service will you offer? Anything less than the
best serves the enemy.

In shopping for a new lawn mower this afternoon, I discussed various brands
with a store owner. Although his equipment cost a few dollars more, he offered top-
quality service. In the same location for thirty years, he offered service that
customers would not likely find elsewhere. His shop and its orderliness, his courtesy,
information, and everything about him signaled that he backed up his word with
first-class service. As I walked out the door, he said, "Whatever one you buy, get the
best so you won't have trouble with it in a few months." This man thought first class.

(See Also: Accountability, Organization, Quality, Stewardship, Value)

Whoever shall compel you to go a mile, go with him two.
MATTHEW 5:41.

The cares of this world, and the deceitfulness of riches, and the lusts of other things entering in, choke the word, and it becomes unfruitful.
MARK 4:19.

He sat down, and called the twelve, and said to them, If any man desires to be first, the same shall be last of all, and servant of all.
MARK 9:35.

SEXISM

(See: Family, Feminism, Women)

SHIPPING

We will cut wood out of Lebanon, as much as you shall need, and we will bring it to you in flotes by sea to Joppa; and you shall carrry it up to Jerusalem.
2 CHRONICLES 2:16.

(See: Business, Imports, International Trade)

SLAVERY

Cum non sis qui fueris, non esse cur velis vivere (Since you are not what you were, there is no reason why you should wish to live).

Man must prefer slavery. Of 4 billion people world-wide, most live under some system of bondage. Even in so-called free sectors, many people push for statism under nice-sounding names like state welfarism, social democracies, the people's republic, or income policies. Throughout history men have opted for the *security* of oppressive dictatorship rather than take on responsibilities of freedom. The American way, a living example, is an embarrassment to communists of what can be accomplished materially and spiritually in a free environment. Since the founding of our nation, the moles have worked hard tunneling under our foundations. Unfortunately, we have legislated immunity for moles and hail tunnels as a purportedly sacred heritage.

In our free society, we produce many times more output per capita than any other place in the world. That percentage is declining as tunnels cause our foundations to collapse here and there. Still, compare our productive output with the Soviet Union, larger in size and population, with its Eastern European captive markets. It has more natural resources than we and makes the stingiest deals in world trade and aid. They cannot even feed themselves. We have bailed out Soviet leadership with food in the 1920s, 1940s, 1960s, 1970s, have supplied about 90 percent of their current technology, constructed their leading truck and automobile factories, and pay their bills at the United Nations. Their per capita income is but a fraction of ours. "When men feel they have no future, they live with a blocked future, with no capacity to build, no capacity to command and—they have surrendered."[1]

Why should anyone prefer the communist system of slavery that delivers deprivation and religious oppression? Jane Fonda, addressing a college crowd in Mount Pleasant, Michigan, said: "If you really understood what Communism is, you would get down on your knees and pray that the United States becomes communistic." I don't know to which god she prays, but read what mine says in ROMANS 13:12 and GALATIANS 4:9.

Unfortunately, in the following biblical verses, you will read that men are attracted by the *security of slavery*. When Israel finally escaped from Egypt, they soon began carping about inconveniences, the food, uncertainties, and made plans to return to Egypt. Why? Sir Joshua Reynolds said, "There is no expedient to which a man will not resort to avoid thinking."[2] Slavery does not require much thought, does it?

> The roots of slavery [are] spiritual: "Whosoever committeth sin is the servant of sin" (JOHN 8:34). Such men are inwardly slaves, slaves to sin. A true slave always seeks a master and the security of a master. The slave mind wants security, a trouble-free, cradle-to-grave or womb-to-tomb security, and it demands a master to provide it.
>
> Slaves, true slaves, want to be rescued from freedom; their greatest fear is liberty. Freedom imposes an impossible burden on them.[3]

"Why should we, contrary to their laws, make our contentment a slave to the power of others?"[4]

[1]Rousas J. Rushdoony, "A Blocked or Open Future?" An address to the Chalcedon Guild Dinner, 1972.
[2]Joshua Reynolds, historically the most important English portrait painter (1723-92).
[3]Rushdoony, *Politics of Guilt and Pity* (Nutley, N.J.: Craig Press, 1970), p. 28.
[4]Michael de Montaigne, *Essays* (1580), Book I, chapter 38, "Of Solitude."

(*See Also:* Communism, Cradle-to-Grave, Idolatry, Planned Economy, Power of State, Socialism, Statism)

Let there more work be laid upon the men, that they labor therein; and let them not regard vain words.... Go, get the straw where you can find it; yet nothing of your work shall be diminished.

EXODUS 5:9, 11.

...Were it not better for us to return to Egypt? They said one to another. Let us make a captain, and let us return to Egypt.

NUMBERS 14:3–4.

If your brother, a Hebrew man, or a Hebrew woman, be sold to you, and serve you six years, then in the seventh year you shall let him go free from you.

DEUTERONOMY 15:12.

...He had nine hundred chariots of iron; and twenty years he mightily oppressed the children of Israel.

JUDGES 4:3.

They and our fathers dealt proudly, and hardened their necks, and listened not to Your commandments, and refused to obey, neither were mindful of Your wonders that You did among them; but hardened their necks, and in their rebellion appointed a captain to return to their bondage; but You are a God ready to pardon, gracious and merciful, slow to anger, and of great kindness, and you forsook them not.

NEHEMIAH 9:16–17.

Therefore My people are gone into captivity, because they have no knowledge; and their honorable men are famished, and their multitude dried up with thirst.

ISAIAH 5:13.

Behold, for your iniquities have you sold yourselves, and for your transgressions is your mother put away.

ISAIAH 50:1.

For of old time I have broken your yoke, and burst your bands; and you said, I will not transgress, when upon every high hill and under every green tree, you wander, playing the harlot. Yet I had planted you a noble vine, wholly the right seed; how then are you turned into the degenerate plant of a strange vine to Me?

JEREMIAH 2:20–21.

They answered Him, We are Abraham's seed, and were never in bondage to any man; what do you mean, You shall be made free? Jesus answered them, Verily, verily, I say to you, Whoever commits sin is the servant of sin.

JOHN 8:33–34.

For when you were servants of sin, you were free from righteousness.

ROMANS 6:20.

…Let us therefore cast off the works of darkness, and let us put on the armor of light.

ROMANS 13:12.

For you suffer, if a man brings you into bondage, if a man devours you, if a man takes of you, if a man exalts himself, if a man smites you on the face.

2 CORINTHIANS 11:20.

Because of false brothers unawares brought in, who came in privily to spy out our liberty which we have in Jesus Christ, that they might bring us into bondage.

GALATIANS 2:4.

But now, after you have known God, or rather are known of God, why turn again to the weak and beggarly elements, where you desire again to be in bondage?

GALATIANS 4:9.

SOCIALISM

George Bernard Shaw wrote, "Compulsory labor, with death as the final penalty, is the keystone of Socialism." Some confused persons believe that socialism crosses a church social with the local United Way. The bad guys are the communists. Communism is what they practice in the Soviet Union. Isn't that country called the Soviet Union of *Socialist* Republics? Most communists today refer to themselves as socialists, the great emancipators of humanity. The bad guys are the Nazis. Even forty years later, Nazism, to most Americans, is far worse then communism and unrelated to socialism. Still the acronym NAZI stands for the National *Socialist* German Workers' Party.

Socialism, like other isms, relies on force to sustain it. Socialists may pat you on the back before pulling your plum out of the pie of private wealth, but they end up with it nevertheless. Although labels change from century to century, distill any to the basics and few differences arise. Read the following.

A KING OF LONG AGO

There once lived a king in a distant land—a just and wise old king, for he had observed and learned much about his people and about himself and his power. His people were free to go their way and were fearful of the king and his soldiers, for his rule granted no privilege to one that was not a privilege to all equally. They were free to petition their king and seek his wisdom in their affairs.

There came one day to the royal court an artisan, a mason, and a lame beggar.

"O great and wise king," they cried, "we are sorely troubled with our plight." "I," said the artisan, "make many useful goods. I use great skill and labor long, and yet when I am finished, the people will not pay me my price."

"And I," said the mason, "am a layer of stone for houses and fine walls, yet I am idle, for no one gives me work."

"I am a poor lame beggar," said the third man, "who seeks alms from those who pass, as they find in their hearts to do so, but alms are so few as to be of great concern lest I perish."

"I can see that your troubles are great," consoled the king. "What would you ask of me?"

Then, they spoke as a group. "Your power is very great, our king, and you can make the people see the folly of their ways and aid us in our troubles."

"Perhaps," said the king, "my power is great, but I must use it wisely or it shall be lost." And he called to the captain of his guard.

"Bring forth three swords," he commanded, "one for each of these three men, and instruct them in their use. These three shall go forth in the land and compel those who will not voluntarily deal with them to obey their command."

"No! No!" the three men called out, "this we did not ask. We are men of honor and could not set upon our fellow man to compel him to our will. This we cannot do. It is you O king, who must use the power."

"You ask me to do that which you would not do because of honor?" questioned the king. "Is honor one thing to a beggar and another to a king? I, too, am an honorable man, and that which is dishonorable for you will never be less dishonorable for your king."[1]

(*See Also:* Cradle-to-Grave, Expropriation, Power of State, Redistribution of Income/Wealth, Statism, Theft, Welfarism)

---

[1]First appearing in the *Rotograph* (Fort Worth, Tex.: Rotary Club), March 16, 1962, it was reprinted in *The Freeman*, July 1962, under the title, "A King of Long Ago," by Lewis Love.

While it is yet in its greenness and not cut down, it withers before any other herb. So are the paths of all who forget God; and the hypocrite's hope shall perish, whose hope shall be cut off, and whose trust shall be a spider's web. He shall lean upon his house, but it shall not stand; he shall hold it fast, but it shall not endure.

*J*OB *8:12–15.*

Blessed is the man who walks not in the counsel of the ungodly, nor stands in the way of sinners, nor sits in the seat of the scornful. But his delight is in the law of the Lord, and in His law does he meditate day and night.

P*SALM 1:1–2.*

Lo, only this have I found, that God has made man upright; but they have sought out many inventions.

E*CCLESIASTES 7:29.*

A sword is upon the liars; and they shall dote; a sword is upon her mighty men, and they shall be dismayed. A sword is upon their horses, and upon their chariots, and upon all the mingled people who are in the midst of her; and they shall become as women, a sword is upon her treasurers; and they shall be robbed.

J*EREMIAH 50:36–37.*

Therefore thus says the Lord, Your wife shall be a harlot in the city; and your sons and your daughters shall fall by the sword, and your land shall be divided by line, and you shall die in a polluted land; and Israel shall surely go into captivity from its land.... The songs of the temple shall be howlings in that day, says the Lord God; there shall be many dead bodies in every place.... Behold, the days come, says the Lord God, that I will send a famine in the land, not a famine of bread, nor a thirst of water, but of hearing the word of the Lord. They shall wander from sea to sea, and from the north even to the east, they shall run to and fro to seek the word of the Lord, and shall not find it.

A*MOS 7:17; 8:3, 11–12.*

The Jews who believed not, moved with envy, took to them certain lewd fellows of the baser sort, and gathered a company, and set all the city in an uproar, and assaulted the house of Jason, and sought to bring them out to the people. When they found them not, they drew Jason and certain brethren to the rulers of the city, crying, These who have turned the world upside down are come hither also; whom Jason has received; and these all do contrary to the decrees of Caesar, saying that there is another king, one Jesus.

A*CTS 17:5–7.*

Not rather (as we be slanderously reported, and as some affirm that we say), let us do evil, that good may come? Whose damnation is just.
ROMANS 3:8.

For I mean not that other men be eased, and you burdened.
2 CORINTHIANS 8:13.

Beware lest any man spoil you through philosophy and vain deceit, after the tradition of men, after the rudiments of the world, and not after Christ.
COLOSSIANS 2:8.

...In the last days perilous times shall come. For men shall be lovers of their own selves, covetous, boasters, proud, blasphemous, disobedient to parents, unthankful, unholy, without natural affection, trucebreakers, false accusers, incontinent, fierce, despisers of those who are good, traitors, heady, highminded, lovers of pleasures more than lovers of God, having a form of godliness, but denying the power thereof: from such turn away.
2 TIMOTHY 3:1–5.

Be not carried away with diverse and strange doctrines. For it is a good thing that the heart be established with grace, not with meats....
HEBREWS 13:9.

SOCIALIST

One time in Puerto Rico, a young American solicited funds from me for the Puerto Rican Socialist Party. Although he spoke no Spanish, the socialists had put him in the hot sun with a metal can. I told him I did not support any government that used force to redistribute wealth and income, especially mine. He replied, "Oh, no, we're not like that. That's what the communists do, but we're not like them. We don't believe in using force." He asked whether I had a bank account. When I replied affirmatively, he said, "You must be a capitalist." So I presented him with this supposition: "Suppose, in this utopian society you're dreaming about, that *your* socialist government decides they need the money in *my* bank account to finance *their* many public health, education, and welfare programs. But I refuse to give up my money."

He replied, "With socialism, everyone is equal. We don't let people accumulate wealth and have big bank accounts. If someone gets greedy and has too much, then he has to pay more in taxes."

"But presume," I pressed, "that I refuse to pay you anything in taxes or surrender my bank account. What would you do then?" I asked.

"Well, we couldn't let you do that. You would have to give it to the government. I suppose if you refused, the government would have to take it away from you." There! He finally said it. They *do* use force! By this time he was becoming a little uncomfortable (see ROMANS 16:18).

Perhaps socialists do not send people to the wall a la Castro or Mao or Stalin; but they confiscate property. How strange that we abhor the idea of taking something by gun point; but (transmuting that act) getting the government to use its police powers to pry income and assets out of private accounts and then to give to us what our neighbors previously possessed, does not seem nearly so bad.

Many socialistic-minded people appear to be fine persons, except for their strange philosophy. The schemes of such intellectuals are no less chaotic or confused. They cloak them in elegant language, intricately weaving half-truths, hypothetical situations, and omniscience into plans that no thinking person, or believer, would ever accept.

(*See Also:* Demagogue, Double Standard, Nonalignment, Socialism, Statist)

Yea, you overwhelm the fatherless, and you dig a pit for your friend.
JOB 6:27.

He devises mischief upon his bed; he sets himself in a way that is not good; he abhors not evil.
PSALM 36:4.

A wise man's heart is at his right hand; but a fool's heart at his left.
ECCLESIASTES 10:2.

Yet the children of your people say, The way of the Lord is not equal; but as for them, their way is not equal.
EZEKIEL 33:17.

But you are departed out of the way; you have caused many to stumble at the law; you have corrupted the covenant of Levi, says the Lord of hosts. Therefore have I also made you contemptible and base before all the people, according as you have not kept My ways, but have been partial in the law.
MALACHI 2:8–9.

For they that are such serve not our Lord Jesus Christ, but their own belly, by good words and fair speeches deceive the hearts of the simple.
ROMANS 16:18.

Having the understanding darkened, being alienated from the life of God through the ignorance that is in them, because of the blindness of their heart; who being past feeling have given themselves over to las-civiousness, to work all uncleanness with greediness.

EPHESIANS 4:18–19.

To the pure all things are pure; but to them who are defiled and unbelieving is nothing pure; but even their mind and conscience are defiled. They profess that they know God; but in works they deny Him, being abominable, and disobedient, and to every good work reprobate.

TITUS 1:15–16.

SOCIAL SECURITY

Not even a sacred cow is as inviolable as our social security system. To touch it is political suicide. Senator William Proxmire, who entertains us with stories of government waste, steers clear of the subject. He writes, "With *Social Security* we reap the most durable and defensible fruits of Franklin D. Roosevelt's New Deal." As a qualifier, he adds, "Though it is now the most costly government program we have, its principle is absolutely right."[1] But is it?

Social security recipients believe they have a right to an old age pension because they paid into it. Actually, a big chunk of dough is paid to people not yet of retirement age: widows, children, and the psychologically and physically disabled. For example, about twelve years ago I reviewed an investment portfolio of a widow. Her husband was killed so there was a cash insurance settlement of $100,000, plus property. She received about $20,000 a year from social security for her two minor children. Recently she had left lucrative employment, which compensated her about $25,000, with fringe benefits. What she and her deceased husband had paid into social security was probably recovered in one year. Still, until the children finish college, she will have received more than a quarter million dollars. Compare that with my neighbors in their eighties, with substantial medical bills, whose *combined* social security hardly pays bare essentials.

Nevertheless, early retirees have received many times over what they paid. If social security is an integral system, then how are deficits compensated? Those who must pay social security taxes have discovered that both the percent on income and the income base have been stretched by Congress, so that now an employee at tops pays nearly $5,000 a year, heading for $7,000 by 1989, as compared with $60 a year in 1937. Oh, I know you think the employer pays half. Where does the employer get the money? Without covering its costs, a firm will discontinue operations. If costs cannot be passed on to final consumers, then they must come from the employee's

---

[1]William Proxmire, *The Fleecing of America* (Boston: Houghton-Mifflin, 1980), p. 178.

paycheck. By paying you less, the employer pretends to pay your half of the tax. You pay it all.

Then when the social security tax can no longer be increased, the government dips into general revenue funds (i.e., other tax money). One day social security will be paid with newly printed money (i.e., inflation). Juan Peron, president of Argentina in the early 1950s, after purchasing British railroads, loaded the system with his supporters, the workers, with lucrative wages and full pension after twenty years, which meant quick retirement for many. In the aftermath of Peron, the government honored pension commitments. They printed more pesos so that pension money bought less and less. Finally pensioners had to seek employment as pensions and pesos became worthless. No wonder some refer to our system as "socialist insecurity"!

Social security is a sham. It depends upon theft. My neighbor does not steal from me. The government does it for him. I don't mind helping him out, and I do; but the social security system survives on financial and moral bankruptcy. Now you may argue that you can do better investing in a private fund than with social security. Are you telling me that you are being robbed? Well, welcome to the club.

(*See Also:* Bankruptcy, Charity, Cradle-to-Grave, Crowd Psychology, Demagoguery, Inflation)

> *But if any provide not for his own, and especially for those of his own house, he has denied the faith, and is worse than an infidel.*
> *1 TIMOTHY 5:8.*

> *If any man or woman who believes has widows, let them relieve them, and let not the church be charged: that it may relieve them who are widows indeed.*
> *1 TIMOTHY 5:16.*

SOURCE

My first book, on finance, was dedicated to the "Source of all wealth." Subsequent books were dedicated to the family, to put matters in proper perspective. Mary Kay Ash, president of her cosmetics firm, often mentions this hierarchy: God first, family second; Mary Kay Cosmetics third.

We must ask some basic questions. Just who is in control? (See DANIEL 2:20–22.) From whom does our law come? (See 1 CORINTHIANS 8:5–6.) Where do we get all of our wealth, our riches, our unlimited prosperity? (See DEUTERONOMY 8:18.) Why should we not follow the commandments of men rather than of God? (See COLOSSIANS 2:20–22.) On whom can we always depend? (See JAMES 1:17.)

In a little booklet entitled *Wonderful Promises*, Rev. Norman Vincent Peale gives thirty-one promises—one for every day of the month—of God. Here are a few of the promises: dynamic life (DEUTERONOMY 30:19–20); hope for the future (2 CHRONICLES 7:14); forgiveness and healing (PSALM 103:3–4); abundant blessings (MALACHI 3:10); life, energy, completeness (ACTS 17:28); peace (PHILIPPIANS 4:7); healing (JAMES 5:15). Why should we make the state, or man, our god, contra the first commandment? They cannot fulfill one of these promises. Why should we confine our relationship with God to five minutes in the evening and an hour or so on Saturday or Sunday? Applied Christianity does not put God afterhours or out of the classroom, or business meetings, or family counsels. After all, He is *The Source*.

(*See Also:* Creation, Foundation, Government, Law, Optimism, Stewardship, Truth)

What nation is there so great, that has statutes and judgments so righteous as all this law, which I set before you this day?

DEUTERONOMY 4:8.

The Lord commanded me at that time to teach you statutes and judgments, that you might do them in the land where you go over to possess it.

DEUTERONOMY 4:14.

You shall remember the Lord your God, for it is He who gives power to get wealth....

DEUTERONOMY 8:18.

...As long as he sought the Lord, God made him to prosper.

2 CHRONICLES 26:5.

Blessed be the Lord, who daily loads us with benefits, the God of our salvation!

PSALM 68:19.

David answered and said, Blessed be the name of God for ever and ever, for wisdom and might are His; and He changes the times and the seasons; He removes kings, and sets up kings; He gives wisdom to the wise, and knowledge to them who know understanding. He reveals the deep and secret things; He knows what is in the darkness, and the light dwells with Him.

DANIEL 2:20–22.

[1]Norman Vincent Peale, *Wonderful Promises* (Carmel, N.Y.: Guideposts Associates, Inc., 1983).

Let every soul be subject to the higher powers. For there is no power but of God; the powers that be are ordained of God.

ROMANS 13:1.

For though there be [those] who are called gods, whether in heaven or in earth (as there be gods many and lords many), but to us there is but one God, the Father, of whom are all things, and we in Him; and one Lord Jesus Christ, by whom are all things, and we by Him.

1 CORINTHIANS 8:5–6.

Wherefore if you be dead with Christ from the rudiments of the world, why, as though living in the world, are you subject to ordinances (touch not; taste not; handle not; which all are to perish with using) after the commandments and doctrines of men?

COLOSSIANS 2:20–22.

Every good gift and every perfect gift is from above, and comes down from the Father of lights, with whom is no variableness, neither shadow of turning.

JAMES 1:17.

SPECIALIZATION

We've often heard the expression jack-of-all-trades, master-of-none when talking about specialization. Production increases as each person concentrates on a few tasks rather than many. The danger of specialization is that demand for that specialty may slump. The specialist can wind up on par with unskilled labor in a glutted market. Still, rewards are greatest to those who achieve excellence.

We tend to doubt the abilities of a jack-of-all-trades. When someone offers to paint my house, repair the plumbing, replace the windows, build a porch, *and* resurface the swimming pool, I'm reluctant to trust him even with my lawn mower. However, a pilot who tells me he can fly twin engines, seaplanes, and corporate jets actually instills more confidence than one who claims experience flying only single-engine Cessna aircraft. A surgeon who specializes only in the left ventricle of the heart would hardly get my business if I needed heart surgery. He might miss something that the eye of a broader specialist would see.

Becoming a specialist does not excuse ignorance in other areas. Some medical specialists who fight for a free market in medicine will attach their names to any leftist organization with humanitarian appeal due to political ignorance. Whatever our specialty, if we know the basics about inflation or free markets, we, at least, can pretend to vote more intelligently. Whatever our specialty, we have no excuse for ignorance of God's law and for not conducting personal and business affairs according to biblical principles.

(*See Also:* Cooperation, Demand and Supply, Division of Labor, Exchange, Organization, Productivity, Quality)

The boys grew; and Esau was a cunning hunter, a man of the field; and Jacob was a plain man, dwelling in tents.

GENESIS 25:27.

He has filled them with wisdom of heart, to work all manner of work, of the engraver, and of the cunning workman, and of the embroiderer in blue, and in purple, in scarlet, and in fine linen, and of the weaver, even of them who do any work and of those who design artistic works.

EXODUS 35:35.

With him was Aholiah, son of Ahisamach, of the tribe of Dan, an engraver, and an artistic workman, and an embroiderer....

EXODUS 38:23.

...You know that there is not among us any who has skill to hew timber like the Sidonians.

1 KINGS 5:6.

David...set masons to hew wrought stones to build the house of God.

1 CHRONICLES 22:2.

There are workmen with you in abundance, hewers and workers of stone and timber, and all manner of artistic men for every manner of work.

1 CHRONICLES 22:15.

Baalath, and all the store cities that Solomon had, and all the chariot cities, and the cities of the horsemen, and all that Solomon desired to build in Jerusalem, and in Lebanon, and throughout the land of his dominion.

2 CHRONICLES 8:6.

Because he was of the same craft, he abode with them, and wrought, for by their occupation they were tentmakers.

ACTS 18:3.

SPECIAL PRIVILEGE

(*See:* Elitism, Rule by Decree, Subsidies)

SPENDING DEFICITS

(*See:* Debt, Inflation, Keynesianism)

STATISM

Not everyone understands the nature and consequences of statism in its myriad disguises any more than they understand the benefits of a free market system. A *state,* to use Robert Carneiro's definition, is an autonomous political unit, encompassing communities, and having a centralized government with the power to tax, draft men for work or war, decree and enforce laws.[1] In other words, the survival of a state derives from its ability to coerce and compel. In a lighter tone, let's define just a few of these isms. Each represents a different face of the same statist head.

    Socialism: You have two cows. The state expropriates one, gives it to your neighbor, and taxes away half of the milk from each of you.

    Communism: You have two cows. The state takes both, assigns you the task of milking and feeding them, and then confiscates the milk for the party elite.

    Fascism (or *National Socialism*): You have two cows. The state confiscates both cows and then shoots you.

    Welfarism: You have two cows. You keep the cows, but the states takes the milk and feeds it to the lazy, criminals, politicians, and bureaucrats.

    New Dealism: You have two cows. The state takes both cows, shoots one, milks the other, and then throws away the milk.

    You noticed the absence of "capitalism" in the list, didn't you? This word, coined by Karl Marx, has so many twisted meanings that it produces more heated confusion than enlightenment. In contrast to the isms, then, how does the *free market* function? You have two cows. You sell one and buy a bull.

    The characteristic common to all isms listed above is *force.* Carneiro writes, "Force, and not enlightened self-interest, is the mechanism by which political

---

[1]Robert L. Carneiro, *A Theory of the Origin of the State* (Menlo Park, Calif.: Institute for Humane Studies, 1970), p. 3.

evolution has led, step by step, from autonomous villages to the state."[2] Some believe that war is the root of the state. The Greek philosopher Heraclitus wrote, "War is the father of all things."[3] I believe that *envy* lies in the heart of statism. "Envy shoots at others and wounds herself," says a Swedish proverb.

If a state government cannot exist for long without consent of the governed, what drives large numbers of people to accept bondage, other than envy or covetousness? "For where envying and strife is, there is disorder and every evil work" (JAMES 3:16). The state takes some or all property from many for state redistribution. Anyone who accepts such property fails the test of the great moral principles so eloquently exemplified throughout the Bible.

Of course, in our modern states, programs of redistribution are cloaked in eleemosynary terminology to veil the real intent of schemes and scams. Those ignorant in their innocence (or vice versa) do not recognize long-range outcomes of these programs. The system of grants, subsidies, welfare, price supports, and protective privileges ensnares us all in its insidious web of deceit. "The best heart may go wrong in dark hours," said Johann Wolfgang von Goethe. Redistribution does not mean that all confiscated properties are equitably [?] redistributed. Most remains in the hands of statists, their agents, friends, and supporters. Senator William Proxmire (Democrat, Wisconsin) estimates that 75 to 80 percent of the funds do not go to people in need.

All this may seem like a harsh indictment. Let's look at the biblical record. A substantial proportion of the Bible is devoted to statism. The Lord clearly shows us that when we abdicate our responsibilities of family and civil government and surrender them for a so-called better life under humanism (i.e., serving other gods), we see the result in EXODUS 1:11: "Therefore they did set over them taskmasters to afflict them with their burdens....

(*See Also:* Directed Economy, Elitism, Humanism, One Worldism, Socialism, Terrorism, Welfarism)

> *Therefore they did set over them taskmasters to afflict them with their burdens. They built for Pharaoh treasure cities....*
>
> EXODUS 1:11

> *You shall not bow down to their gods, nor serve them, nor do their works; but you shall utterly overthrow them, and quite break down their images.*
>
> EXODUS 23:24.

> *Hazael said, Why is my lord weeping? He answered, Because I know the evil that you will do to the children of Israel. Their strongholds will*

[2]Ibid., p. 6.
[3]*Loc cit.*

you set on fire, and their young men will you slay with the sword, and will dash their children, and rip up their women with child.

                                                                                              2 Kings 8:12.

Jehoahaz besought the Lord, and the Lord listened to him, for he saw the oppression of Israel, because the king of Syria oppressed them.

                                                                                              2 Kings 13:4.

The earth is given into the hands of the wicked; he covers the faces of the judges....

                                                                                              Job 9:24.

Envy not the oppressor, and choose none of his ways.

                                                                                              Proverbs 3:31.

To punish the just is not good, nor to strike princes for equity.

                                                                                              Proverbs 17:26.

When the wicked comes, then comes also contempt, and with ignominy reproach.

                                                                                              Proverbs 18:3.

When righteous men do rejoice, there is great glory; but when the wicked rise, a man is hidden.

                                                                                              Proverbs 28:12.

Surely oppression makes a wise man mad....

                                                                                              Ecclesiastes 7:7.

...There is a time wherein one man rules over another to his own hurt.

                                                                                              Ecclesiastes 8:9.

I will give children to be their princes, and babes shall rule over them. And the people shall be oppressed, every one by another, and every one by his neighbor; the child shall behave himself proudly against the ancient, and the base against the honorable.

                                                                                              Isaiah 3:4–5.

Fear, and the pit, and the snare, are upon you, O inhabitant of the earth.

                                                                                              Isaiah 24:17.

Then the princes, governors, captains, judges, treasurers, counsellors, sheriffs, and all the rulers of the provinces, were gathered together to dedicate the image that Nebuchadnezzar the king had set up; and they stood before the image.... Then a herald cried aloud, To you it is commanded, O people, nations, and languages, that...you fall down and worship the golden image that Nebuchadnezzar the king has set up; and whoever does not fall down and worship shall the same hour be cast into the midst of a burning fiery furnace.

DANIEL 3:3–6.

The king shall do according to his will; and he shall exalt himself, and magnify himself above every god, and shall speak marvelous things against the God of gods, and shall prosper until the indignation be accomplished....

DANIEL 11:36.

You shall sow, but you shall not reap; you shall tread the olives, but you shall not annoint thyself with oil, and sweet wine, but shall not drink wine. For the statutes of Omri are kept, and all the works of the house of Ahab, and you walk in their counsels, that I should make you a desolation, and the inhabitants thereof a hissing; therefore, you shall bear the reproach of my people.

MICAH 6:15–16.

...They shall lay their hands on you, and persecute you, delivering you up to the synagogues, and into prisons, being brought before kings and rulers for My name's sake.

LUKE 21:12.

They began to accuse him, saying, We found this fellow perverting the nation, and forbidding to give tribute to Caesar, saying that he himself is Christ a King.

LUKE 23:2.

This is the condemnation, that light is come into the world, and men loved darkness rather than light because their deeds were evil. For every one who does evil hates the light, neither comes to the light, lest his deeds should be reproved.

JOHN 3:19–20.

One of them, named Caiaphas, being the high priest that same year, said to them, You know nothing at all, nor consider that it is expedient for us, that one man should die for the people and that the whole nation perish not.

JOHN 11:49–50.

Have no fellowship with the unfruitful works of darkness, but rather reprove them.

Ephesians 5:11.

For we wrestle not against flesh and blood, but against principalities, against powers, against the rulers of darkness of this world, against spiritual wickedness in high places.

Ephesians 6:12.

I looked, and behold a pale horse; and his name who sat on him was Death, and Hell followed with him. Power was given to them over the fourth part of the earth, to kill with sword, and with hunger, and with death, and with the beasts of the earth.

Revelation 6:8.

He causes all, both small and great, rich and poor, free and bond, to receive a mark in their right hand, or on their foreheads; and that no man might buy or sell, save he who had the mark, or the name of the beast, or the number of his name.

Revelation 13:16–17.

STATIST

Statists have their own supreme god—the state. There are many competing gods, each claiming supremacy. Hence, we find bitter contention between Naziism (National Socialism) and communism, between socialism and welfarism, between Keynesianism and social democracies. Their attempts at system differentiation is marketing, for at the heart each wants, and depends upon, the same thing—that is power and coercion. Mr. Zapp, in the following imaginary dialog, is apparently uninterested in these fine distinctions of the isms. When Mr. Flagg, the statist, approaches him with his own peculiar statist version, Zapp wants no part of it.

Conversations with Flagg, the Government Man

It was late when the door pounding began. An annoyingly loud voice was shouting, "Hear ye, hear ye! All citizens awake." Zapp arose yawning, fumbled for the door lock, and wondered what "citizen" meant. When he opened the door, there stood a small, nervous man. On his ill-fitting loincloth was painted an enormous smiling, cross-eyed dove. In one claw, the dove held seventeen bolts of lightning; in the other, four bludgeons and the jawbone of an ass.

ZAPP: What's going on? It's the middle of the night.

FLAGG: We're starting a government. Hurry! Sign here.

ZAPP: Go away. I'm sleepy.

FLAGG: But this is an emergency. We need a government to defend us against the dirty foreign enemy.

ZAPP: Who?

FLAGG: The people on the other side of the Zucchini Patch.

ZAPP: Some of my best friends live over there.

FLAGG: Don't talk treason. Those people are trying to plunge us into the world's first war.

ZAPP: That's awful. Is our government going to be like that?

FLAGG: Completely different. We believe in peace—the opposite of war. Our government will prevent wars from starting.

ZAPP: How?

FLAGG: Before they can start a war, we march over there and throw spears at them, gouge out their eyes, and kick them.

ZAPP: That ought to make them think twice.

FLAGG: Of course. Wars will start in lots of different ways. For example, the king of Babylon might send a note to the king of Persia, saying, "Let's have lunch."

ZAPP: How could that start a war?

FLAGG: Unfortunately, the Babylonian phrase for "let's have lunch" is the same as the Persian word for your ayatollah is a fink." But mostly, wars will be fought over territory.

ZAPP: You mean like the Zucchini Patch?

FLAGG: Right. Someday you may have the honor of dying to save the hallowed Zucchini Patch.

ZAPP: But I don't even like zucchini. It gives me hives.

FLAGG: Why worry about hives? You'll be dead.

ZAPP: I'd rather have hives.

FLAGG: Imagine. We'll build a big statue of you with an inscription: *"In memory of Zapp, who gave his life's blood to bring us everlasting peace for a few months."*

ZAPP: No thanks. I think I'll not join.

FLAGG: Don't you believe in our glorious way of life?

ZAPP: Look. I'll tell you what. You go home and work on this government idea some more. When you get some of the killing out of it, come back and talk to me.

FLAGG: But our government will be against killing. We'll have police and detectives and judges to protect you.

ZAPP: You'll stop a criminal before he kills me?

FLAGG: Not exactly. We'll step in just after someone kills you.

ZAPP: Well, better late than never.

FLAGG: When we find the killer, we kill him. Killers must be paid in their own coin.

ZAPP: What do you do to a rapist?

FLAGG: And for other crimes we have correctional institutions.

ZAPP: What happens there?

FLAGG: We rebuild criminals so they can live in society with human dignity.

ZAPP: How do you teach them human dignity?

FLAGG: Make them eat bread and water. Make them go to the toilet in the same room where they eat—with guards watching. Take away their names and give them numbers. Cut off their sex lives. Make them crush rocks, build government roads, and walk around in circles. Cut off their communication with the people outside. Put them in a pitch-black dungeon all alone for a few months.

ZAPP: Don't you build anything besides statues, prisons, and dungeons?

FLAGG: Oh sure. We build insane asylums.

ZAPP: What's an insane asylum?

FLAGG: A big building where we keep crazy people.

ZAPP: How do you know they're crazy?

FLAGG: You'd have to be crazy to stay in a place like that.

ZAPP: How do these crazy people get in?

FLAGG: If someone's wife or husband or uncle signs a paper swearing he's crazy, we lock him up.

ZAPP: What if he signs a paper swearing he's not crazy?

FLAGG: We tear it up and throw it away.

ZAPP: Why?

FLAGG: A crazy person will sign anything.

ZAPP: What else do you build?

FLAGG: Well—public schools.

ZAPP: What happens there?

FLAGG: We teach children the things they should know.

ZAPP: Like what?

FLAGG: Oh—like what a wonderful government they have, and how to salute it every morning, and how rotten the other government is, and what to do when you sing the national anthem.

ZAPP: Well, what do you do when you sing it?

FLAGG: You have to stand up, and uncover your bellybutton, and put your right thumb in it.

ZAPP: Why is that?

FLAGG: To symbolize the cord that connects you with your mother country—the state. Just wait until you see 100,000 bare bellybuttons, all doing that at once. It's a stirring sight, believe you me. The emotion of it will bring tears to your eyes. Well, how about joining?

ZAPP: How many portions of food do you get?

FLAGG: Oh, we take all of your food and production. Then we give you some official money.

ZAPP: Money?

FLAGG: Sure, money. Little flat stones.

ZAPP: Oh, good, that's no problem, I know where there are plenty of little flat stones. I'll go get some.

FLAGG: They'd better have my picture on them, or else we'll throw you in prison for counterfeiting.

ZAPP: Oh! Once I get my money stones from you with your picture on them, what do I do with them?

FLAGG: First you have to give a lot of them to the ERS.

ZAPP: What's the ERS?

FLAGG: The Eternal Revenue Service.

ZAPP: What does the Eternal Revenue Service do for me?

FLAGG: It keeps you out of prison.

ZAPP: How?

FLAGG: By collecting your taxes.

ZAPP: What are taxes?

FLAGG: Money you pay to keep out of prison.

ZAPP: That seems like bribery.

FLAGG: Certainly not! Any bribes you pay are over and above your taxes.

ZAPP: Do you tax other things as well?

FLAGG: Yes, of course. That's why we organized the state. We tax little incidentals, like the getting born tax. It costs you four stones for your birth certificate. It proves you were born.

ZAPP: Everyone knows I was born.

FLAGG: You have to have an official birth certificate, for example, to get into our public schools.

ZAPP: Suppose I don't go to school?

FLAGG: All citizens must go to school. School is compulsory. Besides, why waste your school tax?

ZAPP: Is everything compulsory?

FLAGG: Oh, no, of course not. We don't do things like that, like they might on the other side of the Zucchini Patch. Take the library, for instance. You don't have to use the library if you don't want to.

ZAPP: That's nice.

FLAGG: But the library tax is compulsory, whether you use it or not. But, it's the smallest tax we have.

ZAPP: Do you mean there are still more taxes?

FLAGG: Oh, yes. There's the income tax, for example. When you sell something, and money comes in, then we take half of it. And then there's the outgo tax. When you buy something, and money goes out from your pocketbook, then we take 10 percent. By the way, do you smoke?

ZAPP: Some.

FLAGG: There's a cigarette tax. Do you drink?

ZAPP: A little wine occasionally.

FLAGG: Then you'd pay an alcohol tax. You like music and dancing?

ZAPP: Sure.

FLAGG: Entertainment tax. This your hut?

ZAPP: Yessir.

FLAGG: Property tax. That eagle over the door. You'll have to pay a property improvement tax.

ZAPP: Wait a minute. Do I have to pay all of those taxes?

FLAGG: Of course not. This is a free country. You can go to jail instead, and we'll confiscate your property and sell it at the lowest price.

ZAPP: Assume that I just stay in my hut and do nothing.

FLAGG: Retirement tax. Besides, every time you use the bathroom there's a sewer tax. Anyway, how will you earn a living?

ZAPP: I'll just buy and sell things with the people on the other side of the Zucchini Patch.

FLAGG: You'd have to pay import and export taxes.

ZAPP: Suppose I just give everything away instead?

FLAGG: Gift tax. And if someone gives you something, that means an inheritance tax.

ZAPP: You know what I have a notion to do? Just pack up and drive off in my ox cart.

FLAGG: No problem. But there's a travel tax and vehicle tax. Unless you let your ox starve, there's a fuel tax. And if you go to another country, we charge a passport tax and an exit visa tax. Anyway, how will you eat?

ZAPP: I'll return to nature and live off the land. Just hunt and fish.

FLAGG: We have a hunting and fishing tax.

ZAPP: I give up. The way your government has worked things out, I might as well be dead.

FLAGG: A death certificate costs eight stones.

ZAPP: Why do I need a death certificate?

FLAGG: You need the state's permission to be dead, and it allows you to stop using the public library.

ZAPP: Well, at last I finally will be finished with your government and the payment of taxes.

FLAGG: Not quite. There are estate taxes, probate fees, court costs, and surtaxes.

ZAPP: What are surtaxes?

FLAGG: Surtaxes are taxes on taxes, in case we missed something the first time. Sign here.

ZAPP: If I sign, I must obey your laws whether I agree with them or not. And I must pay taxes for life and even after life. Is that correct?

FLAGG: Right.

ZAPP: Even if I pay and pay, I still might be forced to go to war and be killed.

FLAGG: That is a distinct possibility given the bellicose nature of our enemy.

ZAPP: The tax money I pay will be used to build prisons and dungeons, insane asylums, war machines, and support you.

FLAGG: And statues of me, too.

ZAPP: What if I refuse to sign?

FLAGG: Then you are an enemy of the state. We'll have to kill you for treason.

ZAPP: By the way, what do you intend calling this new state?

FLAGG: What do you think of "Freedomland"?[1]

---

[1]Furnished to the author by Larry Roxbury, from *The Rape of the Ape*, (privately circulated), pp. 168–73. Revised for this book.

(*See Also:* Bureaucrat, Communist, Demagogue, Fury of a Bureaucrat Scorned, Politician, Rule by Decree, Socialist)

You shall make no covenant with them, nor with their gods. They shall not dwell in your land, lest they make you sin against Me; for if you serve their gods, it will surely be a snare for you.

Exodus 23:32–33.

The womb shall forget him; the worm shall feed sweetly on him; he shall no more be remembered; and wickedness shall be broken as a tree.

Job 24:20.

The ungodly…are like the chaff which the wind drives away…. For the Lord knows the way of the righteous; but the way of the ungodly shall perish.

Psalm 1:4, 6.

I have hated the congregation of evil doers, and will not sit with the wicked.

Psalm 26:5.

The wicked watches the righteous, and seeks to slay him…. I have seen the wicked in great power, and spreading himself like a green bay tree.

Psalm 37:32, 35.

As a snail which melts away, let every one of them pass away…. Before your pots can feel the thorns, he shall take them away as with a whirlwind, both living, and in His wrath. The righteous shall rejoice when he sees the vengeance….

Psalm 58:8–10.

Deliver me, O Lord, from the evil man; preserve me from the violent man, which imagine mischiefs in their heart; continually are they gathered together for war. They have sharpened their tongues like a serpent; adders' poison is under their lips.

Psalm 140:1–3.

The way of the wicked is as darkness; they know not at what they stumble.

Proverbs 4:19.

The righteous shall never be removed; but the wicked shall not inhabit the earth.

PROVERBS 10:30.

Be not envious against evil men; neither desire to be with them. For their heart studies destruction; their lips talk of mischief.

PROVERBS 24:1–2.

The wicked flee when no man pursues; but the righteous are bold as a lion.

PROVERBS 28:1.

Behold, the Lord's hand is not shortened, that it cannot save, neither His ear heavy, that it cannot hear. But your iniquities have separated between you and your God, and your sins have hid His face from you, that He will not hear. For your hands are defiled with blood, and your fingers with iniquity, your lips have spoken lies, your tongue has muttered perverseness. None calls for justice, nor pleads for truth; for they trust in vanity, and speak lies; they conceive mischief, and bring forth iniquity. They hatch cockatrice' eggs, and weave the spider's web; he who eats of their eggs dies, and that which is crushed breaks out into a viper. Their webs shall not become garments, neither shall they cover themselves with their works; their works are works of iniquity, and the act of violence is in their l.ands. Their feet run to evil, and they make haste to shed innocent blood; their thoughts are thoughts of iniquity; wasting and destruction are in their paths. The way of peace they know not; and there is no judgment in their goings; they have made them crooked paths; whoever goes therein shall not know peace.

ISAIAH 59:1–8.

Also in your skirts is found the blood of the souls of the poor innocents....

JEREMIAH 2:34.

You eat the fat, and you clothe yourself with wool; you kill them who are fed; but you feed not the flock. The diseased have you not strengthened, neither have you healed the sick, neither have you bound up that which was broken, neither have you brought again that which was driven away, neither have you sought that which was lost; but with force and cruelty have you ruled them.

EZEKIEL 34:3–4.

...The wicked shall do wickedly; and none of the wicked shall understand; but the wise shall understand.

DANIEL *12:10.*

Then gathered the chief priests and the Pharisees a council, and said, What do we do? For this Man does many miracles. If we let Him thus alone, all men will believe in Him, and the Romans shall come and take away both our place and nation.

JOHN *11:47–49.*

The kings of the earth stood up, and the rulers were gathered together against the Lord, and against His Christ.

ACTS *4:26.*

They stirred up the people, and the elders, and the scribes, and came upon Him, and caught Him, and brought Him to council, and set up false witnesses, who said, This Man ceases not to speak blasphemous words against this holy place, and the law.

ACTS *6:12–13.*

...Saul...made havoc of the church, entering into every house, and dragging off men and women, committing them to prison.

ACTS *8:3.*

For if the casting away of them be the reconciling of the world, what shall the receiving of them be, but life from the dead?

ROMANS *11:15.*

Have no fellowship with the unfruitful works of darkness, but rather reprove them. For it is a shame even to speak of those things which are done of them in secret. But all things that are reproved are made manifest by the light: for whatever does make manifest is light.

EPHESIANS *5:11–13.*

STEWARDSHIP

Gary North writes that the English word *economy,* which is derived from the Greek word *oikonomia,* means management, and that an *oikonomos* was a steward.[1] Now what is a steward? A steward is a manager. A manager, as we know from professional

---

[1]Gary North, *Unconditional Surrender* (Tyler, Tex.: Geneva Press, 1981), p. 145.

management of our large corporations, does not own the assets but is in charge of and responsible for them. The corporate manager not only guards against losses but is expected to make assets grow, to multiply them.

Is not this the key principle laid down by Jesus in the parable of the talents? Those who multiply their talents and generate a high return on investment get more because they demonstrate capability and responsibility. Suppose you own a business and hire a general manager. To the manager who greatly increases your net worth, you happily give more responsibility and handsome pay. Suppose you mistakenly hire an inept manager who accumulates losses. Will you not take away from him even that which he has? Is not that the principle laid down in the Bible? (See MATTHEW 25:29.)

"This is the biblical doctrine of stewardship," writes Gary North.[2] God created and owns all resources, but we have an obligation to use them wisely. "Each man is fully responsible for his actions. Each person is a steward before God over the resources, including his intellectual and labor skills, under his authority. . . . He bears the costs of his decision. He also reaps the benefits (if any)."[3] God "expects each steward to have increased the number of talents in his possession (MATTHEW 25:20–23). The skills of each man are different, the initial capital is different, and the ultimate rewards are different. The only equality in the parable is the *equality of the law* under which each steward operates."[4]

Only the free market system allows each to fully develop talents and earn the highest return. Dr. North summarizes by writing, "Profitable stewards on a free market are faithful servants. They need not be suffering servants."[5] Man best serves God and other men in a free society founded on the rule of God. It places God first. For this reason the ism believers despise the free market. They despise God. They replace Him with the "messianic state."

(*See Also:* Accountability, Demand and Supply, Law of Increase, Self-Discipline, Strategic Planning)

> *A good man shows favor, and lends; he will guide his affairs with discretion.*
>
> PSALM 112:5.

> *He becomes poor who deals with a slack hand; but the hand of the diligent makes rich.*
>
> PROVERBS 10:4.

[2]Ibid., p. 145.
[3]Ibid., p. 155.
[4]Ibid., p. 158.
[5]Ibid., p. 166.

Better is a dry morsel, and quietness therewith, than a house full of sacrifices with strife.

PROVERBS 17:1.

For whoever has, to him shall be given, and he shall have more abundance; but whoever has not, from him shall be taken away even that which he has.

MATTHEW 13:12.

He also who received seed among the thorns is he who hears the word; and the care of this world, and the deceitfulness of riches, choke the word, and he becomes unfruitful.

MATTHEW 13:22.

STRATEGIC PLANNING

Strategic planning is forward planning to achieve specific objectives. Fulfillment of tomorrow's desires depends on decisions made today. There are no future decisions. Decisions are made now; but there will be future results that occur as a consequence of how we order, plan, and manage today. Successful businesses engage in strategic planning as part of an ongoing process. Management states its goals for both the near term and the long range. It then sets about developing plans and acquiring means for reaching those goals.

Successful managers also develop *contingency plans* to deal with unforeseen events and surprises. They meet future challenges because they have planned to meet them. Unsuccessful managers deal with each situation as it arises. Frequently surprised when a crisis arises, they often manage from crisis to crisis, being pulled and pushed by the ill winds of others and seldom have their firms under control.

How should we behave as Christians? Let's ask: How does God do it? And then emulate the Master Architect. Take a close look at GENESIS 1. Notice the time sequencing of activities. By studying it carefully, you can appreciate the order in which creation unfolded. If God had created man before vegetation, and the animals before the land, there would have been no food supply. God, in His infinite love, settled these matters we regard as trivial. Notice the development of the food chain, the ecosystem, the interdependence and relationships among each level of creation, so that man, coming last in this concatenation of events, had everything laid out for him in neat order. Would *you* have planned it that way?

God certainly employs strategic planning and strategic management. He has shown us, in part, how to succeed in our affairs. Leading orderly lives in tune with God's divine long-range plan, we will indeed be fruitful and multiply.

(*See Also:* Creation, Free Society, Management, Organization, Risk Aversion, Savings, Stewardship)

God said, Let there be light; and there was light....
  God made the firmament, and divided the waters which were under the firmament from the waters which were above the firmament; and it was so.
  ...God said, Let the waters under the heaven be gathered together into one place, and let the dry land appear; and it was so....
  God said, Let the earth bring forth grass, the herb yielding seed, and the fruit tree yielding fruit after its kind, whose seed is in itself, upon the earth; and it was so....
  God said, Let there be lights in the firmament of the heaven to divide the day from night; and let them be for signs, and for seasons, and for days, and years....
  God said, Let the waters bring forth abundantly the moving creature that has life, and fowl that may fly above the earth in the open firmament of heaven. And God created great whales, and every living creature that moves, which the waters brought forth abundantly, after their kind, and every winged fowl after its kind. And God saw that it was good. And God blessed them, saying, Be fruitful and multiply; fill the waters of the seas, and let fowl multiply on the earth.
  ...God said, Let the earth bring forth the living creature after its kind, cattle, and creeping things, and beast of the earth after its kind; and it was so.
  ...God said, Let us make man in our image, after our likeness; and let them have dominion over the fish of the sea, and over the fowl of the air, and over the cattle, and over all the earth, and over every creeping thing that creeps on the earth.
                                    GENESIS *1:3, 7, 9, 11, 14, 20–22, 24, 26.*

SUBSIDIES

Give a man a fish today, and he'll be hungry again tomorrow. Teach him to fish, and he'll feed himself for a lifetime. *Subsidies* imply that a person or business cannot make it without assistance. Subsidies voluntarily given are not our subject. Subsidies, grants, and special privileges of civil government cause considerable harm. This is our subject.

In the first place, civil government cannot subsidize. A government has nothing to give. It produces no income. Consequently, to subsidize or grant financial privilege, a government depends upon expropriation, or it creates costs and then shifts them. A direct subsidy would be money given to a local institution (public or private) to construct a new building. The money was taken from many through taxes. Certainly some contractors, administrators, and a few in the local community benefit from this subsidized project, but many people all over the country involuntarily gave up little things, like a contribution to a charitable organization, or an anniversary dinner out, or a new pair of shoes, for the benefit of a few.

The government also uses import tariffs, quotas, and other protective mechanisms to shield a domestic industry from foreign competition. Prices of protected goods always rise. Many consumers pay for benefits of a few investors and of some members of organized labor. When governments limit the number of licensees of any business activity or grant a local monopoly, the subsidized activities reap benefits at the cost of many. An extra fifty cents in cab fare may not mean much; but there are thousands of these nickel-and-dime items that chew up our income faster than Pac Man.

Most people have their noses in the hog trough, while grunting dissatisfaction with all those government subsidies given to others. Farmers know that high taxes, inflation, interest, and export policies grind up their profits; but when they drive their tractor brigade to Washington, D.C., what do they ask for? More farm support! Labor leaders shout for more federal spending for defense contracts and public works. Where a service competes with the government, they want the government to raise workers' wages.

The first question to ask yourself is: Am I a part of the problem? You are not in a very strong position if you complain about government subsidies while participating in them. In the long run, of course, governments cannot subsidize, but they can tyrannize. One leads to the other, and the price of state subsidies is summarized in Daniel 2:12. As it says in Galatians 4:9, once you learn the truth, how can you return to ways of slavery?

(*See Also:* Elitism, Equality, Private Property, Statism, Taxation)

Children in whom was no blemish, but well-favored, and skillful in all wisdom, and cunning in knowledge, and understanding science, and such as had ability in them to stand in the king's palace, and whom they might teach the learning and the tongue of the Chaldeans. And the king appointed them a daily provision of the king's meat....
Daniel 1:4–5.

For this cause the king was angry and very furious, and commanded to destroy all the wise men of Babylon.
Daniel 2:12.

If some of the branches be broken off, and you, being a wild olive tree, were grafted in among them, and with them partook of the root and fatness of the olive tree, boast not against the branches. But if you boast, you bear not the root, but the root you.

ROMANS 11:17–18.

But now, after that you have known God, or rather are known of God, why do you turn again to the weak and beggarly elements, where you desire to be again in bondage?

GALATIANS 4:9.

SUICIDE

If any man defile the temple of God, him shall God destroy; for the temple of God is holy, which temple you are.

1 CORINTHIANS 3:17.

(*See:* Abortion, Capital Punishment, Creation)

SUPPLY

By supply, of course, we refer to the diverse and abundant supply of goods and services in our country. Under competitive market conditions, supply is a schedule of quantities of a product that suppliers may offer at various prices. In a market of many small sellers of a product, such as egg producers, no one seller can really influence price. Therefore, the individual seller reacts to the market price. He concentrates on cost control, which he can influence. Such a seller, then, is concerned not about marketing but production. A good cost-control system means the difference between profits in good times and survival in bad times, compared with poor management, which survives in good times but bankrupts in bad times.

Even in markets where sellers may establish price, there is a trade-off between how much buyers will purchase and how much the seller would like to sell. In other words, if a seller sets the price, he has no control over how much will be bought. If the seller sets a production target, he cannot exercise control over price. The buyer still reigns supreme in the market.

The only time a seller can dominate the buyer and control both price and quantity is when a government grants a special monopoly privilege and then, through coercion, forces the public to buy that product or service. Two good examples are federal reserve money and first-class mail delivery. Public utilities represent cases where, although a state rate commission may set maximum rates based on costs, these costs rise rapidly due to monopolistic power of unions and their ability to escalate wages. Management of utility companies settle union disputes quickly because unwieldy settlements do not come out of company profits. These costs are passed on directly to the consumer through higher rates. Therefore, in a system of state privileges and subsidies, supply is restricted. In a free society, supply is not only abundant but goods and services are cheaper with a greater variety to choose from.

(*See Also:* Capital Formation, Demand and Supply, Price Mechanism, Production)

> *...I have prepared for the house of the Lord a hundred thousand talents of gold, and a thousand thousand talents of silver, and of brass and iron without weight, for it is in abundance: timber also and stone have I prepared; and you may add to it. Moreover, there are workmen with you in abundance.... Of the gold, the silver, and the brass, and the iron, there is no number....*
>
> 1 CHRONICLES 22:14–16.

> *When goods increase, they are increased who eat them; and what good is there to the owners thereof, saving the beholding of them with their eyes?*
>
> ECCLESIASTES 5:11.

> *I am glad about the coming of Stephanas and Fortunatus, and Achaicus; for what was lacking on your part they supplied.*
>
> 1 CORINTHIANS 16:17.

> *...By an equality, that now at this time your abundance may supply their lack, that their abundance also may supply your lack....*
>
> 2 CORINTHIANS 8:14.

> *My God shall supply all your need according to His riches in glory by Jesus Christ.*
>
> PHILIPPIANS 4:19.

SURETY

A *surety* is a guarantee given to assure that an undertaking or contract will be fulfilled as promised. It may be an item of private property of the one offering the guarantee, or it may be another person who becomes legally responsible for the debt (see PROVERBS 20:16). For instance, a cosigner takes on this contingent liability, a potential obligation should the original signer default (see PROVERBS 22:26). A bail bond works similarly (see ACTS 17:9). Typically, those in the surety business will take in cash payment, a portion of the required bond, which payment remains to compensate the bondsperson for services rendered, like an interest payment. A surety bond guarantees performance of a contract or obligation (see JOB 17:3). Any property held in suretyship must be returned to the original owner in the original condition when terms of contract have been completed. While the property remains in the lender's hands, he is responsible for its safekeeping (see EXODUS 22:10–12).

(*See Also:* Contract, Debts, Pledge, Private Property, Responsibility, Stewardship)

> If a man delivers to his neighbor an ass, or an ox, or a sheep, or any beast, to keep; ... and if it is stolen from him, he shall make restitution to the owner.
>
> EXODUS 22;10, 12.

> Lay down now a pledge, put me in a surety with You. Who is he who will strike hands with me?
>
> JOB 17:3.

> Take his garment that is surety for a stranger; and take a pledge of him for a strange woman.
>
> PROVERBS 20:16.

> Be not one of them who strikes hands, or of them who are sureties for debts.
>
> PROVERBS 22:26.

> When they had taken security of Jason, and of the other, they let him go.
>
> ACTS 17:9.

TAXATION

Should you pay taxes? Glancing through Senator William Proxmire's book, *The Fleecing of America,* that answer is a big *yes* for many: e.g., public educators and teachers' unions; military; bureaucracies; state and local politicians; health professionals; medical research organizations; big labor and big business; friends of the inarticulate poor; and so forth. That answer is a big *no* in other titles such as Irwin Schiff's, *The Biggest Con: How the Government Is Fleecing You;* Frank Chodorov's, *Taxation Is Theft;* Gerald Carson's, *The Golden Egg;* Robert Kuttner's, *Revolt of the Haves;* plus others. Authors and economists tend to support taxation on principle and at great lengths "prove" that tax reduction does not stimulate the economy. Many conclude that high or low taxes have no effect on capital investment and economic growth. Others argue that since we get back tax money through various social programs, we have not really given up anything.

Taxes evoke the specter of the IRS extracting its toll from incomes of citizens and residents. Actually, income taxes provide less than one-half of the total money spent by civil governments. Much originates in indirect (i.e., hidden) taxes, including inflation. Visible and direct taxes include income and social security taxes, sales and property taxes. One of these is allowed by God, the others are not. Civil authorities sometimes try to confuse Christians by quoting "Render unto Caesar what is Caesar's" to justify taxation. Believers must render "to God the things that are God's." God, not Caesar, is Lord, Master, and Owner. Those who slop in Caesar's hog trough of special privilege and subsidies certainly owe Caesar much, including their freedom.

Two kinds of taxes appear in the Bible. One is a head tax on every male over age twenty, of one-half shekel of silver, about 110 grains, payable to the civil government (EXODUS 30:11–14). Primarily it supported the military. It fell on all equally: no progressive taxation here (EXODUS 30:15). The second tax, the tithe, is God's tax, which some treat as a tax on income, others a capital gains tax. Property and all other taxes are forbidden in the Bible. The state replaces God by taxing income. From believers, "the state has a right to collect a minimal head tax from its citizens, but, while *perhaps* the state can require a tithe of all men, . . ., it *cannot* stipulate where that tithe shall go. The state thus controls the use of the head tax; the tither controls the use of the tithe tax."[1]

Scholars distinguish three tithes. First is the Lord's tithe, 10 percent of which went to the priesthood. Parts of that tithe paid for education, for example, which the church organization may provide. The second, a festival tithe, allowed the family to rejoice before the Lord. The third, a poor tithe, given every three years, sufficient to *sustain* the poor, did not raise them to equality with contributors. These approximate 23 percent. Total tax, therefore, given to state control was 110 grains of silver. Other than 1 percent of income to the priesthood, all other taxes remained under family control for education, contributions, and so forth. Free-will offerings were *over and above* taxes and tithes. It is important in God's order not to decapitalize the family.

Today our society is being similarly decapitalized. The state takes about 45 percent of a man's income, and the church claims to be the legitimate repository of the tithe and claims 10 percent or more. With some sects, it runs up to 30 percent. As a result, what remains is usually only sufficient to maintain the family in its living expenses, not to recapitalize the family and society. Whenever and wherever church and state (or temple) reach this point, civilization begins to decapitalize and crumble. God's ordination is a very modest head tax for the state, and a tenth of a tithe, 1 percent of one's income, for the church. To go beyond this is to begin digging the grave of a civilization.[2]

(*See Also:* Inflation, Inheritance, Property Taxes, Slavery, Statism, Theft)

This stone, which I have set for a pillar, shall be God's house; and of all that You shall give me I will surely give the tenth to You.
                                                                GENESIS 28:22.

When you take the sum of the children of Israel after their number, then shall they give every man a ransom for his soul to the Lord, when you number them, that there be no plague among them, when you number them. This they shall give, every one who passes among them that are numbered, half a shekel after the shekel of the sanctuary (a shekel is twenty gerahs): a half shekel shall be the offering of the Lord. Everyone who passes among them that are numbered from twenty years old and above shall give an offering to the Lord. The rich shall not give more,

---

[1] Rousas John Rushdoony, *The Institutes of Biblical Law* (Nutley, N.J.: The Craig Press, 1973), p. 283.

[2] Rushdoony, *Law and Society* (Vallecito, Calif.: Ross House Books, 1982), p. 130.

and the poor shall not give less than half a shekel, when they give an offering to the Lord, to make atonement for your souls.

Exodus 30:12–15.

Levy a tribute to the Lord of the men of war who went out to battle; one soul of five hundred, both of the persons, and of the beeves, and of the asses, and of the sheep: take it of their half, and give it to Eleazar the priest for a heave offering of the Lord. Of the children of Israel's half, you shall take one portion of fifty, of the persons, of the beeves, of the asses, and of the flocks, of all manner of beasts, and give them to the Levites, which keep charge of the tabernacles of the Lord.

Numbers 31:28–30.

Jehoiakim gave the silver and the gold to Pharaoh; but he taxed the land to give the money according to the commandment of Pharaoh. He exacted the silver and gold of the people of the land, of every one according to his taxation, to give to Pharaoh.... He did that which was evil in the sight of the Lord....

2 Kings 23:35, 37.

Be it known now to the king, that, if this city be built and the walls set up again, then will they not pay toll, tribute, and custom, and so you shall diminish the revenue of the kings.

Ezra 4:13.

Some said, We have borrowed money for the king's tribute, and upon our lands and vineyards. Yet now our flesh is as the flesh of our brethren, our children as their children; and lo, we bring into bondage our sons and daughters to be servants, and some of our daughters are brought into bondage already. Neither is it in our power to redeem them, for other men have our lands and vineyards.

Nehemiah 5:4–5.

The former governors who had been before me were chargeable to the people, and had taken of them bread and wine, beside forty shekels of silver; yea, even their servants bare rule over the people, but so I did not, because of the fear of God.

Nehemiah 5:15.

Whoever keeps the fig tree shall eat the fruit of it....

Proverbs 27:18.

Will a man rob God? Yet you have robbed Me. But you say, Wherein have we robbed You? In tithes and offerings. You are cursed with a curse, for you have robbed Me, even this whole nation. Bring all the tithes into the storehouse, that there may be meat in My house, and prove Me now herewith, says the Lord of hosts, if I will not open you the windows of heaven, and pour you out a blessing, that there shall not be room enough to receive it. I will rebuke the devourer for your sakes, and he shall not destroy the fruits of your ground; neither shall your vine cast her fruit before the time in the field, says the Lord of hosts.

MALACHI 3:8–11.

When they were come to Capernaum, they who received tribute money came to Peter, and said, Does not your master pay tribute? He said, Yes. When he was come into the house, Jesus prevented him, saying, What do you think, Simon? Of whom do the kings of the earth take custom or tribute? Of their own children, or of strangers?

MATTHEW 17:24–25.

Tell us therefore, What do you think? Is it lawful to give tribute to Caesar, or not? But Jesus perceived their wickedness, and said, Why tempt me, you hypocrites? Show me the tribute money. They brought to him a penny. And so he said to them, Whose image and superscription is this? They said to him, Caesar's. Then he said to them, Render therefore to Caesar the things which are Caesar's; and to God the things that are God's.

MATTHEW 22:17–21.

It came to pass in those days, that there went out a decree from Caesar Augustus, that all the world should be taxed. (And this taxing was first made when Cyrenius was governor of Syria.) All went to be taxed, every one to his own city. And Joseph also went up from Galilee, out of the city of Nazareth, into Judea, into the city of David, which is called Bethlehem (because he was of the house and lineage of David), to be taxed with Mary, his espoused wife, being great with child.

LUKE 2:1–5.

They began to accuse him, saying, We found this fellow perverting the nation, and forbidding to give tribute to Caesar, saying that he himself is Christ a King.

LUKE 23:2.

…He was led as a sheep to the slaughter, and like a lamb dumb before his shearer, so opened He not His mouth.

ACTS 8:32.

*For I mean not that other men be eased, and you be burdened; but by
an equality, that now at this time your abundance may supply their
lack, that their abundance also may supply your lack....*

                                                        2 CORINTHIANS 8:13–14.

*For the Scripture says, You shall not muzzle the ox that treads out the
corn. And, the laborer is worthy of his reward.*

                                                             1 TIMOTHY 5:18.

TAX COLLECTOR

"In Sieburg, Germany, a unique tax museum, ... exhibits a relief piece depicting the Sumerians kneeling to pay their cattle tax. Collection methods were harsh. A bas-relief from an Egyptian pharoah's tomb shows the tax men beating a taxpayer, one stroke for every day his taxes were in arrears. For more serious offenses noses and ears were cut off.... The Roman tax-gatherers did not hesitate to extract information and enforce payment through applying torture when they deemed it appropriate."[1] In America today, tax collectors have smashed car windows and dragged a pregnant woman over glass, closed bank accounts, ruined businesses, put people out of work, and evicted persons from their homes.

Of IRS collection officers, Gerald Carson writes, "They could destroy a small businessman's credit overnight, for they can, if they choose, seize a bank account, garnishee wages, take a taxpayer's automobile, and padlock his place of business without a court order."[2] Their power is awesome and tactics frightening. While they may not apply physical torture, their psychological turn of the screw frightens many Americans. No wonder that throughout ages the tax collector has not been everyone's favorite person!

(*See Also:* Expropriation, Fury of a Bureaucrat Scorned, Power of State, Statist, Taxation)

*Though wickedness be sweet in his mouth, though he hide it under his
tongue, though he spare it, and forsake it not, but keep it still within his
mouth; yet his meat in his bowels is turned. It is the gall of asps within
him. He has swallowed down riches, and he shall vomit them up
again; God shall cast them out of his belly. He shall suck the poisons of
asps; the viper's tongue shall slay him. He shall not see the rivers, the
floods, the brooks of honey and butter. That which he labored for shall*

[1] Gerald Carson, *The Golden Egg* (Boston: Houghton Mifflin Company, 1977), pp. 14–15.
[2] Ibid., p. 196

he restore, and shall not swallow it down; according to his substance shall the restitution be, and he shall not rejoice therein. Because he has oppressed and forsaken the poor; because he has violently taken away a house which he built not. Surely he shall not feel quietness in his belly; he shall not save of that which he desired. There shall none of his meat be left. In the fullness of his sufficiency he shall be in straits. Every hand of the wicked shall come upon him. When he is about to fill his belly, God shall cast the fury of His wrath upon him, and shall rain it upon him while he is eating. He shall flee from the iron weapon, and the bow of steel shall strike him through. It is drawn, and come out of the body; yea, the glittering sword comes out of his gall; terrors are upon him. All darkness shall be hid in his secret places; a fire not blown shall consume him; it shall go ill with him who is left in his tabernacle. The heaven shall reveal his iniquity; and the earth shall rise up against him. The increase of his house shall depart, and his goods shall flow away in the day of his wrath. This is the portion of a wicked man from God, and the heritage appointed to him by God..

Job 20:12–29.

They encourage themselves in an evil matter; they commune of laying snares privily; they say, Who shall see them?

Psalm 64:5.

Let the extortioner catch all that he has; and let the strangers spoil his labor.... Because that he remembered not to show mercy, but persecuted the poor and needy man, that he might even slay the broken in heart.

Psalm 109:11, 16.

If you have nothing to pay, why should he take away your bed from under you?

Proverbs 22:27.

Fear, and the pit, and the snare, are upon you, O inhabitant of the earth.

Isaiah 24:17.

Then came also publicans to be baptized, and said to him, Master, what shall we do? He said to them, Exact no more than that which is appointed you.

Luke 3:12–13.

Levi made him a great feast in his own house; and there was a great company of publicans and of others who sat down with them. But their

*scribes and Pharisees murmured against His disciples, saying, Why do
you eat and drink with publicans and sinners? Jesus answering said to
them, They who are whole need not a physician; but they who are
sick. I came not to call the righteous, but sinners to repentance.*

LUKE 5:29–32.

*Their throat is an open sepulchre; with their tongues they have used
deceit; the poison of asps is under their lips, whose mouth is full of
cursing and bitterness; their feet are swift to shed blood; destruction
and misery are in their ways; and the way of peace have they not
known; there is no fear of God before their eyes. Now we know that
whatsoever things the law says, it says to them who are under the law;
that every mouth may be stopped, and all the world may become
guilty before God.*

ROMANS 3:13–19.

*But now I have written to you not to keep company, if any man who is
called brother be a fornicator, or covetous, or an idolator, or a railer, or
a drunkard, or an extortioner, with such a one do not eat.*

1 CORINTHIANS 5:11.

*Let him who stole steal no more; but rather let him labor, working with
his hands the things which are good, that he may have to give to him
who needs.*

EPHESIANS 4:28.

*Be sober, be vigilant, because your adversary the devil, as a roaring
lion, walks about, seeking whom he may devour.*

1 PETER 5:8.

TECHNOLOGY

Herbert W. Armstrong tells of an interview in 1914 after the Ford Motor Company
instituted a plan devised by John R. Lee—the sensational $5.00 a day pay scale. "I
understand you are now paying by far the highest wage scale in the automobile
industry," said Mr. Armstrong to Mr. Lee.

"On the contrary," he said. "We are paying the *lowest!*"

Armstrong was taken aback. "But isn't the union scale $3.75 per ten-hour
day?"

"Correct," Lee affirmed.

"And are you not now paying $5.00 per day for only a nine-hour day?"

"Right again, but we don't figure what we *really* pay on that basis. We compute it on the basis of what we get for each dollar spent. You see, our sales volume is now great enough to enable us to install a new conveyor belt or assembly-line system of production. We take full advantage of the fact that fewer men can produce much *more* by machines than a greater number of workmen by hand. We start each car at one end on a conveyor belt system. Each workman has to do his part as it passes him. This way we regulate the speed of production. Actually, we now are getting twice the man-per-day production for $5.00 than our rivals get per man per day working one hour longer than our employees. That means that other manufacturers in our industry pay for two days $7.50 for the same production we get in one nine-hour day for $5.00. So we pay $2.50 less per day for the same results others pay in two ten-hour days!"[1]

This interview clearly illustrates benefits of technology. Technology sometimes means invention of new things, such as the microprocessor computer chip introduced in 1971, or the zipper in 1913, or the video disc invented by John Logie Baird in 1928; or it may mean new processes, such as the autochrome process making color photography available to the public in 1907, or manufacturing design. Time is our most precious resource. How can we accomplish more, or produce more, in less time, using less human energy? Technology often results in more output with fewer raw materials, thereby lowering production costs and saving resources. Examples of the latter are mining technology—economical refining of lower grades of minerals— or reduction of computer size—a desk-top model replacing a room full of equipment.

In God's free society, technological applications result in more goods, at cheaper prices, and saving man's energy and time. Prices of goods drop, and the value of incomes rise. In a statist society, the state taxes technological gains; inflates the supply of currency; and causes higher prices, fewer goods, and lower real wages.

(*See Also:* Business, Capital Formation, Free Enterprise, Quality, Supply)

> *I have filled him with the spirit of God, in wisdom, and in understanding, and in knowledge, and in all manner of workmanship: To devise artistic works, to work in gold, and in silver, and in brass, and in cutting stones, to set them, and in carving of timber, to work in all manner of workmanship.*
>
> Exodus 31:3–5.

> *Them has he filled with wisdom of heart, to work all manner of work, of the engraver, and of the clever workman, and of the embroiderer....*
>
> Exodus 35:35.

[1]Herbert W. Armstrong, "Prepare to Greatly Reduce Your Standard of Living!" *The Plain Truth,* May 1983, 19–21, 28–29. Permission to reprint by the Worldwide Church of God.

The house, when it was in building, was built of stone made ready before it was brought there....

                                                                                    1 KINGS 6:7.

The rest of the acts of Hezekiah, and all his might, and how he made a pool, and a conduit, and brought water into the city....

                                                                                    2 KINGS 20:20.

David prepared iron in abundance for the nails for the doors of the gates, and for the joinings, and brass in abundance without weight.

                                                                                    1 CHRONICLES 22:3.

He made in Jerusalem engines, invented by skillful men, to be on the towers and upon the bulwarks, to shoot arrows and great stones. His name spread far abroad.

                                                                                    2 CHRONICLES 26:15.

The things that have been, it is that which shall be; and that which is done is that which shall be done; and there is no new thing under the sun. Is there anything whereof it may be said, See, this is new? It has already been of old time, which was before us.

                                                                                    ECCLESIASTES 1:9–10.

He spoke also to them a parable: No man puts a piece of a new garment upon the old; if otherwise, then both the new makes a tear, and the piece that was taken out of the new agrees not with the old. And no man puts new wine into old bottles; else the new wine will burst the bottles, and be spilled, and the bottles shall perish.

                                                                                    LUKE 5:36–37.

TERRORISM

The only thing modern about terrorism is the term, its practice resulting from the chaos of an immoral populace and an apostate government. Ezekiel wrote, 2,500 years ago: "Make a chain, for the land is full of bloody crimes, and the city is full of violence.... Destruction comes; and they shall seek peace, and there shall be none" (EZEKIEL 7:23, 25).

Separating himself from God's law and order, the terrorist represents the ultimate and logical end of statism. The statist sees no law higher than his own shifting edicts. In fact, the state practices its own style of terrorism against anyone who opposes it. Confiscation of property and income, called *incomes policy*, is no less an act of terrorism than gunning down a handful of people. The latter makes newspaper headlines and evokes public outrage. The former is buried in dull economic lectures, understood by neither professor nor student, and unheard by the public.

The Bible condones neither. The bloody kind bears no distinction from any other kind of murder (see 2 SAMUEL 4:11). Paul reminds us that each is subject to higher powers, ordained by God (ROMANS 13:1). Righteous rulers are not a terror to good works (ROMANS 13:3); to evil ones, God promises that "the high ones of stature shall be hewn down" (ISAIAH 10:33). When Christians roll over and play dead, permitting unbelievers to take over our God-given legal institutions and to impose humanistic order, corruption, and poverty, terrorism will reign. Under God's discipline, turning our attention to peaceful production and exchange, we will be overwhelmed by God's abundance. Terrorists will be dealt with as quickly as King David dispatched them. "Therefore, let us follow after the things which make for peace, and things wherewith we may edify one another" (ROMANS 14:19).

(*See Also:* Corruption, Envy, One Worldism, Power, Statism, Tax Collector)

The sword without, and terror within, shall destroy both the young man and the virgin, the suckling also with the man of gray hairs.
                                                    DEUTERONOMY 32:25.

They conspired against him, and stoned him with stones at the commandment of the king in the court of the house of the Lord.
                                                    2 CHRONICLES 24:21.

Terrors shall make him afraid on every side, and drive him to his feet. His strength shall be hungerbitten, and destruction shall be ready at his side. It shall devour the strength of his skin, even the firstborn of death shall devour his strength. His confidence shall be rooted out of his tabernacle, and it shall bring him to the king of terrors.
                                                    JOB 18:11–14.

It is drawn and comes out of the body; yea, the glittering sword comes out of his gall; terrors are upon him.
                                                    JOB 20:25.

The rich man shall lie down, but he shall not be gathered; he opens his eyes, and he is not. Terrors take hold on him as waters, a tempest steals him away in the night.
                                                    JOB 27:19–20.

Behold, the Lord, the Lord of hosts, shall lop the bough with terror; and the high ones of stature shall be hewn down, and the haughty shall be humbled.
                                                    ISAIAH 10:33.

Make a chain, for the land is full of bloody crimes, and the city is full of violence. Wherefore I will bring the worst of the heathen, and they shall possess their houses, I will also make the pomp of the strong to cease, and their holy places shall be defiled.

EZEKIEL 7:23–24.

There is Elam and all her multitude round about her grave, all of them slain, fallen by the sword, who are gone down uncircumcised into the nether parts of the earth, which caused their terror in the land of the living; yet have they borne their shame with them who go down to the pit.

EZEKIEL 32:24.

For rulers are not a terror to good works, but to evil. Will you then not be afraid of the power? Do that which is good, and you shall have praise of the same.

ROMANS 13:3.

If you suffer for righteousness' sake, happy are you; and be not afraid of their terror, neither be troubled.

1 PETER 3:14.

TESTIMONY

Proper functioning of a Christian court depends upon accurate testimony of witnesses. Witnesses who do not testify honestly are accessories to crime (see PSALM 50:18). A person is convicted on the word of two or three witnesses: There is no mention of confession, coerced self-incrimination, torture, or wire-tapping. Even a confession, given voluntarily, must be reinforced by the word of witnesses. The Fifth Amendment to the Constitution is indeed biblical. It prevents compelling a person to witness against himself. Believers are also not obligated to tell the truth to an apostate enemy who intends to destroy the believer.

(*See Also:* Court System, Freedom, Justice, Law and Order, Restitution, Surety)

If a man delivers to his neighbor an ass, or an ox, or a sheep, or any beast, to keep, and it dies, or is hurt, or driven away, no man seeing it; then shall an oath of the lord be between them both, that he has not put his hand on his neighbor's goods; and the owner of it shall accept thereof, and he shall not make it good. And if it be stolen from him, he shall make restitution unto the owner thereof. If it be torn to pieces, then let him bring it for witness, and he shall not make good that which was torn.

Exodus 22:10–13.

Whoever kills any person, the murderer shall be put to death by the mouth of witnesses; but one witness shall not testify against any person to cause him to die.

Numbers 35:30.

When you saw a thief, then you consented with him....

Psalm 50:18.

...In the mouth of two or three witnesses shall every word be established.

2 Corinthians 13:1.

Against an elder receive not an accusation, but before two or three witnesses.

1 Timothy 5:19.

He who despises Moses' law died without mercy under two or three witnesses.

Hebrews 10:28.

THEFT

Theft, in any guise, is condemned. For example, robbing God is failure to give God's tithe. Tithes finance the social order according to the rule of God. The penalty for failure to tithe is high taxes exacted by human government. Even paying that tax does not relieve us of the tithe obligation.

Slander is another form of theft. Stealing and cheating, together with lying, are kindred sins. Slander, of course, robs a person of reputation.

Injustice is likewise theft. Anyone who has dealt with corrupt bureaucrats or judges immediately recognizes that anyone in a position of power such as a judge is the worst kind of thief. A corrupt judge not only fails to render justice according to God's law but ruins lives and fortunes of the very ones he should be protecting.

Whoever accepts government subsidies, welfare, or largesse is a thief; the subsidy derives from expropriated money. The eighth commandment clearly says: "Thou shalt not steal" (Exodus 20:15). No list of exceptions follows this single statement. It applies to everyone—business, government, institutions, nonprofit organizations, and every individual.

(*See Also:* Bribery, Capital Punishment, Corruption, Dishonesty, Law, Restitution, Taxation, Testimony)

If the theft be certainly found in his hand alive, whether it be ox, or ass, or sheep, he shall restore double.

Exodus 22:4.

The former governors that had been before me were chargeable to the people, and taken of them bread and wine, beside forty shekels of silver; yea, even their servants bare rule over the people; but so did I not, because of the fear of God.

Nehemiah 5:15.

If I have eaten the fruits thereof without money, or have caused the owners thereof to lose their life, let thistles grow instead of wheat, and cockle instead of barley.

Job 31:39–40.

The robbery of the wicked shall destroy them, because they refuse to do judgment.

Proverbs 21:7.

…Woe to him who increases that which is not his!…

Habakkuk 2:6.

The thief comes not, but for to steal, and to kill, and to destroy. I am come that they might have life, and that they might have it more abundantly.

John 10:10.

Let him who stole steal no more; but rather let him labor, working with his hands the thing which is good, that he may have to give to him who needs.

Ephesians 4:28.

TINSTAAFL

"There is no such thing as a free lunch (TINSTAAFL)" is the individualist's answer to state welfarism. But some do receive free lunches, you may argue. In the first place, someone, somewhere had to invest time, money, and labor to produce that lunch.

The government did not. The government produces nothing (except headaches, perhaps). Therefore, for civil government to provide free lunches, it first must acquire the means. The most expedient method is to confiscate someone else's lunch, that is, his production, for redistribution.

All statist systems operate in this manner because they play a *negative* sum game. Even utopian idealists can promise no better than a *zero* sum game (that is, a theoretical promise unrealizable in practice). Welfarists argue that the value of goods confiscated is worth less to the loser than those who receive these freebies gain. The essay in the "Welfarist" section describes a man who painfully gave up butter. There were times when he even paid three times the going price of margarine just to savor the taste of butter.

Does the person receiving the handout really get a free ride? No. He too pays a price—the price of freedom lost. W. Somerset Maugham wrote, "If a nation values anything more than freedom, it will lose its freedom; and the irony of it is that if it is comfort or money it values more, it will lose that, too."[1] Is that not what PROVERBS 19:15 warns of as well? The cost of the free lunch is loss of freedom. Tom Anderson sums it up best: "Mousetraps furnish free cheese, but the mouse's happiness is shortlived. For mice or men, there is no such thing as a free lunch."

(*See Also:* Envy, Foreign Aid, Redistribution of Income/Wealth, Welfarism)

> *That I will not take anything, from a thread to a sandal strap, and that I will not take anything that is yours lest you should say, I have made Abram rich.*
>
> GENESIS 14:23.

> *If a soul sins, and commits any of these things which are forbidden to be done by the commandments of the Lord, though he wishes it not, yet is he guilty, and shall bear his iniquity.*
>
> LEVITICUS 5:17.

> *...We will go by the high way, and if I and my cattle drink of your water, then I will pay for it....*
>
> NUMBERS 20:19.

> *You shall buy meat of them for money, that you may eat; and you shall also buy water of them for money, that you may drink.*
>
> DEUTERONOMY 2:6.

[1]W. Somerset Maugham, *Strictly Personal* (194), chap. 31, in John Bartlett, *Bartlett's Familiar Quotations,* 13th ed. (Boston: Little, Brown, 1955), p. 875.

...Neither take a gift; for a gift does blind the eyes of the wise, and perverts the words of the righteous.

DEUTERONOMY 16:19.

Slothfulness casts into a deep sleep; and an idle soul shall suffer hunger.

PROVERBS 19:15.

Love not sleep, lest you come to poverty; open your eyes, and you shall be satisfied with bread.

PROVERBS 20:13.

I tell you, you shall not depart thence until you have paid the very last mite.

LUKE 12:59.

Render therefore to all their dues; tribute to whom tribute is due; custom to whom custom; fear to whom fear; honor to whom honor. Owe no man anything, but to love one another, for he who loves another has fulfilled the law.

ROMANS 13:7–8.

For you are bought with a price; therefore glorify God in your body, and in your spirit, which are God's.

1 CORINTHIANS 6:20.

For every man shall bear his own burden.

GALATIANS 6:5.

Be not deceived; God is not mocked; for whatever a man sows, that shall he also reap.

GALATIANS 6:7.

Neither did we eat any man's bread for nothing; but wrought with labor and travail night and day, that we might not be chargeable to any of you.

2 THESSALONIANS 3:8.

For even when we were with you, this we commanded you, that if any would not work, neither should he eat.

2 THESSALONIANS 3:10.

TRADE

Solomon sent to Huram the king of Tyre, saying, As you did deal with David my father, and did send him cedars to build him a house to dwell in, even so deal with me.

2 CHRONICLES 2:3.

(*See:* Barter, Exchange, International Trade)

TRANSFER PAYMENTS

Owe no man anything, but to love one another, for he who loves another has fulfilled the law.

ROMANS 13:8.

(*See:* Social Security, Subsidies, Welfarism)

TRUTH

There has been frequent mention in this book of a free market. Is it possible to have a totally free market of ideas, which are put into practice? In other words, can we have a free market of truths? This implies absence of an absolute truth. To buyers of ideas, any truth is plausible; and another set of truths is also correct to those who believe in them. Let's examine this idea briefly on two levels.

First, if you report something accurately, you perceive a truth, which may vary with someone else's version. For instance, in a crowded room, you step on someone's foot. Your version, your truth: It was an accident, a miscalculated step. The other person may perceive your foot-stepping act as deliberate with intent to inflict pain. Wherein lies the truth? At the human level, many truths may prevail. Hence, a humanistic government can claim relativistic morals, arguing that no one has a monopoly on truth.

Second, away from the human realm, we accept God's truth as absolute, even though we may not always understand it. Even agnostics must agree that God's principles of law and governance are unequalled by our cleverest philosophers. God's laws can function perfectly in any part of the world, under any human government. No other system can ever promise greater freedom or abundance. *One God, one law, one truth!* Should we lie about it?

(*See Also:* Foundation, Freedom, Honesty, Justice, Law, Moral Principles, Remnant, Source)

You shall not steal, neither deal falsely, neither lie to one another.
                                                                        LEVITICUS 19:11.

Just balances, just weights…shall you have….
                                                                        LEVITICUS 19:36.

You shall know the truth, and the truth shall make you free.
                                                                        JOHN 8:32.

You are of your father the devil, and the desires of your father you want to do. He was a murderer from the beginning, and does not stand in the truth, because there is no truth in him. When he speaks a lie, he speaks from his own resources; for he is a liar and the father of it. But because I tell the truth, you do not believe me.
                                                                        JOHN 8:44–45.

…You say rightly that I am a king. For this cause was I born, and for this cause I have come into the world, that I should bear witness to the truth. Everyone who is of the truth hears my voice.
                                                                        JOHN 18:37.

Therefore God also gave them up to uncleanness, in the lusts of their hearts, to dishonor their bodies among themselves, who exchanged the truth of God for a lie, and worshipped and served the creature rather than the Creator….
                                                                        ROMANS 1:24–25.

For though I might desire to boast, I will not be a fool, for I will speak the truth….
                                                                        2 CORINTHIANS 12:6.

Am I therefore your enemy because I tell you the truth?
                                                                        GALATIANS 4:16.

UNDEVELOPED COUNTRIES

(*See:* Economic Growth, Poor Nations, United Nations)

UNIONISM

(*See:* Labor Market, Wages, Work)

UNISEX

The woman shall not wear that which pertains to a man, neither shall a man put on a woman's garment: for all who do so are an abomination to the Lord your God.

DEUTERONOMY 22:5.

(*See:* Feminism, Homosexuality, Youth Cultism)

UNITED NATIONS

In his book, entitled *A Dangerous Place*, Daniel Patrick Moynihan traces the growth of communist influence in the United Nations.[1] He shows how propaganda excited Third World nations to employ language of freedom in the interest of its suppression. Of course, the United Nations, as any atheistic institution, has always been a dangerous place for freedom-loving believers. Rus Walton calls the United Nations a captive of the Communist-bloc nations, "the fox in the hen house."[2] About the United Nations, William F. Buckley wrote, "The United Nations is the most concentrated assault on moral reality in the history of free institutions, and it does not do to ignore that fact or, worse, to get used to it."[3]

Of course, we know that Alger Hiss, convicted communist, represented the United States during writing the U.N. charter. The Soviet Union is the only member country with *three* votes, not one. Tax-free salaries are extremely high, and much of this financial burden is carried by the American taxpayer. Since its inception, the military affairs of the United Nations have always been in communist hands. The post of Undersecretary-General of Political and Security Council Affairs has been held by Russian Soviets, with the exception of a communist Yugoslav. The Undersecretary controls all military and police functions of the United Nations, supervises all disarmament programs, and monitors all atomic energy placed under U.N. care.

Many U.N. member nations deny God. They spurn religious freedom in their countries. They sponsor murder and terrorism, engage in policies to reduce the entire world to slavery while speaking of peace, and are determined to destroy the American way of life. Why should any believer support it?

(*See Also:* Communism, Demagoguery, Double Standard, Nonalignment, One Worldism, Statism, Terrorism, World Government)

> *For the congregation of hypocrites shall be desolate, and fire shall consume the tabernacles of bribery. They conceive mischief, and bring forth vanity, and their belly prepares deceit.*
>
> Job 15:34–35.

> *The nations shall rush like the rushing of many waters; but God shall rebuke them, and they shall flee far off, and shall be chased as the chaff*

[1]Daniel Patrick Moynihan. *A Dangerous Place,* (Boston: Little, Brown, 1978)

[2]Rus Walton, *Fundamentals for American Christians* (Marlborough, N.H.: Plymouth Rock Foundation, 1979).

[3]William F. Buckley, *United Nations Journal: A Delegate's Odyssey* (New York: Putnam, 1974).

of the mountains before the wind, and like a rolling thing before the whirlwind.

ISAIAH 17:13.

The way of peace they know not; and there is no judgment in their goings....

ISAIAH 59:8.

I sat not in the assembly of the mockers....

JEREMIAH 15:17.

After this...I beheld a fourth beast, dreadful and terrible, exceedingly strong. It had huge iron teeth; it was devouring, breaking in pieces, and trampling the residue with its feet. It was different from all the beasts that were before it, and it had ten horns.

DANIEL 7:7.

Thus shall he do in the most strongholds with a strange god, whom he shall acknowledge and increase with glory; and he shall cause them to rule over many, and shall divide the land for gain.

DANIEL 11:39.

The horsemen lift up both the bright sword and the glittering spear; and there is a multitude of slain, and a great number of carcases; and there is no end of their corpses; they stumble upon their corpses: because of the multitude of the whoredoms of the well-favored harlot, the mistress of witchcrafts, that sells nations through her whoredoms, and families through her witchcrafts. Behold, I am against you, says the Lord of hosts....

NAHUM 3:3–4.

I stood upon the sand of the sea, and saw a beast rise up out of the sea, having seven heads and ten horns, and upon his horns ten crowns, and upon his heads the name of blasphemy. And the beast which I saw was like a leopard, and his feet were as the feet of a bear, and his mouth as the mouth of a lion; and the dragon gave him his power, and his seat, and great authority. I saw one of his heads as it were wounded to death; and his deadly wound was healed; and all the world wondered after the beast. They worshipped the dragon which gave power to the beast; and they worshipped the beast, saying, Who is like the beast? Who is able to make war with him? And there was given to him a mouth speaking great things and blasphemies; and power was given to him to continue forty and two months. He opened his mouth in blasphemy against God, to blaspheme His name, and His tabernacle, and those who dwell in heaven. It was given to him to make war with the saints, and to overcome them; and the power was given him over all kindreds, and tongues, and nations.

REVELATION 13:1–7.

The ten horns which you saw are ten kings, which have received no kingdoms as yet, but receive power as kings one hour with the beast. These have one mind, and shall give their power and strength to the beast. These shall make war with the Lamb, and the Lamb shall overcome them, for He is Lord of lords, and King of kings; and they who are with Him are called, the chosen, and faithful.

REVELATION 17:12–14.

U.S.A.

Contrary to unbelievers' efforts to change history and deny our Christian roots, the founders of the United States of America were men of extraordinary vision who created a form of civil government whereby those they ruled could legally and peacefully remove rulers from power. Our noble heritage, firmly planted in Christian principles, should be remembered.

First Charter of Virginia: 1606. Specified that the Virginia colony should bring glory to Almighty God and advance the Christian faith.

Mayflower Compact: 1620. Forty-one pilgrims prepared the first written constitution. It began: "In the name of God, Amen, Having undertaken for the Glory of God and advancement of the Christian faith...."

New England Charter: 1620. "...to advance the enlargement of Christian religion, to the glory of God Almighty."

The Carolinas' Charter: 1622. Settled for "the propagation of the Christian faith."

Fundamental Orders of Connecticut: 1643. "...confederation together to maintain and preserve the liberty and purity of the gospel of our Lord Jesus which we now profess."

Constitution of the New England Confederation: 1643. "Whereas we all came into these parts of America with one and the same end and aim, namely to advance the kingdom of our Lord Jesus Christ and to enjoy the Liberties of the Gospel in purity with peace."

The Continental Congress: 1775. This body officially called all citizens to fast and pray and confess their sin that God might bless them.

Declaration of Independence: 1776. Four specific references to dependence of nation on God.

Chaplains in the Armed Forces: 1776. General George Washington issued an order placing a chaplain in each regiment.

Thanksgiving Day Proclamation: 1789. "Whereas it is the duty of all nations to acknowledge the providence of Almighty God, to obey His will, to be grateful for His benefits, and humbly to implore His protection, aid and favors...."

Inaugural Address: 1789. Every president since Washington has included in his inaugural address references to his and the nation's dependence upon God.

Daniel Webster: 1820. "...more than all, a government and a country were to commence, with the very first foundations laid under the divine light of the Christian religion.... Who would wish that his country's existence had otherwise begun? ... Let us not forget the religious character of our origin."

Motto on coins: 1863. Secretary of the Treasury, Salmon P. Chase, instructed the U.S. mint to begin inscribing "In God We Trust" on all coins.

Gettysburg Address: 1863. "...that this nation, under God, shall have a new birth of freedom and that government of the people, by the people and for the people, shall not perish from the earth."

U.S. Supreme Court: 1892. Justice Brewer, delivering the court's opinion (143 U.S. 457), stated: "These, and many other matters which might be noticed, add a volume of unofficial declarations to the mass of organic utterances that this is a Christian nation."

Pledge of Allegiance: 1954. The words "under God" were adopted by Congress on June 14.

National Motto: 1956. A joint resolution was adopted by Congress on July 20, establishing "In God We Trust" as the national motto of the United States.

Proclamation: 1983. Under President Ronald Reagan, 1983 was declared Year of the Bible.

Newsweek (December 27, 1983) said, "Perhaps even more than the Constitution, the Bible ... is our founding document: the source of the powerful myth of the United States as a special, sacred nation, a people called by God to establish a model society, a beacon to the world.... Bible study was the core of public education and nearly every literate family not only owned a Bible but *read it regularly* and reverently."[1] *Newsweek* then said that the Bible "has virtually disappeared from American education. It is rarely studied, even as literature, in public classrooms...."[2] President Reagan in 1983 said, "Can we resolve to read, learn and try to heed the greatest message ever written—God's Word in the Holy Bible?" He added, "Has anyone stopped to consider that we might come closer to balancing the budget if all of us simply tried to live up to the Ten Commandments and the golden rule?"

Finally, we should heed the warning inscribed on the Thomas Jefferson memorial: "God who gave us life gave us liberty. Can the liberties of a nation be secure when we have removed a conviction that these liberties are the gift of God?"

(*See Also:* Creation, Discipline, Family, Freedom, Government, Individualism, Justice, Rule of Law)

[1] Kenneth L. Woodward, "How the Bible Made America," *Newsweek*, December 27, 1983, 44–51.
[2] Ibid.

Yet they would not hearken to their judges, but they went a whoring after other gods, and bowed themselves to them: they turned quickly out of the way in which their fathers walked, obeying the commandments of the Lord; but they did not so.

JUDGES 2:17.

For the kingdom is the Lord's, and He rules over the nations.

PSALM 22:28.

Blessed is the nation whose God is the Lord, and the people whom He has chosen for His own inheritance.

PSALM 33:12.

I will say of the Lord, He is my refuge and my fortress; my God, in Him will I trust.

PSALM 91:2.

Behold, how good and pleasant it is for brethren to dwell together in unity!

PSALM 133:1.

Four great beasts came up from the sea, each different from the other. The first was like a lion, and had eagle's wings. I watched till its wings were plucked off....

DANIEL 7:3–4.

Therefore I say to you, The kingdom of God shall be taken from you, and given to a nation bringing forth the fruits thereof.

MATTHEW 21:43.

But he who looks into the perfect law of liberty and continues in it, and is not a forgetful hearer but a doer of the work, this one will be blessed in what he does.

JAMES 1:25.

UTILITY

He said to them, Is a candle brought to be put under a bushel, or under a bed? And not to be set on a candlestick?

MARK 4:21.

(*See:* Exchange, Investment, Law of Increase)

VALUE

What is an ounce of lead worth to you? In its natural state, probably nothing. Refined and molded into a bullet, possibly less than fifty cents. In your own body, less than nothing: You'd be glad to pay a handsome sum to have it removed, making it worth a few thousand dollars to the operating surgeon. Its form, place, and use will change its value. Lead is a cheap element. Can an ounce of it ever be worth several million dollars? Yes, in the right place at the right time. For example, the assassin's bullet in the skull of a world leader at a critical time can be worth not only a substantial sum to the killer but even more to the conspirators. Therefore, time, too, figures in value. In other words, value arises by having useful products in the right place, at the right time. Does this really *determine* value?

Orthodox Marxist economics states that value derives from the amount of labor contained in the item. Hence, an item that requires many hours of handcrafting would be worth many times an item fabricated with a few hours labor. Obviously, such theoretical nonsense encourages inefficiency and labor-intensive techniques of production. Some years ago in Mexico, an acquaintance of mine was preparing an art exhibition of his watercolor paintings. He had acquired some friends who delighted in Marxist philosophy. Noting that some of his higher-priced ones, of $400 or more, actually required less than an hour of labor, I asked him, "Aren't you ashamed charging high prices for artwork you completed in twenty minutes?" He gave me the best five-minute lecture on free market economics and subjective value that I have heard, although he had never studied economics. For *his* products, he knew what determined value. But he could not enlarge that concept to an entire society.

Value is in the mind of the beholder. If you like the painting—either for beauty or investment—an exchange becomes possible. When new fashions hit the market, they are priced very high at first. The innovators and impatient willingly pay that high price in order to be among the first to exhibit new and stylish clothes. As imitators manufacture and widely market new styles, price drops. Consumers who are slow to catch onto new trends or who are more patient or who have less money enter this second-level market. Finally, the same clothes hang in bargain basements and discount stores when, an old style, it passes and another one renews the cycle. In other words, identical clothing carries different values in different places to different people at different times. To each party in a transaction, the value of the thing acquired must exceed the value of the thing given before an exchange occurs. In a free society, everyone gains.

(*See Also:* Exchange, Inequality, Market Economy, Price Mechanism, Wages)

For as much money as it is worth he shall give it to me for a possession of a burying place among you.

GENESIS 23:9.

...The land is worth four hundred shekels of silver....

GENESIS 23:15.

You are the salt of the earth; but if the salt has lost its flavor, wherewith shall it be salted? It is therefore good for nothing, but to be cast out, and to be trodden under foot of men.

MATTHEW 5:13.

Are not two sparrows sold for a farthing, and one of them shall not fall to the ground apart from your Father's will? ...Fear not therefore, you are of more value than many sparrows.

MATTHEW 10:29, 31.

The kingdom of heaven is like a merchant, seeking goodly pearls, who, when he had found one pearl of great price, went and sold all that he had, and bought it.

MATTHEW 13:45–46.

Many of them also who used curious arts brought their books together, and burned them before all men; and they counted the price of them, and found it fifty thousand pieces of silver.

ACTS 19:19.

VETERANS' BONUS

Take the sum of the prey that was taken, both of man and beast,...and divide the prey into two parts: between them who took the war upon them, who went out to battle, and between all of the congregation.
NUMBERS 31:26–27.

(*See:* Draft, Military, War)

VOCATION

(*See:* Labor Market, Specialization, Work)

VOLUNTARISM

A society organized entirely on the basis of voluntary relationships has considerable superficial appeal. Those relationships may turn out quite dangerous. Many *voluntarily* joined Germany's National Socialist movement; they believed that a 1,000-year Reich was manifest destiny. Can Christianity function within *any* civil government structure? The Bible requires a restructuring of society. A statist government operates contrary to a society organized and functioning under biblical laws. These disparate societies cannot coexist. The humanistic state, from its perspective, struggles for survival against Christianity. A Christian society, in an elusive quest for a so-called peaceful coexistence, that compromises one of God's laws transgresses the whole law. (See James 2:8–12.)

Although founded on Christian principles, which it more or less adhered to for nearly 150 years, the United States, now having adopted a humanistic government, is gradually outlawing Christianity. The main thrust is evident in the state school system. Too, humanistic laws in the courts and humanistic regulations in the bureaucracies have largely replaced Christian law. We have seen stepped-up harassment and persecution of pastors and church congregations. The next step will be persecution of Christians whose divisive and minoritarian beliefs are destructive to the state. If Christians allow this trend to continue, Christianity will become prohibited due to its incompatibility with the religion of statism. Voluntarism, therefore, is viable only within the framework and discipline of God's order, wherein each individual responds for his actions in an ethical system.

(*See Also:* Cooperation, Individualism, Law and Order, Liberty, Market Economy, Remnant, Source)

> *If his offering be a burnt sacrifice of the herd, let him offer a male without blemish; he shall offer it of his own voluntary will at the door of the tabernacle of the congregation before the Lord.*
>
> LEVITICUS 1:3.

> *Then the people rejoiced, for that they offered willingly, because with perfect heart they offered willingly to the Lord....*
>
> 1 CHRONICLES 29:9.

> *Neither was there any among them who lacked, for as many as were possessors of lands or houses sold them, and brought the price of the things that were sold, and laid them down at the apostles' feet; distribution was made to every man according as he had need.*
>
> ACTS 4:34–35.

WAGES

Who determines wages? This is a tricky question. If you are self-employed, you know. If you work for any state agency, the answer below does not apply. Who pays your salary? Suppose you sell paint. The paint manufacturer does not pay your salary, neither does the distributor or store owner. Your customers do! If customers like your product and service, they buy; they put money in the cash drawer, from which your wages are paid. If your product and service are lousy, customers go elsewhere. Without sales you cannot earn wages and eventually will lose employment. High wages, on the other hand, attract employees. When engineers earn high salaries, a rush of students to learn engineering soon produces an abundance of them. Wages stop climbing, demand for engineering services diminishes, engineers are laid off, and the cycle repeats.

When the Ford Motor Company began its phenomenal wage of $5.00 a day, before long other automobile manufacturers initiated efficient manufacturing techniques. Otherwise, they could not have remained price competitive and would have found it increasingly difficult to retain trained labor at $3.75 a day. By controlling costs, Ford offered a low-priced vehicle, thereby expanding its market, which secured jobs and raised wages.

Another means for increasing your wages is to make yourself sufficiently unique and desirable. A few professional managers demand and receive high salaries as chief executives. A few lawyers, by specializing, have even achieved national fame, becoming wealthy in the process. A television program on wealthy persons interviewed Kenny Rogers, Liberace, Loretta Lynn, *inter alios*. At that time, Rogers had for sale his three California houses for $32 million. All three had come from poor backgrounds. Especially the latter two grew up with poverty. They became rich because of their market appeal. Customers paid their wages. Liberace alone has played directly for more than 25 million persons. These individuals can demand high prices for their services because people willingly pay for them. Consumers demand, entertainers supply. But let a pastor become popular, ministering to millions of people and generating millions of dollars, and the press and humanists will viciously attack. But let taxes be raised to increase the benefits, wages, and retirement pensions of bureaucrats; scarcely a murmur arises.

(*See Also:* Contract, Employee, Free Market, Labor Market, Management, Organization, Productivity, Profit)

Laban said to Jacob, Because you are my brother, should you therefore serve me for nothing? Tell me, what shall your wages be?
GENESIS 29:15.

Your father has deceived me and changed my wages ten times....
GENESIS 31:7.

Pharaoh's daughter said to her, Take this child away and nurse it for me, and I will give you your wages....
EXODUS 2:9.

...You shall give to every man according to his service....
NUMBERS 7:5.

Micah said to him, Dwell with me, and be to me a father and a priest, and I will give you ten shekels of silver by the year, and a suit of apparel, and your food....
JUDGES 17:10.

As a servant earnestly desires the shade, and as an employee looks for the reward of his work.
JOB 7:2.

Woe to him who builds his house by unrighteousness, and his chambers by wrong, who uses his neighbor's service without wages, and gives him not for his work.
JEREMIAH 22:13.

The soldiers likewise demanded of him, saying, What shall we do? He said to them, Do violence to no man, neither accuse any falsely, and be content with your wages.
LUKE 3:14.

...The laborer is worthy of his hire....
LUKE 10:7.

He who reaps receives wages, and gathers fruit to life eternal: that both he who sows and he who reaps may rejoice together.

JOHN 4:36.

...Every man shall receive his own reward according to his own labor.

1 CORINTHIANS 3:8.

The husbandman who labors must be first partaker of the fruits.

2 TIMOTHY 2:6.

WAR

The President said, "I hate war. Eleanor hates war." Before long he had launched us on an irreversible course toward World War II. LBJ's campaign promise not to involve "American boys" in war in Vietnam won him a landslide election. Soon troops followed advisors. These presidents appealed to what we prefer: man's desire for peace.

From a biblical standpoint, wars (disciplining actions) reflect the judgment of God. When people obeyed God, they were rewarded with peace. Where war was necessary against corrupt states, God's people suffered few losses; and where outnumbered, a few could rout many.

How does this square with the sixth commandment: "Thou shalt not kill"? Calvin points out that we should not unjustly do violence to others. Hence, the hundreds of political and economic wars and badly labeled revolutions of this century represent unjust violence—terrorism under the guise of liberation.

On the other hand, is it ever right to kill? Capital punishment and defensive war are legitimate because they react to terrorism of criminals, whether that terrorism is conducted against individuals or a nation. Too, we have a legitimate obligation to prevent violence. Those who themselves would not harm a fly and stand aside watching their neighbor being savagely beaten by criminals would not have obeyed this commandment. Peace, yes! But not at *any* price!

(*See Also:* Capital Punishment, Draft, Golden Rule, Law and Order, Military Defense, United Nations)

When you go out to battle against your enemies, and see horses, and chariots, and a people more than you, be not afraid of them, for the Lord your God is with you, who brought you up out of the land of Egypt. It shall be, when you come near to battle, that the priest shall approach and speak to the people, and shall say to them, Hear, O

Israel, you approach this day in battle against your enemies. Let not your hearts faint, fear not, and do not tremble, neither be terrified because of them, for the Lord your God is He who goes with you, to fight for you against your enemies, to save you.

DEUTERONOMY 20:1–4.

Rebuke the company of spearmen.... Scatter the people who delight in war.

PSALM 68:30.

For by wise counsel you shall make war....

PROVERBS 24:6.

Why do we sit still? Assemble yourselves, and let us enter into the defensed cities, and let us be silent there, for the Lord our God has put us to silence, and given us water of gall to drink, because we have sinned against the Lord. We looked for peace, but no good came; and for a time of health, and behold trouble!

JEREMIAH 8:14–15.

I say to you my friends, Be not afraid of them who kill the body, and after that have no more that they can do. But I will forewarn you whom you shall fear: Fear him, which after he has killed has power to cast into hell.

LUKE 12:4–5.

Then he said to them, Nation shall rise against nation, and kingdom against kingdom.

LUKE 21:10.

WEALTH

Measured wealth is largely a state of mind. Suppose you own a luxury home in some country valued in the millions. Why is it worth so much? Its value depends upon if others desire the property and are willing to pay its high price. Now presume that tourists discover a new foreign spa and no longer visit the island country where your property is located. Your wealth has diminished. Why? Nothing about the property has changed; but there are no buyers.

Or, presume that your net worth is half a million. In the absence of other information, you count yourself as at least comfortable although not wealthy. Then one day you learn that the median measured wealth is 1 million. Suddenly you find yourself among the lower, or poorest, one-half of the country. You believe you are far less rich than before. Again nothing has changed except your state of mind. If your uncontrollable desires far outreach your present circumstances, you are poor. On the other hand, this kind of wealth can be sharply increased instantly by desiring much less than you now own.

Produced wealth—machinery, equipment, building, and so forth—result from our system of free markets in labor, capital, and property. Under the rule of God we save, invent, build, and work for both a better present and for a bigger inheritance than we received. Multiplication of our energies under freedom produces a wealth of factories, livestock, technology, and the intellectual and physical liberty to use them to our greater capacity. However, none of these are permanent wealth, like "permanent" life insurance. Our permanent treasuries are those laid up in heaven.

(*See Also:* Abundance, Capital Formation, Investment, Law of Increase, Prosperity, Savings)

Abram was very rich in cattle, in silver, and in gold.

GENESIS 13:2.

The Lord has blessed my master greatly; and he is become great; and he has given him flocks, and herds, and silver, and gold, and menservants, and maidservants, and camels, and asses.

GENESIS 24:35.

You think in your own mind, My power and the might of my hand has gotten me this wealth. But you shall remember the Lord your God, for it is He who gives the power to get wealth that He may establish His covenant, which He swore unto your fathers, as it is this day. It shall be, if you do at all forget the Lord your God, and walk after other gods, and serve them, and worship them, you shall surely perish.

DEUTERONOMY 8:17–19.

You shall return and obey the voice of the Lord, and do all His commandments. The Lord your God will make you plenteous in every work of your hand, in the fruit of your body, and in the fruit of your cattle, and in the fruit of your land, for good....

DEUTERONOMY 30:8–9.

The Lord makes poor and makes rich; He brings low and lifts up. He raises up the poor out of the dust, and lifts the beggar from the dunghill, to set them among princes, and to make them inherit the throne of glory....

1 SAMUEL 2:7–8.

A little that a righteous man has is better than riches of many wicked. For the arms of the wicked shall be broken; but the Lord upholds the righteous. The Lord knows the days of the upright; and their inheritance shall be for ever.

PSALM 37:16–18.

Be not afraid when one is made rich, when the glory of his house is increased, for when he dies he shall carry nothing away; his glory shall not descend after him.

PSALM 49:16–17.

Blessed be the Lord, who daily loads us with benefits, even the God of our salvation.

PSALM 68:19.

Praise the Lord, Blessed is the man who fears the Lord, who delights in His commandments. His seed shall be mighty upon the earth; the generation of the upright shall be blessed. Wealth and riches shall be in his house; and his righteousness endures forever.

PSALM 112:1–3.

There is he who makes himself rich, yet has nothing; there is he who makes himself poor, yet has great riches.

PROVERBS 13:7.

Better is a little with the fear of the Lord than great treasure and trouble therewith.

PROVERBS 15:16.

The rich man's wealth is his strong city, and as a high wall in his own conceit.

PROVERBS 18:11.

Wealth makes many friends; but the poor is separated from his neighbor.

PROVERBS 19:4.

A good name is rather to be chosen than great riches, and loving favor rather than silver and gold. The rich and poor meet together; the Lord is the maker of them all.... By humility and the fear of the Lord are riches, honor, and life.... The rich rules over the poor, and the borrower is servant to the lender.... He who oppresses the poor to increase his riches, and he who gives to the rich, shall surely come to want.

PROVERBS 22:1–2, 4, 7, 16.

Lay not up for yourselves treasures upon earth, where moth and rust corrupt, and where thieves break through and steal; but lay up for yourselves treasures in heaven, where neither moth nor rust corrupt, and where thieves do not break through to steal: for where your treasure is, there will your heart be also.

MATTHEW 6:19–21.

For whoever has, to him shall be given, and he shall have more abundance; but whoever has not, from him shall be taken away even what he has.

MATTHEW 13:12.

Which of you with taking thought can add to his stature one cubit? If you then be not able to do that thing which is least, why take thought for the rest? Consider the lilies how they grow. They toil not, they spin not; and yet I say to you, that Solomon in all his glory was not arrayed like one of these. If then God so clothes the grass, which is today in the field, and tomorrow is cast into the oven, how much more will He clothe you, O you of little faith?

LUKE 12:25–28.

For where your treasure is, there will your heart be also.

LUKE 12:34.

…For to whom much is given, of him shall be much required; and to whom men have committed much, of him shall they ask the more.

LUKE 12:48.

…A man can receive nothing, except it be given him from heaven.

JOHN 3:27.

WELFARISM

Dr. Walter E. Williams of Temple University said that if we were to give the more than one-quarter trillion of federal dollars now spent on welfare directly to the poor, each family of four would receive about $40,000 a year. But they don't see the money. Who does? Is it any wonder that the two counties in Maryland and Virginia, serving as bedroom communities for Washington, D.C., bureaucrats, politicians, and governmental consultants, boast the highest per capita incomes in the United States? "It's like feeding the sparrows through the horses."

You may mistakenly believe that welfarism, another in the long list of isms, means charity. *Charity* means sowing love and demonstrating it by providing for your own family, and then voluntarily helping, according to your means, widows, orphans, and the poor. *Welfarism,* on the other hand, is socialism, where a hungry bureaucracy redistributes wealth and income to itself, firstly and mostly, and then to others. One of the more insidious forms of statism, it cloaks its grab for power under the guise of doing good. It undermines the very foundation of a free society. The following story well illustrates its destructive nature.

A Modern Fable

Once upon a time there was a Little Red Hen who scratched about and uncovered some grains of wheat. She called her barnyard neighbors and said, "If we work together and plant this wheat, we will have some fine bread to eat. Who will help me plant the wheat?"

"Not I," said the Cow. "Not I," said the Duck. "Not I," said the Goose.

"Then I will," said the Little Red Hen, and she did. After the wheat started growing, the ground turned dry, and there was no rain in sight. "Who will help me water the wheat?" said the Little Red Hen.

"Not I," said the Cow. "Not I," said the Duck. "If there were a God, like you say, He'd make it rain," said the Pig. "Equal rights," said the Goose.

The wheat grew tall and ripened into golden grain. "Who will help me reap the wheat?" asked the Little Red Hen.

"Not I," said the Cow. "I belong to the union," said the Duck. "Out of my classification," said the Pig. "I'd lose my state ADC and federal support money," said the Goose.

"Then I will," said the Little Red Hen, and she did.

When it came time to grind the flour, "Not I," said the Cow. "I'd lose my unemployment compensation," said the Duck.

When it came time to bake the bread, "That's overtime for me," said the Cow. "I'm a dropout and never learned how," said the Duck. "I'd lose my welfare benefits," said the Pig. "If I'm the only one helping, that's discrimination," said the Goose.

"Then I will," said the Little Red Hen. She baked five loaves of fine bread and held them up for her neighbors to see.

"I want some," said the Cow. "It's not fair if you don't give me some," said the Duck. "Communal property," said the Pig. "You are violating my Civil Rights if you don't give me my share," said the Goose. "No," said the Little Red Hen. "I can rest for awhile and eat the five loaves myself."

"Excess profits," cried the Cow. "Capitalist leech!" screeched the Duck. "You robbed The People," grunted the Pig. "Equal rights!" screamed the Goose. And they hurriedly painted picket signs and marched around the Little Red Hen, singing, "We Shall Overcome." And they did.

For when the Farmer came to investigate the commotion, he said, "You must not be greedy, Little Red Hen. Look at the oppressed Cow. Look at the disadvantaged Duck. Look at the underprivileged Pig. Look at the less fortunate Goose. You are guilty of making second-class citizens of them."

"But—but—but I earned the bread," said the Little Red Hen. "I worked for it. No one helped me."

"Exactly," the wise Farmer said. "That's the great free enterprise system; anybody can earn as much as she, he, or it wants. You should be happy to have this much freedom. In other barnyards, you have to give all five loaves to the Farmer. Here, in our system, you give four loaves to your suffering neighbors."

And they lived happily (more or less) ever after, including the Little Red Hen, who smiled and smiled, and clucked, "I am privileged to live in this great barnyard. I am grateful to be free."

But her neighbors often wondered why she never baked any more bread.[1]

Doesn't this story really highlight the messages below of JOB 31, PROVERBS 19, 21, 24, 26, and 28? Read God's curse in GENESIS 3:14–19 and the fourth commandment, especially EXODUS 20:9. We must work for our bread and live by the sweat of our brow. Notice, too, how the statist (the farmer) distorted truth, the real meaning of free enterprise, and substituted welfarism—the system imposed on Little Red Hen. Loving our neighbor does not mean putting ourselves on all fours to support the indolent. Neither does it mean putting our neighbor on all fours to support our demands. No practicing Christian will, either!

(*See Also:* Cradle-to-Grave, Directed Economy, Equality, Humanism, Poverty, Redistribution of Income/Wealth)

His sons are far from safety, they are crushed at the gate, and there is no deliverer. Because the hungry eat up his harvest, taking it even from the thorns, and the robber swallows up their substance.

JOB 5:4–5.

If I have eaten the fruits thereof without money, or have caused the owners thereof to lose their life; let thistles grow instead of wheat, and cockle instead of barley....

JOB 31:39–40.

Look at the ant, you sluggard; consider her ways and be wise: which, having no guide, overseer, or ruler, provides her supplies in the summer, and gathers her food in the harvest. How long will you sleep, O sluggard? When will you arise out of your sleep?

PROVERBS 6:6–9.

He who gathers in summer is a wise son; but he who sleeps in harvest is a son who causes shame.

PROVERBS 10:5.

---

[1] Taken from "A Modern Fable," *Coeval Economics,* ed. Robert P. Vichas (Berkeley, Calif.: McCutchan Publishing Co., 1970), pp. 35–36.

Many entreat the favor of the prince; and every man is a friend of him who gives gifts. All the brethren of the poor do hate him; how much more do his friends go far from him? He pursues them with words, yet they abandon him.

PROVERBS 19:6–7.

A slothful man hides his hand in his bosom, and will not so much as bring it to his mouth again.

PROVERBS 19:24.

The desire of the slothful kills him, for his hands refuse to work. He covets greedily all the day long, but the righteous gives and spares not.

PROVERBS 21:25–26.

I went by the field of the slothful, and by the vineyard of the man void of understanding; and, lo, it was all grown over with thorns, and nettles had covered the face thereof, and the stone wall thereof was broken down.

PROVERBS 24:30–31.

As the door turns on its hinges, so does the slothful turn upon his bed. The slothful hides his hand in his bosom; it grieves him to bring it again to his mouth. The sluggard is wiser in his own conceit than seven men who can render a reason.

PROVERBS 26:14–16.

To have respect of persons is not good, because that man will transgress for a piece of bread.

PROVERBS 28:21.

By much slothfulness, the building decays; and through the idleness of the hands, the house drops through.

ECCLESIASTES 10:18.

They hatch vipers' eggs, and weave the spider's webs. He who eats of their eggs dies, and from that which is crushed a viper breaks out. Their webs shall not become garments, neither shall they cover themselves with their works. Their works are works of iniquity, and the act of violence is in their hands.

ISAIAH 59:5–6.

They shall not build and another inhabit; they shall not plant, and another eat....

ISAIAH 65:22.

Will you profane Me among my people for handfuls of barley and for pieces of bread, to slay the souls that should not die, and to save the souls alive that should not live, by your lying to my people who hear your lies?...

Because with lies you have made the heart of the righteous sad, whom I have not made sad, and strengthened the hands of the wicked, that he should not return from his wicked way, by promising him life. Therefore you shall see no more vanity, nor divine divinations, for I will deliver my people out of your hand, and you shall know that I am the Lord.

Ezekiel 13:19, 22–23.

He said to them, The kings of the Gentiles exercise lordship over them; and they who exercise authority over them are called benefactors. But you shall not be so; but he who is greatest among you, let him be as the younger; and he who is chief, as he who serves. For who is greater, he who sits to eat, or he who serves? Is it not he who sits to eat? But I am among you as he who serves.

Luke 22:25–27.

Jesus answered them saying, Verily, verily, I say to you, You seek me, not because you saw the miracles, but because you did eat of the loaves, and were filled. Labor not for the meat that perishes, but for that meat which endures unto everlasting life, which the Son of man shall give to you: for him has God the Father sealed.

John 6:26–27.

Then says one of his disciples, Judas Iscariot, Simon's son, who would betray Him, Why was not this ointment sold for three hundred pence, and given to the poor? This he said, not that he cared for the poor, but because he was a thief, and had the bag, and he used to take what was put into it. Then Jesus said, Let her alone. Against the day of My burying has she kept this. For the poor you always have with you; but Me you have not always.

John 12:4–8.

For I mean not that other men be eased, and you burdened.

2 Corinthians 8:13.

Nevertheless, what says the Scripture? Cast out the bondwoman and her son, for the son of the bondwoman shall not be heir with the son of the freewoman. So then, brothers, we are not children of the bondwoman, but of the free.

Galatians 4:30–31.

For even when we were with you, this we commanded you, that if any would not work, neither should he eat. For we hear that there are some who walk among you disorderly, working not at all, but are busybodies. Now them who are such we command and exhort by our Lord Jesus Christ, that with quietness they work, and eat their own bread.

2 Thessalonians 3:10–12.

But if any provide not for his own, and specially for those of his own house, he has denied the faith, and is worse than an infidel.

1 Timothy 5:8.

WELFARIST

A welfarist seeks to turn God's order on end and to supplant God with his own heaven-on-earth welfare state. His parlance is a study of contradictions. The welfarist claims that by denying the first commandment of God, the government will supply the needs of its subjects. God promises to fulfill our needs and He does. The welfarist promises to fulfill our needs, but he can't. The welfarist, seeking temporal power and its perquisites, knows well that grandiose language must substitute for unfulfillable promises. Because a government is incapable of producing anything of material consequence, it must rely on the real producers of society. Hence, order is reversed: Producers are turned into captives; the welfarist and his constituency become the masters. The following condensed essay illustrates a vital point.

I Like Butter

The whole thing started because I like butter. I developed a taste for butter in my youth, only to find it beyond my means in these more prosperous middle years.

The whole truth is we could afford to splurge and buy a pound of real butter on special occasions (like Thanksgiving and Christmas if they didn't come so close together), but the genuine article, at 150 percent above the price of a substitute spread is definitely not a good buy. After all, we have to live within a budget, since we have no authority to levy taxes.

To say that I have learned to like the substitute spread would be rank hypocrisy. Through the years I have learned to accept the fact that it is more in line with our after-taxes income. That is, I learned to accept this fact with reasonably good grace until the "down-and-outers" moved in across the street.

A few days after these people moved in I opened the refrigerator one evening and received a severe shock. Most of one shelf was filled with butter—one pound sticks, stacked like cordwood. After a brief period of confusion, which any family man can visualize better than I can tell, the wife made me understand that the butter was "surplus commodity" and belonged to the people across the street. It seems they received more butter than they could store, so the lady of the house made a deal with my wife for storage space. In return we could use all the butter we needed, since the supply was more than ample and sure to be replenished regularly.

Actually the "down-and-outers" are no more than contributing factors, vessels as it were, who have become willing wards of the state. In many ways this particular family appeared to be as nice as one could hope to meet. The wife and five children are sociable and intelligent. The man doesn't beat his wife, gamble away his welfare checks, or drink excessively. He takes the family to church, plays with the kids, likes all sports, is always present when surplus commodities are handed out, and will sometimes do odd jobs for people in the community if they promise not to inform the welfare department. Even though they live in an apartment built with tax money; draw monthly checks; obtain food, schoolbooks, lunches, and the like from the same source, they are the least repulsive parasites I have met.

At this juncture I assume you may be about to cast me as a Scrooge; may I assure you such would be a grave injustice. In all truth I have no quarrel with the gay troubadour, jug of wine, loaf of bread type. It's their life: let them live it. But! When I am forced to pay for the butter that goes on their bread, while having to settle for a less desirable spread myself—that I don't like.

With all the persistence and order of thought generally reserved for matter and form, I pursued the illusive truth about butter: "surplus commodity" is a misnomer for a product that has been supported off the market. This is what actually happens: Everyone earning a salary is separated from a part thereof by the powers that be. Said powers buy butter with some part of this money, at a price well above what it might bring in a free market. Obviously, they are using the people's money to maintain the price beyond those means left to wage-earner's discretion. This unnatural course of events tends to cause huge accumulations of butter. In casting about for the ideal disposition, the powers apparently decided to add insult to injury by giving the butter to those least likely to have paid any taxes toward its purchase.

In a matter of this magnitude, one must approach the apparent conclusion from every conceivable angle. For this reason I hesitate to submit as absolute truth the apparent fact that the ox has been muzzled. [1 TIMOTHY 5:18.]

Rabid enthusiasts of the proposition, that all men should lower their aim to conform to the lowest among them, claim that compassion pure and simple is their prime motivation. They insist the way of life which built the greatest country on earth was founded on the preamble of "every man for himself and let the devil take the hindmost." In this enlightened age, they propose to remedy this by herding the win, place, and show entries into the gutter with the "also rans."

Armed with the illusion of compassion, the equalizers have shown us the hungry child begging for food, the aged and infirm seeking shelter, the farmer toiling in rags. The burden of responsibility is too heavy, they have said; your government must relieve you of this great weight.

Their noble theory deals in opinions, not facts. It proposes to eliminate want, but without want there is no incentive to strive. It hopes to strike out fear, ignoring the fact that fear of failure breeds pride of success. No one shall know hunger, an enticing phrase, but the ox cares not who fills his manger—the ward of the state is little concerned whether his master wears an eagle or a hammer and sickle on his hat. Government is responsible for your welfare; this theory speaks loud and clear. But without responsibility there can be no self-respect. Lack of self-respect removes the opportunity to attain freedom. Freedom alone is able to ignite that vital spark of greatness in men and nations.[1]

(*See Also:* Cradle-to-Grave, Demand and Supply, Equality, Expert, Inflationist, Poverty, Tinstaafl, Welfarism, Work)

Does the wild ass bray when he has grass? Or does the ox low over his fodder?

JOB 6:5.

He preys on the barren who bear not, and does not good to the widow. But God draws the mighty away with His power; He rises up, but no man is sure of his life. He gives them security, and they rely on it; yet His eyes are on their ways. They are exalted for a little while, then they are gone. They are brought low; they are taken out of the way like all others; they dry out like the heads of grain.

JOB 24:21–24.

They gave me also gall for my meat; and in my thirst they gave me vinegar to drink. Let their table become a snare before them; and that which should have been for their welfare, let it become a trap.

PSALM 69:21–22.

…They assemble themselves for corn and wine, and they rebel against Me…. They return, but not to the most High. They are like a deceitful bow. Their princes shall fall by the sword for the rage of their tongue….

HOSEA 7:14, 16.

Beware of false prophets, who come to you in sheep's clothing, but inwardly they are ravening wolves. You will know them by their fruits. Do men gather grapes of thorns, or figs of thistles? Even so every good tree brings forth good fruit; but a corrupt tree brings forth evil fruit. A good tree cannot bring forth evil fruit, neither can a corrupt tree bring forth good fruit. Every tree that brings not forth good fruit is hewn down, and cast into the fire. Wherefore by their fruits you shall know them.

MATTHEW 7:15–20.

For many walk of whom I have told you often, and now tell you even weeping, that they are the enemies of the cross of Christ, whose end is

[1] Essay condensed from Jess Raley, "I Like Butter," *Essays on Liberty*, Vol. X, published by the Foundation for Economic Freedom, Irvington-on-Hudson, N.Y. For further recommended reading on the same subject, see Robert P. Vichas, "Puerto Rico: Land of Food Stamps," *Human Events*, 38 (June 1978), 10 ff.

destruction, whose God is their belly, and whose glory is in their shame, who mind earthly things.

PHILIPPIANS 3:18–19.

WISDOM

In a study of Proverbs, Derek Kidner highlights five dimensions of wisdom. First, wisdom emphasizes instruction, or training. Second, wisdom means discipline, i.e., verbal correction, a face of wisdom we ordinarily shun. Third, it is "wise dealing.., i.e., good sense, practical wisdom, *savoir-faire.*" Fourth, wisdom refers to "the power of forming plans," or shrewdness and discretion. Fifth, similar to the first one, it means knowledge and learning.[1] However, we must be careful not to equate wisdom with a university education. That has been discussed elsewhere in this book. All learning, knowledge, wise-dealing, and planning must rise to biblical standards to be wisdom, "for the Lord gives wisdom: from His mouth comes knowledge and understanding" (PROVERBS 2:6).

(*See Also:* Education, Expert, Judgment, Maturity, Pollution, Source, Truth)

To man, he said, Behold, the fear of the Lord, that is wisdom, and to depart from evil is understanding.

JOB 28:28.

…Days should speak, and multitude of years should teach wisdom. But there is a spirit in man; and the inspiration of the Almighty gives them understanding. Great men are not always wise; neither do the aged understand judgment.

JOB 32:7–9.

Receive my instruction, and not silver, and knowledge rather than choice gold. For wisdom is better than rubies; and all things that may be desired are not to be compared to it. I, wisdom, dwell with prudence, and find out knowledge of witty inventions. The fear of the Lord is to hate evil: pride and arrogancy, and the evil way, and the froward mouth, do I hate.

PROVERBS 8:10–13.

[1]Derek Kidner, *Proverbs: An Introduction and Commentary* (Chicago: Inter-Varsity Press, 1964), pp. 36–40.

There is gold, and a multitude of rubies; but the lips of knowledge are a precious jewel.

PROVERBS 20:15.

I gave my heart to seek and search out by wisdom concerning all things that are done under heaven.... I have seen all the works that are done under the sun; and, behold, all is vanity and vexation of spirit.... I gave my heart to know wisdom, and to know madness and folly; I perceived that this also is vexation of spirit. For in wisdom is much grief; and he who increases knowledge increases sorrow.

ECCLESIASTES 1:13–14, 17–18.

Wisdom is good with an inheritance; and by it there is profit to them that see the sun. For wisdom is a defense, and money is a defense; but the excellency of knowledge is, that wisdom gives life to them who have it.

ECCLESIASTES 7:11–12.

Wisdom strengthens the wise more than ten mighty men who are in the city. For there is not a just man upon earth, who does good, and sins not.

ECCLESIASTES 7:19–20.

If the iron be blunt, and he does not whet the edge, then must he put to more strength; but wisdom is profitable to direct.

ECCLESIASTES 10:10.

Where is the wise? Where is the scribe? Where is the disputer of this world? Has not God made foolish the wisdom of this world?

1 CORINTHIANS 1:20.

Howbeit we speak wisdom among them who are perfect; yet not the wisdom of this world, nor of the princes of this world, that come to nothing. But we speak the wisdom of God in a mystery, even the hidden wisdom, which God ordained before the world to our glory, which none of the princes of this world knew.

1 CORINTHIANS 2:6–8.

...Knowledge puffs up, but charity edifies. If any man thinks that he knows anything, he knows nothing yet as he ought to know.

1 CORINTHIANS 8:1–2.

If any of you lack wisdom, let him ask of God, who gives to all men liberally, and upbraids not; and it shall be given him.

JAMES 1:5.

The wisdom that is from above is pure, then peaceable, gentle, willing to yield, full of mercy and good fruits, without partiality, and without hypocrisy.

JAMES *3:17.*

WOMEN

In MBA (Master of Business Administration) classes attended by working students, female students often compete on male terms, that is, by becoming highly competitive, masculinized women. They presume that colorful language and role playing affirm their business prowess. One popular view of women, amply reinforced by evolutionists, is that of a woman under male domination, cave-man style. However, during the Age of Reason (19th century), women were placed on a pedestal, which brought about their diminished status.

"The all too familiar view of women suddenly emerging in the nineteenth century from a long historical night or to a sunlit plain is completely wrong.... Up to the eighteenth century women usually figured in business as partners with their husbands, and not in inferior capacities. They often took full charge during prolonged absences of their mates."[1]

The so-called Age of Reason reduced women to an unenlightened and unreasoned existence. Feminists, while perhaps highlighting some key issues, foster regressiveness.

> The tragedy of the women's rights movement was that, although it had serious wrongs to correct, it added to the problem, and here the resistance of man was in as large a measure responsible. Instead of restoring women to their rightful place of authority beside men, women's rights became feminism: it put women in competition with men. It led to the masculinization of women and femininization of men, to the unhappiness of both."[2]

The woman's role is that of mother, wife, and helpmeet; a good wife is worth far more than rubies (see PROVERBS 31:10).

(*See Also:* Children, Draft, Family, Feminism, Marriage, Youth Cultism)

Adam said, This is now bone of my bones, and flesh of my flesh; she shall be called woman, because she was taken out of man.

GENESIS *2:23.*

[1]Ferdinand Lundberg and Marynia F. Farnham, M.D., *Modern Woman: The Lost Sex* (New York: Harper & Row, Pub., 1947), pp. 130, 421.

[2]Rousas John Rushdoony, *The Institutes of Biblical Law* (Nutley, N.J.: The Craig Press, 1973), pp. 351.

The Lord God said to the woman, What is this that you have done? The woman said, The serpent beguiled me, and I did eat.... To the woman He said, I will greatly multiply your sorrow and your conception; in sorrow you shall bring forth children, and your desire shall be to your husband, and he shall rule over you.

GENESIS 3:13, 16.

...If a man dies, and has no son, then you shall cause his inheritance to pass to his daughter.

NUMBERS 27:8.

...All the wives shall give to their husbands honor, both to great and small.

ESTHER 1:20.

As a jewel of gold in a swine's snout, so is a fair woman who is without discretion.

PROVERBS 11:22.

Who can find a virtuous wife? For her worth is far above rubies. The heart of her husband safely trusts her; so he will have no lack of gain. She does him good, not evil, all the days of her life. She seeks wool and flax, and willingly works with her hands.

PROVERBS 31:10–13.

I find more bitter than death the woman, whose heart is snares and nets, and her hands as bands; whoso pleases God shall escape from her, but the sinner shall be taken by her.

ECCLESIASTES 7:26.

Which yet my soul seeks, but I find not: one man among a thousand have I found; but a woman among all those have I found not.

ECCLESIASTES 7:28.

Wives, submit yourselves to your own husbands, as to the Lord. For the husband is the head of the wife, even as Christ is the Head of the church; and He is the Savior of the body.

EPHESIANS 5:22–23.

In like manner also, that women adorn themselves in modest apparel, with shamefacedness and sobriety, not with braided hair, or gold, or pearls, or costly array. But (which becomes women professing god-liness) with good works.

1 TIMOTHY 2:9–10.

Withal they learn to be idle, wandering about from house to house, and not only idle, but tattlers also and busybodies, speaking things which they ought not.

1 TIMOTHY 5:13.

The aged women likewise, that they be in behavior as becomes holiness, not false accusers, not given to much wine, teachers of good things, that they may teach the young women to be sober, to love their husbands, to love their children, to be discreet, chaste, keepers at home, good, obedient to their own husbands, that the word of God be not blasphemed.

TITUS 2:3–5.

WORK

Three verses interest us on work. First, in GENESIS 3:19, in his role and his duty to God, man must work. Work disciplines. From it man learns. However, we must not become workaholics and forget our link to God. EXODUS 20:9, therefore, commands us to take a day off and remember our Creator. So that we don't take off too many days of rest and develop bad habits, 2 THESSALONIANS 3:10 lays it out rather clearly: If we don't want (but are able) to work, then we are not entitled to eat and live off the labor of others.

The Bible says two things about work. Both run contrary to much of contemporary ethics. One is that we must work: No free rides; no reference to endless vacations; no message about retirement, early or late. "Six days shalt thou labor, and do all thy work" (EXODUS 20:9). Second, the Bible does not make reference to job security, the right to employment (meaning someone else's obligation to meet a payroll).

However, current humanistic laws make receiving sustenance a right, which translates into an obligation of those who do work to support those who refuse. Our present laws and welfare programs could not be further from biblical principles. For those who cannot work—the infirm, children, the aged—the Bible tells us to assist them through private voluntary charity. With a federal welfare program having grown from only a few dollars to $300 billion·in one lifetime, we should expect poverty, unemployment, and the plight of the disadvantaged to have disappeared, or so our social engineers predicted. This would happen, they said, if we spent more and more money on these social programs. What has happened and why?

For a rudimentary minicourse, let's take the agricultural subsidy and price support programs as an example in welfare economics. Economics tells us that if producers receive a higher price than the market price through subsidies, we can expect the supply of subsidized products to expand. At one time agricultural surpluses became so huge that Congress invented Public Law 480 to dispose of surplus commodities. At the time of PL480, the public and press worried about balance of payments deficits. So, PL480 allowed us to "sell" grain for soft currencies (i.e., inconvertible money), which money was eventually returned to the "buying country." On our balance of payments books, legerdemain made it appear as though exports had risen by sale of surplus grains, when, in fact, they were gifts.

If we subsidize unemployment, or welfare babies, or poverty, we can, according to basic economic laws, expect the number of unemployed, welfare babies and so-called poor to rise. And it has. Similarly, if laws make it impossible to dismiss employees, persons with guaranteed (by the government) employment will not be encouraged to work, and production will fall. For instance, what are the three major problems with Soviet workers? Corruption, alcoholism, and absenteeism. We find that all socialist countries have these problems. Why should we expect different results when we cease following God's plan for a free and productive society?

God commands us to take charge and subdue the earth: hardly a committee task. The committee meetings and discussions took place long ago. Now is the time for us Christians to get busy and carry out this mandate. We have stalled long enough, waiting for Sam to do it.

God's command is a just one. Without work, we would have extreme shortages of housing, widespread famines, illnesses of all kinds, and certainly unemployment. The cruelest punishment for someone incarcerated is not confinement but lack of creative things to do. Such an environment—in or out of prison—leads to riots and anarchy, vice and corruption, indolence and immorality, further loss of freedom, totalitarianism, and unbelief in the Creator and the abundance possible under the rule of God.

(*See Also:* Abundance, Discipline, Employee, Freedom, Labor, Market Economy, Production, Supply, Wages)

In the sweat of your face shall you eat bread, until you return to the ground....

                                                               GENESIS 3:19.

Remember the Sabbath day, to keep it holy. Six days you shall labor and do all your work, but the seventh day is the Sabbath of the Lord your God. In it you shall do no work: you, nor your son, nor your daughter, nor your manservant, nor your maidservant, nor your cattle, nor your stranger who is within your gates. For in six days the Lord made the heavens and the earth, the sea, and all that is in them, and rested the seventh day. Therefore, the Lord blessed the Sabbath day and hallowed it.

                                                               EXODUS 20:8–11.

Man goes forth to his work and to his labor until evening.

PSALM 104:23.

He who gathers in summer is a wise son; but he who sleeps in harvest is a son who causes shame.

PROVERBS 10:5.

Love not sleep, lest you come to poverty; open your eyes, and you shall be satisfied with bread.

PROVERBS 20:13.

He who tills his land shall have plenty of bread.

PROVERBS 28:19.

Yea, I hated all my labor which I had taken under the sun, because I should leave it to the man who will be after me.

ECCLESIASTES 2:18.

There is one alone, and there is not a second; yea, he has neither child nor brother, yet is there no end of all his labor; neither is his eye satisfied with riches; neither says he, For whom do I labor, and bereave my soul of good? This is also vanity, yea, it is sore travail.

ECCLESIASTES 4:8.

Whatsoever your hand finds to do, do it with your might; for there is no work, nor device, nor knowledge, nor wisdom, in the grave, where you are going.

ECCLESIASTES 9:10.

By much slothfulness the building decays; and through idleness of the hands, the house drops through.

ECCLESIASTES 10:18.

Then says he to his disciples, The harvest is truly abundant, but the laborers are few.

MATTHEW 9:37.

For even when we were with you, we commanded you this: If anyone will not work, neither shall he eat. For we hear that there are some who walk among you in a disorderly manner, not working at all, but are busybodies. Now those who are such we command and exhort through our Lord Jesus Christ that they work in quietness and eat their own bread.

2 THESSALONIANS 3:10–12.

WORLD GOVERNMENT

Christians yearn for peace. Communists, too, want peace. Both sides see world government as an instrument in this peace. MICAH 4:1–3 describes the world government and peace desired by Christians. Each side refers to a different kind of world government. Their respective concepts of peace are incompatible.

Does the United Nations fit the Christian model of the communist model for world government and peace? The League of Nations, by choosing the superstate concept, long ago rejected God. Its offspring, the United Nations, denies God. During its first twenty-five years of existence, more than seventy-five wars erupted and more than half the world has become enslaved by some variety of communism. The United Nations is truly modern society's tower of Babel.

(*See Also:* Demagoguery, Elitism, One Worldism, Peace Treaty, Planned Economy, Slavery, Statism)

You have committed fornication with the Egyptians your neighbors, great of flesh, and have increased your whoredoms, to provoke Me to anger.... Because your filthiness was poured out, and your nakedness discovered through your whoredoms with your lovers, and with all the idols of your abominations, and by the blood of your children, which you did give them.... I will also give you into their hand, and they shall throw down your eminent place, and shall break down your high places; they shall strip you also of your clothes, and shall take your fair jewels, and leave you naked and bare.
EZEKIEL 16:26, 36, 39.

In the latter days it shall come to pass that the mountain of the Lord's house shall be established atop the mountains, and shall be exalted above the hills; and people shall flow to it. Many nations shall come and say, Come, and let us go up to the mountain of the Lord, to the house of the God of Jacob; He will teach us His ways, and we shall walk in His paths. For out of Zion the law shall go forth, and the word of the Lord from Jerusalem. He shall judge among many peoples, and rebuke strong nations afar off. They shall beat their swords into plowshares, and their spears into pruning hooks. Nation shall not lift up sword against nation; neither shall they learn war any more.
MICAH 4:1–3.

Peace I leave with you, my peace I give to you, not as the world gives, give I to you. Let not your heart be troubled, neither let it be afraid....

Hereafter I will not talk much with you, for the prince of this world comes, and has nothing in me.

JOHN 14:27, 30.

These things I have spoken to you, that in Me you might have peace. In the world you shall have tribulation; but be of good cheer, I have overcome the world.

JOHN 16:33.

For when they shall say, Peace and safety, then sudden destruction comes upon them, as travail upon a woman; and they shall not escape.

1 THESSALONIANS 5:3.

WRITER

...By these, my son, be admonished: of making many books there is no end....

ECCLESIASTES 12:12.

(*See:* Educator, Individualism, Professor)

XENOPHOBIA

Xenophobia, hatred of foreigners, translates into fanatical nationalism. The state replaces God and family. As the fire of propaganda, fed by demagogues, consumes people with an arsenal of national hatred, otherwise peaceful people, trapped by suspicion and hatred of "the enemy," and terrified by the threat of attack, prepare to defend their state in the name of frenzied patriotism.

Modern nationalism, to coalesce people of diverse interests, relies on bonds of common language, religion, customs, and xenophobia. Preservation of self and family is both a duty and moral obligation. However, true patriotism must stand on the moral foundation of God's law.

(*See Also:* Demagoguery, Double Standard, Elitism, Military Defense, Slavery, Statism)

> He heard the words of Laban's sons, saying, Jacob has taken away all that was our father's; and of that which was our father's has he gotten all this glory.
>
> GENESIS 31:1.

> The bloodthirsty hate the upright....
>
> PROVERBS 29:10.

> If the world hates you, you know that it hated me before it hated you.
>
> JOHN 15:18.

> For we ourselves also were sometimes foolish, disobedient, deceived, serving diverse lusts and pleasures, living in malice and envy, hateful, and hating one another.
>
> TITUS 3:3.

> Whoever hates his brother is a murderer....
>
> 1 JOHN 3:15.

YOUTH CULTISM

Youth cultism, which especially flourished during the 1960s and 1970s, when mothers competed with daughters and when fathers sought friendship (not parenthood) with their sons, is an expression of an unhealthy desire to remain young in spirit. It is a revolt against maturity. "Youth" is raised to a level of worship and adulation. Parents abdicate familial responsibilities: Husbands defer their responsibility to their wives, and wives defer responsibility to their minor children. This behavior is satanic. Satan, as you recall, offered Eve the opportunity of becoming a god and of having continual rejuvenation, an opportunity for mankind to recreate itself.

A free society functions when mature individuals accept responsibilities as independent, stable persons in the family and community. To remain a child forever, dependent upon others, leads to a statist society where freedom is an obscure, abstract concept. What characterizes childhood? Immaturity (1 CORINTHIANS 13:11); dependence on others (1 THESSALONIANS 2:7); need for instruction (PROVERBS 22:6); need to be disciplined (MATTHEW 11:16–19); instability (EPHESIANS 4:14); and foolishness (PROVERBS 22:15). When youthful appearance is a necessity for promotion in business and government and for success, certainly a prudent person who must deal with unbelievers will play at Halloween year round, as long as it does not distort reality, and he assumes the mature responsibility required of him by God.

(See Also: Children, Cradle-to-Grave, Crowd Psychology, Hippies, Idolatry, Maturity, Responsibility)

The lions do lack, and suffer hunger; but they who seek the Lord shall not want any good thing. Come, you children, listen to me; I will teach you the fear of the Lord.

PSALM 34:10–11.

Foolishness is bound in the heart of a child, but the rod of correction shall drive it far from him.

PROVERBS 22:15.

Woe to you, O land, when your king is a child....
                                                            ECCLESIASTES *10:16.*

I will give children to be their princes, and babes shall rule over them. The people shall be oppressed, every one by another, and every one by his neighbor; the child shall behave himself proudly against the ancient, and the base against the honorable.
                                                            ISAIAH *3:4–5.*

The new wine mourns, the vine languishes, all the merryhearted do sigh.
                                                            ISAIAH *24:7.*

...They respected not the persons of the priests; they favored not the elders.
                                                            LAMENTATIONS *4:16.*

Whereunto shall I liken this generation? It is like children sitting in the markets, and calling to their fellows, and saying, We have piped to you, and you would not dance.
                                                            MATTHEW *11:16–17.*

When I was a child, I spake as a child, I understood as a child, I thought as a child; but when I became a man, I put away childish things.
                                                            1 CORINTHIANS *13:11.*

That we henceforth be no more children, tossed to and fro, and carried about with every wind of doctrine, by the sleight of men, and cunning craftiness, whereby they lie in wait to deceive.
                                                            EPHESIANS *4:14.*

Young men likewise exhort to be sober minded. In all things showing yourself a pattern of good works: in doctrine showing uncorruptness, gravity, sincerity, sound speech, that cannot be condemned; that he who is of the contrary part may be ashamed, having no evil thing to say to you.
                                                            TITUS *2:6–8.*

For every one who uses milk is unskillful in the word of righteousness, for he is a babe.
                                                            HEBREWS *5:13.*

ZAIN

We end with the seventh letter of the Hebrew alphabet: "Thy statutes have been my song." The verses below from Psalm 119 complement the theme of this volume—the Bible's message for living in a free society today. The psalmist sings of hope because he knows that everything good comes from God through man's obedience and adherence to God's laws. When men mold the world in their own likeness, the psalmist sings: "Horror hath taken hold upon me."

God guided our forefathers into creating a practical demonstration—America, the Beautiful—of how freedom, prosperity, and blessings flow to us when we put our trust in the Lord and not in human institutions. (Please read Psalm 115 carefully.) America has detoured from those early foundational principles. It has abdicated responsibilities as a light, hope, and example to the rest of the world.

God has allowed the world to develop its own alternative humanistic life styles, which provide a real demonstration of the slavery, deprivation, and loss of hope that result from the isms. People the world over, in turning their backs to the God of light, have become hypnotized with seductive promises of the powers of darkness: communism, socialism, or the new grand plan. Put this book in their hands and tell them about true liberty and the rewards of faithfulness cited in Psalm 128. Tell your friends that we can still regain and live in a free society. "With men this is impossible; but with God all things are possible" (MATTHEW 19:26).

(*See Also:* Abundance, Foundation, Free Society, Liberty, Remnant, Source, Stewardship)

> *Remember the word to Your servant, upon which you have caused me to hope.*
>
> *This is my comfort in my affliction: for Your word has quickened me.*
>
> *The proud have had me in great derision; yet have I not turned aside from Your law.*

I remembered Your judgments of old, O Lord, and have comforted myself.

Horror has taken hold of me because of the wicked who forsake Your law.

Your statutes have been my songs in the house of my pilgrimage.

I have remembered Your name, O Lord, in the night, and have kept Your law.

This I had, because I kept Your precepts.

PSALM 119:49–56.

AUTHOR'S OFFER

The author has arranged for the purchaser of this book to receive free copies of *The Envoy*, a publication focusing on government and the Bible. To receive your free copies, compliments of the author, write to:

> Author's Offer
> *The Envoy*
> 1001 Jefferson Plaza, Suite 112
> Wilmington, Delaware 19801

Please address your request as above and include your complete mailing address and zip code. No other correspondence is necessary unless you wish to communicate with the author.

> *Let us hear the conclusion of the whole matter: Fear God, and keep His commandments, for this is the whole duty of man. For God shall bring every work into judgment, with every secret thing, whether it be good or whether it be evil.*
> *ECCLESIASTES 12:13–14.*

411